The History of Television, 1880 to 1941

ALBERT ABRAMSON

The History of
Television, 1880 to 1941

McFarland & Company, Inc., Publishers
Jefferson, North Carolina, and London

Library of Congress Cataloguing-in-Publication Data

Abramson, Albert.
The history of television, 1880 to 1941.

Bibliography: p. 327.
Includes index.
1. Television—History. I. Title.
TK6637.A27   1987   621.388′009   86-43091

ISBN 0-89950-284-9 (acid-free natural paper) ∞

Printed in the United States of America

McFarland   Box 611   Jefferson NC 28640

This volume is gratefully dedicated to those television pioneers who so graciously allowed me to come into their lives to relate their contributions to the history of television:

Manfred Von Ardenne • Alda Bedford • D.C. Birkinshaw • Tony Bridgewater • Arch Brolly • Mrs. Philo Farnsworth • Lesly E. Flory • Harley Iams • Ray Kell • Thomas M.C. Lance • Harry Lubcke • Hans G. Lubszynski • Joseph D. McGee • Robert Morris • George Morton • Albert F. Murray • Albert Rose • Solomon Sagall • Otto Schade • Kenjiro Takayanagi • Arthur Vance • E.C.L. White • W.D. Wright • Vladimir K. Zworykin

DA

Acknowledgments

I wish to thank the following persons and their organizations for their cooperation. Without them, there would have been no book.

Mr. Al Pinsky, Public Relations at RCA, David Sarnoff Research Laboratories: for the utmost cooperation while I was in Princeton, New Jersey. With no thought of obligations, he opened every door for me.

Ms. Birdy Rogers, Head Librarian at the Patent Room, Los Angeles Public Library: for her patience over seven years of helping me in my search for patents.

Mr. Jerry Sears, Counsel, United States Patent Office, Department of Commerce, Washington, D.C.: for granting me access to hundreds of patent files and interferences.

Ms. Anita Newell, Archivist, Westinghouse Electric, East Pittsburgh: for granting me access to the Westinghouse microfilm files.

Mr. Brian Samain, Public Relations, EMI (now Thorne, EMI), London: for giving me access to the EMI Archives. Special thanks to Mr. Leonard Petts, Archivist at Hayes, Middlesex.

Dr. Marcy Goldstein, Archivist, Bell Telephone Laboratories, Short Hills, New Jersey: for access to the notebooks and records of the Dr. Herbert E. Ives television project.

To the following television historians for their invaluable advice and suggestions: Mr. Tony Bridgewater, Mr. Gerhart Goebel and Mr. George Shiers.

To the following friends who worked hard at translating technical articles and patents into understandable English: Günter Schmitt (German), Therese Weiderholt (French), John Inonue (Japanese), Sharon Behry (Russian), and Joe Arvisu (Portuguese).

I wish to thank the various sources for giving me permission to reproduce copyrighted photographs and illustrations. Where it was not possible to find the original copyright owners, I offer my apologies for the noninclusion of their names. Picture credits are as follows:

Scientific American: pp. 12, 37, 42, 49. *Prometheus*: pp. 30, 31. *Modern Electrics*: p. 32. *L'Illustration*: p. 33. P.K. Gorokhov, *B.L. Rosing*; Moscow, 1964: p. 36. Radio Corporation of America (RCA): pp.

vii

80 (top), 142 (bottom), 144, 184 (top), 251. Tony Bridgewater: p. 61. *Journal of the Röntgen Society*: p. 39. *Electrical Experimenter*: p. 44. *Radio Broadcast*: p. 59. A. Dinsdale, *Television 1928*: p. 61, 69, 117 (top). *Radio News*: pp. 58, 90, 219. Gerhart Goebel: p. 71. C.F. Jenkins, *Radiomovies, Radiovision, Television*, 1929: pp. 77, 114. G. Eichhorn, *Wetterfunk, Bildfunk, Television*, 1926: p. 81. *Television* (London): p. 88. General Electric Company: pp. 93, 109, 126, 154. Westinghouse Electric Company: pp. 80 (bottom), 142 (bottom). *Science and Invention*: pp. 88 (bottom), 91, 103. AT&T (reproduced with permission of AT&T Corporate Archives): pp. 100, 101, 116. Japanese Victor Corporation: pp. 102, 176. Jay Faulkner: pp. 106, 117 (bottom), 221. *Revue Général d'Electricité*: p. 98. Katalina Glass: p. 119. Les Flory: pp. 138, 166, 183 (top), 184 (bottom). Manfred von Ardenne: pp. 141, 156. *Radio Industries*: p. 159. Harley Iams: p. 184 (top). Royal Television Society: p. 216. *Television Today 1935, Vol. I*: p. 196. *Television & Short-Wave World*: p. 228. *Electronics & Television & Short-Wave World*: p. 263.

Finally, thanks to my dear wife, Arlene, who never lost faith in me during those trying times when it looked as though I was never to get it done.

Albert Abramson, 17 Jan 1987

Table of Contents

Foreword

It would be difficult to cite any technological innovation whose impact on the fabric of daily living has been as pervasive as that of television. In the space of only some decades, this highly sophisticated system was invented, developed and succeeded literally in providing a window on the world to all of its inhabitants.

How did this profound gift to mankind come about? You will search your libraries in vain for a worldwide, authoritative and detailed account of this dramatic development. Albert Abramson had scoured the world to interview the fast-disappearing scientists whose imagination and enterprise combined to make television a reality. These interviews were supplemented by an extensive and intensive search of the scientific literature. The list of well over a thousand references reinforces the factual validity of Abramson's story.

The highly detailed story should serve many purposes, among which is an unmatched collection of source material. The reader has a generous supply of detail with which he can support his own interpretation of the meaning of this vast development.

I found, for example, that the common and oversimplified practice of citing some individual as the "father" of television is a patent distortion of history. To try to squeeze the numerous contributions into the narrow confines of one individual does an injustice to the rich texture of the facts—a remarkable interaction of several hundred major scientists striving towards a common goal, each in his own fashion. The competition was intense. Here was a striking game played out. The aim of each individual was to enhance his own prestige, which, coincidentally could be done only by serving society. (Abramson's treatment of the many personal conflicts is meticulously even-handed.)

So, too, among the many private corporations and the competition was often a life-and-death struggle for the survival of all or part of the corporation. In the end, the beneficiary was always society. What better arrangement than that the intense drives to satisfy individual and corporate needs should be channeled into serving society?

These are some of the themes that Abramson's story of the birth of television implicitly supports. It is a story long overdue.

Dr. Albert Rose

Introduction

Throughout the preparation of this book on the history of television, I faced a fundamental problem: how to present a great mass of what appears to be "obviously" unrelated material in a palatable and entertaining manner. Yet I wanted to avoid the fictions with which many historians embellish their facts—the mythical anecdotes and quotes for which there is little or no factual basis. While such fictions make for interesting reading, the reader is ill served.

I had spent a great deal of time in researching the vast treasure trove of literature to be found in the libraries and archives of the large corporations and interviewing the surviving pioneers. I felt no need to "create" drama, realizing that the real drama lay in the facts themselves. Every event, whether it was a simple article or a complicated patent, was an adventure into the future. The pioneers involved were treading on ground that had never before been covered. They were creating a new form of communication that man had intuitively desired for thousands of years—namely, to reach beyond the horizon and see and hear his fellow man, who might be thousands of miles away.

No one person invented television; most of the inventors were ahead of their time and technology; some were idle dreamers, others were practical men who could turn their ideas into machinery. Ideas did not always occur in logical order. So I decided to present the actual facts from primary sources as they appeared chronologically and let the reader vicariously participate in the medium's progress. For the reader and the future historian, I have included a host of references that could be checked out at some later date. Also one will find in the notes most of the comments and opinions that are helpful in explaining certain events.

I have striven to be objective, factual and impartial, allowing only my conscience and the facts that I have uncovered to be my guide. The source material I have used consists principally of documentary evidence such as:

(1) patent applications, patent interferences, and of course the patents themselves;

(2) engineering notebooks and logs as well as letters and cor-

respondence of the various inventors found in several industrial archives;

(3) the great body of general information found in the technical
journals;

(4) the vast amount of knowledge to be found in the newspapers and
magazines of the times; and finally,

(5) the extensive interviews that I conducted with the surviving
pioneers in the United States, Great Britain, Japan, and Germany. My
only regret is that I did not start my research some ten years earlier in order
to get to know more of the television pioneers who were still alive.

I have made certain assumptions: first, that each pioneer or inventor
is aware of (a) prior art and (b) prior literature through his own research
of patents and related materials; second, that he is indeed the actual inventor and the facts are as recorded. Any attempts at predating or changes
after the fact are given no consideration.

All claims were put into three categories:

(1) I report as fact all ideas and/or machines and how well they
worked, when these are fully supported by (a) dated and witnessed
laboratory notes, (b) dated and signed applications for patents, (c) photos
and blueprints of apparatus, and (d) demonstrations, whether public or
private, as reported by reliable, disinterested witnesses.

(2) I report as marginal claims that cannot be substantiated except by
secondhand information such as undated photos and notes or by the
reports of involved witnesses. These claims are presented when the matter
is important enough to be included in the body of this book, and it is left
to the reader to decide for himself whether the facts are as quoted.

(3) I reject out of hand all claims in which an idea, invention, or
device was supposedly conceived many years in the past, and the inventor
has only his memory to guide him.

I have used all of the above as a means of providing checks and
balances of one against the other, so enabling me to present the story as
authentically and truthfully to the historical record as humanly possible.
With these facts in mind, I have made many presumptions based on the
facts as I have seen them, and have come up with what I feel are logical
conclusions. Only time will tell how correct they are. In no case do I attempt to justify or criticize any patent office or legal decision.

I assume full responsibility for all statements made and for any errors
that may have occurred. Any additional information will be greatly
appreciated.

Albert Abramson

Chapter 1

Archaeology and Prehistory of Television: 1671–1879

For some ninety years audiences all over the world have enjoyed watching motion pictures of every size and shape. These same audiences have also been watching television in one form or another for some fifty years. Yet, while it took only some six years for the motion picture to evolve from a laboratory experiment to a full-grown commercial venture, it took almost a half-century for television to reach a maturity that the motion picture achieved almost overnight. The reason is easy to understand: the motion picture, being an optical-mechanical-chemical medium, was easier to accomplish than television, which was based on optical-electrical principles.

As a result, any history of the motion picture usually disposes of the technological achievements (the camera, film and viewing devices) in the first few pages of the book. It would then continue with the works of the early directors, cameramen, stars and producers who built the industry to its present position.

The history of television is different. Television took a long time gestating. It grew with the technology of the times; its disciplines came from a broad spectrum of the arts and sciences that were more often than not unrelated.

C.W. Ceram pointed out in his classic book *Archaeology of the Cinema* that man has "a fondness for mechanistic theories of evolution, from a tendency to see the history of civilized man as a continuously progressive process going on for five thousand years."[1] But this progression is a myth. The early history of television is made up of discoveries that at the time seemed absolutely unrelated to each other. To find a bridge for them was impossible. Time was needed to fit the pieces together into a sort of jigsaw puzzle.

As a consequence, there has been no serious history of early television. Most histories of television state merely that it evolved from radio broadcasting, leading the reader to believe that television was the natural progeny of radio.

It is true that the great electrical trusts finally developed television in their laboratories, and the radio broadcasters took it over as their own. But in so doing, they had to convert from an aural to a visual medium. This conversion was not a simple imitation of motion pictures. The motion picture had already developed a large literature of its own. It had evolved a grammar and syntax that were unique. It had matured as a purely visual medium. The coming of sound to motion pictures was fought with a vigor. No "competent" director needed speech to tell his story.

Still, there was a symbiotic relationship between the new medium of television and the motion picture. Television applied the motion picture grammar to radio programming, converting news, sports, and especially drama, into visual form with the greatest of ease.

Man's desire for communication with his fellow man had not included the motion picture, which was not a direct medium. Any event filmed had to be played back at a later time. This was in contrast to the telephone and the radio, which allowed instant communication. So the motion picture became a medium for education and entertainment rather than communication. What was still needed was a means of seeing one's correspondent at the very moment one was speaking to him. This was the original intent of television. But while the desire was there, the technical means were not.

As a result, the motion picture arrived long before television. But as satisfactory as it was, it left a void; it was not instantaneous. The strip of film stood in the way. Thus men wondered what it would be like to have a device that could transmit its image at the very moment it was being picked up.

One answer was offered by Henry D. Hubbard, Secretary of the United States Bureau of Standards. On May 9, 1921, Mr. Hubbard addressed the Society of Motion Picture Engineers. At this time, the motion picture was some 30 years old, dating from Edison's invention of 1891. Hubbard's lecture on "The Motion Picture of Tomorrow" included his prediction of the motion picture camera of 1950, some 30 years in the future.

> Dare we expect a camera with automatic focusing, automatic aperture adjustment, a camera recording in full color with bivisual stereoscopic effect, exactly as recorded, automatically to be filed, and exhibiting it immediately; a camera with self-sensitizing plates on which not separate pictures but a continuously changing picture is formed and erased after being telegraphed to a storage room; a camera equipped with mechanism for automatic cleaning of the glass surfaces, and the whole not to exceed in size the smallest Kodak of today[?][2]

By 1950 there was in existence a camera that fulfilled the majority of Mr. Hubbard's predictions — but not in the motion picture industry. For the motion picture camera of 1950 was still the same instrument Hubbard had known in 1921. Of course, there had been subtle refinements in the basic machinery, mainly consisting of a motor drive on the inside and the addition of sound recording equipment on the outside, and recording in full color had become part of the regular shooting process. However, it was essentially the same tool. Such amenities as automatic focus, automatic aperture adjustment and bivisual stereo effect had long been accomplished in the laboratories but were not part of the daily motion picture technique. Instead, a whole new industry had arisen to create Mr. Hubbard's desired camera of the future.

The visual arts — the motion picture and television — are actually two sides of the same coin. Yet they came from different roots. The motion picture had arisen from a combination of photographic techniques combined with mechanical means for propelling a strip of light-sensitive emulsion through a camera; and after suitable processing, the developed strip of images being driven through a viewing device of one sort or another. Television evolved from the field of electrical communication, a direct descendant of the electrical telegraph, the telephone and finally "facsimile" or the transmission of still pictures.

It appears from Hubbard's predictions that he expected radical changes in the motion picture as he knew it. He predicted the demise of film as the storage medium, being replaced with "self-sensitizing" plates, being "telegraphed" to a storage room exactly as recorded, and being exhibited immediately.

Motion picture film is neither "telegraphed" nor exhibited immediately. It cannot be "erased," or "filed," nor can it form a continuously changing picture. Only a storage medium based on magnetic recording principles can do these things.

The camera that fulfilled Hubbard's predictions was the electronic television camera, which had been developed for a quite different purpose. Its main use was to "telegraph" or send its pictures (an ever-changing view) to either a control or recording room depending on how it was being used. The function of recording can be remote, with the only connection being either direct-wire or radio-relay. The "emulsion" is the camera tube itself, the choice of color or monochrome depending on it. The recording medium is a very passive element, simply recording precisely whatever the camera presents to it.

Through the magic of electronics, the images from several cameras can be blended, mixed or otherwise put together in such a fashion that even the normal editing process of the motion picture can be done by the pressing of a button or without ever touching the tape itself. Mr. Hubbard's prediction of a machine "not to exceed in size the smallest Kodak of today" was first fulfilled in July 1980 by the Sony Corporation of Japan. They had just introduced a self-contained Video Camera/Recorder weighing some 4.4 pounds for home movie use to be available by the year 1985.[3]

It seems that the motion picture as it is known today will be undergoing major changes in the future. The trend from film to tape has been predicted for many years and is finally starting to take place.[4] At the present, video recording of images is slowly replacing the traditional film techniques. In the gathering of news for instance, there has been almost a 100 percent changeover from film to videotape. Many of the studios in Hollywood are setting up videotape units to record movies using video techniques rather than the old-fashioned film methods.

It is possible that the motion picture based on film as we know it is nothing more than a stop-gap measure which served a short but useful life, while the true motion picture medium of the future—one based on electrical principles—was nurtured and developed, with the electronic discipline learning from the old film-based medium the visual techniques that made the motion picture so unique.

There is no question that the art of the motion picture is based on the use of film and film editing. Yet today, there is nothing that can be done on film that can't be done quicker and more economically on videotape. The electronic medium has not only taken over film's role but is sending it on its way to oblivion. The question in 1987 is not "will videotape replace film" but when? That the handwriting is on the wall is made evident by the fact that even America's number one film manufacturer has long been secretly engaged in research in the field of video technology and is preparing itself for the inevitable changeover from light-sensitive emulsions to electronic conversion materials.[5]

The history of the motion picture explains why it took precedence over that of television. It is commonly agreed that the motion picture was based on three discoveries: the magic lantern, the Stroboscope (or wheel of life), and photography. The magic lantern was introduced by Father Athanasius Kircher, who in 1671 described the principle that a brightly illuminated object placed before a magnifying lens will project its inverted image onto a screen in a dark room, the image being enlarged according to the relative distance of the screen and of the object to the lens. By the end of the seventeenth century, magic lanterns were quite common throughout Europe. They normally projected pictures painted on glass until the development of photography.

This development began in 1727, when Johann H. Schulze discovered the chemical effect of sunlight on silver salts. In 1802 Thomas Wedgwood was able to produce pictures on glass. In 1814 Sir Humphrey Davy reported on the sensitivity of silver iodine to light. Sir John Herschel related in 1839 that sodium hyposulphate was able to fix chloride of silver. In 1839 real photography began with the work of Joseph Niépce and Louis Jacques Mandé Daguerre. They were able to make a permanent print of an image from a camera obscura. Also in 1839 Henry Fox Talbot was able to make any number of positive prints on silver-chloride paper. In 1851 Frederick Scott Archer developed the wet plate process. This made use of a glass plate with a film of wet collodion. In 1871 R.L. Maddox used silver-bromide plates with a gelatine coating as a binding agent. This was the dry plate process that cut exposure time down to about a hundreth of a second.

In 1824/25 Peter M. Roget delivered a paper in which he discussed wheel phenomena in regard to the "persistence of vision" in moving objects. (Other papers on the same subject were given by Joseph Plateau and Michael Faraday.) To exhibit this phenomenon, Plateau invented a "magic disc" called the Fantascope or Phenakistiscope in 1832. In this same year, Simon Ritter von Stampfer invented his "Stroboscope," which was similar to Plateau's device. It had a series of drawings around the edge of the disc with a series of slits cut through the disc's perimeter. As the drawings were viewed through the slits, one got the impression of continuous movement. In 1834 William George Horner improved on this machine with his Zootrope or Zoetrope. Here the drawings were on a band inside the drum which were viewed through slits cut into the upper half of the drum opposite the images.

It appears that as early as 1849 Plateau suggested the use of Daguerreotypes with his Phenakistiscope. However, by 1853 Baron Franz von Uchatius had instead combined the magic lantern with the Phenakistiscope. He was the first man to achieve moving images on a screen visible to the audience. He mounted hand-painted slides on a disc which was rotated by hand. A second disc containing slits (the shutter) was also rotated. As the two discs were turned, the slides were projected from a light source through a lens onto a large screen. There was a second model in which the disc was stationary and a series of lenses were rotated in the same manner.

In 1877 Charles Emile Reynaud developed his Praxinoscope. In this device, Reynaud substituted a polygonal drum of mirrors which spun at the center of the outer drum. Light reflected from a lamp mounted above it gave a bright and clear impression of movement.

In 1878 Eadweard Muybridge, with the help of John D. Isaacs, set up a battery of cameras hooked up to take a series of successive pictures of moving objects. This was the famous experiment carried out by Muybridge for Leland Stanford to find out if all four hooves of a horse left the ground at any one time. (The resulting photographs proved once and for all that they did.)[6]

Simultaneously with these developments, important discoveries were being made in the field of electrical communication. Man's desire to see and communicate beyond the horizon led him to devise ways and means to accomplish these aims. The invention of the telescope let man see objects that could not be reached physically: the moon, the planets, the sun and the stars. The discovery and harnessing of electricity gave man the first practical methods for communication beyond the horizon. In 1837, Samuel F.B. Morse demonstrated his new electrical telegraph, which was a rather simple device using a unique code made up of dots and dashes. The Morse code became an international language. This was a tremendous accomplishment. It wasn't too long before means were devised to record the dots and dashes on long strips of paper to be read at a later time.[7]

By 1843, Alexander Bain had invented an "automatic copying telegraph." It consisted of pendulums, one at the transmitter and the other at the receiving end, kept in step by magnetic catches that would hold either pendulum from starting until the other had returned to its starting position. At each swing, the message block was lowered a short distance so that the falling arc swept over an adjacent line.

At the transmitting station, the swinging arcs of the pendulum carried a small contactor which rode over printing type, making the appropriate electrical contacts to be transmitted to the distant receiver. Here the receiving pendulum was tracing a path across a piece of chemically treated paper. Since the pendulum was tracing the type, it only sent signals when in contact with the metal surfaces. At the receiver, this was translated into a series of lines which would give the impression of the original message.[8]

Bain had very little success with this machine even though it had all of the elements necessary to send visual information. In 1846, he devised a simpler "chemical telegraph," which eliminated the need for synchronization between transmitter and receiver by using the action of electricity on paper treated with certain chemicals to produce dots and dashes.[9]

In 1848, Frederick C. Bakewell invented a more advanced "electric telegraph" for sending copies of writing, print, or of other characters, symbols or designs. He also planned to use pendulums as a means of synchronization. Bakewell's machine used two synchronously rotating metal cylinders, one at the transmitter and the other at the receiving end. Both machines had a metal stylus or needle which traced a spiral path across the cylinders by means of a lead screw.

At the transmitter a specially prepared message was made by writing on tinfoil with varnish or other insulating material. The tinfoil was rolled on a cylinder and explored by the stylus, which sent a continuous signal except when it was passing over the varnish.

At the receiver, a sheet of chemically prepared paper was placed on the drum and the stylus put into contact with it. As the needle of the transmitter traced the drawing, current passed when the tinfoil was contacted and turned off when the needle hit a varnished surface. Thus current flowed intermittently in the circuit and at the receiver caused a reproduction of the picture to be made.[10]

A machine very similar to Bain's 1843 invention was patented by Giovanni Caselli of Florence, Italy, in 1865.[11] Caselli's 1861 invention, called the Pantelegraph, was built and operated for several years in France but was abandoned when it did not realize the hopes of its promoters.[12] In 1869 L. d'Arlincourt patented a visual telegraph which used tuning forks for synchronization.[13] It was not until 1876 that Alexander Graham Bell unraveled the secret of the speaking telegraph or telephone.[14]

Along with the historic developments in photography and electricity, many important advances were made in the allied fields of physics and chemistry. In 1817 Jons J. Berzelius isolated the element selenium.[15] In 1828 William Nicol invented the special polarizing prism that bears his name.[16] In 1839 Edmond Becqueral described the electrochemical effect of light. This became known as the photo-voltaic effect.[17] In 1845, Michael Faraday demonstrated that a beam of plane-polarized light passing through a transparent medium would be rotated if placed in a powerful magnetic field. This became known as the Faraday effect.[18]

In 1873 Willoughby Smith, chief electrician of the Telegraph Construction and Maintenance Company, used selenium rods as high resistance for continuity checks of the Atlantic cable. This checking proved to be very unreliable due to wide variations in resistance. Observation of the changes in the resistance of the crystalline selenium bars were made by Joseph May. He reported that a stick of crystalline selenium offered considerably less resistance to a battery current when exposed to light than when kept in the dark. This phenomena became known as the photoconductive effect. This report on the sensitivity of selenium to light was soon to manifest itself in the first schemes for a "visual telegraph."[19]

John Kerr discovered in 1875 that an electric potential applied to certain dielectrics caused rotation of the plane of polarized light. This was the electro-optical effect in liquids.[20] In 1877 Kerr worked on the magneto-optical effects by reflection. This was the rotation of a plane of polarization when plane-polarized light was reflected from the pole piece of a magnet.[21]

Other researchers began experiments with electrical discharges at low pressures. The first step was taken in 1858 by Julius Plücker and Heinrich Geissler. Plücker designed a sealed glass tube which was filled with gas at low pressure with an electrode at each end. When a certain voltage was applied to the electrodes, the gas in the tube ionized, current flowed and the tube glowed with a characteristic color. This became known as the Geissler tube.[22]

Experiments with similar tubes were made in 1869 when Wilhelm Hittorf discovered that a solid body would cast a shadow on the walls of the tube.[23] In 1876, E. Goldstein concluded that the rays came from the cathode and called them cathode rays.[24] Further work was done by William Crooks, who in 1879 suggested that the rays were actually negatively charged particles projected with high velocity by the electric forces near the surface of the cathode.[25]

A device called the telectroscope was first mentioned in 1877 as an apparatus for sending images or pictures at a distance. This was reported in *L'Aneé Scientifique et Industrielle*, June 1877, in an article by the editor, L. Figuier. He described an apparatus supposedly made by Alexander Graham Bell capable of visual transmission.

The apparatus he described was composed of two chambers, one at the sender and the other at the receiver, connected by a bundle of fine wires. The transmitter consisted of a multitude of wire ends which formed a plane surface. The receiver consisted of a multitude of "vibrations lumineuses" (spark gaps?) which would correspond to the light and color of the object being transmitted. It was claimed that Bell had actually used the device, but Figuier claimed that the lack of details left this very much in doubt. This appears to be the first description of a multi-wire apparatus for the simultaneous transmission of visual images. No mention was made of the material to be used to convert the light to electricity.[26]

On December 24, 1877, Thomas A. Edison applied for his patent on the phonograph. It was announced in the *Scientific American* on November 17, and described in it on December 22, 1877. This was the first practical device for the recording and reproduction of sound.[27]

Wordsworth Donisthorpe wrote a letter to *Nature* on January 12, 1878, outlining a plan for combining the phonograph with a "kinesigraph." This scheme is considered to be the first complete plan for the talking motion picture. In his proposal, Donisthorpe described the means for recording instantaneous photographs at about an eighth of a second, and after fixing, the prints to be put on a long strip or ribbon and wound from one cylinder to another to pass before the eye at the same intervals of time as they were taken.

For playback, he suggested the use of an electric spark to instantaneously light up each picture as it passed before the eye. He added the use of the phonograph to repeat the dialogue of the actors. He mentioned that only the lack of color would render the representation absolutely complete.[28]

Just one month later on February 20, 1878, a Portuguese professor, Adriano de Paiva, published an article in which he described an electric telescope or telectroscope quite similar to the one described earlier by L. Figuier. He did mention the use of a selenium-covered plate to convert the light from the images into electricity.[29]

Later, in November 1878, came the disclosure of another telectroscope from one Constantine Senlecq of Ardres, France. However, it was quite different from both Figuier's and de Paiva's. Senlecq planned to reproduce a picture telegraphically at a distance from a camera obscura. Here would be placed a piece of unpolished glass which would be traced by a small piece of selenium held by two springs acting as pincers in an electric circuit. This tracing point would traverse the surface of the glass and transmit a varying electric current to the receiver. This was to consist of a tracing point of blacklead, connected with a very thin plate of soft iron vibrating as in the telephone, which would draw a fine line on a sheet of paper. Synchronization of the two units would be by "any means of autographic telegraphic transmission." This of course was phototelegraphy (facsimile) and not television.[30]

By the end of 1878, the combination of Bell's telephone and Edison's phonograph combined with the progress being made in photography led the magazine *Punch* to print a cartoon of a new Edison "invention," the "telephonoscope." Here was depicted two-way television on a wide screen

His proposal was certainly one of the keystones of the modern television system. It outlined the following elements: (a) a transducer for converting light into electricity, (b) a means for scanning to systematically dissect the picture into its basic elements, (c) a means for synchronizing the transmitter with the receiver, (d) a light valve or modulator at the receiver to convert the electrical signals back into visible light, and finally (e) some kind of screen to display the reconstructed image.[7]

In 1880, Adriano de Paiva published the first brochure ever written about electrical television. This was *La Téléscopie Electrique, Basée sur L'Emploi du Selenium*, published in Porto by Antonio Jose da Silva.[8]

On February 11, 1881, C. Senlecq outlined a newer version of his telectroscope. He described the use of a multitude of small bores, each of which was filled with selenium which was led to the contacts of a linear commutator. There was to be a second contact line for sending pulses to an electromagnet at the receiver. Here the signal was sent sequentially to wires embedded in a hard rubber plate. These wires were to make an image on specially prepared paper. In addition, Senlecq proposed to use platinum wires which were supposed to glow in accordance to the picture signals and create a visual image. He indicated the use of a Ruhmkorff coil to generate sparks corresponding to the transmitter current.[9]

In 1881 Shelford Bidwell is said to have given a demonstration of still picture transmission and reception to the Physical Society in London. At the transmitter, a shadowgraph image was projected onto the front of the box with a pinhole aperture containing a selenium cell. The receiver consisted of a platinum-covered brass cylinder mounted horizontally on a spindle. A picture projected by a magic lantern was focused by a lens through cutouts of tinfoil onto the cylinder through a pinhole aperture to a size two inches square. During rotation of the cylinder, every part of the projected image was to be scanned. A platinum point was attached to a flexible arm and traced out the lines on the paper with an intensity which varied in accordance with the current through the selenium cell.[10]

Another scheme was proposed in April 1882 by William Lucas. This was mainly concerned with an optical receiver. He believed that the transmitter could be the same as Bidwell's cylinder model. In the receiver, the light was to be modulated by a crossed pair of Nicol prisms operated by the incoming signal via an electromagnet. The modulated beam was then to be deflected by vertical and horizontal prisms to cast a moving spot of light which traced a horizontal pattern on a screen. Lucas did not elaborate as to how the moving prisms were to operate.[11]

On January 6, 1884, Paul Nipkow in Berlin applied for German Patent No. 30105. This is the master television patent, for it showed for the first time a means of systematically scanning an image into its elemental points through the use of a perforated disc.

The scanning disc had 24 holes in a spiral near the outer rim. From station I (the transmitter) light from the subject would pass through the

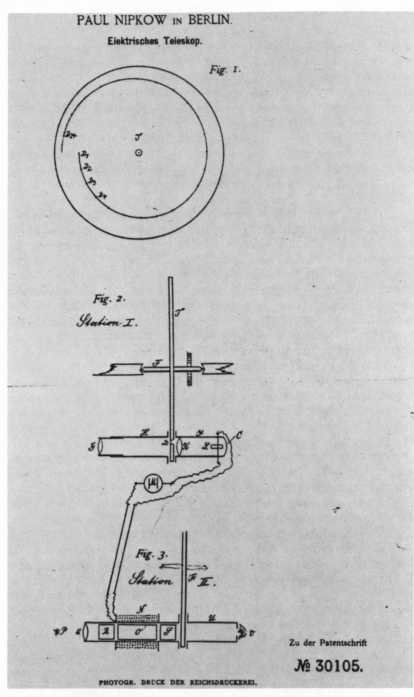

Paul Nipkow's German Patent No. 30105, showing the first means of systematic-ally scanning an image onto its elemental points through the use of a perforated disc.

disc and lenses G and K onto a selenium cell. The disc would rotate at a constant speed, and the output of the cell L was connected by an electrical circuit to the receiver at station II (the "receptor," in the patent), where another disc rotating at a constant speed was illuminated by a polarized light source. P is the source of light, and the light goes through convex lens Q, Nicol prisms R and S. The plane of polarization is rotated by means of coil N around body O made of flint glass according to the Faraday effect. This was the light valve or modulator. The image was to be viewed through disc T through eyepiece U.

Nipkow also mentioned replacing the selenium cell with (a) a carbon cell developed by Sumner Tainter; (b) a carbon drum with a microphone mounted on its membrane or a carbon drum that is sealed by the membrane of a telephone; or (c) a Thermophone receiver or Thermobatterie (the use of a heated body through a darkened tube which generates varying currents when heated and cooled).

Nipkow suggested replacing the disc by a pan- or copy telegraph. He also suggested replacing the polarization system with a telephone with a reflective member or a telephone with members that open and close by means of a tube that furnishes the needed air to a burning body. This was an application of a manometric device such as the "talking arc."[12] Nipkow never built such a device but did spend his hard-earned money on a patent.

On January 8, 1885, an article on "The New Telephotograph" by P.I. Bakmet'yev appeared in *Elektrichestro*. This appears to be the first article in a Russian journal describing several schemes for seeing at a distance. The author mentioned a method for phototelegraphy using a spiral scan with several sensors in a multi-wire setup. He also showed a version of the early Senlecq scheme which used a single selenium resistor and a single point to reconstruct the picture.[13]

Also in 1885, Shelford Bidwell described his version of the Nipkow patent in *La Lumière Electrique*. He had added means for synchronizing the two discs. He did not specify a selenium cell but some form of microphone which was supposed to react to light and cause current to flow in a circuit. At the receiver, another telephone coil was to vibrate a mirror, which was to pass reflected light through the disc.[14]

On August 29, 1885, Sumner Tainter applied for a patent for a method of magnetic recording. It included means for magnetic recording by causing the records to produce changes in the field of a magnetic needle, thereby inducing electric currents in a coil in said field and converting said currents into sound waves. It mentioned the use of a bobbin of insulated wire in the field of the needle and a telephone circuit including the bobbin.[15]

In September 1888 Oberlin Smith wrote the first article on magnetic recording, entitled "Some Possible Forms of Phonograph." The article mentioned several different means of magnetic recording, including the idea for a recording telephone using either a cord, string, thread, ribbon, chain or wire which would become magnetized as it passed through a helix (coil) by means of hand, clockwork or other means. It would be played back in a similar manner.[16]

The television apparatus of Lazare Weiller was described in November 1889. This article depicted M. Weiller's new device called the phoroscope, the first apparatus to use a revolving drum carrying a series of tilted mirrors as a scanning device. Since each mirror was at a slightly different angle from the one preceding it, it was able to scan the entire scene in each rotation. The light from the scene went from the mirrors to a selenium cell, where the electric current was distributed through a commutator.

Synchronization was by means of the Hughes and Baudot regulators used in telegraphy. At the receiver, the currents were converted back into light by means of a manometric flame actuated by a telephone receiver. The varying light from the flame was directed to the mirrors on the receptor, thus recreating the original picture.[17]

Another television device, called the telephane, was described in December 1890 by Henry Sutton of Australia. Sutton described rotating Nipkow discs which were synchronized by use of La Cour's phonic wheels with a Delany regulator (tuning forks?).

For the modulation of the light source, Sutton planned to use the Kerr effect, the use of two Nicol prisms which would polarize the light. Between the two prisms would be some form of tube filled with carbon sulphate. This tube would be surrounded by a coil of wire, which would rotate the polarized light when activated by an electrostatic field.[18]

Much progress had been made in the recording and projection of moving objects. In 1881 Eadweard Muybridge had gone to Paris and met Etienne Jules Marey. Marey was a French physician and physiologist, and was very enthusiastic about Muybridge's new projection device. In 1882 Marey had devised a "photographic gun," a camera with a cylindrical chamber in which a dry plate revolved. With this device he was able to photograph birds in flight at about 12 pictures per second. By mounting these pictures on a serial disc, he was able to show the objects in motion.

It is claimed that Marey had great influence on Muybridge by impressing on him the value of his process for observing physiological studies and other scientific purposes. In July 1882 Marey proposed the use of sensitized paper in his camera. But this paper was not satisfactory for a variety of reasons.[19]

In 1884 Ottomar Anschutz, a professional photographer, devised an ingenious camera for taking rapid pictures using a "focal plane" shutter. From 1885 on he specialized in the photography of men and animals in motion.

Anschutz invented his "Elektrischer Schnellseher" or electric tachyscope in 1887. This electric rapid viewer used a stroboscopic disc with a shutter that was operated by an electrical discharge tube rather than the usual slit.[20]

Anschutz had built an apparatus using the Geissler tube to replace the optical shutter. From 14 to 24 diapositives were mounted along the circumference of the disc. At the highest point a piece of circular opal glass 10cm in diameter was positioned. Directly behind it was a Geissler tube, wound spirally to a circular face of the same diameter. As the disc was set into motion, the Geissler tube had a strong induction current sent through it, broken in about 1/1000 of a second, and it glowed as each slide was in the proper position. As the disc was spun so that each picture followed another in about 1/30 second, the opal glass began to glow with a seemingly continuous light. The series slides would now be seen in motion in "elegant measure and excellent completion."

This device by Anschutz was not only the very first optical machine to use an electric shutter but had great influence on the course of the motion picture. It was first shown in Berlin in March 1887.[21]

Also in May 1887, the Rev. Hannibal Goodwin of Newark, New Jersey, applied for an American patent for the production of light-sensitive strips.[22]

In 1888 Etienne Marey had considerable success with his process called chronophotography. This was a device using a roll of sensitized paper film which was pulled through the camera by means of an intermittent mechanism. This machine, called the Chronophotographe, was quite successful, being the first camera to use both an intermittent movement and a strip of light-sensitive paper.[23]

Eadweard Muybridge had visited Thomas Edison in February 1888 and is supposed to have talked of a method of combining his Zoopraxiscope with the Edison phonograph.[24] It appears that Edison set his assistant, W.K.L. Dickson, to work on this project sometime in 1887 or 1888.

It is claimed that Edison had Dickson either build a tachyscope or purchase one for experimentation. Edison was fascinated by Anschutz's device, and his first efforts at the motion picture used the Geissler tube in the exact same manner.

Dickson's first effort was to use the phonograph of Edison and photograph miniature pictures on it using Carbutt celluloid film with some form of stop/start movement. For playback he used a Geissler tube with electrical contacts to illuminate his tiny pictures. There were no problems of synchronization, as the phonograph and the cylinder with the pictures were driven from the same shaft.[25]

In 1889, Edison visited the Paris Exposition and met Etienne Marey, who showed him the results he had obtained with his new camera. He displayed scenes using a Plateau disc combined with a projector and disc illuminated by a Geissler tube. Marey's use of paper film was not lost on Edison. In 1889, Edison filed four caveats dealing with a motion picture device. The fourth one, filed on November 2, 1889, related to both the use of film in a long band and an intermittent movement.[26]

Theories about these matters became a reality in September 1889 when Edison ordered some of the new roll film being made by George Eastman of Rochester, New York. W.K.L. Dickson (Edison's assistant) proceeded to build a camera (the Kinetograph) to take pictures with this new film and a viewing device (the Kinetoscope) to display them. The camera had an intermittent movement and used perforated transparent film. The viewer moved the film continuously in an endless loop and used a revolving shutter to interrupt the light between frames.[27]

Thomas Edison had not been the only one working on the motion picture. A Frenchman, Ducos du Hauron, had applied for a patent on a motion picture device as early as 1864. Wordsworth Donisthorpe had applied for a British patent in 1876.[28] Augustin le Prince had applied for an American patent in November 1886 for motion pictures and projection. Others, such as William Friese-Greene, had applied for a patent in 1889 for a camera using perforated film strips. Such a machine perforated the film only on the corners and was propelled by rollers. A crank caused the film to move as well as the shutter to operate.

There were others, of course, but it is generally conceded that it was Edison who made the motion picture practical. His introduction of perforated film solved a myriad of problems.[29]

The premiere of the Kinetoscope took place on April 14, 1894. Strangely enough, Edison had few or no plans for the projection of images. Thus it happened that several independent inventors hit upon the idea of an intermittent mechanism to allow the film to pause for the time necessary for projection onto a large screen. Among these inventors were Thomas Armat and Charles Francis Jenkins in Washington; Woodville Latham in New York; Robert W. Paul in London; and the Lumière Brothers, Louis and Auguste, in Lyons, France.[30]

Many important discoveries in electricity were made during this period. One of the most important was made by Thomas A. Edison, who discovered that electricity would flow in an incandescent lamp to a conductor placed inside the lamp. While experimenting with his electric light bulb, Edison noticed that the inside of the bulbs became blackened by a dark deposit on the glass. Trying to find the cause of this phenomenon, he discovered that current would flow from the heated element to a conductor placed anywhere in the bulb. Even though he was so busy that he never continued work on this project, his discovery became known as the Edison effect and was to be the forerunner of the two-electrode vacuum tube.[31]

In 1887 Heinrich Hertz discovered that if ultraviolet light fell on a spark gap, an electrical discharge took place more easily than when the gap was in darkness.[32] Further work on this effect was done by Wilhelm Hallwachs in 1888. In that year he made the first apparatus for demonstrating the so-called photoelectric effect. He observed that a well-insulated and negatively charged body lost its charge when illuminated with ultraviolet light.[33]

In 1889 Julius Elster and Hans Geitel discovered that certain electropositive metals such as sodium, rubidium, and cesium exhibited photoelectric activity when illuminated with ordinary light. In 1890 they enclosed an alkali amalgam in an evacuated envelope and thus produced the first photometric device.[34]

Also in 1890 A. Stoletow devised the first true photoelectric cell. It had a metal plate connected in series with a very sensitive high-resistance galvanometer, a battery and a gauze screen. When the plate was illuminated, the galvanometer registered a current, indicating that the plate emitted electrons under the influence of light.[35]

Prof. E. Branley in Paris constructed an insulating tube in 1890/91 containing metal filings which, when subjected to an electrical discharge, increased the tube's conductivity. Because the filings drew together, this device became known as the "coherer." It was later used to detect radio waves.[36]

Noah Steiner Amstutz of Cleveland, Ohio, applied for a patent for the first device for transmitting single-line halftone photographic images on March 17, 1891. His transmitter consisted of a cylinder upon which was wrapped a photograph in relief (prepared in gelatin) with a stylus which traveled over its surface responding to its varying depth. Attached to the stylus was a series of resistance coils, so that as the stylus moved, it produced different amounts of resistance into the circuit thus modulating the picture with a varying current.

At the receiver, a stylus with a V-shaped tracing tool cut a series of parallel lines into some type of "plastic material" which when printed produced lighter or darker lines depending on the amount of current being transmitted. Suitable means of synchronizing were mentioned. This appears to be the first facsimile transmitter for sending photographs with halftones. It is claimed that Amstutz sent the first successful pictures over a 25-mile line in some eight minutes in May 1891.[37]

Also in 1891, A. Blondel introduced the first "oscillograph," a recording device which had a small vibrating mirror mounted on a pair of conductors, held close together in a magnetic field. As the amplitude of the vibration depended upon the amount of electricity sent into the device, it could reflect a varying image onto a piece of film or something similar. This device was improved by W. Duddell in 1893 to a form similar to that used today.[38]

Louis Marcel Brillouin proposed in 1891 another television scheme which used two lensed discs rotating at different speeds. This was a system devised to dissect and scan an image. Brillouin proposed the use of a selenium cell to translate the light into electric currents. At the receiver, a similar set of lensed discs was to use a "mirror galvanometer" as a light valve. The mirror galvanometer was a narrow vertical mirror in the form of a wedge that was moved by the coil and opened and closed in response to the transmitted signal, thus modulating the light source.[39]

In 1893, Leon Le Pontois described his telectroscope. It employed Nipkow discs and alternating-current motors controlled by tuning forks for synchronizing the transmitter and receiver. The subject was flooded with "hot light," while the selenium cell was placed in a receptacle containing a cooling mixture. Light modulation depended upon a complicated monometric arrangement with relays in pressure chambers supplied with hydrogen and oxygen. This furnished light for a cylinder of carbonate of calcium in a projection lantern fitted with a ground glass screen for direct viewing.[40]

There is mention of one Quierno Majorana in 1894, whose device for seeing at a distance used rotating discs with intersecting slots for analysis of the image.[41]

Also in 1894, an article by Charles Francis Jenkins appeared, describing his device for transmitting pictures by electricity, called the Phantascope. It was quite similar to the 1880 Carey apparatus in that it was a multi-wire device using a multitude of selenium or sulphur wires connected electrically to a multitude of filaments which would glow in accordance to the amount of light that struck the transmitter. At this time Jenkins, along with Thomas Armat, was engaged in the design and operation of one of the first motion picture projectors made. This was also called a Phantascope.[42]

Carl Nystrom filed for a patent on a machine called the Telephotograph on January 11, 1895. It was to use a selenium cell that was to traverse back and forth on the edge of a rotating drum so as to scan a scene. The currents from the cell were to be taken from a commutator and sent to a receiver. Here an incandescent lamp of some sort was to follow the same motion as the transmitter and reconstruct the picture. Several schemes were shown for transmitting still pictures as well.[43]

In 1896 Guglielmo Marconi, a young Italian inventor, applied for the first patent covering the new science of radio telegraphy based on the use of electric waves. It covered a complete system for both the transmission and reception of wireless communication. Marconi traveled to Great Britain in mid–February 1896 with a letter of introduction from Alan Archibald Campbell Swinton to W. Preece, engineer-in-chief of the Government Telegraph Service.[44]

J. Ambrose Fleming rotated the image in a Crooks tube by changing the current in a coil wrapped around the tube in 1896. In 1897 Sir William Crooks deflected the image in a similar tube by electrostatic means, and in 1897 J.J. Thomson proved that these rays carried a negative charge.[45]

Also in 1897 Ferdinand Braun perfected the cathode ray tube that bears his name. It had a cold cathode from which electrons were attracted by a high potential from an anode A. These rays went through a perforated diaphragm to a screen made of mica coated with a material which glowed when struck by cathode rays. The beam was deflected in one plane only by either magnetic or electrostatic fields.

As originally used by Braun, the image was viewed through a rotating mirror and was deflected magnetically. Its immediate use was for the study of electrical waveforms. This use had been suggested by H. Ebert sometime in 1897.[46]

On February 24, 1897, Jan Szczepanik and Ludwig Kleinberg of Austria applied for a patent for a method and apparatus for reproducing pictures and the like at a distance by means of electricity. (In Britain, this was the first television patent applied for.) This device was to use two oscillating mirrors. Each was to have a reflecting surface in the form of a narrow linear strip, the rest of the mirror being opaque. The two mirrors were at right angles to each other and, given the proper movements, would scan an image with a zigzag motion.

This image would be reflected to a selenium cell, which would be rotating to overcome its sluggishness. The current from this cell would be sent by line to an electromagnet connected to a similar set of mirrors and provided with an aperture. The light from an incandescent source would go through a prism and pass only through that portion of the spectrum scanned by the rotating selenium cell.

For synchronization, two electromagnets on each of the rotating mirrors would go to some sort of current-interrupting device, i.e., "an induction aparatus, a microphone or some other device M1 or M2 by means of which the current is constantly interrupted or varied in strength." It was planned to send a succession of pictures lasting some 0.1 to 0.5 seconds so that the "impression of a moving picture can be made on the retina of the eye, exactly as in the case of the stroboscope, kinematograph and the like."

It was later reported that this apparatus had actually been built and was to be exhibited at the Paris Exposition of 1900. This exhibition never took place, although it was reported that Szczepanik had been paid over one million dollars for the rights to his invention but would not reveal the details of his apparatus until the exhibition was over.[47]

A description of the "Dussaud Teleoscope" was given in July 1898. The transmitter had a movable shutter consisting of apertures arranged in a spiral on a Nipkow disc. The light from the subject formed an image at the back of the camera and the more or less luminous parts of this image struck in succession "a peculiar system of selenite plates." The shutter was actuated by a Hughes clockwork mechanism.

The current from the selenite would flow to an induction coil in the receiver which was connected to the disc of a telephone. This disc moved an opaque plate provided with transparent lines and displaced it more or less in front of an identical but stationary plate. Thus the pencil of light produced by a lamp (N) was forced to pass through the two opaque plates more or less diminished, according to the current passed through the wire.

Since the light now passed through the shutter (disc) in a path similar to and synchronous with the sender, an identical picture should be reproduced at the receiver at about one-tenth of a second. This was the first television scheme which was to project its image onto a viewing screen similar to that of the motion picture. The apparatus was to be shown at the Paris Exhibition of 1900, but never was.[48]

In 1898 the first Russian television patent was filed by M. Wolfke. It used Nipkow discs and a selenium plate that excited an induction coil. The secondary winding of the coil included a vibrator, which radiated electromagnetic waves. Thus Wolfke's was the first patent to describe a television system using the new art of wireless telegraphy. The Nipkow disc did not have the usual spiral but used a circle of holes offset from center so as to scan the image in an oscillatory fashion. The light modulator was a gas discharge tube (Geissler) to be used as an instantaneous light source. How Wolfke planned to modulate this tube was not described.[49]

Another Russian patent was applied for by A.A. Polumordvinov in December 1889. It was to be used for color or black-and-white television. For monochrome it used the slotted discs of Majorana. For color Polumordvinov proposed to use two concentrically disposed cylinders with slits alternately covered by red, green and violet filters. This was the first proposed "sequential" system of color television.[50]

On December 1, 1898, Vlademar Poulsen of Copenhagen, Denmark, applied for a patent for a method of recording and reproducing sounds or signals. Poulsen stated that it was possible to store signals on a paramagnetic body. He further stated that a steel wire or ribbon which was moved past an electromagnet connected with an electric or magnetic transmitter, such as a telephone, was magnetically excited along its length in exact correspondence with the signals, messages or speech delivered to the transmitter, and that when the magnetically excited wire was again moved past the electromagnet, it would reproduce the said signals, messages or speech in a telephone receiver connected with the said electromagnet.

Poulsen predicted that the "present invention will replace the phonograph hitherto used and provide simpler and better-acting apparatus." Poulsen actually built this apparatus and showed it at the Paris Exhibition of 1900, where he won the Grand Prix.[51]

Thus by the end of the nineteenth century, many of the basic discoveries for television had been made. But the requirements of the infant art were such that many years would pass before the necessary tools would come onto the scene.

feature and in 1905 described a Braun-type tube fitted with a lime-coated hot cathode.[11]

J. Ambrose Fleming applied for a patent in 1904 on a two-electrode vacuum tube to be used as a detector of high-frequency oscillation. Fleming was seeking a better way of detecting the feeble radio waves of that time. When radio (Hertzian) waves were led to a plate, the negative charge tended to stop the flow of electrons from the filament to the plate, which had the effect of cutting the radio frequency in half. This was necessary because the ether waves were sent at too high a frequency to be audible. The two-element tube or diode was known as "Fleming's valve" and could be used to operate headphones.[12]

In 1906, Lee De Forest applied for a patent for a "Two-electrode Audion." He applied for the first three-electrode "Audion" on October 25, 1906, and the first grid-type three-electrode Audion on January 29, 1907. The third element or control grid was De Forest's greatest contribution to the vacuum tube. Up to this time the flow of electrons went from the cathode to the plate. The grid was put in the path of the electrons and when voltage was applied to the grid, it had a tendency to stop the flow. The stronger the grid current, the fewer electrons could get by. No matter how strong the tube current, the sensitive grid could control it.

This new tube, the three-electrode Audion, could do three important things. It could amplify signals to any volume required, hundreds of times if necessary. It could change alternating current to direct current. It could generate high-frequency current. These properties were developed through a period of time, and even De Forest didn't know what a miracle he had performed. At the time, he only knew that he had a better radio detector. He left a certain amount of gas in the tube in the mistaken idea that the gas was necessary to make it function properly.[13]

Another, similar patent was filed in March 1906 by Robert von Lieben for a cathode ray relay. This device was to enable current variations of small energy to release current variations of greater energy at the output of the device. It was a cathode ray tube in which the current was modulated by the magnetic action of a coil "e" on a beam of electrons from cathode "k." Thus it was a true amplifier of electron current.[14]

Georges P.E. Rignoux applied in February 1906 for a television patent using vibrating mirrors very similar to the original Le Blanc scheme. The picture was scanned by two small vibrating mirrors and transduced by a selenium cell at the transmitter. The receiver had a small plate connected to a telephone receiver that vibrated as it received current from the transmitter. This plate was in the path of the light from a small lamp and varied the amount of light that went to two small vibrating mirrors similar to the transmitter. The telephone receiver and its plate comprised the light modulator.[15]

On September 12, 1906, Max Dieckmann and Gustav Glage in Straszburg applied for the first patent using a cathode ray tube as a display device *not* for waveforms. The cathode ray tube had four magnetic coils to control the position of the electron beam. There was no means for modulating the electron beam as it was either on or off. The instrument was controlled by a pen or stylus connected by two sets of sliding resistors which varied the signals (on two axes) sent to the magnetic coils. This was an advanced form of "Telautograph" (Fernschrieber) which was to be used for sending handwritten messages by wire. It was not a television device as it had no provision for scanning of the images, did not depend on the persistence of vision and had no transducer to convert light into electricity; nor could the electron beam be modulated. It simply was the first device on which it was possible to write on the face of the cathode ray tube. Also in 1906, Dieckmann and Glage applied for an electrical valve using cathode rays similar to the von Lieben patent.[16]

Sometime in 1906 F. Lux supposedly built a model of a television device which was to use selenium cells in a multicellular mosaic. An alternating current of discrete frequency was to flow through each cell and was to be modulated by the picture signals from each cell. In a manner not disclosed, these signals were to be sent to a mosaic of light squares which were controlled by the movements of vibrating resonant springs (similar to the vibrating-reed frequency meter), thus varying the brightness of each opening in accordance to the picture signal sent. This would seem to be the first device actually built for viewing at a distance. It was a multi-wire simultaneous system and not a true television system.[17]

Although there were many attempts to synchronize the motion picture with the phonograph, it remained for Eugene A. Lauste to combine the motion picture and sound on the same film strip. Lauste, a former employee of Edison, applied for a patent in 1906 using either a vibrating diaphragm, a reflecting mirror, or the speaking arc (the "talking flame" of König) to record the sound on the film. For playback he planned to use a selenium cell. Later he abandoned the talking flame and used a string galvanometer with excellent results.[18]

On July 25, 1907, Boris Rosing of the Technological Institute, St. Petersburg, Russia, applied for a Russian patent covering a television system using a cathode ray tube for a receiver. The transmitter used two polyhededronal mirrors (the Weiler mirror drum) for dissecting and scanning the image. The dissected images were to be sent by a lens to a selenium cell, silver-chloride Becquerel element or an Elster and Geitel sodium amalgam device. Synchronization was by means of rheostats that varied the resistance with every passage of each face of the mirror. These signals were sent to coils in the receiving tube to deflect the beam in accordance with the scanning of the image.

The receiving tube in this patent was a cold-cathode tube which had its beam deflected by either magnetic coils or plates. The modulation of the beam was accomplished by means of two plates in the neck of the tube situated before the deflection coils. These two plates were to be connected to the output of the photocell and its variations of current were to deflect the beam in such a manner as to vary its position through the diaphragm.

Thus if there were no signal, the beam was to be so deflected that none of it came through the diaphragm, and with full signal the entire beam would emanate from the diaphragm; any degree between was possible. Other means of synchronization and transmission were mentioned. This patent of Rosing was second in importance to that of the original Nipkow patent of 1884.[19]

Great progress was made in 1907 in the art of phototelegraphy. There was the work of both Arthur Korn and Edouard Belin. Korn's system used transmitting and receiving cylinders that turned synchronously. A celluloid film negative was wrapped around the cylinder, which was made of glass. The light from a lamp passed through the film to a fixed selenium cell, varying its output. At the receiver, a sensitized photographic film covered the cylinder, and the light from a lamp was passed through a shutter made of two strips of wire, which opened or shut depending on the current passing through the pole pieces of a strong magnet. It was claimed that this device could transmit halftones with good fidelity.[20]

The Belin system used a thickly coated gelatin-bichromate print, which had a certain amount of relief: light images were elevated, while shades were depressions. The print was wrapped around the transmitting cylinder, which moved uniformly and in a direction parallel to the axis. A sapphire point pressed on the picture, which was connected to a contact piece that slid over the edges of a series of thin copper plates, separated by thin sheets of mica, the whole being a rheostat capable of interposing a resistance ranging from 0 to 4000 ohms in 20 steps. The current regulated in accordance with the electrical variations passed through an aperiodic reflecting galvanometer such as Blondel's oscillograph.

A beam of light concentrated on the galvanometer mirror was reflected to a convex lens so placed as to project an image of the mirror over a small hole in the side of a light-tight box. Inside the box was a rotating receiving cylinder covered with photographic film. Between the hole and the lens and close to the latter was inserted an "optical wedge," consisting of a sheet of glass tinted by gradations from perfect transparency at one end to opacity at the other. A slight deflection of the mirror displaced the reflected rays from the center of the lens towards the edge and caused them to pass through a different part of the optical wedge; thus the intensity of the projected image of the mirror and therefore of the photographic action upon the film was varied in correspondence with the strength of the current.[21]

In February 1908, Charles F. Jenkins applied for a patent on a "Telautograph."[22] On April 1, 1908, Johannes Adamian applied for a British patent for color television. In this patent Adamian described the reflected light from a vibrating mirror thrown onto a series of selenium cells which had graduated resistances. The varying current was to be sent to a pair of Geissler tubes, which emitted different colored light. Actually one was white while the other emitted red light. The picture was dissected by a disk with perforations in a spiral and recomposed by a similar disc at the receiver.[23]

On May 20, 1908, Georges P.E. Rignoux applied for a French patent, the first to describe a system whereby the light from a source was sent to a rotating mirror drum, which then scanned the image to be transmitted. This system later became known as the "flying spot" system. It was intended for cutout figures against an opaque background, and the patent mentions the use of motion picture film.

The light from the source in this system went to a revolving mirror drum, where its reflected light scanned the image to be transmitted. From there it went through a lens to a selenium cell. The current from the cell went to two coils, which produced a magnetic field around a transparent dielectric plate.

At the receiver a light source went through a Nicol prism and the transparent plate surrounded by the magnetic coils and passed through another Nicol prism to a rotating mirror drum, which was turned by synchronized motors and reconstituted the picture on a viewing screen. This was a true "flying spot" system, as the light was reflected from the subject after the subject was scanned, and the mirror drum was situated between the light source and the photocell.[24]

In June 1908 Shelford Bidwell wrote a letter to *Nature* on "Telegraphic Photography and Electric Vision." He reviewed the various schemes for telegraphic transmission of photographs. He mentioned Dr. Korn's method; the "Téléstéréographie" method of Belin; the "Télauto-graveur" of Carbonelle; and finally Berjonneau's "Téléphotographe." Most important, he mentioned the remarks of one M.J. Armengaud, who believed that within a year, people would "be watching one another across distances hundreds of miles apart."

However, Bidwell proceeded to show how impossible this notion was. He described an apparatus that for a two-inch square picture would require 90,000 selenium cells, luminosity-controlling devices, projection lenses and conducting wires. The receiving apparatus would occupy a space of 4000 cubic feet, and the cable connecting the apparatus would have a diameter of 8 or 10 inches. Finally, the cost would be some £1,250,000. He concluded that it could be done in color but in that case, the cost would be multiplied by three.[25]

Bidwell's letter provoked a swift answer in the June 18, 1908, issue of *Nature* from A.A. Campbell Swinton (dated June 12, 1908) who stated

That it is widely impractical to effect even 160,000 synchronised operations per second by ordinary mechanical means, this part of the problem of obtaining distant electric vision can probably be solved by the employment of two beams of kathode rays (one at the transmitting and one at the receiving station) synchronously deflected by varying fields of two electromagnets placed at right angles to one another and energised by two alternating electric currents of widely different frequencies so that the moving extremities of the two beams are caused to sweep synchronously over the world of the required surfaces within the one-tenth of a second necessary to take advantage of visual persistence. Indeed, so far as the receiving apparatus is concerned, the moving kathode beam has only to be arranged to impinge on a sufficiently sensitive fluorescent screen, and given suitable variations in its intensity, to obtain the required result. The real difficulties lie in devising an efficient transmitter which, under the influence of light and shade, shall sufficiently vary the transmitted electric current so as to produce the necessary alterations in the intensity of the kathode beam of the receiver, and further in making this transmitter sufficiently rapid in action to respond to the 160,000 variation per second that are necessary as a minimum. Possibly no photoelectric phenomenon at present known will provide what is required in this respect, but should something suitable be discovered, distant electric vision will, I think, come within the realm of possibility.[26]

At this time, unknown to Campbell Swinton, both Boris Rosing in Russia and Max Dieckmann in Germany were experimenting with cathode ray tubes as a receiver, but no one had ever prescribed the use of a cathode ray tube as a transmitter. This startling letter, dated June 12, 1908, thus marks the beginning of the concept of an all-electric television system including both receiver and camera.

Yet, only two weeks later, on June 25, 1908, Boris Rosing's English patent was issued, describing a cathode ray receiver that fulfilled all of Campbell Swinton's requirements. Of course there was no electric camera in the Rosing patent.

On July 18, 1908, Gilbert Sellers applied for the first American patent for a television system. His patent was for the electrical transmission of graphic messages. He intended to transmit graphic messages, pictures, photos, prints, etc., and visible views of fixed, living and moving objects. Sellers planned to use a mechanism that moved the lens physically to scan the image. A series of revolving selenium cells were to pick up the scanned image.[27]

On December 24, 1908, A.C. Anderson and L.S. Anderson of Copenhagen applied for the first British patent under the heading or classification of "Television." This was a color television patent using either an endless perforated band or a disc with spirally disposed perforations. To produce the color it was planned to have a separate, rapidly rotating disc having apertures that received the light from a prism, which would separate the colors from red to violet. This rotating disc was synchronized with another disc at the receiver that had sectors colored like the solar spectrum, so that as the green image was transmitted, the green part of the disc was to be interposed in front of the image, thus giving a color picture at the receiver. The light valve was a graded transparent plate controlled electromagnetically by the current in the line wire. A selenium cell was to be used at the transmitter, with an ordinary lamp at the receiver.[28]

In the year 1909, three different television systems were actually built and operated. The first (in the order they were published) was that of Max

Georges Rignoux's apparatus, 1909. Top left: Lamp, mirror and object placed in front of the lens of the transmitter. Top right: the mosaic of selenium cells. Bottom: the original letter (left) and its transmitted image.

contact the beam was deflected vertically so that no rays reached the fluorescent screen and no luminous spot was formed. Thus the beam was normally on when no contact was made and off when passing over the object, responding to an "on or off" condition. It was claimed that as the pattern was repeated every tenth of a second, it followed every movement of the pattern being traced.

Dieckmann never applied for a patent on this device, and he turned his efforts to the sending of still pictures for the next fifteen years. It seems to be the first apparatus built that fulfilled all of the requirements for a television receiver, but due to the lack of a light-transducing device, the transmitter was actually a form of the telegraph (being either on or off) and lacked the requirements for a true television system.[29]

The second was the apparatus of Ernst Ruhmer, who gave a demonstration of his equipment on June 26, 1909. His device consisted of a mosaic of 25 selenium cells in rows of 5 each. Each cell when exposed to light was connected to a sensitive relay, which sent an alternating current

Opposite: Ernst Ruhmer and apparatus, 1909.

of certain frequency over a line. This was a form of multiplexing whereby signals of different frequencies could be sent over a single wire and would be detected and separated at the receiver. This was common practice at this time in telegraphic communications.

At the receiver, there was one resonating relay for each selenium cell. Thus the impulse sent from the selenium cell would only operate its own incandescent lamp. Simple geometric figures were transmitted. It was claimed that Ruhmer planned to build a model with 10,000 cells for the 1910 Brussels International Exposition at a cost of $1,250,000. While this crude device could transmit some basic figures and used a light-transducer, it was a simultaneous system that needed no means of synchronization and could not transmit any halftones.[30]

A quite different television device was built by Georges Rignoux in collaboration with physics professor A. Fournier. The transmitter consisted of a bright lamp which reflected the image of the object onto a selenium screen. This screen used a multiple bank of selenium cells, each connected to a separate relay. The relays were connected in sequence to a rotating commutator. As each relay was connected to the commutator it sent its signal through a single wire to the receiver. Here the signals were sent to a magnet which was part of a light valve comprising a Nicol prism, a tube of carbon sulphate around which the magnet was wound (the Faraday effect) and another Nicol prism.

Light from a very bright source was thus modulated by this valve and was sent to a rotating mirror drum, which had as many faces as there were rows of light cells and was synchronized with the commutator at the transmitter. The modulated light was then sent to a screen, where the image was reconstructed. This was a real television system, the first on record as having been built and operated. Even though its transmitter was limited, its receiver could have produced halftones on the screen, if the system had permitted it.[31]

On January 24, 1910, A. Ekstrom applied for a Swedish patent covering the principle of an inverse light system. It was a "flying spot" system similar to that of Rignoux. It was exclusively for the transmission of slides or transparencies, and of course, motion picture film. The patent described how the light from a bright source went to a double oscillating mirror to affect scanning. This was sent through the transparency to the selenium cell. For playback, the light from an arc went through a light valve (some sort of vibrating mirror) or galvanometer. Here a collecting glass (which was a graded transparency) transmitted it from another double rotating mirror to a screen.[32]

Michel Schmierer of Charlottenburg applied in April 1910 for two German patents covering the use of a Braun tube for reception and a scanning device using commutators to effectively scan an image in sequence.[33]

Gustav H. Hoglund of Chicago applied for a television patent on April 18, 1910. Hoglund's transmitter consisted of a shutter made up of an outer disc and an inner disc. The outer disc had a plurality of slots or openings of equal length and width which extended in a stepped line outward from the center of the disc. The inner disc had a plurality of elongated arcuated slots arranged in a spiral stepped formation from the outer edge to the center of the disc.

Since the discs were revolving in different directions it was obvious that the image would be dissected or scanned. It was planned to run the discs in synchronism, using synchronous motors. The light from the scene was then sent to a selenium cell for transmission. At the receiver, a "speaking arc," which was modulated by the received signal, went through a similar set of rotating shutters to a lens system and finally to a ground glass plate. The patent also included a telephone system so that the viewer could talk as well as see the sender.[34]

On June 20, 1910, Alf Sinding-Larsen of Norway applied for a patent for the "Transmission of Moving Objects" using vibrating mirrors and the use of a light-electric cell. It included the use of some form of light pipe made of silver with strongly reflecting inner surfaces. This device was supposedly for the direct transmission of images. Sending the modulated light directly to the receiver would eliminate a light valve there. It could also be used for sending pictures in both directions simultaneously. The use of tuning forks for synchronization was mentioned.[35]

Julius Elster and Hans Geitel reported on a new process for the sensitization of alkali metal cells in 1909/10. The cells were filled with hydrogen at a pressure of $\frac{1}{2}$mm of mercury heated to 350°C, and then a glow discharge was passed through them. Hydrogen was first left inside the cell to provide amplification by ionization. Later the hydrogen gas was pumped out and replaced with argon or helium to get longer lasting results.[36]

Boris Rosing applied for a patent on March 2, 1911, for a means of securing exact synchronization between the transmitter and receiver. This patent was the result of Rosing's work on an actual system of television and included two important inventions to make a system of television practical.

The first was the use of a light-chopper (either a grid in front of the picture or some opaque material) or a rapidly rotating disc or an endless band with apertures. The idea was to provide electrical pulses of constant frequency but of varying duration, in order to avoid the lagging effect due to the reactance of the apparatus.

The second was the use of a variable speed scanning beam in the receiver to effect modulation. In other words, since a slowly moving beam will be brighter and a fast moving beam will be dimmer, Rosing suggested that by varying the speed of the scan he could dispense with the older method of beam modulation. This technique was later known as "variable-velocity" scanning.[37]

It appears that Rosing had carried out experiments with actual models later in 1908 and attempted to transmit simple images (various drawings

Boris L. Rosing

on positive slides, moving fingers, hands, etc.). He continuously improved his system and in May 1911 successfully carried his first distant transmission of images. In his witnessed notebook, he is said to have written, "On May 9, 1911, a distinct image was seen for the first time, consisting of four luminous bands."[38]

Rosing was not using the sluggish selenium cell but a specially rapid photoelectric cell built in his laboratory. The cell consisted essentially of a glass bulb containing rarified hydrogen or helium and sodium, potassium, cesium or rubidium amalgam. The amalgam constitutes the optically sensitive electrode, while for the anode a platinum electrode was fused through the bulb. The amalgam was negatively charged, and when it was illuminated, there occurred, by the Hallwachs effect, a discharge from its surface varying in strength directly in proportion to the intensity of the incident illumination. This photoelectric current follows the variations in the exciting illumination.

Rosing's camera was in a housing with the two mirror drums and their gearing and the electrical connections to the homemade photoelectric cell. The receiver featured a cold cathode Braun tube with plates for beam modulation. The four deflecting magnets were situated in a ring sur-

degree of persistence that it would be possible to reduce the rate of scanning. He also stated that "as each of the metallic cubes in the screen J acts as an independent photocell and is only called upon to act once in a tenth of a second, the arrangement has obvious advantages over other arrangements that have been suggested, in which a single photocell is called upon to produce the many thousands of separate impulses that are required to be transmitted through the line wire per second, a condition which no known form of photocell will admit of." He finally indicated that the sluggishness of either the metallic cubes J or the vapor in K in no way interferes with the correct transmission and reproduction of the images at rest, and only gradually with the reproduction of images that may be in motion.[2]

In 1911 the first book containing a history of television as well as phototelegraphy and telautography was published. This was the *Handbuch der Phototelegraphie und Telautographie* by professors Arthur Korn and Bruno Glatzel. The book included the first complete survey of the most important contributions made to phototelegraphy and television.[3]

The Institute of Radio Engineers was formed in the United States on May 13, 1912. It was the result of the merger of the Wireless Society and the Society of Wireless Telegraph Engineers.

In 1913 American Telephone and Telegraph (AT&T) started to build its first high vacuum tubes for amplifiers. It had acquired the rights to the De Forest Audion. At the same time, Irving Langmuir of the General Electric Company was also working on high vacuum tubes and had applied for an American patent in October 1913.[4] W.D. Coolidge of the General Electric Company was working on high voltage x-ray tubes. He had added a tungsten cathode (heated by electricity) for the purpose of getting electron flow. He also added a focusing shield around the cathode. This tube gave steady operation with none of the eccentricities of the cold cathode tube, in which gas ionization had limited the effective anode voltage. There was also the use of chemical "getters" for improving the vacuum in sealed-off tubes. The current flow could be regulated by a rheostat. Coolidge's seems to be the first practical hot cathode ray tube.[5]

The beginning of World War I in August 1914 appears to have slowed down the number of patents and articles in the field of television considerably. However, several important items of interest did appear.

On June 25, 1914, Samuel L. Hart of London applied for a patent on an autographic device for transmitting pictures of moving objects to a distance electrically. It used a lens device to focus successively the rays from all parts of the field to a stationary, sensitive cell. The transmitter consisted of a series of lenses mounted at different angles to the horizontal with their axes converging to the central part of the segment, where a sensitive cell was placed. It was planned to oscillate the segments in order to cover the entire field of view.

At the receiver, a similar setup was planned with a single lens so positioned that it would receive the light from a special light valve (four types

Georges Rignoux (top center) and his 1914 apparatus. The lower left-hand corner shows the receiving station (e — solenoid; f — Nicol Prism; g — light). The lower center shows the receiving apparatus (c — translucent screen on which images from revolving mirror d are received). The lower right-hand corner shows the transmitting stations (a — magnetic relays; b — bank of selenium cells).

were described). Thus as the lens was oscillated it would recreate the scene. Means of synchronization were also mentioned. Importantly, on page eight it was mentioned that this apparatus could be used as a cinematographic recorder. It could record on a rapidly moving tape, or on a revolving plate or disc similar to that of the phonograph record.[6]

On July 13, 1914, Georges Rignoux reported that his apparatus was operating and that letters or other objects presented to the transmitter had been projected on the screen of the receiving apparatus. Later, on May 22, 1915, Rignoux described his machine in more detail. It had a selenium screen with 64 cells. The cells were connected by wire to a commutator, which rotated at 450 turns/minute. The signals were sent by two wires to a solenoid, which surrounded a hollow core. A Nicol prism polarized the light before it went through the core, and another prism allowed the light from an arc to pass when there was a certain current in the coil. A rotating wheel with eight mirrors reflected the light from the arc to a screen, where it was viewed. A third wire was used to synchronize the two parts of the machine (the motor running the commutator and the motor running the mirror drum). It was claimed that simple letters such as H, T, and U had been successfully transmitted.[7]

On April 1, 1915, Andre Voulgre applied for a French patent on a television system. Apparently the last such patent applied for until the war was over, it featured the use of several rotating bands in order to effect the scanning. In front of the two bands going in opposite directions was a disc with four slits in it. A similar arrangement was at the receiver. The use of a potassium, rubidium, or sodium photocell was mentioned. The light modulator was a mercury vapor lamp, which was powered by the current from the secondary of a coil.[8]

An article by Marcus J. Martin appeared in *Wireless World* in June 1915 in which he discussed the possibilities of television. He concluded that some form of television could possibly work over ordinary wire conductors, but that the idea of wireless television, from a really practical viewpoint, was "absurdly impossible." This article was part of a series written by Martin on the "Wireless Transmission of Photographs."[9]

Another, more important article seems to be the publication of the Campbell Swinton plan for television in the *Electrical Experimenter* of August 1915. Here was shown the Campbell Swinton's complete plan, including a drawing of a man and a woman conversing by means of two-way television and a schematic diagram of the system.

This article carefully explained the basic principles of the new Campbell Swinton system, including the need for two different scanning velocities, the need for synchronization, the charging of the cubes by the light from the camera, the necessary modulation of the receiving tube and finally how it was made possible by the persistence of vision—all of this in a layman's language. The importance of this article was that it appeared in a popular magazine with a large, varied readership, so that its ideas were propagated over a large area. It was not an obscure journal such as that of the Röntgen Society.[10]

On August 20, 1915, a young French scientist named Alexandre Dauvillier applied for his first patent, for an improvement in a radiography and radioscopy system. In order to avoid the "distortion" of the process at that time, he planned to use two perforated discs to scan an image in an x-ray system combined with the "Bucky effect." This early effort lead Dauvillier to combine his work on radiology with the infant art of television.[11]

C. Francis Jenkins founded the Society of Motion Picture Engineers

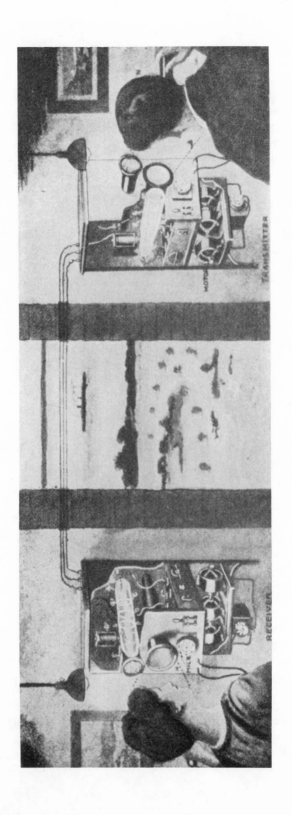

in July 1916. The purpose was "advancement in the theory and practice of motion picture engineering and the allied arts and sciences, the standardization of mechanisms and practices therein."

On November 17, 1917, D. McFarlan Moore of General Electric applied for a patent for a gaseous conduction lamp. The principal idea of the patent was to provide a lamp that would glow at low voltages, had stationary electrodes and was easy to start. This patent appears to be the basis of the early neon bulbs that were used in later mechanical disc systems, the progenitor of the Moore "crater-lamp."[12]

On December 17, 1917, Alexander M. Nicolson of Western Electric applied for a patent on "Television." The image was to be picked up by a single oscillating mirror moved by means of wires in a magnetic field. It would have two simple harmonic motions, fed by a single frequency, with a phase difference of 90 degrees. Thus the image would be scanned in a spiral path. This meant that the scanning velocity was continuously changing as it neared the center of its travel. To allow for this, a special compensating piece of glass or quartz (which became less transparent at its center) was inserted between the mirror and the object being scanned. As the mirror oscillated in the magnetic field, it supplied synchronizing signals of about 1000 cycles with 18/20 scans per second.

The most important part of this patent was the use of a special cathode ray tube. This Braun tube had a hot cathode and a grid which had a negative potential to control the beam. It used magnetic focus, which focused the beam by means of a coil around the neck of the tube. There is no mention of any gas in the tube. This appears to be the first television patent to specify the use of a hot cathode to emit a stream of electrons with a modulating grid to control the flow of electrons to the screen. It also specified the use of vacuum tubes for amplification, detection, modulation, and oscillation.

The output of the photocell produced a drop of potential across a resistor, which was impressed upon an amplifier. This voltage became the picture signal. This patent had all of the necessary ingredients for a practical television picture tube. But there is no evidence that Nicolson ever built or operated such a device.[13]

In August 1918 Jakob Kunz of the University of Illinois applied for a patent for making photoelectric cells using any of a group of alkali metals such as lithium, sodium, potassium, rubidium or cesium. Kunz described the use of an evacuated glass chamber having two electrodes, one of which consisted of a dense film of an alkali metal in a suitable form and condition, lying on the inner surface of the chamber. This could be filled with hydrogen, argon, helium or neon gas. The film electrode was so arranged that the light to be measured would fall upon the same. The other electrode was placed in the immediate vicinity of the film electrode in the

Opposite: Campbell Swinton's two-way television scheme.

form of a screen. Between the two electrodes there was formed a field subject to and sensitive to the influence of light.[14]

The end of the war in Europe in November 1918 found Marconi's Wireless Telegraph Company with a virtual monopoly over wireless communications in the United States. The United States Navy had taken over the Marconi wireless installation in New Jersey when the United States had entered the war. This station was using a 50 kilowatt Alexanderson alternator built by General Electric.

After the war, the Marconi Company tried to buy 24 Alexanderson alternators (now some 200 kilowatts), 14 for American Marconi and the other 10 for British Marconi, with exclusive rights to their use.

When the United States Navy found out about this arrangement, it was decided that General Electric would not sell this equipment to the Marconi Company. Instead it proposed that General Electric set up an American radio operating company which would be controlled by American interests and would exploit the Alexanderson alternator. This resulted in the formation of the Radio Corporation of America (RCA) which was organized on October 17, 1919, in the state of Delaware.

On November 20, 1919, the American Marconi Company was officially merged with the Radio Corporation of America. At this time a cross-licensing agreement was enacted between RCA and General Electric. On July 1, 1920, a cross-licensing agreement was affected between General Electric and the American Telephone and Telegraph Company. A similar agreement was made between RCA and Western Electric (the AT&T manufacturing division).

Edward J. Nally of American Marconi became president of RCA. He had been vice president and general manager of American Marconi. The chairman of the board was Owen D. Young, who was head of the General Electric legal department. Dr. Ernst Alexanderson became RCA's chief engineer, and David Sarnoff became commercial manager.

All patents of the participants were to be freely available to one another for ten years. General Electric was to have all of the rights of wireless telegraphy and the manufacture of receiving apparatus. AT&T was to have exclusive rights in radio-telephony associated with its telephone service, plus the manufacture of transmitter apparatus. RCA had no manufacturing rights and was to operate the transatlantic service of the old Marconi Company. All foreign patents were to be concluded through RCA. RCA was to act solely as a sales and service organization for the group.[15]

The end of the war brought renewed interest in the infant art of television. In February 1919, a patent was applied for by Dionys von Mihály of Hungary. Mihály had been experimenting with the recording of sound on film since 1916, and with the end of the war he turned his efforts to developing a television system. This early patent was for means of synchronization of a television system. There were to be fixed points at the transmitter, a light-sensitive device at the receiver and means to bring the two into phase.

The synchronizing method was two governors coupled to rheostats. The speed was to be regulated by the amount of current passing through the resistors. No means for scanning the picture was shown or described.

In 1920, von Mihály applied for two more patents for a television system. One was for improvements in selenium cells and the like. The other was for a type of oscillograph in the form of a galvanometer with frequency response up to 50 kc/s.[16]

The hot cathode Braun oscillograph of Sir J.J. Thomson was described in April 1919. He was studying explosion phenomena using the piezoelectric effect of crystals under mechanical pressure. By connecting the deflecting plates of his tube to the crystal he was able to get deflection of the electron beam that would indicate the pressure and rapidity of an explosion. This was a pressure-time curve. The electron beam was moved by a sine-wave current, which gave the beam a nonuniform movement. This appears to be the first Braun tube that had a hot cathode and an alternating-current time base generator used for electrical measurements. This experiment was conducted at the Cavendish Laboratory.[17]

In September 1919 H.K. Sandell of Chicago applied for a patent for a multi-transmitter device. It used a mirror drum rotating at a high rate of speed, which sent the light from the scene to a bank of selenium cells. Between the mirror and the cell was a series of slits so that each cell received a small portion of the light from the scene. Each cell was to be connected to its own radio transmitter with an aerial of different amplitude.

At the receiver, a set of electromagnets was connected to the output of each cell and moved a tiny mirror that received its light from a light tube. Each electromagnet was tuned to receive only the wave emitted by the sending circuit of its corresponding selenium cell at the transmitter. Thus the light from the mirror went to a series of slits similar to the transmitter and to the rotating mirror drum. Halftones were dependent on the strength of the currents emitted by the sending apparatus. This being a simultaneous system, no means for synchronization was either mentioned or necessary.[18]

In October 1919 C.F. Jenkins of Washington, D.C., applied for a patent on a motion picture machine. This was to provide means whereby pictures on a constantly advancing motion picture film might be satisfactorily projected upon a screen by a mechanism having no intermittent movement. Jenkins planned to do this by means of an annular prism which progressively varied in cross-section. This change in form of each side was such that the rays were bent, progressively, so that the picture was stationary on the screen as the film was advanced. This device was not only applicable to the motion picture but was soon to be used by Jenkins in a television system.[19]

On November 28, 1919, Franz Skaupy in Berlin applied for a patent for a Braun tube with a glowing cathode for the purpose of sending electrical pictures. The patent disclosed a cathode ray tube of the usual construction with a filament connected to a battery. This same battery was connected to a grid, which was across the coil, which had the picture signal impressed upon it. The aperture electrode attracted the beam from a source of high voltage. The patent shows only one set of deflecting plates and indicates a cylinder to concentrate the beam. There is no mention of gas or vacuum in the specification.[20]

On August 10, 1920, H.J. van der Bijl of Western Electric applied for a patent for a vacuum tube and method of operating same. Essentially it was a form of Braun tube with a hot cathode that had an inert gas in it to facilitate focusing. It contained a filament heated by a battery for maintaining a disc at a positive potential to a cathode and a battery for maintaining a high potential between cathode and anode. A set of plates was provided internally although deflection could be by external magnetic coils. This tube was the basis for the Western Electric oscilloscope, which was to be in common use for the next ten years or so.

Van der Bijl explained that a pure electron discharge produced two bad results: the spreading of the beam due to the mutual repulsion of the electrons, and a tendency for the various parts of the tube, including the receiving screen, to become negatively charged, impairing the efficiency of the tube if not entirely destroying its action.

This patent was accompanied by a separate patent by J.B. Johnson, also of Western Electric, for the circuitry and operation of the van der Bijl cathode ray tube. It was claimed that this tube was to be used for the measurement of indication of the wave-forms or potentials of alternating currents in electric circuits.[21]

On August 18, 1920, S.N. Kakourine applied for a Russian patent on a television system. This was for a system using Nipkow discs with synchronizing means for sending pictures by wireless.[22]

In August 1920 H.C. Egerton of Western Electric applied for a patent on a television system. This patent used a single mirror oscillating in two directions at both the transmitter and receiver. The main feature of the patent was the provision for more than one scan per picture, in order to present an apparently continuous reproduction on the receiving screen so that the observor's eye could detect no lag or flicker. This patent presented means to fill in the area between scans, and it seems to be the earliest patent for what later became known as "interlaced scanning" to eliminate flicker.[23]

In 1920, Miss E.F. Seiler made a detailed and extended investigation in the color sensitivity of alkali metal photoelectric cells. She found that the wavelengths for maximum sensitivity increased in the same order as the atomic numbers of the alkali elements, and that the relative magnitude of the number of electrons released at the maximum decreased from lithium to cesium. This study indicated those alkali metals that would have a color response close to that of the human eye.[24]

An entirely new type of photoelectric cell was revealed by Theodore W. Case in 1920. This was called the Thalofide cell and was composed of

Vladimir Kosma Zworykin, hired by Westinghouse shortly after his 1919 immigration from Russia. This photo was taken about 1911, when Zworykin was studying electrical engineering under Boris Rosing at the St. Petersburg Technological Institute. Later, Zworykin was to give great credit to Rosing for introducing him to the idea of cathode ray television.

thallium, oxygen and sulphur. It had its maximum sensitivity at around 10,000 Angstrom units. The average sensitivity of these cells was such that the dark resistance was lowered some 50 percent in 0.06 footcandles.

In 1921, Case described another type of photoelectric cell. This one was composed of either barium or strontium deposited on a layer of silver. The strontium cell was stated to be quite stable and to have the same color sensitivity as a potassium hydride cell.[25]

Westinghouse Electric and Manufacturing Company of East Pittsburg, Pa., had been left out of the formation of RCA. It had watched the formation of the GE-AT&T-RCA consortium and had decided to buy up all of the electrical patents not controlled by the new corporation. It was able to purchase some of the Fessenden patents and, more importantly, the "feedback" and "superheterodyne" circuits of Major Edwin Armstrong on

October 5, 1920. It also acquired some of the patents owned by Michael Pupin. About this time in 1920, Westinghouse hired Vladimir K. Zworykin, who had recently arrived from Russia.[26]

However, it was the introduction of radio broadcasting in the United States that was to change Westinghouse's fortunes. In August 1920 the Detroit News was operating radio Station 8MK. In Wilkensburg, Pennsylvania, a similar radio transmitter was set up by Frank Conrad of Westinghouse with the call letters 8XK. His broadcasts attracted wide attention in the area, and on September 29, 1920, an advertisement offering parts and gadgets for listeners to Conrad's station brought in a flood of requests. This came to the attention of H.P. Davis, Westinghouse vice president, who asked Conrad if he could build a newer and stronger transmitter at the Westinghouse plant and be ready for the election of November 2, 1920. This was done, and the Department of Commerce assigned the call letters KDKA to the station. The broadcast of this election coverage is generally conceded to be the birth of radio broadcasting as we know it today.[27]

It was ironic that David Sarnoff's 1916 dream of the "radio music box"[28] in the home was brought to reality by General Electric's and RCA's arch rival, Westinghouse. However, Westinghouse was soon to join forces with them. The war had sped up research in radio communication. The three-element vacuum tube was now being used in amplifiers in telephony and telegraphy and wireless transmission. Radio was a reality for both voice and code. With the end of the war, thousands of amateurs were once again sending and receiving messages.

the electron beam. There is no record of this tube ever having been built, and no more was heard of the inventor.[3]

In 1921, Marcus J. Martin published his second book, entitled *The Electrical Transmission of Photographs*. This book was important for two reasons. First, it included a rather comprehensive survey of both phototelegraphy and television to date, and second, it included a complete description of the 1911 Campbell Swinton plan for electric television. Surprisingly, the author credits the Campbell Swinton idea from the period of 1914–1915. This was the fourth printed reference to the Campbell Swinton television scheme, which makes it difficult for any inventor from 1921 on to claim that he was not aware of its existence.[4]

In the United States, the American inventor Charles Francis Jenkins had turned his attention from motion pictures to television. By May 1922 he had reported on his efforts to produce (1) a motion picture machine; (2) a high speed camera; (3) a home machine using lithographed pictures on paper discs; (4) a stroboscope to makè objects stand still; (5) a director for reading ground speed from aircraft; and (6) the use of prism discs to transmit pictures by radio. His prismatic rings were shown in two forms, disc and band.

On March 13, 1922, Jenkins applied for his first patent for transmitting pictures by wireless. It disclosed two prismatic rings, in which one ring would bend the beam in one direction while the second ring would bend it at right angles to the first. At the transmitter, the two prisms, one rotating considerably faster than the other, would analyze the scene and send the light to a photocell.

The receiver, which was essentially the same as the transmitter, had a light valve based on the Faraday principle. It included a Nicol prism polarizer (10, 11) and an analyzer consisting of a coil (12) and a cell filled with bisulphate of carbon (13), which was supposed to vary the light from the source (8) by rotation of the plane of polarization. This light was projected on a screen, which could be phosphorescent or fluorescent. This patent was the beginning of Jenkins' effort to perfect a system for the transmission of motion pictures by radio. This was reported in November 1922. Jenkins filed for many supporting patents in the next few years and started to build operable machines.[5]

A very unusual television patent was filed by Boris Rtcheouloff on June 27, 1922, in Russia. The patent was divided into two sections. The first dealt with a camera tube based on the use of a vibrating spring inside the tube that was to oscillate in two directions under the influence of magnetic coils. At the extreme end of the spring was attached a photoelectric element, which was to scan the scene as the spring vibrated.

The receiving tube was quite similar to the transmitter in that it too depended on the use of a vibrating spring. Here the tip of the vibrating spring had a luminous element attached to it that was supposed to vibrate in synchronization with the camera tube, be modulated by the signal from it, and create a picture on a screen outside of the tube.

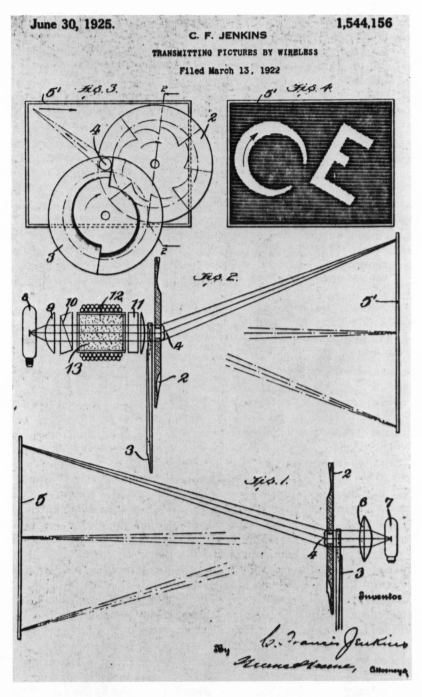

Diagram from C.F. Jenkins' first television patent (filed in 1922).

The second section was for a television magnetic recorder. It described the use of a steel ribbon on which the magnetic oscillations were to be impressed. This steel ribbon was either on an endless loop or was sent from spool to spool.

Three methods of recording were described. The first showed both picture and sound being recorded on an endless loop and then being transmitted by a spool to spool recorder. A system of pole-pieces and coils was used to impress the oscillations onto the steel ribbon. A similar set of pole-pieces and coils was used to recover the oscillations from the steel ribbon. The second method showed the signal from the camera being recorded from spool to spool and then being transmitted. The third method showed both picture and sound being recorded on an endless loop and then being transmitted later to a network of subscribers by means of a number of pickup coils. This was the first patent covering the recording and playback (by magnetic means) of a television signal.[6]

In November 1922 Nicholas Langer described the work being done on a television system in Hungary. Langer had been working on a television system and had joined with Dionys von Mihály in Budapest. Langer described the new system, although Mihály's participation was not mentioned until later.

The device used a vibrating mirror as a transmitter. It consisted of two movements, with the first being some 500 cycles on one axis and the second some 5 cycles/sec on a second axis. Thus some 50-line pictures could be transmitted. A highly sensitive selenium cell, supposed to respond to frequencies of about 10,000 cycles/sec, was used.

At the receiver, a dead beat string galvanometer was required. This consisted of a fine platinum thread suspended between the poles of a powerful electromagnet that carried a small, light aluminum plate at its center. This plate had a small hole drilled in it and was the light modulator. A current passing through the thread diverted it at right angles to the lines of force, and consequently the hole in the plate moved so as to intercept a greater or lesser amount of light depending on the signal from the transmitter. The modulated light was sent to a vibrating mirror similar to that of the transmitter, which was synchronized by means of synchronous motors. The problem of synchronization was conceded to be the most difficult part of the problem.[7]

On December 1, 1922, Edouard Belin gave a simulated demonstration of radio-television at the Sorbonne in Paris. After some 15 years of transmitting still pictures by wire or by radio, Belin had turned his attention to the problem of television. Belin was able to demonstrate the ability to transmit by radio, flashes of light varying in intensity from dark to light.

The apparatus consisted of a transmitter that used a perforated disc about 12 inches in diameter as a light "chopper." This chopper was to systematically interrupt the light signal so that a pulsating (AC) signal was transmitted. Light from a Pointolite lamp passed through a perforated disc rotating at 10 revolutions/sec. It went to a graduated screen (from clear to opaque, as in Belin's phototelegraphic device) to a photoelectric cell, which was connected to a wireless transmitting circuit with a loop antenna.

Another loop antenna picked up the signal connected to a tuner and amplifier. The amplified signal was sent to a mirror galvanometer. As the varying impulses of the signal were received, the mirror was moved, its amplitude being greater with a large signal, and smaller when a small signal was received. A beam of light was reflected from the mirror to another graduated screen (a plate of diamond glass) so placed that with a weak signal, the light would pass through the denser part of the glass, and with a strong signal, light would pass through the clear part of the glass onto a white screen. Thus the light at the receiving end would always correspond to the variations of light at the transmitter. This demonstration lacked two important elements, scanning and synchronization; therefore it was not a true demonstration of television.

It was claimed that if a single point of light could be transmitted, so could a million. Belin went on to state that when the apparatus was developed, the full image reproduced on a screen would really be made up of a series of horizontal lines very close together formed of an immense number of points of light. "M. Belin does not expect that such an apparatus will be reproduced in the very near future," it was noted, "but there is no serious technical difficulty in the way of its construction."[8]

The work of Dr. Max Dieckmann was also reported in 1922. He had been director of the Research Laboratory for Radio Telegraphy and Atmospheric Electricity at Grafelfing, near Munich, during the war. He had been trying to perfect radio apparatus for sending pictures from aircraft and/or ships to ground stations.

Dieckmann's apparatus was a form of telautographic sender and recorder. It consisted of a cylinder that was covered with conductive ink, so that as the stylus came into contact with the conductive part of the picture, a circuit was closed and signals were transmitted. At the receiver, a recording stylus would mark the special paper and thus recreate the picture.[9]

The recent work of Dr. Arthur Korn was also discussed. He had spent the war as a professor of physics at the Berlin Technical High School. He had adapted an apparatus which required a special typewriter to produce his pictures. A rotating cylinder on his transmitter concentrated the light from the picture onto a special selenium cell, which had 18 wires leading to 18 special cells, each of which could only receive its own special signal, depending on the brightness of the signal. At the receiver, these signals were sent to a special typewriter, which would print only the letter corresponding to its brightness. This would build up a likeness of the image at the receiving machine.[10]

On December 27, 1922, Edouard Belin applied for his first modern television patent. This system covered a method of using two exploratory mirrors, oscillating about two perpendicular axes, in proper relation with each other and a stationary photoelectric cell.

At the receiver, a source of light was to be modulated by an oscillograph, where it was sent to a mirror with a graduated transparency, a lens and another mirror in the path of the reflected beam. This mirror was to be in synchronization with the previous mirror in order to properly reconstruct the transmitted picture. For light valves, Belin mentioned (1) an oscillographic mirror, (2) the use of the Braun tube, (3) a graduated screen, and (4) the Kerr phenomenon or similar effects.[11]

On December 29, 1922, another Frenchman, Georges Valensi, applied for the first French patent covering a television receiving tube with a hot cathode. On January 3, 1923, Valensi applied for a second patent for a method of transmission and synchronization for television. Valensi planned to use two opaque synchronized wheels with transparent lines as exploring means. One disc was to have two spiral arcs while the other, with a series of portions of a spiral, was to rotate in opposite directions. These were to cause the scanning to be at a uniform speed and in a sine wave manner. Synchronization was to be similar to the Baudot telegraph system. This patent mentioned that color television would be possible with the use of three photocells and three cathode ray tubes.[12]

On January 23, 1923, Dionys von Mihály of Hungary filed for improvements in Phototelegraphic Apparatus. This was basically the same apparatus that Langer had described late in 1922. It had a transmitter containing an oscillographic mirror, which was to be oscillated on two axes, preferably at right angles, to scan an image. This mirror was to throw successive images of picture elements onto a selenium cell at the transmitting station or to throw a spot of light of varying intensity onto a screen at the receiving station. The mirror was oscillated in the longitudinal axis by an intermittent current supplied to it. The connecting rod was moved by a crank connected to a phonic wheel controlled by a tuning fork. A light relay was to modulate the light going to the screen. An actual device encompassing these principles had been built sometime late in 1922.

Pictures of the device appeared in the book *Das Electrische Fernsehen und das Telehor* by Dionys von Mihály with an introduction by Dr. Eugen Nesper. This appears to be the earliest book published exclusively about television. It contained an excellent history of television as well as a thorough description of all of the Mihály apparatus. Although the book showed pictures of the machine, it was later claimed that because of troubled conditions in Hungary, the final apparatus could not be tested. It was hoped, however, that work would continue into 1924 to obtain perfectly satisfactory results.[13]

Lee De Forest had been experimenting with the recording of sound on film for several years. On March 13, 1923, there was a report on his new process which was called the Phonofilm. Working in conjunction with Theodore W. Case, he had produced equipment which he hoped to install in motion picture theatres across the country.[14]

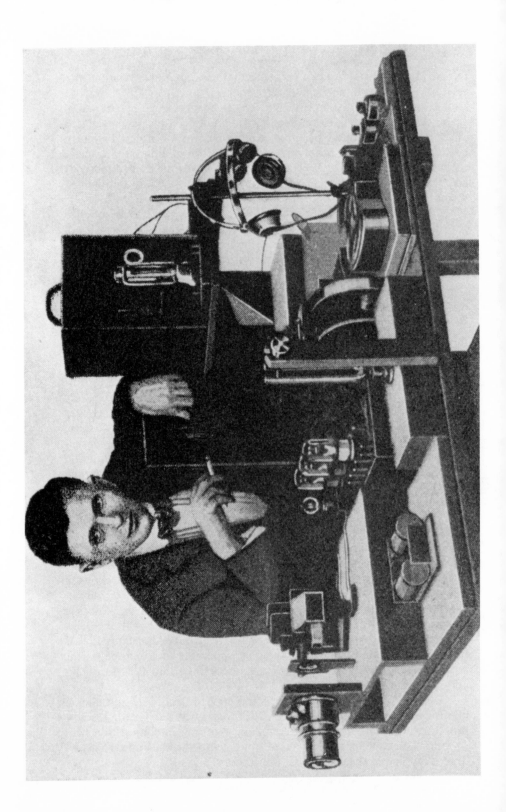

C.F. Jenkins and his 1923/24 apparatus.

On April 18, 1923, W.S. Stephenson and G.W. Walton of London applied for a television patent which provided for straight-line scanning of the image by means of two slotted discs which could be variously arranged to provide the proper movements for both transmission and reception. However, this patent differed from Valensi's in that it described means for successive scanning, i.e., in the same direction or bidirectional as well. Means for color television were also described.[15]

In April 1923 it was reported that C.F. Jenkins of Washington, D.C., had successfully transmitted still photographs by radio using his new apparatus with the prismatic rings. It was claimed that all other machines used pictures on a cylindrical surface, but that Jenkins' were copied from

Opposite: Dionys von Mihály and his TV apparatus.

a flat surface and impressed the photographs on common photographic plates. The photographs were transmitted from a lantern slide to a photoelectric cell made of thallium oxide and sulphur (the Case cell) through the prismatic rings. In front of the cell was an interrupter operating at 540 rev/sec. At the receiver, the modulated current was fed into the special light valve, which had a tungsten filament. The transmitter and receiver were synchronized by means of tuning forks.[16]

It was also claimed at this time that Jenkins had accomplished the radio transmission of the likeness of a young woman to his laboratory some five miles away. The image of her face against a window illuminated by sunlight was scanned by the prismatic rings and sent to a photocell. This image was supposedly sent by means of Jenkins' special radio transmitting apparatus from his Connecticut Avenue laboratory to the lab on 16th Street.

At the receiver, another set of prismatic rings together with a special light valve that glowed red when supplied with two volts reconstructed the image. It was later revealed that this light valve had been specially made for Jenkins by D. McFarlan Moore of General Electric, through L.C. Porter of General Electric Harrison Lamp Works. At this time, Jenkins was enjoying the services of both General Electric and Westinghouse Electric in his research on phototelegraphy and television.

There is no independent confirmation of this first transmission of a woman's image by radio by Jenkins from any other source. Later, Jenkins made claim of a June 14, 1923, date. Whether "live" or a photograph, this was the first transmission of television by radio ever reported.[17]

About this time in 1923, a young Scotsman, John Logie Baird, had decided that he would devote his life to the development of television. After having failed in several other ventures, he decided that the use of the Nipkow disc combined with modern photocells and the thermionic amplifier could produce a workable television system. After several attempts alone, he finally advertised for help in June 1923 in the *London Times*. He received the offer of some technical equipment and attracted the attention of Wilfred E.L. Day, a motion picture entrepreneur who saw in Baird an opportunity to invest in the new field of television. With the financial backing of Day, Baird was set up in a laboratory at 22 Frith Street in London.

Baird filed for his first television patent on July 26, 1923. It used a simple Nipkow disc arrangement at the transmitter. At the receiver, the image was to be displayed on a bank of lamps arranged to form a screen. There was to be an arm moving synchronously with the disc, moving over a series of contacts to complete the circuits of the successive lamps. The differing intensities of illumination of the lamps constituted the picture to be viewed. This was to be the first of a great number of patents taken out by Baird to produce a workable television system.[18]

On August 15, 1923, John H. Hammond, Jr., of Gloucester, Mass., applied for a patent for a system and method of television. This included

John Logie Baird.

monochrome, color, and stereoscopic means. It seems to be the first patent describing the "flying spot" scanning of live objects. One variant called for the projection of a light beam, which would be caused to travel in a predetermined path by the use of vibrating mirrors. The light would be reflected from the object to a photoelectric system. Here it would be converted into electrical signals to be transmitted by either wire or radio. The subject was to be in a dark room surrounded by dull black, light-absorbent walls.

At the receiver, a similar light beam would pass through a pair of Nicol prisms, a polarization cell and a lens system to a set of mirrors similar to those at the transmitter and in synchronization with them. Here the modulated light passed to a screen for viewing. It was planned to send 200 line pictures at 16 frames/sec.

The patent also included a cathode ray tube which had magnetic deflection and magnetic focusing as well as a special means for modulating the beam. An electrode in front of the anode focused the beam upon an aperture in a diaphragm farther down the tube. As the potential of the electrode varied, the diameter of the bundle of rays was altered, thus varying the intensity of the electron beam. It was planned to use a form of spiral scanning.[19]

On November 28, 1923, J.E. Gardner and H.D. Hineline of the Westinghouse Electric and Manufacturing Company of Pittsburgh applied for a patent for the first all-electric "flying spot" system. It used cathode ray tubes at both the transmitting and receiving ends. The film or other transparency was mounted between the screen and an optical system which focused the light from the picture onto a photoelectric cell. The light was thus modulated by the successive points of the picture and was amplified and applied to the grid of a modulator for transmission.

At the receiver, the signal was sent to a similar cathode ray tube in which the intensity of the electron beam was modulated by a grid. Thus the picture was reproduced on the face of the cathode ray tube and focused onto a screen by an optical system. This was a most important patent, the first since that of Rignoux in 1908 to use this method with cathode ray tubes at both transmitting and receiving ends.[20]

On November 29, 1923, Alexandre Dauvillier of Paris applied for patents covering the means for positioning and scanning a beam in a cathode ray tube with that of an exploring beam. One method was the use of a rotating disc to generate the signals necessary to produce currents proportional to the variations of the coordinates of the beam relative to the image to be transmitted. The other was the use of two screens with perpendicular slots displaced at right angles subject to oscillations of different frequencies about two rectangular axes. The German patent showed a very modern Braun tube with negative grid modulation to control the electron beam.[21]

Dauvillier had been working in the Physical Research Laboratories of Louis de Broglie since 1921. In October 1923, M. de Broglie had presented a paper indicating that a stream of electrons should have wave properties similar to a beam of hard X-rays, the wavelength being inversely proportional to the electron velocity. This relation of an electron beam to light radiation was one of the earliest papers relating to what was to be known as "electron optics."[22]

On December 21, 1923, W. Rogowski and W. Grosser in Aachen, Germany, applied for a patent covering a "glowing cathode oscillograph with 'electron focus'." This patent disclosed several methods of concentration of electron beams by a difference of potentials between main and auxiliary electrodes. It stated that by a suitable arrangement and shape of main and auxiliary electrodes and/or diaphragms, there was produced an electric field which converged from the glowing cathode towards one point. This point was formed as an opening in a diaphragm so that the electron beam flowed in large numbers through this opening and could be concentrated again in the rear of the diaphragm, by a longitudinal magnetic field, into a sharp point. This appears to be the earliest patent pertaining to the new field of electron optics.[23]

Radio. They reported that the apparatus was crude and cumbersome. Absent were the famous Jenkins prismatic rings which had been used in facsimile. Instead, both transmitter and receiver used some form of prismed Nipkow disc with 48 lenses in it. The disc revolved at 16 rev/sec, or 960 rpm. However, Hugo Gernsback claimed that it was possible to put small objects in the path of the light and see them on the radio receiver. Watson Davis stated that he could see Mr. Jenkins wave his hand in front of the equipment and see it on the screen.

In operation, a special prismed disc dissected the picture, which was sent to a Case Thalofide photoelectric cell. The picture signal was then transmitted by radio and picked up on a regular radio receiver. The receiver also had a revolving disc with lens prisms driven by a motor. A special lamp was used as a light modulator. Both transmitting and receiving discs were run off the same motor, which meant that no means for synchronization were needed. As far as can be determined, these were the first witnessed demonstrations of radio-television ever reported.[27]

On January 5, 1924, Edouard Belin applied for a patent on the use of a Braun tube as a receptor in a television system. On January 13, 1924, he was quoted as saying that he would be transmitting animated surfaces and human faces within a year. An updated version of his 1922 system was described. Belin had now added rotating prisms at both ends of his system in order to scan a circle. There was no mention of synchronization, as Belin was interested only in proving that he could reproduce light tones anywhere in the arc. He was also using a very sensitive photocell containing a potassium anode and a cathode grid of nickel and platinum with almost no lag.[28]

On January 15, 1924, Edmund E. Fournier d'Albe of Kingston-on-Thames applied for a patent for the telegraphic transmission of pictures and images. D'Albe intended to accomplish this transmission by means of resonators tuned to the different light frequencies. The picture was to be broken up by a set of parallel cylinders, each revolving within a stationary cylinder, but having a different number of perforations. It was planned to revolve the cylinders at different speeds in order to capture a wide range of frequencies. The light fluctuations were to be sent to a single selenium cell for transmission.

At the receiver, a similar set of tuned reeds was to pick up the special frequencies being sent out and operate a small silvered mirror at each resonator, thus recreating the light and shade of the image being transmitted. This was a simultaneous sytem similar to that of Lux and Ruhmer.[29]

The Russian inventor A.A. Tchernischeff also applied for a patent on a modification of a Braun tube for cathode ray television on January 26, 1924.[30]

On February 8, 1924, Laurent and Augustin Sequin of France applied for a patent using cathode ray tubes for both transmission and reception. In this patent, the light from the image was reflected by a small mirror to a grid screen covered with selenium, or perhaps made of two different metals, alkaline salts, etc., so as to create a variable electric charge depending on the amount of light hitting a particular part of the screen. The screen was to be scanned by a cathode ray beam so that a varying current was transmitted by ionization to a receptor plate, which conducted the signal out of the tube. A variant was shown in which the grid screen was solid and deflected the beam to the receptor plate.

The receiver also used a cathode ray beam, which was to move in synchronism with the transmitter. This beam was to be modulated by a set of plates in the path of the beam similar to the Rosing scheme. The beam produced a picture on a fluorescent screen that was reflected to an eyepiece by a mirror.[31]

Also on February 8, 1924, George J. Blake and Henry D. Spooner of London applied for a patent covering a complete television system. The camera tube had a plate covered with selenium or like substance. The light from the scene was directed to this plate and the electron beam impinged on this same surface. Since the resistance of any spot was dependent on its illumination, it was expected that a varying electrical current would be sent to a resistor, which was connected through an amplifier and modulator to a continuous wave wireless transmitter.

Three signals were to be sent, two to represent the scanning frequencies which were to activate the scanning coils. The other was to control the intensity of the scanning beam of the cold cathode Braun tube with magnetic focus similar to that of Boris Rosing's 27,570/07 and 5486/11 English patents.[32]

On March 17, 1924, V.K. Zworykin applied for a patent on a two-way television system. This patent was based on his December 29, 1923, patent in that it combined his camera and receiver into a sending/receiving station for transmitting pictures as well as voice. This patent, which was stalled in its path through the Patent Office, was renewed on June 27, 1931. The renewal included a mention of "photoelectric globules," which did not appear in the original application.[33]

Also on March 17, 1924, Zworykin applied for a patent on a variable-brilliancy light source. This was to use an evacuated envelope containing mercury vapor in an ionized atmosphere, including two electrodes maintained at a difference of potential and means for varying the potential gradient in the portion of the said ionized atmosphere. At the time of this patent, the only variable light source seems to have been the incandescent lamps of D. McFarlan Moore, which had very little brightness. Thus it was important for Zworykin to develop a bright light source that could easily be modulated to complete a practical television system.[34]

In March 1924 Nicholas Langer reported on the progress being made on the Mihály television machine called the "Telehor." Due to material difficulties, it was claimed that the experiments had been interrupted in the middle of 1923, and there is no record of this machine having produced pictures of any kind.[35]

On March 18, 1924, Apollinar and Wladislavus Zeitlin of Berlin applied for the first German patent covering a camera tube. The light from the image was focused obliquely onto a plate covered with a light coat of potassium. This plate was kept at a positive potential by a battery so that it emitted electrons when struck by light. The plate was scanned from the rear by an electron beam, which was to neutralize most of the electrons; those that were not neutralized went to a collector to become the picture signal. The patent mentions use of the Hallwachs effect. The receiver used a cathode ray tube which had a special frequency-dividing tube for equalizing the beam when it was modulated by the picture signal.[36]

On April 10, 1924, Harold J. McCreary of Associated Electric Laboratories of Chicago applied for a patent that included a special camera tube. McCreary's patent featured a photoelectric plate made of insulating material with a large number of conductors passing through it. The light from the scene was projected on the front of the slab, and the electron beam scanned the reverse side. McCreary preferred to coat both sides of the plate with either potassium hydride, selenium, or some similar substance. This was the first patent describing an insulated plate (or target) with pins or other conducting devices going through the plate and with the front side sensitized to light while it was discharged by an electron beam from the back.

Claim Three of the patent specifically called for a plurality of minute wires or pins imbedded in a plate, photoelectric material on the image side of the plate, means for causing a cathode ray to impinge on the other side of the plate, said ray to scan the plate to successively connect said pins to the other side of said circuit. The patent called for sine wave scanning, which gives the effect of a Lissajous figure.

It also included a color version consisting of three of the above camera tubes with proper color filters so that "red, blue, and yellow" signals were sent. At the receiver, three cathode ray tubes, each having a certain coating on the face plate screen (such as bismuth sulphate mixed with calcium oxide; antimony oxide with calcium oxide; and bismuth oxide), would produce the red, yellow and blue images. The three images were to be combined by means of mirrors to form the chromatic image. This was the first patent showing an electrical camera tube using a "two-sided" target and using three tubes to pickup and receive color images. It was a most important patent for its innovative concept.[37]

On April 23, 1924, C.F. Jenkins filed for a patent for an improvement on his Radio Vision apparatus. This was for a combination of his prismatic ring with a lens disc. It appears that the lenses were to be used for the line scanning while the prismatic ring would cause the disc to move in a vertical direction once each revolution. The prismatic plate was a variation of the prismatic ring in the form of a glass ring with variable thickness.[38]

In April 1924, A.A. Campbell Swinton again described his all-electric television scheme. He had now decided to bring his 1911 idea up to date. He again admitted that he had never built the device described and that it was "an idea only." He again related the advantage of having each photocell act independently in that it was called to act once in a tenth of a second, rather than called upon to produce the many thousands of separate impulses which no known form of photocell will admit of. This certainly anticipated the "storage principle" as it allowed the light-sensitive elements to build up a charge during the interval of time that the electron beam was scanning the rest of the photoelectric surface. None of the Nipkow disc systems that had been proposed and built were able to "store" their signal; they were all "instantaneous" in their mode of operation. That is, the incoming and outgoing signals were the same. Later on, camera tubes would be proposed that had either storage or nonstorage capabilities.

Among the many improvements that could be applied, Campbell Swinton stated that other, more sensitive materials could be substituted for rubidium and that the use of revolving potentiometers working on sources of continuous current and so arranged could make the two cathode ray beams move in parallel lines. He described the use of a hot cathode to reduce the voltage to some 300 to 500 volts as well as improvements in the focusing of the beams and improved viewing screens.

In the discussion of his paper, Campbell Swinton concluded how hopeless the task was—but "if we could only get one of the big research laboratories like that of the G.E.C. or of the Western Electric Company—one of those people who have large skilled staffs and any amount of money to engage on the business—I believe they would solve a thing like this in six months and make a reasonable job of it." Campbell Swinton was correct in that it did require the large research laboratories to finally finish up the task, but it was to be some six or seven years before that completion came to pass. Campbell Swinton's paper had an enormous effect on the history of television as it stimulated a great amount of effort on behalf of the large electrical companies as well as many independent inventors.[39]

One of the immediate effects of this Campbell Swinton paper was an article in May 1924 by John L. Baird reporting on his latest experiments with television. His apparatus could transmit only crude outline images. Baird declared that later apparatus could transmit a certain amount of detail. His transmitter was the usual Nipkow disc with four sets of five holes staggered around the circumference. Behind it was a serrated disc that revolved at some 2000rpm to create a pulsing current in order to overcome the lag of the single selenium cell being used.

The receiver consisted of a disc with lamps arranged in a staggered formation similar to that of the disc at the transmitter. These lamps were joined electrically to a commutator at the center of the disc. The disc was run in synchronism with the transmitting disc, and the image was reproduced by the flashing in and out of the lamps, persistence of vision making the whole image appear simultaneously. It was later reported that a visitor to Baird's workshop was able to see the outlines of a "cross," an "H" and the fingers of his hand across the width of the laboratory. This

John L. Baird and his 1925 apparatus, which could transmit crude outline images.

appears to be the first article by Baird about his work on television.[40]

On May 28, 1924, D.E. Howes of the Westinghouse Electric and Manufacturing Company applied for a patent covering post acceleration deflection. Howes proposed an oscillograph tube in which the rays would have different velocities at different parts of their paths. Its object was to successively give electrons a small acceleration to produce cathode rays of small velocity, deflect the rays while they have this small velocity, produce a large acceleration to give the rays a great velocity and finally to have the rays hit the sensitive target with great velocity. This was an important concept as it would allow the deflection of a cathode ray beam with minimum energy while allowing it to be accelerated for high brightness.[41]

About this time in 1924, August Karolus at the Physical Institute of the University of Leipzig started his research into television. He concentrated on the use of a special Kerr cell with Nipkow discs. He applied for patents covering this device and its circuitry in June 1924.[42]

A short history of television was presented in *Wireless World* in June 1924 by James Strachan. He gives credit for the invention of the "telectroscope" to Senlecq and mentions how impractical the many multiple wire systems were and that what was really required was a single line wire system with synchronous apparatus. He concludes by stating the advantage of the thermionic amplifier as a means of amplifying minute currents, and he mentions his great hopes for the "invention" of Campbell Swinton.[43]

On July 11, 1924, Karl C. Randall of the Westinghouse Electric Company applied for a patent for a signaling system. Using the television system of Zworykin, it was designed to supervise the operation of electrical equipment at any substation from a central point. It described the original form of the Zworykin camera tube, which used a simple layer of alkali metal placed upon a layer of aluminum oxide which was on top of a thin sheet of aluminum foil.[44]

In the United States in July 1924, Dr. Ernst Alexanderson of General Electric also became interested in television. His first analysis of the problem led him to favor the transmission of the whole field continuously. This was to flavor his later thinking. He had C.A. Hoxie build a crude device consisting of a Nipkow disc with a number of small holes in connection with a photoelectric cell. In a simulated demonstration on December 10, 1924, Alexanderson was convinced that their photocell was sensitive enough to be practical.

At this time C.F. Jenkins tried to sell his patents to Westinghouse, and they were turned over to RCA (per their agreement) for review. Alexanderson claimed to have seen one of Jenkins' early demonstrations some two years earlier and was not very impressed with the results. He was quite anxious to avoid using the Jenkins patents if at all possible. The optical engineer of the General Electric staff, Dr. Frank A. Benson, had devised a hexagonal rotating prism which Alexanderson felt was better than the Jenkins prismatic rings and could be used without infringing on Jenkins' patent.

As a result, a machine was built using Benford prisms at both the transmitter and receiver. It was tested on January 17, 1925. The image, which was a horizontal bar of light, was passed through a rotating Benford prism through a toothed wheel which gave an alternating signal of 1000 cycles. This output current was amplified and sent to WGY (the GE radio station in Schenectady).

The signal was received on a conventional radio receiver, and the current was used to control the mirror of a standard oscillograph. Through a system of lenses, the image of an arc lamp was reflected by the mirror of the oscillograph and thrown upon a small opening. The light from the opening passed through another rotating Benford prism and was focused upon a screen. It produced light spots over the screen in six separate tracks; however, two were coincidental so that only four tracks were visible on the screen. This is why only a horizontal bar of light was shown. The test was supervised by Dr. Benson with the aid of C.A. Hoxie, Rockwood, Long and others. (Hoxie was the inventor of the "Pallophotophone," an important device for recording sound on motion picture film.)[45]

Also at this time, Max Dieckmann in Germany resumed his television experiments. On August 29, 1924, he applied for a patent for a system using a single mirror that was moved in two directions to cause scanning.

Max Dieckmann.

This was done mechanically by means of an oscillating arm. Coils were attached to the mirror support to provide means for synchronizing the receiver. The light from the subject passed through a lens to the vibrating mirror and finally to a photocell. Three sets of signals were to be transmitted. At the receiver, the two synchronizing signals were sent to coils next to the neck of a Braun tube to deflect the beam. Dieckmann still disclosed a cold cathode Braun tube in which the cathode beam modulator was a pair of deflecting plates similar to his 1909 device.[46]

Some time in the autumn of 1924, a young Japanese electrical engineer, Kenjiro Takayanagi, also started a research program into the possibilities of television. Working in the laboratories of the Hamamatsu Technical College as an assistant professor, he claimed that he had built certain equipment, including a camera tube, in 1924. He stated, however, that as "our vacuum technique did not bear this challenge" at the time he did not achieve any results. He then decided to concentrate on the design of a practical Braun tube for television.[47]

On September 23, 1924, C.A. Hoxie of General Electric applied for a patent for improvements in the method and apparatus for the electrical transmissions of pictures and views. There were means indicated for the transmission of both still and moving pictures. The system had several common elements, the first was the use of a light chopper to produce high frequency waves of varying amplitude. The patent described the use of perforated endless belts and the common Nipkow disc.[48]

In October 1924, L.T. Jones and H.G. Tasker of the Department of Physics of the University of California reported on their experiments with a cathode ray tube using electrostatic focus. While they were able to get good focus, they decided that this kind of thermionic Braun tube was not reliable as an oscillograph for external fields of low frequency. Whether this peculiarity existed with large deflecting frequencies was to be left to a future paper. The tube contained a considerable amount of mercury vapour. Focus was dependent on exciting voltage, filament temperature and possibly driving voltage.[49]

On December 1, 1924, it was reported that RCA had transmitted its first photographs by facsimile from London to New York. This used the new photoradiogram system that had been developed by Richard H. Ranger of RCA. It was claimed that the whole process took twenty minutes.[50]

Just three days later, on December 4, 1924, C.F. Jenkins transmitted a message written in Japanese from station NOF, Anacostia, Wash., to Boston, Mass. This transmission was done with his apparatus, which he claimed was quite different from that used by RCA. Further tests were cancelled due to interference from code and static.[51]

C.F. Jenkins (left) and Dr. George M. Burgess study Jenkins' television apparatus at the June 13, 1925, demonstration.

rotating prismatic ring for the slower frame scanning. The light valve was the glow lamp invented by D. McFarlan Moore. Jenkins claimed that he had been able to transmit pictures from a film projector to a small screen on a radio receiving set as early as March 31, 1925.

On August 12, 1925, Jenkins reported that he was able to transmit outlines of movies with verbal description six miles from his laboratory in Washington, D.C., to his home. Jenkins' television system was able to transmit only silhouettes for several more years.[9]

The Dr. Herbert Ives/AT&T television project was progressing well. In addition to the enormous resources of the Bell Telephone Laboratories, Dr. Ives had a very able staff working with him. Among them were Frank Gray, John R. Hofele, Robert C. Mathes, and Ralph V.L. Hartley.

On June 15, 1925, Frank Gray reported that "photographs of individuals were transmitted so well that they could easily be recognized at the receiving end." On this date he described a new method for transmitting images. He suggested "making an intense spot of light move over the subject in some regular manner, say in a series of parallel lines, and let this alone be the scanning device." This idea was the use of the "flying spot" or "spotlight" method of scanning.

This revolutionary scheme was quickly adapted to the film projector by June 23, 1925, and Gray reported that "the brightness at the disc was greater than the previous setup and will evidently give sufficient light for films." On June 26, 1925, Gray suggested that this same method be used for strong illumination of a subject without injury or inconvenience.[10]

On June 25, 1925, Boris Rosing applied for a patent on an advanced form of Braun cathode ray tube. It appeared to have a long magnetic coil with long deflecting plates combined with magnetic deflection in order to concentrate the beam and provide it with proper focus. It was later stated that Rosing had been provided a laboratory in Leningrad in 1924 and was proceeding with his research into electrical television.[11]

On July 10, 1925, the Bell Telephone Labs reported that they had actually transmitted the first motion pictures with their new television equipment. In fact, it was claimed that within a few weeks the pictures had better details than the still pictures previously transmitted. All that remained was to synchronize the camera with the disc and complete the spiral in 7/8 of the disc rotation.

Dr. Ives also made a novel suggestion on July 10, 1925. He proposed the use of motion picture film as a means of "chemical amplification" whereby motion picture film was exposed, rapidly processed and fed to the projector with only a few seconds delay. Ives felt this was the most feasible way of increasing the sensitivity of the transmitting end.

A similar process was proposed at the receiver whereby the received image was photographed and developed and projected very quickly. There was also a proposal for recording the sound on the same film to keep it in sync with the picture. This method was later known as the "intermediate film process."[12]

On July 13, 1925, V.K. Zworykin of the Westinghouse Electric and Manufacturing Company applied for a color television patent. Based on his 1923 patent application (which was still pending), this advanced version had two new important features.

First, it had an additional analyzing screen such as the Paget type placed between two lenses to focus its image onto the photoelectric plate. The screen was made up of small squares of three different colors: red, blue, and green. It was claimed that each color would be absorbed in such a manner that the light arriving at the photoelectric material would be broken up into a mosaic pattern corresponding to each square of the color screen. When a similar screen was placed in front of the receiving tube, the scene would be reproduced in natural colors.

Second and of more importance, it stated that the photoelectric material, such as potassium hydride, is evaporated on the aluminum oxide or other insulating material and treated to form a colloidial deposit of potassium hydride consisting of minute globules. Each globule is very active photoelectrically and constitutes for all intents and purposes *a minute photoelectric cell*. The patent also stated that the screen could be a fine (300 mesh) screen. The British version of this patent mentioned either a thin aluminum foil or a mesh screen. These were important changes that Zworykin soon tried to incorporate into his earlier (1923) patent application. The introduction of a mesh screen alleviated any of the problems of penetrating a thin aluminum foil. The change from a continuous layer to a mosaic of globules also eliminated the problem of lateral conduction across the signal plate.[13]

On October 2, 1925, Dr. Zworykin applied for an amendment to his 1923 patent application in which he stated that "preferably the photoelectric material is potassium hydride deposited in such a manner that it is in the form of small globules, each separated from its neighbor and insulated therefrom by the aluminum oxide." This amendment was to slow down the patent application for the next 13 years and cause Dr. Zworykin many problems. The United States Patent Office claimed that this was "new material" and not allowable.[14] However, the July 1925 color patent application ran into no difficulties and was granted in Great Britain in 1927 and in the United States in 1928.

There is evidence that during the period of 1924–1925 Dr. Zworykin actually built and operated a television system. It used modified Braun tubes at both the transmitter and receiver. It was claimed that the receiver was built using parts of a Western Electric cathode ray oscilloscope and gave quite satisfactory results.[15]

The transmitting tube was of unusual construction and gave considerably more difficulties, "particularly in the construction of the partition between the cathode ray tube and the photocell. This partition consisted of a metal screen with an insulating layer and photosensitive substance on top of the insulation. Glass cloth gave the most promising results, except for the matter of electric leakage due to the sealing of the tube. Cloth made of quartz or pyrex glass would be more suitable, but no supplier could be found to supply this."[16]

At about this time (the exact date is still in dispute) Dr. Zworykin gave a demonstration of this new system to a group of Westinghouse executives. They included Harry P. Davies (vice president of Westinghouse), Sam M. Kintner (head of the research laboratories), and Otto S. Schairer (director of the Patent Department). Zworykin himself described the demonstration as being very poor. "The scanning rate was low and the 'picture' merely an X-mark. Clearly the system shown was far removed from a practical television system."[17] And so "the work was stopped temporarily in order to work with the mechanical method of picture transmission that was still in progress."[18]

R. E. Hellmund

OK pu

Research Report R-429A.

V. Zworykin,
June 25, 1926.

PROBLEMS OF TELEVISION.

Closing Report.

This order was used for experimental work on rapid picture transmission, using the modified Braun cathode ray tube both for transmitter and receiver. The receiving tube was developed using parts of a Western Electric Cathode Ray Oscillograph and gave quite satisfactory results. The transmitting part of the scheme caused more difficulties, particularly in the construction of the partition between the cathode ray tube and the photo-cell. This partition consists of a metal screen with an insulating layer and photo-sensitive substance on top of the insulation. Glass cloth for insulation has so far given the most promising results, except in the matter of electric leakage due to the difficulty of sealing it into the bulb. The cloth made of quartz or pyrex glass would be much more suitable, but unfortunately a firm could not be located which makes this kind of cloth.

This development has been temporarily discontinued in order to work with the mechanical method of picture transmission, which is still in progress.

The development of both problems will be continued on the new orders 6-4520 and 6-4522.

V. Zworykin

3.

copies to:
J. Carr
7-12-26
2 M.V.
aw.

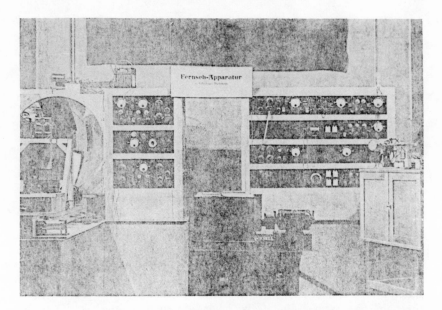

Fernseh-Apparatur

Max Dieckmann's 1925 CRT apparatus. It was on display in August at the German Transport and Traffic Exhibition in Munich.

At no time did Dr. Zworykin ever claim that this demonstration was a success. In fact, quite the opposite was true; his employers left after the demonstration with the admonition that "he go to work on something more useful." He was told to forget television and ordered to work on something like photocells, sound movies or something else that had more commercial promise. In the next year Dr. Zworykin was working on photographic sound recording. However, this failure did not deter Dr. Zworykin at all. He continued his research into television while working full time on other fields of endeavor.

The camera tube used in this demonstration has survived to this day, although it was never produced in any patent interference or litigation. Only Dr. Zworykin's witnesses testified to having seen the device, and it was not clear whether it was the same device or operated under the conditions stated by Zworykin. But for all intents and purposes it was the first electric camera tube ever built and operated.[19]

During August 18–19, 1925, Max Dieckmann had a television apparatus on display at the German Transport and Traffic Exhibition in Munich, Germany. The transmitter consisted of a large parabolic mirror that received the light from an object in the path of a bright light source. This light was reflected to an oscillographic mirror through an aperture,

Opposite, top: The first Zworykin camera tube, ca.1924/25. Bottom: Zworykin memo of 25 June, 1926.

whence it went to a large photocell of the type developed by Elster and Geitel. The mirror was moved by the oscillating mechanism described in Dieckmann's August 1924 patent.

At the receiver, the signals were sent to a cold cathode Braun tube, similar to Dieckmann's older 1909 tube, which had the beam modulated by passing through two capacitive plates where it went through an aperture. The beam was deflected by two sets of magnetic coils, at 500 and 10 cycles/sec respectively, with sine-wave scanning. While it was claimed that this system was able to transmit simple moving silhouette images, there is no evidence that it was *actually operating* at the exposition.[20]

Theodore W. Case, who had been working closely with Lee De Forest on the development of the sound film, also turned to television. On August 25, 1925, Case applied for a patent for a method and apparatus for transmitting pictures. This patent had a camera tube that used a layer of either semitransparent or opaque material of some conducting photoelectric substance such as potassium or any substance that emits electrons under the influence of light. The tube was to be gas-filled to keep the beam from spreading. The picture was to be focused upon a layer, and it was stated that if it were semitransparent, the picture could be focused right through the coating. Or, if the layer was opaque, the picture to be transmitted was to be focused upon the potassium or other coating on the side facing the electron gun using a lens for that purpose.

This was the first American patent to show a layer that was both struck by the light from the image and impinged on by the electron beam. Case mentioned the use of alternating current for deflection purposes and proposed a 600-line picture at 10 frames/sec.[21]

By October 23, 1925, the General Electric Company had surveyed the various means for producing a workable television system. Two methods had been tried: a rotating disc with a D. McFarlan Moore lamp for light control, and a rotating prism for scanning and an oscillograph for light control.

Four methods of scanning were discussed: (a) rotating prisms, (b) rotating lenses, (c) oscillating mirrors, and (d) the cathode ray oscillograph. The rotating prism was to be used for facsimile and general television use, rotating mirrors for large screen television, and oscillating mirrors for amateur use. On October 31, Dr. Ernst Alexanderson first proposed a "multiple beam" method. And at this time a test of the August Karolus light valve (the Kerr cell) was so successful that Dr. Alexanderson recommended purchasing it for some $200,000.[22]

The Bell Laboratories television system of Dr. Herbert Ives was making excellent progress. On November 2, 1925, Frank Gray had arbitrarily replaced the DC component (the background value) at the receiver. This important concept made it possible to receive television pictures with a full range of tones.[23] And on November 30, 1925, picture signals were transmitted by radio on 200 meters (in-house) with good success. At this time synchronous motors had been procured, and the film projector was synchronized with the scanning discs. All experiments were done with the transmitter and receiver in different parts of the laboratory. In addition, a flat cathode neon glow lamp had been developed which covered the rectangular area scanned by the discs and allowed the picture to be seen by several viewers.[24]

In November 1925 there were more patent applications by Russian inventors. On November 8, 1925, Grabovsky, Popoff and Piskounoff applied for a television patent along the lines of Campbell Swinton. Its camera tube used a continuous mosaic rather than the metallic cubes of Campbell Swinton. A similar patent was applied for on November 28, 1925, by A.A. Tchernischeff.[25]

In December 1925 W. Rogowski and W. Grosser of the Electrotechnical Institute of Technology High School, Aachen, Germany, described a new oscillograph of the Braun type that gave a very intense spot. The article described the various methods of concentrating the beam. Their tube had an auxiliary electrode and also a coil outside of the tube and concentric with it to concentrate the cathode beam, thus giving a more intense spot on the screen.

This tube was of the high vacuum (no gas) type. It used magnetic focus and magnetic deflection. Also, the screen was made of a special material that would not give off gas. The long tube was to keep the beam free of electric charges from the glass. It was claimed that photographs were taken of frequencies as high as 100,000 periods/sec. This appears to be the first high vacuum, magnetically focused oscillograph tube built and operated.[26] However, in spite of the apparent advantages of this new tube, the Western Electric gas-focused tube probably was more stable and consistent in its operation and continued to be the most widely used oscillograph tube.

On December 18, 1925, it was reported that Prof. E. Belin had given a demonstration of a device which was supposed to prove that the principle of television had been solved. However, this was merely a device which used a mirror drum that in addition to its rotation was given an oscillatory motion so as to cover an entire image. There were no electrical components involved; it was only a simulation of how Belin proposed to transmit a television image by substituting a photocell for one of the mirrors (the image then to be reproduced in some unexplained manner).[27]

On January 20, 1926, John L. Baird applied for a British patent covering the "flying spot" (the inverse system of Rignoux) method of television scanning.[28] It is not known when Baird first got this idea. But like most inventors, he was probably familiar with the inventions of the past. At this time, Baird had gone about as far as he could with his crude, insensitive equipment. By reversing the scanning process, as did Dr. Gray of the Bell Telephone Labs, he obtained the results he had been seeking. By scanning the object with a concentrated beam of light *through* the Nipkow disc, he was able to get his first "real" images, i.e., pictures with halftones.

All the evidence indicates that he first actually used this method for scanning an actual object ("Bill," his ventriloquist's dummy) and a young office boy (William Taynton) on October 2, 1925. Baird had no interest in motion picture film (even for experimental purposes as the Bell Telephone Labs had), believing that television should be *instantaneous*.

For the first time in history, a "live" television picture did not have to depend on the feeble electrical currents generated by the direct reflection of light from the subject to create a picture signal. By rapidly scanning the subject with an enormously bright light through a disc (or mirror drum) and having the photocells collect the reflected light, a stronger signal was generated, one in which the gray scale could be reproduced.

This new method also eliminated the enormous heat from the bright lights. The one apparent drawback was that the subject had to be in a darkened area to be effective. This discovery prompted Baird to quickly attempt the first public demonstration of "real television," i.e., with halftones.[29]

On January 23, 1926, it was reported that Baird had perfected a television apparatus and had given practical demonstrations of transmission of both sound and pictures between rooms. On January 26, 1926, Baird gave a demonstration of his television apparatus to some 40 members of the Royal Institution at his laboratory in Frith Street, Soho. This was the first *public demonstration* of true television ever witnessed. The images of living human faces, not as outlines or silhouettes but complete with tonal gradations of light and shade and detail were transmitted between two rooms. The description in the *London Times* stated that the pictures were "faint and often blurred." No mention was made as to how many lines were being scanned or at what frame rate.[30]

All of Baird's publicity indicated that Baird had invented a super-sensitive photocell which he kept a secret. No one ever saw his transmitter or his cell. His apparatus was always covered with screens of one sort or another, with the excuse that "extraneous light was not wanted and would interfere with the image." There was even a story that Baird had been experimenting with a cell made of visual purple, which was nonsense. It was also claimed that Baird had invented some "exotic" circuit using a transformer that magically solved his problems.

Later it was stated that Baird was very frightened of industrial espionage, but it would be more truthful to indicate that Baird and his financial backers wanted to keep his simple (but most effective) method a secret for as long as possible in order to head off any possible competition. For it was soon realized that the "flying spot system," while patentable, could not be protected. One result seems to be a profusion of equipment made for publicity purposes only. Certain models were often re-built or re-labeled so as to not reveal the real apparatus.[31]

At this time (December 1925) a Dr. R.T. Beattie of the Admiralty Research Laboratory (ARL) at Teddington, England, had given a demonstration of a crude television device. It appears that as early as 1923 ARL began secret work on television systems. The purpose was for the "spotting of aircraft while at sea." Other research was conducted by the Air Ministry Laboratory, Imperial College, London. After much research a basic television system was assembled early in 1925 and was operating by December.

The device used Nipkow discs 20 inches in diameter having 40 holes running at a rate of 5 frames/sec. The transmitter used a gas-filled (helium) photocell having a coating of rubidium and a sensitivity of 3.3 microamperes/lumen. The receiver used a neon lamp of the Osglimbeehive type as a light valve. Picture size was some 4cm by 4cm. However, the Baird demonstration of January 26, 1926, as crude as it was, proved to be far superior to their results and prompted the ARL (as well as the Air Ministry) to suspend their own efforts and wait for future developments to be made by Baird and other private experimenters.[32]

On February 9, 1926, Reginald S. Clay of London applied for a patent for a means of synchronizing television systems. This patent was important as it described straight-line scanning with a quick return. Clay planned to transmit an additional pulse during the period of darkness at the end of each scanning line which was to be used to keep the beam in phase. The patent was particularly concerned with the use of a cathode ray tube. Clay mentioned methods for modulating the electron beam by magnetic means so that it did not change speed as it changed brightness.[33]

On February 10, 1926, Frank Gray of the Bell Telephone Labs reported on the first use of his new flying spot process on living persons. One of his first subjects was J.R. Hofele. For reasons that remain unknown, the Bell Labs had only started to process Gray's idea as a patent on January 14, 1926.[34]

On March 2, 1926, Dr. Gray gave a description of a complete system using the new flying spot scanner. He noted that the results were the same as if the subject were illuminated from light coming from the photoelectric cell. He claimed that by using a single photoelectric cell some $13'' \times 1\frac{1}{2}''$, "a person can be seen and his motions followed quite easily. The subject is scarcely aware that he is being subjected to the scanning process."[35]

On March 9, 1926, Marius Latour applied for a patent in which he proposed to separate the images in order to transmit them. He mentioned the use of interlace to present a homogenous picture. Each picture was divided into a plurality of fractions and explored by a multiplicity of photocells. The concept of interlace, or the nonsequential scanning of the image, was to have much significance later on.[36]

On May 8, 1926, Robert C. Mathes of the Bell Telephone Labs reported on a proposal to reduce the bandwidth of a picture signal by sending it over a number of channels. Mathes suggested that a better way would be to use a number of columns and to send the signal from a single scanning element to charge up a group of 50 condensers, each of which acquired the charge corresponding to one of the picture elements in each column. Then another set of brushes would discharge the stored impulses to produce signals 1/50th of the frequency required. This storing of the charge corresponding to a picture element was a very important concept which later became the focus of many patent interferences. While there is no evidence that this plan was ever reduced to practice, Mathes' idea was one of the first proposals of the "charge storage principle" on record.[37]

On May 21, 1926, Henry J. Round of the Marconi Wireless Company applied for a British patent for a method of picture telegraphy. The patent called for a plurality of "light tubes" massed at one end to receive the light from the picture. Each light tube had its own photocell, which charged a condenser. The currents from the condenser were then amplified and discharged by a rotating commutator and sent to a transmitter. The variations in light and shade were thus transmitted by a brush rotating at, say, 8 to 10 times/sec.

At the receiver, another rotating commutator, running synchronously, was used either: (a) to carry a moving light source that sent the varying light impulses to the "cipher" end of the light tubes, or (b) to connect a plurality of stationary light sources by means of brushes so as to light up the "cipher" end of the light tubes in sequence.

Claim Five of the British patent stated that "photocells are connected each to charge a condenser." This appears to be the first patent incorporating means for using the "storage principle" whereby each condenser would be continually recharging itself during the time interval when the scanner (whether mechanical or electrical) was systematically discharging the other condensers. As such it was a very important television patent even though it described an otherwise impractical device.[38]

On June 2, 1926, C.F. Jenkins of Washington, D.C., applied for a television patent using a series of light-conducting elements such as rods or tubes in a rotating device to create a visual representation. The rods were to be disposed radially, and in different planes, within a rotating element. At the center of the device was to be a light valve supplied with pulsating current that represented the picture signal. It was planned to synchronize all of these elements so that a moving picture was projected onto a screen K.[39]

Frank Gray also reported on June 21, 1926, that the Bell Telephone Labs was building a "large screen" of 100 neon lamps as a receiver. This consisted of ten vertical sections of glass tubing joined to form a continuous tube. Each was filled with neon gas and had a single spiral electrode running through it. Ten exterior electrodes were placed on the glass in the form of rectangular pieces of tinfoil. Signals were sent from a commutator by means of a rotating brush. Although limited to 100 elements, simple moving objects could be seen in a well-lit room. It was planned to build a larger, 2,500-element screen.[40]

On June 25, 1926, the *Electrician* featured a photograph taken in the laboratories of Baird Television Ltd. This seems to be the first published picture taken from a receiver of a human face with a semblance of halftones and detail. Baird of course knew nothing of the work being done in the Bell Telephone Labs and while he enjoyed (and demanded) the publicity and acclaim, the Bell Labs kept their work shrouded in secrecy.[41]

On July 1, 1926, AT&T and RCA signed an agreement in which, for one million dollars, the Bell system turned over its radio facilities (including station WEAF) to RCA and withdrew from broadcasting. It also gave up its rights to manufacture receiving sets to RCA. In return, RCA agreed to use the Bell wires exclusively and not to compete with the telephone company for telephone business.[42]

On July 14, 1926, the first simple television shadow images were shown on a standard Western Electric oscillograph tube at the Bell Telephone Labs. The transmitter was a rotating disc with 5 spirals of 10 holes each. Connected to it was a rotating disc with 500 contacts. These were touched by a brush to discharge a condenser to supply current for the scanning plates. By this method, shadow images of the letter "A" and a hooked piece of wire could be seen on a field about one inch square.[43]

On July 24, 1926, the Bell Telephone Labs reported that they had received television images on a cathode ray tube that had been modified with the addition of a grid near the filament in the form of a circular perforated plate. Moving images could be viewed by several persons at a time. On July 31, 1926, the Bell Telephone Labs tried their cathode ray receiver with the 50 hole disc. This time the picture tube had a wire gauze placed across the end of the screen. The picture voltage was applied between the gauze and the accelerating anode. The results were not very good, although hands in motion and very dim images of a person's face could be seen. It appears that the strength of the beam displaced and spread the spot and thus prevented good reproduction of the images.[44]

On July 26, 1926, Eduoard Belin gave a demonstration of his new cathode ray television system to Gen. Gustave A. Ferrie, head of the French Military Telegraph, Prof. Charles Fabrie of the Sorbonne and Rene Mesny of the French Academy of Sciences. This new television system revealed that Belin had been joined by Fernand Holweck, who had been chief of staff of the Madam Curie Radium Institute. Holweck was noted for his high vacuum pump as well as for creating many electron tubes which were continually evacuated. It is not known just when Holweck first became associated with M. Belin. The Belin Laboratory was at Malmaison near Paris, but the demonstration was given at the laboratory of Madame Curie.

The new television scheme was now called the "Belin and Holweck" system. The demonstration was under the direction of M. Gregory N. Ogloblinsky, who had constructed the apparatus and was chief engineer of the Laboratory des Etablissments Eduoard Belin. Gone were the rotating mirrors and discs of the early Belin schemes, none of which ever produced a real television image.

Instead, the light from a Garbarini arc went through a set of condensing lenses through a diaphragm with a hole 0.1 cm in diameter. There were two little mirrors, one placed above the other, the very narrow lower

mirror vibrating at 500 cycles/sec and the upper mirror, slightly larger, operating horizontally at about 10 oscillations/sec. The upper mirror had a microphone attached to it by means of a light metallic bar. Pressure on the membrane at the end of each oscillation of the mirror sent current (a low-frequency pulse) to the receiving apparatus. The two mirrors were driven by a 500-cycle alternator as they were connected mechanically. The two mirrors produced a scanning action that covered the whole transparency. This system was patterned after the flying spot method of Rignoux. The resulting beam was fed to a photocell (composed of a cathode of metallic potassium and an anode of nickel cadmium) which converted the varying light into a signal that was then sent to a vacuum tube amplifier to be transmitted.

Reception was by means of a metallic cathode ray oscilloscope built by Holweck. It was connected to a helical vacuum pump to continuously evacuate the tube, also designed and built by Holweck. The filament required a potential of about two volts. A difference of potential was applied between the grid and filament to control the brightness. A disc with a small hole acted as the plate. It had a little copper tube that was surrounded by a small coil to magnetically focus the beam. The plate had a voltage of about 1000 volts, supplied by a special battery. The modulated beam was moved by two ordinary coils supplied with 500-cycle current from a high speed motor and 10-cycle current from a low speed motor. These motors were kept in sync by the action of the 10-cycle pulse being sent along with the 500-cycle sine-wave. It was claimed that only pictures without halftones were sent. The 33-line pictures were able to show images of hands and fingers and the outline of a human face.[45]

On August 2, 1926, the television apparatus of Alexandre Dauvillier of the Louis de Broglie Laboratories was revealed. The transmitter was that of the August 31, 1924, German patent which used two vibrating mirrors that transmitted the light from the subject to a photoelectric cell. Dauvillier used sine-wave scanning at 800 cycles horizontally with 10 frames/sec vertically to produce a 40-line picture. A photocell of potassium hydride was at a distance from the diaphragm to get more illumination. The phase relationship of the transmitter to the receiver was within 5 lines.

The receiving tube was similar to that of Dauvillier's February 11, 1925, application. The difference of potential of the photocell was applied between the diaphragm and the Wehnelt cylinder by means of a regulated potentiometer. It was claimed that the modulation was sufficiently sensitive that application of maximum emission would not displace or distort the spot. The fineness of the spot was regulated by a coaxial magnetic coil. The tube had a particle of calcium inserted within it in order to maintain a low pressure. (This was later known as a "getter.") The screen was made

Opposite, top: Edouard Belin in his laboratory. Bottom: Fernand Holweck (left) with Gregory N. Ogloblinsky with the Belin CRT receiver.

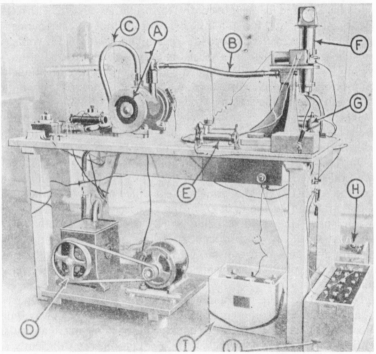

The Belin and Holweck cathode ray apparatus. Top: the transmitter: A—alternator that drives mirrors; B—microphone of low frequency mirror; C—transparency support; D—diaphragm; E—alternator rheostat; F—objective lenses; G—arc lamp. Bottom: the receiver: A—Holweck molecular pump; B—tube connecting with oscillograph; C—tube connecting pumps; D—preparatory pump; E and G—rheostats; F—oscillograph; H, I, J—batteries for concentrating coil, filament and low frequency coil.

A 1927 photo of Alexandre Dauvillier with his television apparatus.

of willemite. Actual experience with a display screen made of metal showed that a current of 1 microampere with some 300 volts on the plate gave a very brilliant spot. The cathode beam was accelerated *after* modulation and *before* deflection. "Trying acceleration after deflection does not give good results," it was reported.

Dauvillier's cathode ray tube was quite modern; it was sealed off, thus being portable, was of high vacuum (no gas), used magnetic focus, had a willemite screen and was made of Pyrex glass. But Dauvillier deplored the enormous amount of light necessary to produce suitable currents for his cathode ray tube. He was quite discouraged by the fact that an increase in sensitivity at the transmitter on the order of 1000 times would be necessary before a practical television system was possible.

M. De Broglie (who read the paper) admitted that of the systems of Mihály, Jenkins, or Belin that only Baird was able to transmit a normal picture. The use of the flying spot scanner made this transmission possible, and neither Baird nor the Bell Telephone Labs had any intention of revealing this method for the time being.[46]

On August 9, 1926, Baird obtained a license from the BBC to transmit television over station 2TV to Harrow. The transmitter operated on 200 meters with 250 watts of power. This seems to be the first license ever issued to transmit television signals.

In September 1926 A. Dinsdale reported that he had witnessed a demonstration of Baird's system in which it was claimed that faces were perfectly distinguishable, with smooth gradations of shade, bright highlights, dark shadows and perfectly recognizable beyond all question or doubt. He stated that Baird had now formed a company and that rapid progress was being made towards commercial application of his apparatus.[47]

On September 18, 1926, a television device designed by Dr. Ernst Alexanderson of General Electric with seven multiple beams and a drum with 24 mirrors was tested in a simulated manner. At this time, only one beam of light was sent through the seven holes.[48]

Obviously relating to the cathode ray activities of the two French pioneers Belin and Dauvillier was a letter written by Campbell Swinton to Nature on October 9, 1926, stating that "not long after 1897, after the invention of the Braun tube, [he] had built a home made Braun oscillograph in which a metal plate . . . coated with selenium was traversed by the end of a cathode ray beam." He claimed he had the assistance of Prof. G.M. Minchin. He also tried a cathode ray tube purchased from Germany, but that tube in its "hard" form proved intractable with no results. This report was, of course, contrary to his statements in both 1911 and 1924, in which he had stated that he had never built any apparatus.[49]

On October 15, 1926, John L. Baird applied for a patent for improvements in "Recording of Views of Objects or Scenes, or Optical Images or the like." This was to be done by recording the varying electrical picture signals on a gramophone or like element. This is the first patent taken out on what later became known as the "video disc."

Baird described several variations of the disc, such as having the sound and picture on separate tracks; combining them in a single groove where the side walls (for example) were used for the sound record and the bottom of the groove for the sight record; or having the grooves of the sight and sound records be parallel grooves of a double spiral, or on opposite sides of the disc, or at opposite ends of a cylinder.[50]

On October 18, 1926, Hans Busch presented a paper, "Calculation of the Path of an Electron Beam in an Axial Symmetrical Electromagnetic Field." In an attempt to calculate the equation $n = e/m$, Busch gave the results of both magnetic and electrostatic fields on an electron in an axial symmetrical but otherwise random field. Busch presented proof that a narrow electron beam merging from a point of the axis of symmetry and parallel to it will be focused in a point in such a field. He also stated that e/m can ascertain the distance between the point of origin and the focal point within certain accuracy. This article is generally conceded to be the first to explain the new field of "electron optics." Busch mentioned the prior work of Rogowski and Grosser.[51]

Dr. Ernst Alexanderson with his multi-spot projector.

On October 19, 1926, Dr. Ernst Alexanderson of General Electric applied for his first television patent. It was a multiple beam process in which the basic idea was to split up the transmitted image into four parts and send each of these beams to its own photocell. It was planned to transmit each of these signals simultaneously on separate carrier waves by means of multiplexing (the Hammond method is mentioned). The four carriers were to be demodulated and sent to four separate oscillographs, where they were to be modulated separately. The four light beams were then to be sent to four mirrors and to a common lens and travel in four parallel paths across the screen. A rotating mirror drum or disc or lens disc was to be used to scan and reconstruct the images.

Dr. Alexanderson expected that the amount of illumination on the screen would not be merely in direct proportion to the number of mirrors but approximately in proportion to the square of the number of the mirrors. In a modification, there was a description of the use of a special Kerr cell with seven pairs of electrodes to be used to control seven bands of light.[52]

In October of 1926 Kenjiro Takanayagi of the Hamamatsu Technical School of Japan started his first actual experiments with cathode ray television. He claimed he transmitted his first picture onto a Braun tube on December 25, 1926. This was the Japanese character katakana "i" inscribed on a mica plate.[53]

On November 10, 1926, Frank Gray at the Bell Telephone Labs suggested to Dr. Ives the idea of placing a light valve in front of a cathode ray tube viewing screen. Since they had been unsuccessful in modulating the electron beam without serious distortions, why not just present a bright (unmodulated) screen and view it through the light valve, thereby eliminating all of the problems of modulation and deflection?

On November 16, 1926, Frank Gray reported on the progress that had been made on cathode ray reception. The Bell Telephone Labs now had two special tubes which they were using for their experiments. The first had a grid near the filament on which the picture signal was impressed. The second had two parallel wire gauzes near the screen on which the picture voltage was impressed. Neither tube gave good results; only simple subjects were reproduced, and they did not show halftones in a satisfactory manner.

On November 27, 1926, Frank Gray reported that the large two-foot grid screen had been built. It worked, although it was inferior in its imagery. Then, in December 1926, with the big screen functioning and the line coupling apparatus worked out, it was planned to stage an actual demonstration at an early date. This was set for April 1927.[54]

On December 4, 1926, F.W. Reynolds of the American Telephone and Telegraph Company applied for a patent on "Electrooptical Transmission." This patent described a unique electric camera tube. It consisted of a multiple-unit photoelectric element comprising a large number of fine tubular units and a light-transmitting and electrically conducting auxiliary electrode within the large end of the transmitting tube. The photoelectric element was to be made of a large number of relatively fine and long glass or quartz tubes with a film of rubidium, potassium or other photoactive material deposited on the inner walls of these units. The auxiliary unit could either be a light-transmitting conducting film of platinum on the inner side of one end of the tube or on a separate transparent plate within the tube, or an open mesh screen of fine wires.

It was planned that the cathode ray impressed on the opposite end of the photoelectric units in any suitable manner would be modulated or have their intensity changed in passing through the photoelectric units approximately in proportion to the intensity of the light falling upon a unit of the photoelectric element through which the cathode rays may be passing. A pulsating current would flow between a cathode and an electrode, which would represent the light falling at any instant on the element being scanned. Scanning would be spiral or substantially parallel. Reynolds planned to use LaCour motors to run in synchronization along with a tuning fork to insure proper phase relationships. This patent quickly ran into an interference with Dr. Zworykin of Westinghouse, which Reynolds lost.[55]

There were two important articles on John L. Baird's work in December 1926. Both told of the progress made during the past year. But in neither was there mention of the use of the "flying spot" method to solve the problem of the insensitivity of the existing photocells. In Baird's article in *Experimental Wireless*, he stated that the problems were solved but that as a result of the patent situation he was not at liberty to divulge how it had been accomplished.[56]

On December 15, 1926, Dr. Ernst Alexanderson revealed for the first time in a speech given in St. Louis, Missouri, that he and General Electric had been engaged in television research. He indicated that he was working on telephotography and that by speeding up the process some sixteen times, "television becomes an accomplished fact." However, the problem was complicated by the need to use mechanical moving parts. It was known that "a cathode ray can be deflected by purely electromagnetic means, and the use of the cathode ray oscillograph has been suggested." But he was not willing to wait for a discovery that might never come.

Alexanderson described his multi-beam projector with great anticipation. However, a demonstration of this machine at 16 pictures/sec on December 24, 1926, gave very poor results. It appeared as though a wave of light was passing over the screen. So it was planned to interlace the lines to reduce this effect. In spite of the hopes (and publicity) that Alexanderson had for this machine, there is no record of it ever giving a successful demonstration.[57]

On December 24, 1926, Boris Rtcheouloff, now of London, applied for a British patent updating his 1922 Russian patent application. He still used vibrating springs at both the transmitting and receiving tubes under the control of alternating currents from magnets. On January 4, 1927, Rtcheouloff applied for another British patent on his magnetic recorder. This also was almost identical to his earlier Russian patent which had not yet been issued.[58]

On January 7, 1927, Philo T. Farnsworth of the Television Laboratories, San Francisco, California, applied for a patent covering a television system. Farnsworth was a young experimenter who had dreamed of a television system since his high school days. He had come to San Francisco and had convinced a group of backers that he could produce a workable television system within a few short years. He lacked formal education but was full of new, innovative ideas.

Philo Farnsworth devised a novel system that was not based on the

Fig.4

Fig.5

Fig.7

Fig.8

Fig.6

Fig.9

Fig.10

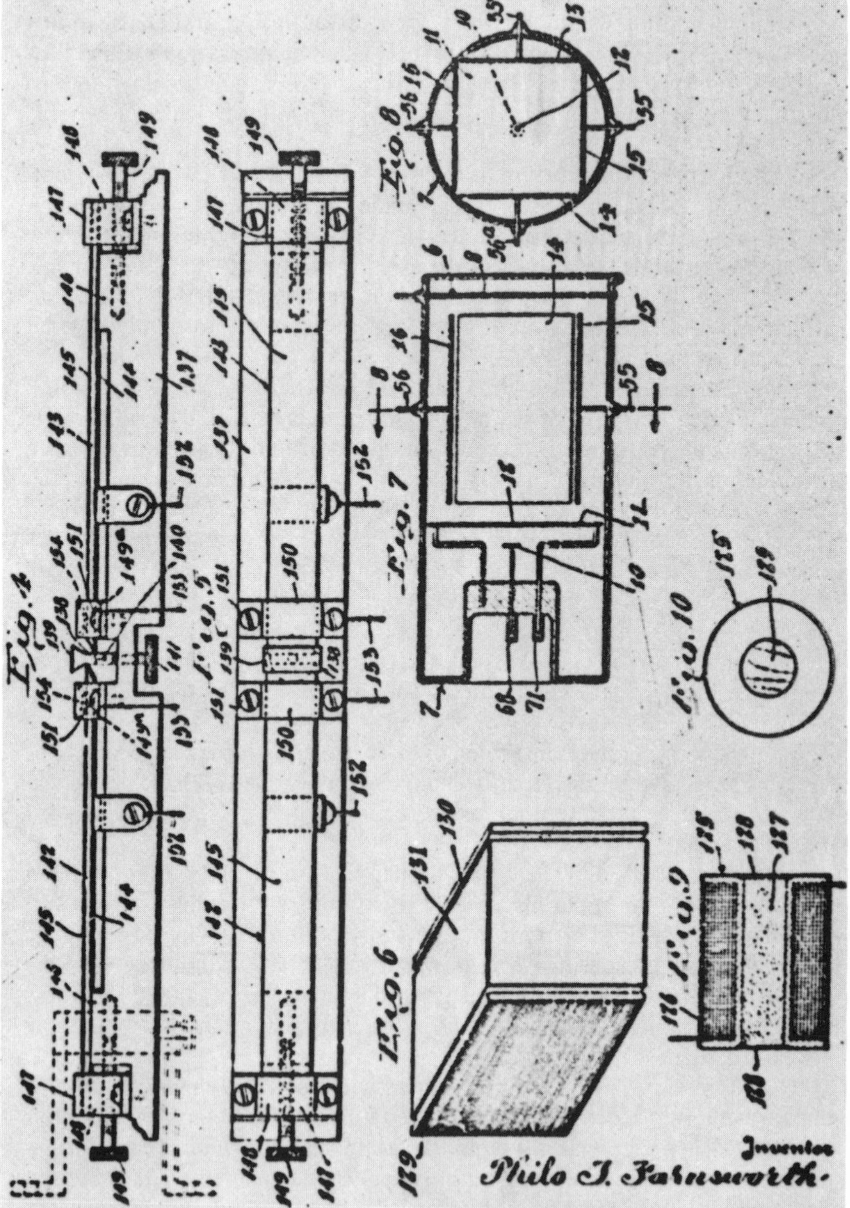

Inventor

Philo T. Farnsworth

By Lyon & Lyon

ideas of Campbell Swinton. The camera tube (which was later to be called an Image Dissector) was essentially the same as that of Max Dieckmann and Rudolf Hell. However, their patent had not yet been issued and, as often happens in the field of invention, was almost identical. Still, where Dieckmann failed to get his tube to operate, Farnsworth was to succeed.

Basically the camera tube had a light-sensitive plate (6) formed of a fine mesh (8) covered with a light-sensitive medium such as sodium, potassium or rubidium. An electric shutter was (11) formed by a metallic plate in which there was an aperture (12). Between the shutter (11) and the light-sensitive plate (6) there were four plates to deflect the electron stream in two directions. The action of the four plates was to cause the electric image to be passed systematically in front of the aperture so as to analyze or dissect the scene to be transmitted. The tube was to be of the high vacuum type to permit a high potential without ionization.

Farnsworth also planned to use straight-line scanning of about 500 lines horizontally at 10 cycles/sec vertically. Thus he expected to accomplish uniform lighting of all portions of the image to be produced.

The receiver was to use as a source of light an arc with a shutter (121). The light from the shutter was to pass through a polarizer in the form of a Nicol prism. It was planned to use two cooperating oscillographs to form a correct picture upon a screen. This receiving system was divided out of the original patent application. In studying the existing patents, Farnsworth was so concerned with the 1917 Nicolson patent covering a Braun tube as a receiver that he went to great lengths not to include a hot cathode Braun tube in his first patent application.

It is to be noted that Farnsworth never used anything but a cathode ray tube as a receiver. He did experiment with gas-filled tubes, both for transmitter and receivers. He also used rotary generators to produce his early scanning voltages.[59]

The *New York Times* reported on January 11, 1927, that Dr. Alexanderson of General Electric had given a speech on radio-photography and television to a group of radio engineers. He described his still picture method and his hopes for a television system. He showed his multi-beam projector in a simulated demonstration by spinning the drum to cause the light spots to move and fill the screen.[60]

On January 17, 1927, Dr. Ives of the Bell Telephone Laboratories made a suggestion for the simultaneous transmission and reception of color television images. He proposed the use of three photoelectric cells, each sensitive to one special color and connected to three sets of amplifiers and transmission channels. At the receiving end, the large grid neon tube would be made of three grids arranged so their linear portions alternated.

Opposite: Philo Farnsworth's first patent. The first practical Image Dissector came out of this patent.

The 1927 cathode ray tube of Dr. Alexandre Dauvillier.

By the use of different gasses, it would be possible to get alternate strips of red, green and blue colors. It was planned to use three sets of distributors running on the same axle.[61]

John L. Baird filed for a patent on January 26, 1927, for a magnetic recording system capable of recording a single frame or of playing back a recording at high speed. It was in the form of a plate of magnetic material that had several record and playback heads so arranged as to play back at high speed.[62] Another patent for magnetic recording of picture signals was applied for in France on February 5, 1927, by Leon Thurm.[63]

On March 4, 1927, the Etablissements Edouard Belin applied for a patent for improvements and procedures in apparatus for radiovision. It was mainly concerned with improvements in the performance of the cathode ray tube. It was to result in an efficient concentration of the beam and the good quality of the spot produced by the light of the screen.

The tube was to be in several sections, with each part insulated from the other. The screen was to be connected to the body of the the tube by means of a connection "L." There were to be two differences of potential starting with V' and proceding towards the screen. A difference of potential between filament and grid was potential V". A second difference of potential between the body and plate "P" was potential V'''. There was also the mention of the use of a long-persistence phosphor. Since the patent did not specify either the use of gas or magnetic focus, it is assumed that the principle of "electron focus" was used. This idea was well established in

Europe at this time. The patent was issued to Etablissements Edouard Belin, and there is no way of finding who the actual inventor was. This turned out to be a very important patent.[64]

In March 1927 *Science and Invention* had an article describing the cathode ray television system of Alexandre Dauvillier. It showed photographs of the actual equipment for the first time.[65]

In March 1927 Hans Busch reported on "The Action of the Concentration Coil with the Braun Tube." He had investigated the effects of electrostatic and magnetic fields in concentrating the cathode ray tube in a Braun tube. He proved that a short, narrow coil acts on the electron path exactly as a lens to light rays, the formula $1/f = 1/a + 1/b$ being similarly valid.

An electrostatic field acts on the electron path as a medium of definite refractive index in optics. Investigation has shown that much larger diaphragms can be employed, thereby increasing the luminosity of the fluorescent spot without impairing the sharpness. Busch described a Braun tube in which an aperture of 8mm diameter produced a spot of 0.3mm, and the beam current was about 10 percent of the tube current.[66]

On April 7, 1927, the Bell Telephone Laboratories of American Telephone and Telegraph gave a demonstration of their television system over both wire and radio circuits. The demonstration was under the direction of Dr. Herbert E. Ives and Dr. Frank Gray. Pictures and sound were sent by wire from Washington, D.C., to New York City. There was also a wireless demonstration from Whippany, New Jersey, to New York City, some 22 miles away.

The principal event was a speech by Herbert Hoover, then secretary of commerce, which originated in Washington, D.C. This was followed by a program of amateur vaudeville which originated in Whippany and was transmitted by radio.

The pictures were received on sets with a screen some two by three inches in size by means of a scanning disc, and on the large two-foot glass tube screen as well. The 50-line pictures were transmitted 18 times/sec. The wired pictures were sent by special circuits with the picture signal on one line and special synchronizing signals (60 and 2000 cycles) sent on another. A third line was for voice transmission. The radio transmission from station 3XN sent the picture signal on 191 meters (1570kc), the sync signals on 1600 meters (185kc), and the voice on 207 meters (1450kc).

The quality of the pictures reproduced on the small scanning disc sets were described as "excellent daguerreotypes which have come to life and started to talk." The details of the faces appeared in clear-cut black lines against a shining gold background. However, the picture quality of the large screen was much inferior, with features considerably blurred by the enlargement. It was claimed that there was no difference in quality between the pictures sent by either wire or radio.

The flying spot system developed by Dr. Gray was revealed as the means for picking up the images at the transmitter. It was included among

Dr. Frank Gray (standing) and John R. Hofele. Dr. Gray's "flying spot" scanning device made the Bell Labs 1927 demonstration a success.

a host of technical achievements that made the demonstration such a success. There were no exaggerated claims made for any major technical breakthroughs. Mention was made of the fact that the Bell Telephone Laboratories had been working on the project for several years and the demonstration required the services of almost 1000 men.[67]

It was in fact the best demonstration of a mechanical television system ever made to this time. It would be several more years before any other system could even begin to compare with it in picture quality.

In April 1927 Kenjiro Takayanagi of the Hamamatsu Higher Technical School of Japan carried out successful experiments using a cathode ray receiver. Takayanagi had built quite an ingenious system around a Tokyo Denki gas-filled oscillograph tube. He used a 40-hole Nipkow disc that rotated at 14 rev/sec. A flying spot system of Rignoux was used with two GE photocells. The use of the Nipkow disc meant that Takayanagi had to have a linear time-base generator. This was supplied with horizontal pulses from the rotating disc, which came from a row of holes that faced a photoelectric cell. The vertical pulse came from a larger hole in the disc. The scanning currents and sync pulses were fed to the cathode ray tube, and it was claimed that they worked quite satisfactorily.

Opposite: Dr. Herbert E. Ives at Bell Labs' 1927 demonstration of television over both radio and wire circuits.

Kenjiro Takayanagi's 1927 CRT apparatus.

This is the first recorded use of horizontal and vertical pulses generated by means of a photocell.

The received image was about 4 by 5 cm square on a green screen, the number of picture elements about 1600. The images were recognizable as faces, and "identification was somehow possible." Takayanagi predicted that future Braun tubes would be both high vacuum and high voltage. And there would have to be some 100,000 elements for the picture to be practical.[68]

At this time only Takayangi in Japan and the Bell Telephone Labs in the United States were using Nipkow discs for scanning, with Braun tubes for reception. As a result, they were using unidirectional, linear scanning. Belin and Holweck as well as Dauvillier in France were using vibrating mirrors for scanning, with Braun tubes for reception with sine-wave scanning. Farnsworth, who was just starting his experiments with cathode ray tubes, was also using sine-wave scanning in conjunction with his first electric camera tubes. All of the other pioneers, including Baird, Alexanderson, Jenkins, von Mihály, and Karolus, were using some form of Nipkow disc, prism or mirror drum for their television experiments. Max Dieckmann seemed to have stopped working on a television system.

On April 20, 1927, Campbell Swinton wrote to Dr. Alexanderson discussing the merits of cathode ray television. He hoped that someone would "be induced to follow the cathode-ray idea up seriously." Not knowing of the laboratory efforts of Dr. Ives, who was actually working on cathode ray television at the time, Campbell Swinton stated his hopes to Dr. Alexanderson, who unfortunately never thought much of the idea.[69]

Meanwhile, experiments were still being conducted with cathode ray reception at the Bell Telephone Labs. On May 1, 1927, Frank Gray related the advantages of using a uniform sweep in one direction with a cathode

Valensi's 1927 apparatus. A — receiving lamp; B — fluorescent screen; C — coils of magnetic field; D — reflection apparatus; E — explorer disks; F — synchronizing circuit; G — receiving circuit; H — collimator; I — synchronized motor; J — photoelectric cell; K — 8-cycle alternator; I — 800-cycle alternator; M — amplifier.

ray tube. He described the method they were using, which had a commutator rotating synchronously with the scanning disc at the transmitting end. A condenser was charged and quickly discharged through a resistance. The voltage across the resistance was applied to one pair of metal plates in the cathode ray tube. As a result, the beam moved across the tube with a practically constant velocity and was quickly jerked back to repeat the motion again. A similar movement of the beam was used in a vertical direction. This resulted in a beam tracing the screen repeatedly in the same direction, at a constant velocity, in a series of parallel lines one after the other. It was possible to receive simple television pictures on a tube operated in this manner.[70]

Early in May 1927, Dr. Alexanderson had Ray D. Kell, who was working in the Testing Department of General Electric, come to work for him on his television project. By May 21, 1927, Kell and Paul A. Kober had developed and demonstrated a television system of 48 lines. It was projected onto a small screen by means of a high-frequency mercury light that Kober had brought from the Harrison Tube Plant. Mr. Kell was soon to be guiding the General Electric/Alexanderson television project.[71]

It was reported that on May 24, 1927, John L. Baird had transmitted television images from his laboratory in London to Glasgow, Scotland, a distance of some 438 miles. This was done using ordinary telephone lines. It was claimed that the images were "recognizable" and steady in position.[72]

In June 1927 J.L. Baird reported that he had abandoned the rotating disc of lenses in favor of two rotating slotted discs with a block of cellular or honeycomb appearance. This was supposed to break up the strips or line images into finer images made up of dots. A similar block at the receiver was used to recreate the picture.

At this time it was also reported that Baird had devised a "phonoscope" for recording the television signal. This was a machine for preserving radio pictures by means of phonograph records. Although it was stated that some records had been made and that every object seemed to have its own "sound" there were no reports of actually playing the recordings and seeing the visual images. An illustration showed a disc cylinder of the old Edison type, not the flat disc of Berliner. This was the first of a long series of "new ideas" created to keep Baird's financial backers content.[73]

In July 1927 the television scheme of Georges Valensi, chief engineer of the French Post Office, was described. Valensi was credited with being one of the first inventors to have the idea of using cathode rays for television apparatus. His transmitter was restricted to either slides or opaques. Two powerful lamps illuminated the image, which was intercepted by two "stroboscobic discs." These discs produced straight-line scanning of the image which was then passed through a collimator lens to a photocell. The discs were connected to the two circuits for creating the magnetic deflection of the electron beam in the Braun tube. A slow motor of 8 cycles/sec and a high speed motor of 800 cycles/sec were geared together so that only one synchronized signal was necessary to be sent to the telephone line.

The receiving apparatus consisted of a special Braun tube made by Mr. Johannes of Paris. It used a small amount of gas to concentrate the beam. Only 12 volts were necessary to modulate the beam. An anode voltage of 800 volts was applied to the perforated plate. Four magnetic coils located near the screen were fed wave profiles of isosceles triangles (straight lines) in perfect synchronism with the transmitter.

No description of the pictures shown was given in this article. It was mentioned that recent experiments had somewhat neglected the cathode ray tube, and the developments of M. Valensi seemed to indicate that in that tube probably lay the solution of the television problem, with regard to cheap, compact and lightweight apparatus. The apparatus was built in collaboration with the Etablissements Gaiffe-Gallot-Pilon.[74]

In September 1927 an article on the apparatus of Eduoard Belin indicated that he was continuing his work on his television apparatus. The scanning rate was now 10 cycles vertically and 200 cycles horizontally, which meant a picture of 40 or less lines. This was an improvement in that a radio transmitter had been previously designed to operate on wave lengths from 250 meters to 30 meters. The transmitter used a water-cooled vacuum tube built by Holweck to keep down excessive heating on the lower wavelengths.[75]

On September 5, 1927, at the annual meeting of the British Association for the Advancement of Science, J.L. Baird demonstrated his newest system of television, called Noctovision. This differed from ordinary spot light scanning (Baird still had not revealed that he was using this method) in that the subject sat in darkness and was subjected to a powerful beam of infrared radiation. This eliminates the bright lights but creates problems due to the special response of the infrared as compared to daylight. This demonstration was not very successful, with quite a bit of flicker and apparent fading of the picture.

Baird had now settled into a pattern of producing many variations of his basic television system in order to keep his financial backers happy. (This practice was to have severe repercussions during the next few years.) Baird had promised to show his Phonovisor but did not. However, the reviewer congratulated Baird for providing the most popular of the scientific exhibits at the Leeds meeting.[76]

Of far more importance were the event taking place in the laboratories of Philo T. Farnsworth in San Francisco. It is claimed that on September 7, 1927, he was able to transmit an "image" from one of his early camera tubes. It was no more than a moving blob of light that was reproduced on a receiving tube, but it proved that his new system would work.

At this time Farnsworth had the only operating camera tubes in the world. Due to the insensitivity of his tubes, only pictures from slides (at first) and, later on, motion pictures could be used. He had assistance from Herbert Metcalf and Bill Cummings. It is claimed that the first tube was built at California Institute of Technology by Cummings in 1926. It was used for tests, but never transmitted a picture. Farnsworth also had the aid of his brother-in-law, Cliff Gardner, who had learned the art of glassblowing and was now building the dissector tubes.[77]

On September 14, 1927, Ralph Hartley and Herbert E. Ives of the Electrical Research Products (a subsidiary of the Bell Labs) applied for a patent for a system of television using motion picture film at either or both ends of a television system. At this time, the prospects for the "live" pickup of faces and events was quite dim. Even though the flying spot principle had made it possible to transmit pictures with halftones, it was limited to a small area swept by the flying spot.

It was therefore planned to use the greater light-gathering capabilities (higher sensitivity) of motion picture film and quickly process it so that it could be transmitted by an existing television system. Motion picture film was to be recorded in an ordinary camera. After quick processing, the film was to be projected through a mechanical film scanner (Nipkow disc), where its picture was converted into a picture signal. The accompanying

Philo Farnsworth's first Image Dissector tube, ca.1926.

sound track would also be recorded so that both picture and sound would be in sync.

A second variation was to be used for large screen television. In this method, the transmitted picture was also photographed from the face of the disc by a film camera, quickly processed, and sent to a special film projector, where it was projected onto a large screen by means of the usual arc lamp. Here also, the sound track was placed on the film in its proper position so that when the film was played back it was in sync. This was the first patent covering the recording of a television image for the express purpose of displaying it on a large screen.[78]

On November 12, 1927, Robert C. Mathes of the Bell Telephone Laboratories applied for a patent for increasing the brightness of images on screens such as the Bell Labs large screen device. It was to have means for producing a field of view, the use of a plurality of condensers and means for charging the elements in succession periodically in accordance with the tone values of elemental areas of the field of view. It would also have a plurality of voltage-controlled repeaters associated conductively with the condenser elements and means, controlled by the repeaters, for producing an image of the field of view. Mathes claimed that the image produced by this method was considerably brighter than the image produced when only one element was being actuated at a time and that it reduced flicker. Both a multi- and a single-channel method were described. This was a unique use of the "charge storage" principle at the receiving end.[79]

In November 1927 C.F. Jenkins published an article on "Radio Vision." He gave the April television demonstration of the Bell Laboratories great praise. He indicated that he was hard at work on the projection of motion pictures by radio, and he published photographs of his transmitting and receiving equipment.[80]

On December 31, 1927, August Karolus of the Telefunken Company applied for a patent combining a Kerr cell with a cathode ray tube. Karolus stated that since the same pencil of cathode rays is to be influenced both for the purpose of picture composition and of brightness control, it must fail to fulfill the desired end for the following reason: since the means provided to control the light intensity of the fluorescent spot, that is, the strength of the electron current, alter at the same time as the velocity of the electrons, the deviation of the ray by electric or magnetic fields is made rather uncertain inasmuch as the deflection is a function of the electron speed. Thus the travel of the light spot on the screen fails to be in exact synchronization with the transmitter. Karolus therefore suggested that the cathode ray tube send out a constant stream of electrons free from any deviations and that a Kerr cell be placed between the viewer and the screen, where it would be modulated by the picture signal. This he hoped would solve the problem.[81]

August Karolus shared the same feelings about cathode ray television as did Dr. Alexanderson and many of the leading television pioneers at this time: it promised the solution to the television problem, but fulfillment was just a visionary dream.

Chapter 7
The Introduction of the Kinescope: 1928–1929

On January 7, 1928, Alexandre Dauvillier published a three-part paper on "La Télévision Electrique" in *Revue Général d'Electricité*. The first part was the finest history of television since Korn and Glatzel's 1911 book. Like most inventors, Dauvillier had compiled a long list of patents and papers on the history of television. He covered the work from Bain in 1848 to that of Schoultz, Blake and Spooner, the Seguin brothers, and Zworykin. The second part disclosed the efforts of the author to produce a practical television system based on the use of the cathode ray tube. The third part reported the author's efforts at producing X-ray apparatus using television techniques as early as 1915.[1]

On January 9, 1928, Philo T. Farnsworth applied for his second patent application. This was for an improved dissector tube in that it indicated that the light from the scene impinged directly on the active light-sensitive surface. It also mentioned the use of secondary emission, which gives from five to twenty times as much current as can be obtained from photo-emission alone. The dissector tube, being an instantaneous device, was to be plagued by a lack of sensitivity and caused Farnsworth to devise many new secondary emission schemes to overcome this deficiency.[2]

On January 13, 1928, the General Electric Company gave a demonstration of television from its Research Laboratories station in Schenectady. The broadcast was under the supervision of Dr. Alexanderson. The picture was transmitted from 2XAF on 37.8 meters. The sound was sent on WGY's regular frequency of 379.5 meters. The picture was 48 lines at 16 frames/sec. A flying spot system was used at the studio, and it was claimed that the pictures could represent every detail in faces.

The special receivers used the neon lamp of D. McFarlan Moore. The image was about 1½ inches long and 1 inch wide, with a magnifying glass being used to bring the image size up to about 3 inches. It was claimed that three receivers in different parts of Schenectady were receiving pictures as good as those in the laboratory. They were located in the homes of Dr. Alexanderson and General Electric executives E.W. Allen and E.W. Rice,

Ernst Alexanderson (left) and Ray Kell with a 1927 experimental home television receiver.

Jr. This was the first demonstration of television by radio using "home receivers" instead of laboratory instruments.[3]

On January 20, 1928, Paul Selenyi of "Tungsram" Budapest-Upjest, Hungary, described a cathode-ray tube which was used to present figures on the end of the tube by dusting the outer surface of the tube with powdered sulphur. Selenyi used a V-shaped glowing cathode which was surrounded by an electrode and connected to a metal cap. The cathode rays passed through a circular opening in a cylinder maintained at a voltage of some 150–300 volts above that of the cathode. The inner surfaces of the glass bulb were coated with magnesium, and this metallic film formed the anode to which a pressure of 3000–4000 volts was being applied. It was claimed that with a ray strength of 1 microampere a marking velocity of 30km/sec. was obtained.

A patent was filed by Selenyi on February 1, 1928, covering this tube for drawing electrical pictures. A further article described a tube with an accelerating field and one free of lines of force. The patent described the use of an electrode to concentrate the beam and a magnetic coil to focus the beam. There were means for varying the brightness and for deflecting the beam in accordance to the phenomenon desired. There was reference to the electric transmission of pictures.[4]

On February 9, 1928, it was announced that John Baird had successfully transmitted an image from London to a receiving station at Hartsdale, New York, at midnight, London time. This was transmitted on 45 meters using 2kw of power. It was claimed that recognizable images were seen at the receiving end.[5]

Following this, it was later claimed that a television image was received on board the liner *Berengaria* while a thousand miles at sea. This was done on March 7, 1928, by Capt. Oliver G. Hutchinson of the Baird Television Development Company. This was in keeping with the Baird policy of exploring every facet of the new field of television (and getting much-needed publicity) to keep the public's curiosity alive.[6]

All of this publicity was planned to sell receivers and stock in Baird Television. They put a homemade receiver kit on sale in February 1928 at Selfridge's Store in London. Also, shares of stock in the Baird Company were being sold by ads, which were more often than not misleading. In March 1928, the magazine *Popular Wireless* offered the Baird Company £1000 if it would simply televise 5 simple objects over a distance of 25 yards. This challenge was never accepted. By June 1928, it was reported that "the Baird system is hopeless, after all."[7]

On February 25, 1928, the Bell Telephone Labs gave a demonstration of their system of television using crystal-controlled quartz oscillators to effect synchronization between the transmitter and the receiver. These special oscillators were developed by J.W. Horton and W.A. Marrison. These oscillators also included frequency-reducing circuits, which could generate from any vacuum tube a current whose frequency was a simple fraction of it, such as a quarter, a fifth or a sixth. It also included special circuits to slowly change the speed of the motor to affect desired framing of the picture.[8]

V.K. Zworykin of the Westinghouse Electric and Manufacturing Company applied for a patent on a novel photoelectric tube on March 3, 1928. It consisted of a base layer of magnesium, which was then covered with a thin film of certain metals such as cesium or rubidium or potassium or a combination of them in order to get almost any desired relation between wavelength of radiation and electron emissivity. Zworykin preferred to use cesium trinitride. He claimed that his method would produce a sensitive, stable photocell that would be simple and cheap to manufacture. This appears to be the first reference to a cesium magnesium cell, which was considerably more efficient than the potassium hydrogen cell that was in more common use. Zworykin claimed that his gas-filled cells yielded about 25 microamperes/lumen, while his vacuum cells yielded about 2 microamperes.[9]

Dr. Alexanderson of General Electric reported that on March 13, 1928, there was a demonstration of large screen (18 inches square) television at Schenectady. It was on 48 lines and used the Karolus light control.

Alexanderson stated that this was probably the first time that a picture of such size and quality had been projected. He credited Ray Kell for working out the arrangement.[10]

On March 20, 1928, Ray D. Kell of General Electric applied for his first patent covering a color television system. It was a two-color system in which the light from the scene was scanned by a disc with two sets of spirally arranged holes, in an interlaced scanning sequence. A disc with the two sectors provided the interlaced holes with light from one color to the first set of holes and light of the other color to the other set of holes. At the receiver, a similar disc with spirally interlaced holes had two lamps (of different colors) that illuminated the holes in sequence following the signals from the transmitter.[11]

On April 3, 1928, Philo Farnsworth lost his first patent interference to Dr. Zworykin of Westinghouse. This was interference #54,922. He lost another interference, #55,448, to Dr. Zworykin on July 11, 1928. The loss of an interference in the United States Patent Office meant that certain claims had to be given up, the rest of the patent being allowed.[12]

On April 17, 1928, Philo T. Farnsworth applied for a patent for electrical discharge apparatus. In this patent, he discussed how by applying a coaxial uniform, magnetic field, longitudinal to the path of the discharge around his tube, he was able to focus the electrical image to a sharp point. He claimed that applying this field caused two things to happen: first, the diffused spot focuses to a sharp image, and second, the plane of the deflection causes the alternating transverse field to rotate. He stated that an image formed in this fashion suffered from slight aberrations, the same as if focused by an ordinary lens. He described the paths of the electrons as being in helixes that depend on the electrical strength of the field applied. This appears to be the first patent covering this important application of "electron optics" to a television cathode ray tube.[13]

Philo Farnsworth applied for a patent for a synchronizing system on April 25, 1928. This patent described a shaded border around the picture to be transmitted, which by its nature would have a different frequency from that of the picture itself. It was proposed that a signal would consist of series of high frequencies (1500 cycles for horizontal scan) followed by the random picture frequencies, which would be modulated by the low frequencies (15 cycles for vertical scan) and transmitted. The receiver was to have means for selecting these separate frequencies.

This patent showed for the first time in an application by Farnsworth a hot cathode Braun tube that was magnetically focused by a long coil. This long focus coil was used by Farnsworth for both his camera (dissector) tube and his picture (receiver) tube.[14]

On April 26, 1928, Ricardo Bruni of Italy applied for a television patent of an all-electrical method of television using what Bruni called Photoscopes at both the transmitting and receiving ends. In the camera tube, a target was covered with selenium, which was scanned by a beam of electrons from a filament. The target was at an angle to the beam so that the image from the scene and the electron beam impinged on the same side. The receiving Photoscope was also tilted to the beam, and it was planned that by synchronizing the two tubes, the pictures would be made visible by means of phosphorescent material and viewed through a lens.[15]

In April 1928 the Radio Corporation of America applied for a television station permit for a station to be operated by its Research and Test Department at Van Cortlandt Park in New York City. This laboratory, which had been under the direction of Dr. Alfred N. Goldsmith since 1924, was charged with the testing and evaluation of existing products and the planning of new ones. The television transmitter and scanning equipment were to be installed at 411 Fifth Avenue, the home of RCA Photophone, where convenient studio facilities were available.

The transmitter was built by the staff of Theodore A. Smith, who was in charge of the new television engineering group. It was to use the 48-line, 16 frames/sec system developed by General Electric, who furnished all of the scanning equipment and who were also building some 48-line receivers. The transmitter was to operate on 2000 to 2100kc (142.8 meters). The Federal Radio Commission issued the call letters W2XBS for this facility. This appears to be the first permit ever issued in the United States for a television station.[16]

On May 5, 1928, C.F. Jenkins gave a demonstration of the projection of motion pictures by television to members of the Federal Radio Commission. His transmitting apparatus consisted of an ordinary 35mm film projector with the intermittent removed, a 48-hole scanning disc about 15 inches in diameter and a very powerful arc lamp. The film passed by the lenses at 15 frames/sec while the disc rotated at 900 rpm. The light from the arc went through the film and was registered on a photocell, which transmitted the picture information.

A new television receiver, shown for the first time, consisted of a hollow drum some seven inches in diameter and about five inches wide. In the center of the drum was a hollow spindle with a thin wall. Within this drum were inset 48 short quartz rods, which were to conduct light to holes on the periphery of the drum. At the very center of the drum was a special neon tube with four targets facing upwards. With a revolving commutator, each of the four targets received its proper picture signal, which was transmitted by the quartz rods to a mirror sitting at an angle of 45 degrees. A magnifying lens was set up in front of the mirror to enlarge the picture. When the lens disc and the rods were properly aligned, a beam of light was transmitted across the mirror. It was claimed that silhouettes were clearly transmitted and the illusion of motion was excellent.

This appears to be the first television device to use transluscent rods for the transmission of light to the screen. Jenkins announced that he intended to manufacture and sell "Radio-Movies" instruments on a commercial basis and sell them as an accessory to the regular broadcast receiver.[17]

There were two important demonstrations of television in 1928. The

C.F. Jenkins with his Radiomovies transmitter of 1928. Lenses were in a circle, and the film moved continuously.

first was by Kenjiro Takayanagi of the Hamamatsu Higher Technical School in Japan. He gave a demonstration of his cathode ray television system before the Japanese Society of Electricity in May 1928. He had improved his system since April 1927, and it was now capable of displaying moving images of hands and faces. He was transmitting 40 line pictures at 14 rev/sec. His article describing this system showed the first published pictures from the screen of a cathode ray tube.

Takayanagi continued to improve his system and by the end of 1928 was transmitting pictures of "recognizable" quality—not merely shadowgraphs, but pictures with halftones. Clearly he had the most advanced cathode ray system in the world at the time. He continued to

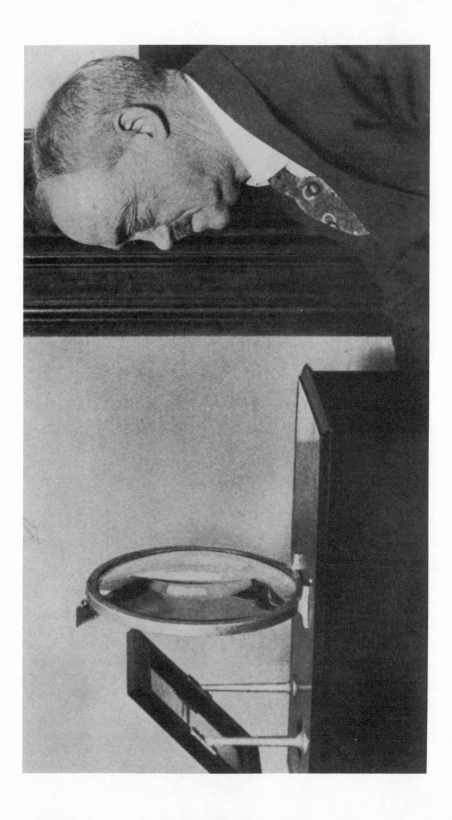

improve his system and by the end of 1928 was capable of transmitting pictures of "good" quality.[18]

On May 11, 1928, Dionys von Mihály gave a demonstration of television in Berlin which was witnessed by 50 people. Von Mihály had abandoned his older machine, which it seems had never actually worked, and was now using the conventional Nipkow disc scanning 30 lines at 10 frames/sec. Von Mihály used an alkali-metal photocell at the transmitter and a glow lamp similar to that of D. McFarlan Moore at the receiver. The demonstration consisted mainly of moving silhouettes and transparencies on a screen some 4 cm by 4 cm. This appears to be the first public demonstration of a working television system in Germany, and it was credited with creating great interest in the new medium.[19]

The Bell Telephone Laboratories had built a 36-inch scanning disc with larger scanning holes. It was fitted with a five-inch lens. A Case Thalofide photocell was used to translate the images into picture signals. On May 10, 1928, this disc was taken out of doors and set up on the roof of the Bell Laboratories Building. With it, they were able to transmit full-length pictures of men swinging tennis rackets and other such motions. This appears to be the first successful transmission of "live" pictures using sunlight rather than artificial light. The success of this experiment led Dr. Ives to plan a demonstration for the public within four to six weeks.[20]

However, it was later claimed that the first demonstration of daylight television was given to the press in London on June 18, 1928, by John L. Baird. This is supposed to have occurred on the roof of Baird's laboratories in Long Acre and to have been sent to a room four floors below. In spite of the fact that there was no mention of this "demonstration" in either the *London Times, N.Y. Times* or *Nature* for 1928, it was reported in *Television* in London by three authors.[21]

On May 22, 1928, Roy Bishop of the Farnsworth Laboratories wrote a letter to Mr. C.E. Tullar of the patent department of General Electric, trying to interest him in the Farnsworth television scheme. It was claimed that Farnsworth had given a private demonstration to Dr. James Cranston and Dr. L.F. Fuller of G.E. on March 1, 1928. It couldn't have gone too well, as they were having heating problems with the coils of the dissector tube. Also, according to Farnsworth's records, the first "real" pictures from the Image Dissector did not occur until the week of May 7–13, 1928.

It appears that Albert G. Davis, vice president of General Electric, did not think Mr. Farnsworth's television scheme amounted to much, but he felt that Farnsworth had done some pretty scientific work with limited facilities. Therefore, General Electric indicated they would be happy to take Farnsworth on the staff with the understanding that they would buy whatever he had invented up to that time, but that "whatever he invents while in our employ comes to us under the regular engineering contract."

Opposite: A 1929 photo of C.F. Jenkins with his new drum receiver.

Bell Labs outdoor demonstration, 10 May 1928, on the roof of the Bell Laboratories building.

Top: The Baird outdoor television demonstration of 1928, which took place on the roof of the Baird laboratories. Baird is in the center; British Actor Jack Buchanan is on the left. Bottom: Philo Farnsworth's 1928 television camera. Farnsworth gave a private demonstration with this camera in 1928.

It is known that Farnsworth's financial backers had decided quite early that his television project be turned over to one of the large electric companies in anticipation of the enormous development costs involved.[22]

In June 1928, Campbell Swinton published an article, "Television by Cathode Rays." He claimed again that he had actually tried some experiments in 1903–04 using a cathode ray tube covered with selenium and traversed by the electron beam. It produced no results when hooked up to a sensitive galvanometer. This was done with a cold cathode tube operating under high voltages and no means of amplification.

He then went on to relate a short history of television, including the 1925 patents of Blake, Spooner and V.K. Zworkyin. He stated that Zworykin's patent had a convention date of July 13, 1923, which was in error — it was July 13, 1925. Campbell Swinton considered it a "very interesting" specification. He stated that cathode ray transmitters, though suggested and even patented, had not been exhibited or even claimed actually as having been made to function. At this time, Campbell Swinton was unaware that the only cathode ray transmitters in the world were being built and operated in San Francisco by Philo T. Farnsworth.[23]

On June 5, 1928, J.L. Baird of Television Ltd. applied for a patent on a color television system. It was for a sequential method of color television in which the scanning disc had three sets of spirally arranged holes. Each set of holes covered the whole image in an interlaced manner. There were light filters of blue, red and green covering the three sets of holes. By means of a commutator and slip rings, the signals were sent to a receiver with a disc similar to the transmitter. Here the signals were sent to appropriately colored lamps to recreate the original scene.[24]

Dr. Lewis R. Koller of the GE Research Laboratories presented a paper on June 7, 1928, to the Radio Division of the National Electrical Manufacturing Association (NEMA). He explained the principles of photoelectric cells and stated that a cell made with a silver bulb coated with a thin layer of some material such as one of the alkali metals (lithium, potassium, rubidium, cesium, etc.) would be particularly photosensitive. He mentioned that a potassium cell did not see light the way the eye did as it was far more sensitive to blue and less to red light. Cesium photocells were most desirable for any work involving color. He mentioned the particular application to both television and the talking picture.

Dr. Koller described a cell with a silvered inside surface upon which a monatomic film of cesium was coated, with the cesium and silver acting as the cathode. Several curves of sensitivity were shown, the gas-filled tubes being higher than the pure vacuum tubes. A typical vacuum cell could have about 1 microampere sensitivity, while a similar gas-filled tube would have about 12–13 microamperes. It appears that the cesium-magnesium photocells of Dr. Zworykin were being tested by both Westinghouse and General Electric. The introduction of the cesium-silver photocell at this time made possible many advances in both television and

Kolomon Tihany, Berlin, 1928. In that year, Tihany applied for patents that included descriptions of several novel and important photoelectric camera plates.

motion pictures. The more common potassium hydride photocell had neither the sensitivity nor the color response needed.[25]

On June 11, 1928, a Hungarian, Kolomon Tihany, applied for patents for complete electric television systems using a cathode ray transmitter and receiving tubes. Tihany described at least four varieties of photoelectric camera plates, each of which was quite novel and important.

The first variation indicated a structure of metallic particles which were insulated from one another and had photoelectric coatings. The second used insulating filaments in a network, with the photoelectric coating being at certain intervals. The third showed an insulating diaphragm with thin layers of photoelectric coating and a thin continuous metallic layer (4) being earthed for increasing the capacity. The fourth called for the use of a glass plate with square alkali metal cells, having a reverse side of metallic coating to increase the capacity and a grid (41) in front of the carrier to collect the electrons released by action of the light. The electron beam impinged on the alkali cells and was then reflected from the carrier plate to either a Faraday or Perrin cylinder. The last two variations were quite important as they showed means to store and intensify a charge.

Tihany showed all of the elements necessary to produce a practical camera tube of the storage type, and it is claimed that he actually built some tubes to prove his thesis. However, there is no proof that they ever did work.[26]

The television apparatus of Ulises A. Sanabria was shown at a

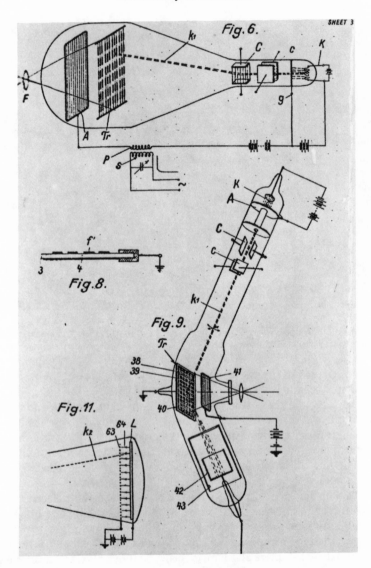

Diagram from Kolomon Tihany's 1928 patent application for an electric television.

meeting of the Radio Manufacturers Association (RMA) in Chicago on June 13, 1928. This was the first time that television equipment was shown at a radio convention. The machine was built by A.J. Carter Company of Chicago. The transmitter had three spirals of holes of 15 each to produce a 45-line picture at 15 frames/sec.[27]

On June 22, 1928, Coryton E.C. Roberts of London applied for a patent on a camera tube of the dissector type. It described a camera tube in which the entire electron stream was projected through an aperture in an anode "A" in sequence to create picture signals. It showed various means for moving the electron stream across the aperture, and several interesting variations were described. It is known that Roberts later built several tubes of this kind but never did get any of them to work.[28]

On July 3, 1928, it was reported that John L. Baird gave the first demonstration of color television to the press and a party of scientists. The transmitter used a scanning disc with three sets of spirals, each spiral being covered with a colored filter (green, red and blue). A similar disc was used at the receiver, except that the color was provided by three special cells, neon for red, helium for blue and mercury for green. It was claimed that a demonstration of faces and flowers was vividly shown.[29]

On July 12, 1928, the Bell Telephone Laboratories gave a demonstration of outdoor television to the press from the roof of the Bell Telephone Laboratories in New York. It was claimed that the camera was portable enough to be taken anywhere for broadcasting. Scenes of a sparring match, a golf exhibit and other motions were demonstrated. Dr. Frank Gray operated the camera while Dr. Herbert E. Ives controlled the receiver.[30]

C.F. Jenkins applied for a patent on a cell persistence transmitter on July 16, 1928. In this patent, Jenkins described a means for storing the charges in a multitude of cells until they were discharged. He stated that as the light charged the cell to its full capacity, it could be discharged by a commutator, each cell being discharged in turn. If this current light translation occurred at the right time, to illuminate an elementary area of the transmitter, then an exact facsimile of the scene at the transmitting station would be reproduced at the receiving station.

A multi-lamp receiver with some 2,304 bulbs was actually built to be operated by a commutator in a fashion similar to the Bell Telephone Labs large screen device. Later, it was claimed that a camera made up of a multiplicity of photo cells was to be built. But no more was ever heard of it. This patent became the subject of interferences #62,727 and #67,440 with Dr. Zworykin of Westinghouse, which Jenkins lost.[31]

On July 26, 1928, Dr. Alexanderson made some tests of the General Electric television equipment in ordinary daylight. He first used the 24-line scanning disc mounted in a box. He could transmit simple figures of men boxing. Later, he used the 48-line transmitter, and he claimed that one could clearly see the skyline of the factories and smoke from the chimneys. Dr. Alexanderson presumed that the Bell Telephone Labs results were from some "radical improvements in photoelectric cells."[32] The Bell Telephone Labs never did reveal that they were using the Case Thalofide cell with such remarkable results.

On August 8, 1928, the Westinghouse Electric and Manufacturing Company of East Pittsburgh demonstrated a system of "radio-movies" at their radio station KDKA in East Pittsburgh, Pa. The demonstration was under the auspices of Harry P. Davis, vice president of Westinghouse, who gave credit to Dr. Frank Conrad for bringing the device to its present state of perfection. The broadcast was sent two miles by land line to the broadcasting station, and then two miles back to the receivers. The system operated on three frequencies: picture signals on 150 meters, sound on 63 meters and a special synchronization signal on 90 meters.

Dr. Conrad was transmitting a 60-line picture at 16 frames/sec. A special 35mm film projector was used with a 60-hole disc. The light from the film went to a cesium photocell and became the picture signal, which was converted into electrical impulses and broadcast. A 5000-cycle signal from a tuning fork was transmitted on a special carrier wave. This was used at the receiver to synchronize the synchronous motors used there. At the receiver, a special "mercury arc" was to be used to provide the light for the picture. The image of the arc lamp was projected through the scanning disc and allowed the image to be projected onto some kind of screen or ground glass.[33]

The Radio Corporation of America was still trying to equal the technical performance of the Bell Telephone Labs television system. It was to take the efforts of both General Electric and Westinghouse to do so. Since General Electric was obviously ahead with the transmission of "Radio Television" (produced "live" directly from the studio), it remained for Westinghouse to perfect the technique of "Radio Motion Pictures" from 35mm film. It appears that the Westinghouse television project had been dormant since Zworykin's failure in 1925/26 and that this effort had only recently been undertaken.

Conspicuously missing from the Westinghouse television demonstration of August 8, 1928, was Dr. V.K. Zworykin. He had not been part of the Westinghouse television project under Dr. Conrad, having been engaged in research on photocells, film sound-recording and picture-facsimile apparatus. Dr. Zworykin was in Europe during the summer of 1928 inspecting various electrical laboratories. He visited Germany, Belgium, Hungary, Great Britain and France. It is known that he was particularly interested in the work being done in France by Dauvillier, Valensi, and Belin and Holweck, all of whom were engaged in cathode ray research.

In Paris Zworykin visited the laboratories of Etablissements Belin and was shown all of their work in progress. He saw the Belin phototransmitter, which was very similar to a device Dr. Zworykin had been working on for Westinghouse. Here he met Gregory N. Ogloblinsky, chief engineer for Belin, as well as Fernand Holweck and Pierre Chevallier.

He was shown a very crude cathode ray tube that used electrostatic means for focusing the beam. It appeared to be a two-piece glass tube that was continuously pumped to maintain a vacuum. It had a glowing cathode encased in a metal structure. Two disc anodes were used to focus and accelerate the beam. Only one set of deflection plates was built into the tube. The fluorescent screen appeared to be insulated from the rest of the tube by the glass structure. There was no connecting anode from the screen to the cathode that would have allowed the electron charge on the screen to be returned to the electron gun.[34]

While the idea for electrostatic focus was common in Europe since 1926 (see the work of Rogowski and Grosser) or in America (with the work of R.H. George in 1927/28), it appears that Holweck and Chevallier were among the first to build such a tube and actually get it to operate.[35]

Dr. Zworykin was quite elated with this disclosure and returned to the United States sometime early in September 1928 with (1) a Holweck vacuum pump, (2) a Holweck demountable cathode ray tube, and (3) Gregory N. Ogloblinsky as a future Westinghouse recruit. Ogloblinsky was soon to become a most valuable addition to Dr. Zworykin's staff.[36]

Dr. Zworykin saw in electrostatic focus the answer he was seeking for a practical television picture tube. It would eliminate all of the problems associated with the gas-focused Western Electric tube of Johnson.

Dr. Zworykin planned a permanently sealed, high vacuum tube with a pure electron discharge. In addition, he decided on separation of the function of beam modulation, deflection of the beam while at low electron velocities, and finally, electron beam acceleration for high brightness by means of a high-voltage second anode in the form of a metallic coating on the inside of the glass bulb. This would provide a path for the electrons to return to the electron gun, thus preventing the screen from charging up. As is true of many great inventions, while all of these elements were in existence, it took Dr. Zworykin's genius to put them together properly. This was Dr. Zworykin's greatest triumph.

Harley Iams, who had been working with Zworykin on facsimile at Westinghouse, was put to work on the television scanning deflection circuits sometime in November 1928. It is claimed that Dr. Zworykin soon fabricated a crude tube from a Dewar flask in order to prove that it would work.[37]

In spite of the great promise of this new tube, Zworykin could not get Westinghouse to go ahead with his new idea. Therefore Sam Kintner, vice president of Westinghouse, suggested to Dr. Zworykin that he go to New York to visit David Sarnoff. This famous meeting (of which the exact date is impossible to document, but which has been narrowed down to sometime late in December 1928 or at the latest, January 1929) took place before Sarnoff left for Europe to participate in the German Reparations Conference from February 1, 1929, through June 1929.

David Sarnoff, who was then executive vice president of RCA, asked Dr. Zworykin how much it would cost to produce a workable television system. He was told that "it could be done in two years at a cost of some one hundred thousand dollars." Zworykin informed Sarnoff that the "basic instrument was already operative but required extensive and expensive development." (There have been inferences that a crude camera tube was the instrument referred to by Zworykin, but it is known that Zworykin had no camera tube either being built or working at this time. He did have a crude picture tube built from the Dewar flask operating in his laboratory). David Sarnoff was convinced and had Westinghouse give Zworykin additional financing, staffing and equipment. In addition, an order was soon given for a shipment of glass picture tube blanks from the Corning Glass Company.[38]

On August 10, 1928, Francis C.P. Henroteau of Ottawa, Canada, applied for a United States television patent (serial number 298,809), which was never granted. This was basically concerned with a nonconducting photoelectric screen that was scanned and discharged by a beam of light. Henroteau sent copies of this application to C.F. Jenkins on August 16, 1928; to Dr. Lewis Koller of General Electric on August 30, 1928; to Dr. Zworykin of Westinghouse on October 1, 1928; and to Lee De Forest on December 14, 1928. This patent application was abandoned and a new one applied for in May 1929.[39]

It is claimed that John L. Baird actually demonstrated stereoscopic television at the Baird Laboratory in Long Acre on August 10, 1928. He used a scanning disc with two sets of spiral holes, each spiral having its own light source. Thus two sets of images were transmitted simultaneously. At the receiver, a similar disc with two sets of holes in spirals was set up with each hole staggered so that a single neon tube was used for both images. Thus an alternating image was presented to both eyes. An ordinary stereoscopic viewing device, consisting of two prisms, caused the images to be blended into a three-dimensional one. One observor claimed that "the illusion is very striking."[40]

On August 21, 1928, General Electric attempted the first outside remote broadcast using television cameras. This was to cover the acceptance speech of Governor Al Smith at the capitol in Albany for the Democratic nomination for the presidency.

The "camera" was the new portable flying spot scanner of General Electric. It was a simple box in which the light from a 1000 watt bulb was projected through a 24-hole scanning disc. This box was accompanied by two tripod-mounted photoelectric cells, which were to pick up the reflected light from the subject and convert it into electrical signals.

Technically, although it was a daylight pickup, the main source of light came from the camera, the same as used indoors with a flying spot scanner. The transmitter camera, which was operated by Ray Kell, sent its signal by wire some 18 miles away to where Alda Bedford was to monitor it and have it broadcast on Station WGY. According to Kell, the rehearsals went well, but the real event was spoiled when the enormous arc-lights of the newsreel cameras wiped out the picture.[41]

D.N. Sharma of Edinburgh applied for a patent for apparatus using cathode rays on August 24, 1928. The camera tube was very similar to Dauvillier's 1925 patent (see page 74) in that there was a special "composite plate" which was to reflect the light from the scene to a photocell.

This special transparent or semitransparent plate was to be made of such material as zinc-sulphate with a trace of Thoria, etc. A cathode ray beam was to scan this special plate and as this plate received the light from the scene it would have a pattern of the scene impressed on it. As the cathode beam scanned the rear of the plate, it was to render the plate more or less opaque (depending on the amount of light that struck each portion). As the face plate varied its brightness, a photoelectric cell which faced it was to provide a varying signal, which became the picture signal. There is no record of this device ever having been built.[42]

On August 24, 1928, Philo Farnsworth of the Crocker-Bishop Research Laboratory of San Francisco gave a private demonstration of the Farnsworth television system to two members of the Pacific Telephone Company, Mr. J.E. Heller and L.A. Gary. They reported that the picture was of rather low intensity on a screen about 1.25 by 1.50 inches. Images were hard to identify, but motion was easily followed. They were impressed by the photoelectric transmitter tube (the dissector) and that all scanning was done electrically.[43]

This was followed by a demonstration to the press on September 3, 1928, and reported in the *San Francisco Chronicle*. This article featured the first photograph of an electric camera tube. Philo was shown holding a dissector in one hand and a cathode ray receiving tube in the other. In the background was one of his early "cameras."

The article stated that the system was capable of sending some 20 pictures/sec with about 8000 elements of light. (This would be about a 50- or 60-line picture.) The image was described at only 1.25 inches square with "a queer looking little image in bluish light now, that frequently smudges and blurs." However, it was claimed that the basic principle had been achieved and that perfection was but a matter of engineering. It mentioned that the laboratories were at 202 Green Street in San Francisco and that the financial backers were W.W. Crocker and Roy N. Bishop. At this time, Philo Farnsworth had the only operating camera tubes in the world. Yet, to this day, Farnsworth's pioneering efforts have gone relatively unknown and unappreciated.[44]

On August 31, 1928, there was a television demonstration given for the first time at the Berlin Radio Exhibition. The equipment of Dionys von Mihály was operating and on display. There was also the television equipment of Dr. August Karolus of Telefunken. It was a device using a mirror drum and the Karolus light valve. It could project pictures as large as 10 by 10 centimeters. Only diapositives (transparencies) were transmitted, and it was claimed that the results were not as good as Baird's television.[45]

The General Electric station in Schenectady, WGY, "telecast" the first television drama on September 11, 1928. This was a presentation of "The Queen's Messenger" by J.H. Manners. The picture and sound were broadcast over separate channels. Three "cameras" were used, each containing a twelve-inch, 24-hole scanning disc driven by a small synchronous motor. Behind the disc was a 1000 watt lamp, the light of which was concentrated by a lens. Another lens on the outside of the box projected the light onto the subject. Each was mounted on wheels and had its own bank of photocells in a wooden box mounted on a tripod. Each cell was about seven

inches in diameter. (These were the same as used in the Albany "remote" pickup.) There was one camera for each of the two characters. The third camera was used for closeups of the hands or props. The director had a monitor screen to watch the progress of the program and controls for fading from one camera to another.

The program was witnessed by a group of newspapermen and scientists gathered in one of the buildings of the General Electric Company, a short distance from the transmitter. It was claimed that the pictures were small, sometimes blurred and confused, not always in the center of the screen and hard on the eyes because of the flicker.[46]

One of these General Electric cameras was on display at the Radio World's Fair held in New York City on September 21, 1928. It was part of the General Electric exhibit, which also included a demonstration of a large-screen television projector of Dr. Alexanderson. (This was not the Alexanderson seven-beam device.) It was claimed that this machine projected pictures some 12 by 12 inches onto a silver screen by a 5-inch projecting lens.

There was also a television exhibit by the A.J. Carter Company, which had built the Ulisis Sanabria equipment. Its disc had three scanning spirals. Each of these had 15 scanning holes and was driven at 15 pictures/sec. This gave a 45-line picture. A third exhibit was given by the Daven Radio Corporation, which was using equipment with 48 holes on a 24-inch disc.[47]

On October 2, 3, and 4, 1928, General Electric attempted a series of long-distance transmissions of television signals over ordinary telephone lines. The test originated from a portable 24-line General Electric camera set up in a booth at the NBC studio at 711 Fifth Avenue in New York.

The first test was from the NBC studio to the WGY studio in Schenectady. It was claimed that a face was recognizable, with very bad line reflections and four pronounced transients. A fan-shaped figure was received, which was very sharp but distorted due to the fact that the high frequencies were retarded more than the low frequencies.

A second test was transmitted some 3000 miles from NBC in New York to Chicago, back to NBC, and finally to Schenectady. This was a total failure as no faces were recognizable and even the most simple geometrical figures could not be distinguished. The tests conducted by Ray Kell and Merle Trainer proved that pictures sent over a long telephone line without phase correction were impractical.[48]

On October 4, 1928, Dr. Gillis Holst of Eindhoven, the Netherlands, applied for a patent on an early form of "image tube" for photographic recording. It was to be used for converting visible images to electrical images, both still and moving. In operation, the optical image was sent to a

Opposite: Behind the scenes at the telecast of the first television drama: The Queen's Messenger, *September 11, 1928. Three cameras were used, with picture and sound broadcast separately.*

plate, where it was converted into a charge pattern that was then sent en masse to an anode, which then emitted visible rays for viewing. The purpose was to provide means whereby the actinic effect of light rays may be materially increased.[49]

At this time in 1928, there were about 12 stations actually broadcasting pictures in the United States at some time during the day or were about to do so. Six stations were using 48-hole scanning; three were using 24-hole scanning; and one each were using 60, 45, and 36 holes. The number of pictures/sec varied from 7½ to 21.

As a result, the Radio Manufacturers Association (RMA) formed a "Television Standards Committee" on October 9, 1928, to try to solve this problem. In order to slow the spread of television in the broadcast band, stations were allowed to broadcast only one hour per day and forbidden to do so between the hours of 6 and 11 P.M. The Federal Radio Commission restricted the hours of all still-picture transmission and television until January 1, 1929. After that date all television would be in a special band above 1500 kc.[50]

On October 10, 1928, John L. Baird applied for a patent for a television recorder. This patent was concerned with a self-contained player for gramophone records. This invention later was called Phonovision. On October 17, 1928, the BBC turned down the Baird Corporation's request for a television station.[51]

G.W. Walton applied for a patent for a television system using simultaneous scanning and reproduction of a strip on October 25, 1928. The strip could be recorded on film as a one-dimensional picture. It would be received and scanned on a similar film and reconverted to a conventional two-dimensional picture.[52]

The Bell Telephone Labs reported on October 29, 1928, that work was progressing on a 72-hole disc to replace the 50-hole disc which was then in use. It would require a bandwidth twice that of the older 50-hole system. It was demonstrated to Mr. F.B. Jewett on November 22, 1928.

On October 31, 1928, Dr. Frank Gray of the Bell Telephone Labs reported on means for the recording of television images on film by the use of a strip source of light using a continuous motion of the film. The labs had previously considered means for the slow recording of television images on film that could be transmitted by telephone wires to theaters all over the country, thus making it possible to transmit newsreels within a few hours. It was hoped to send 200-line pictures at anywhere from 5 minutes to 12 minutes per foot.[53]

On November 28, 1928, Philo T. Farnsworth applied for a patent, the first one to show the standard form of dissector that was to be used for the next several years. It had an added feature of dual apertures which were supposed to separate the high and low frequencies.[54]

John Hays Hammond, Jr., applied for a patent for a system of television on December 6, 1928. Most of the patent dealt with the recording of events in order to present them under better conditions than would

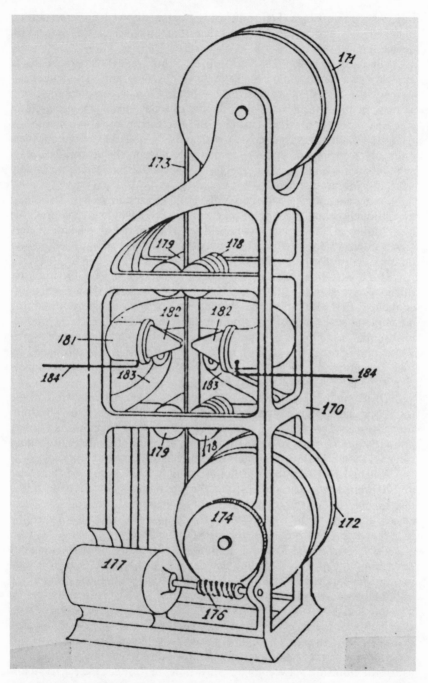

"Figure 12" from John Hays Hammond's television patent (filed in 1928) shows Hammond's representation of a video recorder.

otherwise be possible. "Figure 12" of the patent shows his representation of a video recorder, the first American patent covering this important device.[55]

On December 12, 1928, M. Knoll, L. Schiff, and C. Stoerk of Berlin applied for a patent on a new cathode ray oscillograph. The patent described several cathode ray oscilloscopes as well as a complete television system. In addition, it mentioned the use of a new arrangement based on electrostatic effect for the focusing of the electron beam. This consisted of fixing at certain intervals, coaxially with and symmetrically to one another, pairs of electrodes of suitable form (e.g., alternately perforated metal cylinders with small washers of large diameters), connected alternately with appropriate voltages.

In this manner were produced divergent electric fields with stress acting obliquely to the direction of the beam in such a way as to compress the beam radially. If the voltage were sufficiently high, one single pair of electrodes might suffice to effect this concentration. The divergent fields could be obtained by various types of electrodes.

If a controlling voltage were supplied to such a device, the intensity of the electrons in the beam, and thereby the intensity of the focal spot, could be varied without inertia. The patent also showed a figure containing a complete television system. Another figure showed a circuit for producing oscillations of linear voltage for use in television and picture telegraphy work, and another the wave-shape of the linear oscillation produced by such a connection. Waves were linear and followed a sawtooth pattern.[56]

On December 14, 1928, Ray Kell of General Electric reported on the results he had obtained using a standard Western Electric oscillograph tube. He stated that he had tried to put a grid into a tube but had finally given that up. Instead, he had added a vacuum tube into the circuit feeding the television signal to the shield to vary the brilliance of the spot.

Kell had devised a linear scanning circuit to feed currents of 480 cycles and 20 cycles to the plates in the tube. By making contact with the scanning disc at 480 times/sec he claimed that the electron beam followed very closely the spot at the transmitter. Kell claimed that with this device, he had "been able to produce pictures of fair quality."[57]

Fritz Schröter of Telefunken GmbH in Berlin applied for a patent describing a television recording device on December 23, 1928. It used a photochemical process in which a glow tube (using a filament) impressed its light onto a strip of photographic emulsion in such a manner as to create a visible image.

It was an accurate system in that it had six rotating glow lamps that scanned across the emulsion. There was a slit between the emulsion and the lamps in order to maintain straight lines. Another variation showed the use of the emulsion between two electric poles to produce the electrical impulses (six positive poles passing a negative pole) to create a picture on the top side of the paper, which became immediately visible.[58]

Philo T. Farnsworth received nationwide publicity in January 1929. On February 15, 1929, he hired Harry L. Lubcke, a young electrical engineer from the University of California. Lubcke's main project was to help Farnsworth develop a completely electric scanning generator.

Farnsworth had been using 500-cycle motor generators to generate his sine-wave scanning currents. The use of sine-wave scanning created several problems; it produced double images, since it was impossible to keep the two-half cycles in exact phase, and it produced "shaded" pictures as a result of the variable speed with which it scanned the picture. Farnsworth then turned to tuning forks as a means of synchronization and finally to vacuum tubes to produce his scanning pulses.

By July of 1929, Farnsworth and Lubcke had developed an electric scanning generator that produced sawtoothed currents and special pulses to eliminate the return scan line. This gave Philo Farnsworth the first all-electric television system in the world. He now had in his laboratory an all-electric camera device (the dissector tube), a magnetically focused high vacuum cathode ray viewing tube, and a vacuum tube scanning and pulse generator. There were absolutely no moving parts in the system.[59]

In January 1929, the terms for the purchase of the Victor Talking Machine Company of Camden, New Jersey, by the Radio Corporation of America were set. The purchase price was some $154 million, which was paid to the banking house of Speligman and Speyer. It appears that in October 1927 the RCA board of directors, at the request of David Sarnoff, had recommended that RCA be provided with a separate manufacturing unit to which the General Electric Company and Westinghouse Electric would transfer elements of their radio facilities and staff. A second committee in April 1928 recommended this consolidation in principle but put a ceiling of $25 million on RCA production.[60]

However, by 1929 the purchase not only entailed the vast manufacturing plants in Camden, New Jersey (that Sarnoff had long coveted) but also principal interest in the Victor Talking Machine Company of Japan and the Gramophone Company Ltd. of Great Britain.

It also included a well-organized system of distributors and dealers. The Gramophone Company Ltd. had made an agreement with the Marconi Company to acquire the business and rights of the Marconiphone Company in the field of home entertainment. Therefore David Sarnoff became a director of the Gramophone Company Ltd. in March 1929. One immediate result was that the Gramophone Company started to receive the RCA patents and began a limited research program into television.[61]

The Marconi Wireless Telegraph Company, as the RCA licensee in Great Britain, was also receiving the RCA patents and registering them in Marconi's name. The General Electric Company was assigning their patents to the British Thomson-Houston Company, while Westinghouse Electric was either keeping them under their own name or in the name of Metropolitan Vickers.

David Sarnoff had very little interest in the talking machine. He made immediate plans to begin the manufacture of radio sets at Camden. All television development was to be moved to Camden during the first part of 1930. This included the important work that Dr. Zworykin and his staff were now doing at Westinghouse in East Pittsburgh.[62]

Actual work on the new Zworykin television system began on February 1, 1929, with the arrival of the first shipment of glass bulbs from the Corning Glass Company. As Dr. Zworykin did not have a camera tube working at the time, he decided to use a standard Simplex movie projector that had had its intermittent removed as a source of picture signals. An oscillating mirror was to scan the motion picture frame. A relay lens system focused the beam onto one part of the photocell.

It was planned to use sine-wave scanning for the horizontal scan as it simplified the scanning process with both the oscillating mirror and the scanning coils being fed by the same simple sine-wave generator. Vertical scan was a linear process, however, with a toothed wheel driven by the film to indicate the start of each frame. A contact on the wheel would discharge a condenser circuit, causing the beam to travel upwards during the time of one motion picture frame.

This process was described in a patent applied for by Dr. Zworykin on March 26, 1929. While the patent went into great detail about the transmission system using a film projector there was very little said about the receiving tube. The patent was mainly concerned with the synchronization of the film frames. Details were given only of a control grid being connected to the negative end of the battery and an alternating potential representing the picture signal. There was no hint given of a revolutionary new picture tube.[63]

As promised by David Sarnoff, Dr. Zworykin had several engineers assigned to his project. Among them was Harley Iams, who had started the project in November 1928. John Batchelor arrived in April 1929, Arthur Vance in May 1929, Gregory N. Ogloblinsky in July 1929 and Randall Ballard in September 1929. W.D. Wright was the optical engineer for the group. Batchelor and A.J. Harcher were building the picture tubes. Video amplifiers, deflection circuits and high voltage supplies were designed and built by Arthur Vance. The power supplies were built by Skypzak. The radio receiver design was by Ballard. The general layout of the receivers was designed by Harley Iams and a student engineer by the name of Pepper. (Because of ill health, Iams left the project in December 1929, as did W.D. Wright, who had to return to England because of family problems.)

The first satisfactory picture tube was produced by the middle of April 1929. The film projector was completely assembled by the end of April. The development of a suitable electrical circuit was undertaken, and on May 10, 1929, the first demonstration was given of a movie film over three separate pairs of wires. Finally a circuit for the transmission of moving pictures over a radio channel was developed using a single radio channel for both picture signals and synchronization.[64]

Dr. Frank Gray and John R. Hofele of the Bell Telephone Labs applied for patents on February 2, 1929, which were important as they were the first to reveal the spatial distribution of the video signal. They proved that information in the signal was bunched at certain intervals, leaving huge gaps with relatively little information.[65]

On February 3, 1929, it was reported that the General Electric Company had transmitted both the picture and voice of the noted film director D.W. Griffith from their studios in Schenectady to Los Angeles by means of their short wave station W2XAF operating on 31.48 meters. The voice was carried by station 2XO on 22.5 meters. Although the audio was fine for the entire fifteen minutes, the picture lasted only a few minutes. This seems to be the first nationwide telecast of both sight and sound.[66]

On February 11, 1929, Frank Gray revealed that the Bell Telephone Labs had developed equipment suitable for the "real-time" recording of television images on 35mm motion picture film. By the use of a special quartz, capillary, mercury lamp, and a special rotating disc with a series of slots, it was possible to form a beam of light in successive parallel lines across a piece of continuously moving film.

Dr. Gray claimed that they were actually recording 50-line television images at 18 images/sec. (Samples of these recordings have survived.) Thus the art of "television film recording" was born in the Bell Labs some time early in February of 1929. This apparatus was considered to be part of the Bell Telephone Labs scheme for the projection of television images on a large screen almost simultaneously with their reception.[67]

On February 11, 1929, Leon Nemirovsky of Paris applied for a patent for a secret transmission system using a rotating magnetic wheel with a multitude of recording and reproducing coils.[68]

Jean Thibaud presented an article on February 27, 1929, which showed the effect of the longitudinal magnetic current on a slow (low-voltage) electron beam. This article mentioned the research on "electron optics" (this seems to be the first time this term was actually used in the literature) and the (1927) work of Hans Busch and others. There were figures showing the effects of the longitudinal magnetic field on the beam either to concentrate or magnify it. The spiral path of the beam under the influence of the magnetic field was also described. The article also explained the similarity between the action of a magnetic field to that of a lens to light.[69]

The First Annual Exhibition of the Television Society was held on March 5, 1929, at the Engineers Club in London. Historical devices of Mr. Llewelen B. Atkinson were shown. These were apparatuses presumably devised some 47 years before (1882). The apparatuses consisted of mirror wheels at both transmitter and receiver. In order to avoid electrical reproduction, the light from the scene went to a point representing a selenium cell and back to the transmitter. A crude form of light modulator was also displayed. Capt. Wilson of the Baird Television company showed a complete shadowgraph transmitter and receiver. A Mr. Troutbeck of

Standard Telephones and Cables showed a cathode ray oscilloscope loaned from his company.[70] Baird Television Ltd. gave another demonstration to the BBC in March 1929 in an effort to get facilities granted. The generally poor quality of the Baird system in London had led the Postmaster General to make a statement concerning participation with the Baird Company. He regarded the Baird system as "a noteworthy scientific achievement" but considered that the system had not reached a sufficiently advanced stage to warrant its occupying a place in the broadcasting of programs. He had no objection, however, to Baird using a BBC station for this purpose outside of broadcasting hours.[71]

Having had very little luck with the British Post Office, Baird decided to take his equipment to Germany. It seems that the secretary of state and high commissioner of broadcasting, Dr. Hans Bredow, and two assistants had been in London in December 1928 and had witnessed a successful demonstration of the Baird system and had invited Baird to bring his equipment to Berlin and use their Witzleben transmitter.

Baird did so, and he used the Berlin transmitter from May 15, 1929, to June 13, 1929, when he apparently discontinued its use as a result of many difficulties. At this time, von Mihály also had permission to use the Berlin transmitter for his "Tele-Cinema" and did not fare as well as Baird did.

But Baird's statements to the press that "other Broadcasting authorities are more interested in my television transmission than you are" was not lost on the BBC. With great reluctance, the Post Office agreed to allow Baird to use their facilities at radio station 2LO with signals from Baird's Long Acre laboratory using the 30-line, 12½ frame/sec system. The most important result of Baird's trip to Berlin was the formation of Fernseh A.G. on June 11, 1929. This was formed with Baird Television, Zeiss Ikon, Robert Bosch, and Loewe Radio and registered on July 3, 1929.[72]

The installation of television equipment by the Van Cortlandt Park Laboratory at 411 Fifth Avenue was completed by mid–March 1929. RCA had decided to go with the Westinghouse standard of 60 lines at 20 frames/sec (instead of General Electric's 48 lines at 16 frames/sec) and on April 13, 1929, had presented a paper calling for some tentative standardization of the television signal.[73]

On April 14, 1929, Dr. Alfred Goldsmith reported on the progress being made by RCA's station 2-XBS, indicating that some form of television receiving device would be ready for market at an early date. This newspaper report so distressed Gen. J.G. Harbord, president of RCA, that he wrote a letter of admonishment to Dr. Goldsmith, telling him that from now on all of his publicity releases would have to be cleared first with RCA. This action of course was a result of RCA's and Sarnoff's policy not to interfere with the highly successful radio operation of the National Broadcasting Company.[74]

R.H. Thun of Germany applied for a British patent on May 18, 1929, for a method of variable scanning or variable velocity in which the brightness of the portion of the picture being scanned was varied by the speed of the scanning device while its brightness remained constant.[75]

On May 25, 1929, J.W. Horton of Electrical Research Products applied for a patent for an intermediate film system (similar to their September 14, 1927 patent) except that this was for a color intermediate film system. It showed three sets of photocells at the transmitter and three sets of light valves at the receiver. At this time, Bell Labs were finishing up work on a three-color television system and it was claimed to be in operation by June 10, 1929.[76]

On May 29, 1929, F.C.P. Henroteau of Ottawa, Canada, applied for a patent for a television process in which a nonconducting photoelectric screen had an image formed on it. A beam of light passed through a filter and a slit through an aperture in a rotating disc, causing an emission of electrons. The beam was cut off by this disc and the mosaic was charged by the light from the scene. A shutter then cut off the view and the cathode was scanned from two rotating discs which caused regular displacement of the beam. It was planned that the intensity of the beam should be greater than the light from the scene.

A British patent was allowed on October 6, 1930, but although the American patent was also allowed, Henroteau's attorneys decided to withdraw the patent but not abandon it.[77]

The French Television Society was formed on May 30, 1929. The first president was Edouard Belin. Among the charter members were Edouard Branley, Pierre Chevallier, Alexandre Dauvillier, Louis Lumière and Georges Valensi.[78]

On June 27, 1929, the Bell Telephone Laboratories gave a demonstration of color television. It was claimed that the same light sources, scanning disc and synchronizing systems as the monochrome system were used. New were the type and arrangement of the photoelectric cells and the type and arrangements of neon and argon lamps at the receiving end.

A new type of photoelectric cell was revealed that used sodium rather than potassium. The Bell Telephone Labs chose sodium as it was easier to work with than either rubidium or cesium, and they claimed that it had response into the deep red. These cells were developed by A.R. Olpin and G.R. Stilwell.

This was a simultaneous color system, the first one in television history. The three primary colors were displayed at the same time, rather than in sequence as Baird had done in his earlier color demonstration. Three sets of photocells were used, each covered with a set of colored filters (orange-red for red, yellow-green for green, and greenish-blue for blue). A bank of photocells—fourteen with red filters, eight with green filters, and two with blue filters—was used according to the relative sensitivity of the cells. Three sets of amplifiers were used to transmit the signals. A mirror arrangement was set up with three lights—two argon, one with a blue filter and one with a green filter—and a neon lamp for red.

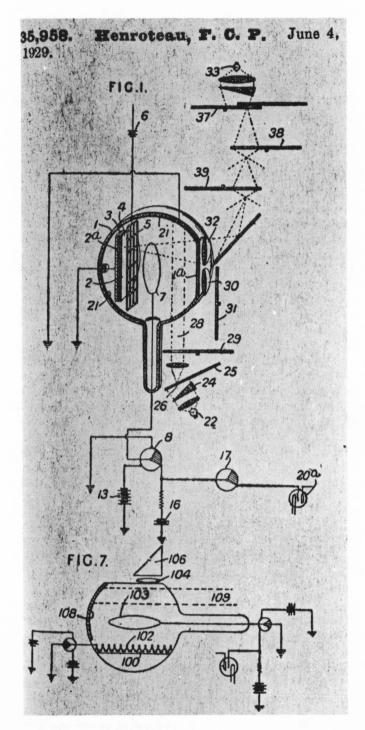

Diagram from F.C.P. Henroteau's camera patent (filed in 1929).

A standard 16-inch scanning disc was used, and it was claimed that when properly adjusted, an image was seen in natural colors with the general appearance of a small colored movie screen. The system used the 50-hole disc rotating at 18 rev/sec. The scene was viewed through a pair of semitransparent mirrors set on an angle of 45 degrees. The Bell Telephone Labs claimed that the colored images produced by this method were "quite striking in appearance, in spite of the rather low brightness and small size characteristic of the present stage of development."[79]

By June 1929, the RCA television station W2XBS was now telecasting some two hours daily (7 to 9 P.M.) between 2000 and 2100 kcs (142) meters. It was reported in July that not only was "conservative RCA" broadcasting television on a regular schedule but there were rumors of "impending RCA television receivers."[80]

All was not well at RCA when David Sarnoff returned from Europe in June 1929. A new plan involving the Victor Company had been formulated that perpetuated the old system of having three sets of engineers and managers, each going his own way in the Camden plant. Sarnoff objected strenuously, and offered to resign if the plan was not changed to have a single, united management under his control.

On October 4, 1929, Sarnoff's plan was adopted, and on December 26, 1929, a new entity, RCA Victor Company, was incorporated. RCA owned 50 percent of the company, General Electric owned 30 percent, and Westinghouse, 20 percent. However, this new plan was soon to run into two difficulties. The first was the onset of a deepening depression in the United States, and the second was the filing of an antitrust suit by the United States Department of Justice.[81]

On June 27, 1929, T.A. Smith of the Radio Corporation applied for a patent for a method of interlacing (staggered manner so that successive lines are reproduced out of sequence). It was claimed that this arrangement reduced or eliminated picture flicker at the receiving station.[82]

V.K. Zworykin of Westinghouse applied for a second patent on his new system on July 5, 1929. This was the same basic patent as the March 26, 1929, application with the addition of separate synchronizing pulses, one for each oscillation of the mirror and one pulse for the end of each complete frame. It was planned to send all of the signals on a single radio wavelength.[83]

This was successfully accomplished, and pictures by radio were demonstrated to a group of General Electric and RCA engineers, including Dr. Alfred Goldsmith, on August 17, 1929. Management was so pleased that they asked for nothing to be changed except to package the parts into six home receivers to be sold by Christmas, 1929.[84]

On July 19, 1929, T.A. Smith of RCA applied for a patent for a television system using a film projector similar to Dr. Zworykin's except that it used a Nipkow disc and a mask to limit the beam to the picture portion of the frame. However, the use of a Nipkow disc predicated the need for a linear scan with quick return. This was similar to the film projector

Gregory N. Ogloblinsky, hired by Westinghouse as part of Zworykin's research group in 1929.

systems of C.F. Jenkins, Dr. Ives and Dr. Gray of the Bell Telephone Labs, and Dr. Conrad of Westinghouse.[85]

Dr. Zworykin, having had considerable success with his new picture tube, now decided to develop a cathode ray tube for the transmitter as well. With the knowledge he had gained in the development of his picture tube, i.e., the use of electrostatic means for sharp focus and the use of a pure electron discharge in a vacuum, as well as the newly developed techniques for using cesium as the photoelectric substance, Dr. Zworykin started experimenting with the demountable Holweck cathode ray oscillograph purchased from Belin in France.

Gregory N. Ogloblinsky had arrived at Westinghouse from Paris, and actual work was started in July 1929. "After a study of its performance and proper alterations, a transmitter was assembled for 12-line pictures." From all indications, it was constructed using the Holweck demountable tube into which was inserted a crude mosaic consisting of several rows of rivets or pins placed within an insulated target. The side of the plugs facing the lens was photosensitized with a layer of cesium. The beam was focused upon the rear of the target. Some form of screen was used to collect the discharged electrons and provide the picture signal.

According to the report, "the result proved to be quite promising. A rough picture was actually transmitted across the room using cathode ray tubes for both transmitter and receiver." It also mentions that an interesting principle (charge storage?) was found and verified experimentally. "The solution of the direct vision problem is thus considerably advanced and may be the next point of attack in the practical development of television." No more work was done on the camera tube until the move to Camden in January 1930.[86]

Dr. V.K. Zworykin and Pierre Chevallier were not the only inventors working on cathode ray tubes using electrostatic focus at this time. In January 1929 Roscoe H. George of the Engineering Experiment Station, Purdue University, Lafayette, Indiana, described a new type of hot cathode oscillograph. The important feature of the new oscillograph tube was the "new" electrostatic method of focusing the beam. It was a metallic tube that was continuously pumped. The oscillograph would operate at any beam potential from 500 to 20,000 volts.

Dr. George had been working on an oscilloscope since 1927, and it was claimed that a portable machine of this type had been in operation since August 27, 1928. The circuitry included automatic devices for recording lightning surges that start the beam some ¼ to ½ microseconds after the surge voltage begins to rise from zero.

George indicated that the focusing of the electron beam had always been the most difficult problem in cathode ray design, since the positive ion method of Johnson does not function well at beam potentials in excess of 200 volts and the magnetic method becomes unsatisfactory at potentials much less than 10,000 volts. The oscilloscope was run from a 110-volt line and the vacuum produced by means of a rotary oil pump.

On September 14, 1929, Roscoe H. George applied for a patent on this device. The patent related to the principle of electrostatic focus, which was quite important, but nowhere was there mentioned means for modulating the beam. So it appears that George was mainly concerned with a fixed high brightness cathode ray oscillograph tube as a means for recording certain high speed electrical phenomena.[87]

The Berlin Radio Exhibition was held in August of 1929. The German Post Office sponsored the television exhibit. It furnished a 30-line, 12½ frame signal from a telecinema transmitter. On display was the von Mihály apparatus, which received the Post Office transmission on a special receiver. Its quality was considered quite good.

Dr. August Karolus of Telefunken had two sets of receivers on display, one that received the Post Office transmissions and a separate one that operated on 48 lines. The receivers used his special Kerr cell, which projected a picture some three feet square. It was claimed that the 48-line receiver had the best picture at the show.

For the first time, Fernseh A.G. had an exhibit which included receivers of the Baird design, the only difference being that the scanning direction was horizontal rather than vertical. It was indicated that some production of receivers was contemplated at the time.[88]

On August 20, 1929, the Baird Television Development Company had transmitted their first talking pictures using a Mechau projector. Up to this time, Baird had shown very little interest in transmitting motion picture film. It was claimed that voices were very clear and that the pictures as good as could be expected at this state of the art.

The Baird Television Company had also sent much experimental equipment to New York City and gave a demonstration of both sight and sound on September 2, 1929. This was sent by wire from the Paramount Building to a laboratory at Forty-Fifth Street.[89]

On September 30, 1929, the first experimental broadcast took place from the Baird studio in Long Acre through London station 2LO using the 30-line, 12½ frame system. Only the picture was telecast since only one transmitter was available. It was claimed that "fairly clear images" were transmitted. This was quite a victory for the Baird Television Company.[90]

Pierre E.L. Chevallier applied for a French patent for a cathode ray tube incorporating electrostatic focus on October 25, 1929. Basically, this patent related to the reduction of the section of the electron beam, or what may be characterized as focusing of the electron beam. Chevallier described means of focusing the beam by means of difference of potentials to create an electrostatic field to focus the projected electrons to a sharply defined point.

The patent showed two versions: first, a completely metallic tube that was continuously pumped, and second, a glass tube that was to have its interior metallized. However, the same mode of operation was claimed for both. The proper ratio of voltages for focusing the beam was from ¼ to ½ of the potential applied to the tube wall and the cathode. The modulating voltage was to be negative for proper control of the beam. This patent referred to certain researches involving the use of a cathode ray oscillograph.

It is almost certain that Chevallier, working with Holweck, had a crude version of this tube operating in the Belin Laboratory in Paris when Dr. Zworykin visited it in the summer of 1928. How advanced it was, or how well it operated, has never been ascertained. There is no evidence that Belin ever tried to develop it further in spite of its potential.

A patent was filed and was issued in France on February 16, 1931. On June 16, 1931, the RCA patent department became involved in the American patent application, processed it and gave it the title "Kinescope."[91]

Another researcher, Manfred von Ardenne of Berlin, delivered a manuscript on October 2, 1929, describing a new cathode ray tube for photographic recording. Von Ardenne stated that this tube provided extreme brightness for instantaneous exposure. He claimed this brightness was due to (1) the use of a calcium tungstate ($CaWO_2$) screen which possessed a higher photographic sensitivity than zinc sulphate, (2) the use of electrostatic concentration of the beam using a Wehnelt cylinder with negative bias with a trace of a rare gas to prevent divergence of the ray after leaving the anode, and (3) the use of potentials of up to 4500 volts.

Manfred von Ardenne, 1930, with a developmental cathode ray tube.

Since this tube still relied on the gas to focus the beam, it was closely related to the Johnson Western Electric tube. It was claimed to have a sensitivity of 1.5 millimeters with an anode voltage of 400 volts. This tube was later (1931) to be placed on the market by E. Leyboldt Nachfolger A.G. of Bayenthal, Cologne, Germany, and was to be used quite extensively by the British at that time in their early research in radar detection. It was very useful for oscillographic purposes that did not demand modulation of the beam.[92]

On November 16, 1929, V.K. Zworykin of the Westinghouse Electric and Manufacturing Company applied for a patent for a vacuum tube. Dr. Zworykin claimed that up till now it had been substantially impossible to focus the cathode ray to a well-defined spot while still maintaining proper control of the intensity of the ray. Dr. Zworykin stated that he now proposed a cathode ray tube improved in the following ways: (1) capable of operating under acceleration potentials of thousands of volts; (2) not

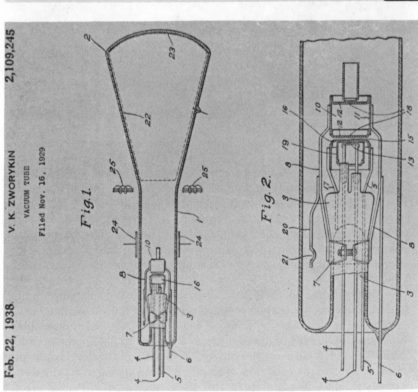

Feb. 22, 1938. V. K. ZWORYKIN 2,109,245

VACUUM TUBE

Filed Nov. 16, 1929

Fig.1.

Fig.2.

requiring continuous pumping, (3) having electrodes simple in construction and having small volume, (4) focusing the ray totally unaffected by the control potentials, (5) having a spot that is well defined at all points of deflection on the screen, (6) having an acceleration potential so large in respect to the intensity controls that the deflection of the beam is not influenced by said control potentials and is the same for all intensities, and finally (7) having a tube wherein the electrons are accelerated in two stages, one at low potential and another at high potential, and wherein deflection of the electrons occurs between the two said stages.

Dr. Zworykin described a tube of high vacuum, containing no gas. It had a second accelerating anode in the form of a coating of metal on the inside of the large portion of the tube. All of the deflection devices, one magnetic for horizontal deflection, and the other electrostatic for vertical deflection, were external to the tube. It was suggested that the screen could have a long persistence phosphor in order to decrease the number of frames/sec. It could have a cooling fan, or be provided with a cooling jacket if the beam had to remain in one position too long. The patent was granted with six claims, Claim Four relating to the electrostatic field effective to focus the ray onto the screen.[93]

On November 18, 1929, Dr. Zworykin delivered a paper describing his new picture tube to the Institute of Radio Engineers at Rochester, New York. First he described the transmitting equipment. An ordinary 35mm film projector with its intermittent removed used a vibrating mirror to focus the light from the film onto a photoelectric cell. A scanning speed of some 480 cycles was used. This was sine-wave scanning, but Dr. Zworykin claimed that the nonuniform distribution of light across the picture was not readily apparent to the eye, so no precautions were used.

A description of the receiver, with its picture tube or "Kinescope" as it was now called, was given. It had been found that three sets of signals (picture, horizontally scanning frequency, and framing impulse) could be combined into one channel. At the receiver, the output of the radio receiver was amplified and divided into three parts: the synchronizing frequency, the framing impulses, and the picture frequencies. The synchronizing frequency was applied to the deflection coils, the framing impulse and the picture signal to the control electrode of the Kinescope. The same voltage that modulated the control grid was impressed upon a bandpass filter, which was tuned to the frequency of the AC voltage used for the framing impulses. The output of this filter was amplified, rectified and used to unbias a discharging triode, which was normally biased to zero plate current and which took its plate voltage from the condenser that provided the vertical scanning voltage.

The advantages of the new Zworykin television system were: (1) the

Opposite, left: Diagram from V.K. Zworykin's patent (filed in 1929) for the Kinescope, the cathode ray tube that changed television history forever. Right: Zworykin with his Kinescope.

V.K. Zworykin and 1929 home receiver.

picture was green (rather than red as with a neon light source); (2) it was
visible to a large number of people; (3) there were no moving parts; (4) the
framing of the picture was automatic; and (5) it was brilliant enough to
be seen in a moderately lighted room.

There have been several reports that Zworykin gave a "demonstration" of the Kinescope on November 18, 1929, at Rochester, New York.
But careful investigation shows that only a paper was read. (Too many
times the press was careless in announcing a so-called "demonstration"
when only a lecture was given.) While Westinghouse did have several
working receivers at the time, there is no evidence that any were on display
at the meeting.[94]

Seven receivers had been built by November 1929, with one of them going into Dr. Zworykin's home four miles from KDKA for experimentation. It was reported that KDKA had been broadcasting motion pictures daily from August 25, 1929, using the Conrad television system. Dr. Zworykin used the Westinghouse television transmitter late at night (between 2 and 6 P.M.) some three times a week to telecast quite satisfactory pictures. This was on the 150 and 90 meter wavelength. Dr. Zworykin claimed that film of 60-line definition (at 12 frames/sec) was quite well received at his home. This appears to be the first reception of television by radio to an all-electric receiver, with absolutely no moving parts.

In addition, at this time, a second film transmitter was built for transmitting both pictures and sound. A special film was prepared for use with the 12 pictures/sec frequency, and it was claimed that sound pictures were transmitted across a laboratory room.[95]

However, the disclosure of the Kinescope changed the history of television for all time. For Dr. Zworykin had produced a simple but ingenious picture tube which made it possible to have a practical receiver in the home of the viewer, a device which the average person could operate, that required absolutely no technical knowledge to run, and could be viewed under almost normal lighting conditions. Zworykin's tube was the most important single technical advancement ever made in the history of television.

Yet it was greeted with skepticism by most of the "experts" working in television at the time. They knew only too well of the limitations of the "standard" cathode ray tubes available and found it hard to believe that Dr. Zworykin had actually accomplished a breakthrough. Some of this can be blamed on the secrecy that quickly descended over the Kinescope. It was reported that even as Dr. Zworykin was giving his speech, someone from the Westinghouse Patent department was giving him signals not to go on with his lecture. There were absolutely no public demonstrations of this device until May 1932, and most of the descriptions of its operation came from reporters, none of whom had ever seen the tube in operation.[96]

On November 20, 1929, W.J. Hitchcock of General Electric applied for a patent for camera tubes having targets and a minimum of capacity to their surroundings and well insulated from each other. This was to be done by means of a plurality of small conducting sections or spots mounted on vitreous supports.[97]

The Baird Company gave a demonstration of its television equipment in New York City on December 20, 1929, featuring Mayor Jimmy Walker. It featured "live" telecasts of both picture and sound. It was claimed that "the image was recognizable and the music in perfect step with the picture."[98]

In December 1929 the magazine *Radio* published a photograph of a Farnsworth television image. It was claimed that the original was approximately 3½ inches square and consisted of 20,000 elements. This appears to be the first photograph published of an image produced by an all-electric television system with no moving parts.[99]

Also in December 1929, Isaac Shoenberg left the Marconiphone division of the Marconi Wireless Telegraph Company after 15 years and joined
Columbia Graphaphone Company as the manager of patents at the request of Louis Sterling.[100]

In France almost all work on television was at a standstill. It appears
that the loss of Gregory Ogloblinsky to Westinghouse signaled the tem-
porary cessation of French research into cathode ray television. No more
was heard of the work of Belin and Holweck. Dauvillier had turned to the
field of cosmic physics. The only experimentation being done was by one
Rene Barthelemy of the Compagnie pour la Fabrication des Compteurs et
Matériel d'Usines à Gaz of Montrouge, who was concentrating on the
synchronization of mechnical television scanning systems.[101]

In the United States, the important work on cathode ray transmitters
was being done by Dr. Zworykin at Westinghouse in Pittsburgh and Philo
Farnsworth in San Francisco. The only other work on cathode ray receivers was that of Frank Gray of the Bell Telephone Labs and Kenjiro
Takayanagi in Japan.

It appeared that at this time, television was finally going to emerge
from the laboratory and take its place in the entertainment industry. But
the end of 1929 found the United States and Europe about to enter a deep
economic depression. This depression was to have a profound effect on the
fledgling television industry.

Chapter 8
Back to the Laboratory: 1930–1932

On January 3, 1930, David Sarnoff became president of the Radio Corporation of America. At this time, all television activities of RCA were to be concentrated in the new facilities at Camden, New Jersey. In addition, General Electric was to turn over its Harrison Tube Plant and Westinghouse Electric its Lamp Works at Indianapolis to RCA.

Dr. W.R.G. Baker of General Electric became chief engineer of RCA Victor. Two engineering groups were set up at Camden under L.W. Chubb. There was an Advanced Development Division, headed by Albert F. Murray. Under Murray were (a) Radio Receivers, under George Beers; (b) Acoustics, under Dr. Irving Wolf; and (c) Television, under Dr. V.K. Zworykin. Albert Murray seems to be the only executive coming from outside the General Electric/Westinghouse Electric empire. He had been assistant chief engineer of the Wireless Specialty Company of Boston, owned by John Hayes Hammond, Jr., who was one of the large RCA stockholders.[2]

There was also a General Research Group under the direction of Elmer W. Engstrom, who came from RCA Photophone. The Technical and Test Department, under Dr. Alfred N. Goldsmith, continued to run the RCA television transmitter from 411 Fifth Avenue.

In January 1930 John Baird's television experiments over the Brookman's Park transmitter were then extended to two half-hours per week for night transmission. In March 1930, two wavelengths were assigned to the Baird system so that both sound and picture could be transmitted together. This transmission started on April 1, 1930. Vision was on 356.3 meters and sound on 261.3 meters.[3]

Also in January 1930, it was announced that Jenkins Television was producing television sets. Jenkins had two transmitters in operation: W3XK in Washington, D.C., and W2CXR in Jersey City.

On January 14, 1930, Jenkins applied for a patent which proposed to use his rotary drum–type scanner as a means of flying spot scanning. He claimed that the light pipes would conduct the entire amount of light to the subject without material loss of intensity.[4]

General Electric made two long-distance tests of television images from Schenectady on February 18, 1930. The first was from Schenectady to Australia, relaying the image back to Schenectady, where it was monitored in the laboratory. The second test was from Schenectady to California and back. The image was a simple rectangle drawn on white paper. The received image alternated from single to multiple images and at times was quite sharp. The California test gave better results.[5]

Alan Archibald Campbell Swinton died on February 19, 1930.[6] He was never to know that at this time camera tubes very similar to the ones he described in 1911 were being built in the RCA Laboratories by V.K. Zworykin in Camden, New Jersey. It is claimed that Dr. Zworykin started work on two-sided camera tubes as soon as he moved into the new laboratories in Camden.

On March 3, 1930, P.T. Farnsworth applied for a patent covering an electron multiplier. This was to be done by modulating an electron stream, and using a pair of opposed surfaces to liberate electrons by secondary emission. The final electron flow was a function of the potential through which the electrons fell between impacts, and the number of impacts.[7]

Hans Hatzinger of Frankfort am Main, Germany, applied for a patent for a scanning device on March 25, 1930. This was in the form of a multitude of mirrors arranged in a spiral along an axis. This seems to be the first mirror wheel patent. It was presumed that this device would produce brighter pictures than either the Nipkow disc or mirror drum.[8]

At this time, there were several reports on the new picture tube of Dr. Zworykin. In the United States, an article in *Radio-Craft* in February 1930 was followed by a similar article in *Radio News*. In Europe, however, an early article by W.G.W. Mitchell in *Television* gave no real information as to its performance and was very misleading. For instance, there was nothing said of its two anodes, the use of electro-static focus, or the fact that it was gas-free. Another article by Dr. Neuberger in *Fernsehen* (the first German television journal) was along the same lines. Thus the European reports did nothing to indicate the tremendous breakthrough that had been accomplished.[9]

However, reports of the new Zworykin tube seemed to have two immediate results. On March 26, 1930, Dr. Frank Gray of the Bell Telephone Labs reported on the work that had been done with a "new" Bell oscillograph, which was of the high vacuum type (no gas), used magnetic focus and had a lead in front of the hot filament in order to control the beam. Gray reported that this new tube, "gives television images equal in quality to those on the disk and of the same order of brightness."[10]

In Japan, Kenjiro Takayanagi also started to build high vacuum cathode ray tubes. He filed two patents on March 28, 1930, for tubes of this type. It is reported that by May 1930 he was able to demonstrate bright and distinct pictures on tubes some 15 and 30 cm in diameter.[11]

April 1, 1930, was the official date of the changeover of all television research from the General Electric Company, Westinghouse Electric & Manufacturing Company, and the Test and Development Division of Van

Courtlandt Park to the new laboratories of RCA in Camden, New Jersey.[12]

At this time, as a result of the business connection between RCA and the H.M.V. Gramophone Company, RCA extended an invitation to A.W. Whitaker, who was in charge of Advanced Development (Research), to come to the United States and see the work being done by General Electric, Westinghouse and RCA in Camden, New Jersey. On April 2, 1930, he witnessed Zworykin's television system and reported that, "his high voltage cathode ray tube presented a 5 inch image and was so bright that it could be viewed in a brightly lighted room." This seems to be the first report on the new Zworykin Kinescope.[13]

On April 3, 1930, Dietrich Prinz of Berlin applied for a patent for means of synchronizing the horizontal and vertical scanning frequencies in a television system. They were locked together through frequency multiplication and demultiplication devices. As far as can be determined, this is the first patent covering this important feature. Although it was assigned to Telefunken, it became part of the RCA patent structure due to the relationship between Telefunken and RCA.[14]

The Television Society in London held its second Annual Exhibition at University College on April 9, 1930. There were exhibits by Capt. Wilson, C.P. Garside, T.C.M. Lance and C.F.C. Roberts. It appears that Roberts had a display of his "dissector" tubes, none of which were working."[15]

On April 9, 1930, the Bell Telephone Laboratories gave their first demonstration of a new two-way television system. There was an increase in the number of scanning lines from 50 to 72, which gave twice the image detail. It was claimed that a bandwidth of some 40,000 cycles was necessary in order to transmit this amount of detail. Synchronization was by means of a 1275-cycle alternating current, controlling motors rotating at 18 frames/sec. The flying spot featured a blue color to which the eye was relatively insensitive.

The system was in operation between the Bell Laboratory Building and the main offices of the American Telephone & Telegraph Company in New York City. A demonstration of this new system called the "Ikono-phone" was reported later in May 1930.[16]

Early in April 1930 an opportunity came for Dr. V.K. Zworykin to visit the Green Street laboratories of Philo T. Farnsworth in San Francisco. The early effects of the deepening recession were being felt, and some of the stockholders of the Farnsworth Television Laboratories were anxious to sell out and were actively seeking new ownership. The firm of Carroll W. Knowles Company had acquired an option to buy the stock of Farnsworth Television Laboratories and had sent out an invitation to RCA to inspect the laboratories and its patents. It appears that this was done without Philo Farnsworth's knowledge.

However, when Farnsworth found out that Dr. Zworykin was to come, it is reported that he was delighted and prepared to show him all he had accomplished. Farnsworth knew of Dr. Zworykin's work (from the many patent interferences between them) and had very high regard for him. As a result, he welcomed Dr. Zworykin as a future ally or at least as a source of much-needed financing. Also, Farnsworth felt that Dr. Zworykin would understand his language and would have proper appreciation of what he had attained.

On April 16, 1930, Dr. Zworykin arrived in San Francisco and spent three days at the Green Street laboratory. He was gracious in his praise of Farnsworth's results and seemed tremendously impressed with what he saw. He was shown in detail all that had been accomplished. Sitting at Farnsworth's desk on the first day after his arrival, in the presence of Jesse McCarger (president of Television Laboratories), Donald Lippincott (patent attorney) and George Everson (financial backer), he paid him high tribute by picking up the dissector tube and saying, "This is a beautiful instrument, I wish that I might have invented it." This of course, pleased Philo Farnsworth very much.

Later, Cliff Gardner showed Dr. Zworykin the success that he had had in sealing an optically clear disk of Pyrex glass onto the end of the dissector tube. Dr. Zworykin had been assured at both Westinghouse and RCA that such a seal could not be made. So it was arranged to have Gardner show Dr. Zworykin how he accomplished the sealing process.

Dr. Zworykin seemed to be very impressed with the dissector tube. Simple and straightforward in design, it was a remarkable camera tube. With sufficient light (from film or slides) it was an excellent transmitter. It had no "shading" problems (uneven distribution of the electrical charges making up the picture), delivered a clear distinct picture, was inherently a direct-coupled device with a constant (black) reference level and could deliver all of the background information. However, Dr. Zworykin was not at all impressed with Farnsworth's cathode ray picture tube, which could produce only small, dim pictures compared to his newly developed Kinescope.

On his way home, it is reported that Dr. Zworykin stopped in Los Angeles and wired Dr. E. Wilson of Westinghouse (they had developed the cesium-magnesium photo cell together) and requested him to make up several dissectors for future experimentation. Of course, this is standard practice—for one laboratory to build or construct devices of another laboratory in order to verify or challenge its findings. It is known that several were built and operated. (One has survived to this day, after having been discarded by the RCA Patent Department.)

While Farnsworth was still using some form of potassium hydride as his photoelectric element for his tubes, it appears that Dr. Wilson was able to use the new cesium surfaces that had been developed in both the General Electric and Westinghouse laboratories and as a result produced much more sensitive tubes.[17]

Dr. Zworykin wrote a report on the Farnsworth system, which must have raised much curiosity about it. Dr. Zworykin obviously could not admit that the dissector tube at this time was much superior to the crude, two-sided experimental camera tubes he was building in the RCA Laboratories. However, he could comment that his new developmental Kinescope was far superior to the Farnsworth picture tube, or "Oscillite," as it was to be known.

The report is not available, and all we can find is the reaction from Dr. Alexanderson, who stated, "Farnsworth had evidently done some very clever work, but I don't think that television is going to develop along these lines." He continued, "I think that Farnsworth can do greater service as a competitor to the Radio Corporation group by settling this provided he has financial backing. If he should be right, the Radio Corporation can afford to pay more for his patent than we can justify now." Of course, it is known that Dr. Alexanderson was not in favor of any cathode ray system (including Dr. Zworykin's) at this time.[18]

At any rate, RCA then sent Albert Murray and T. Goldsborough (the RCA patent attorney) to San Francisco to again investigate the Farnsworth patent applications. One thing is certain: the advanced look at the Farnsworth system certainly spurred Dr. Zworykin to improve his new television system.

Upon his return, Dr. Zworykin continued his efforts to build a practical camera tube. On May 1, 1930, Zworykin filed for his first patent on a camera tube since July 13, 1925. This was for a very different type of two-sided tube. It was thought that the great advantage of a two-sided tube was that the target plate would insulate the beam from the photo surface. It was feared that the electron beam or the gas from the oxide would poison the photo surfaces and render the tube inoperable.

The tube could be made in two forms, either "linear" or "planar." The "linear" form was to be used for scanning motion picture film. It would be composed of a single line of cells. As the beam repeatedly scanned this row of cells, the upward movement of the film compensated for any need of vertical scanning by the electron beam. Tubes of this type were the easiest to construct; thus the first camera tubes built in early 1930 were in this form.

The full screen or "planar" device was to be of such size as to capture the entire view. This meant as many rows of cells as there were scanning lines. This kind of device was very difficult to build. It is known that several of the "linear" camera tubes were built to prove that the principle was sound.

The patent application showed a camera tube that resembled Dr. Zworykin's Kinescope. It was a hard tube (gas-free) and had a second anode for focus and acceleration. The target was two-sided, consisting of a multitude of pins or rivets which penetrated the supporting plate. One side of the target was to be photosensitized with cesium oxide, and the other side was to be a common plate that was connected through a resistance to an amplifier. In front of the target was a plate or screen that furnished the polarizing voltage and was connected to the other side of the resistance through a battery. This plate furnished the picture signal.

A cathode ray beam from an electron gun was to scan the rear of the plate systematically. Each of the rivets or pins was to act as a single photoelectric cell, as they were isolated from each other. They were to form an electrostatic pattern according to the amount of light each cell was subjected to. They were to be charged continuously and only discharged when the beam struck the rear of the plate. Unfortunately, the problems of building uniform and blemish-free targets of this type were enormous.[19]

All accounts of these early devices suggest that they operated, but not very well. They certainly were not as good as the Dr. Wilson Image Dissectors they were testing at the time. In fact, Dr. Zworykin wrote Harley Iams on June 20, 1930, that "Ogloblinsky got very nice results with the transmitting tube, which is a modified Farnsworth type." He continued, "The sensitivity is quite high, and I hope to get a direct vision pretty soon." Of course, direct vision was Dr. Zworykin's dream — that is, to be able to pick up a "live" image direct from a scene by means of its own reflected light.[20]

On May 5, 1930, Philo Farnsworth applied for two patents (one with Harry Lubcke) covering the production of electrical scanning generators which produced slope-wave (sawtooth) currents to control the scanning of the electron beam, means for extinguishing the beam during the return portion of the cycle and use of an extinguishing impulse to synchronize both transmitter and receiver.

According to the records, generators of this type had been constructed and used in the Farnsworth Laboratory as early as July 1929. These appear to be the first sawtooth generators *not* using pulses from a disc or photocell, but generated electrically. The patent also included means for suppression of the DC component (the black level) at the transmitter and reestablishing it at the receiver.[21]

On May 20, 1930, Dr. Frank Gray of the Bell Telephone Labs made a summary of the various means for electrically scanning a picture. It appears that Dr. Gray had been interested in electrical scanning since April 29, 1929, but this was the first time that an interest in this approach was seriously considered.

Dr. Gray mentioned scanning by a moving beam of radiation as well as a cathode ray beam. He suggested the use of the photosensitivity of insulators and/or high resistance plates, and the interactions of two different types of radiation on a light-sensitive material. He stated that "storage of photoelectric charges over an image cycle presents the possibility of greatly increasing television signals and perhaps transmitting television signals under ordinary conditions of illumination."[22]

Even though all RCA television research was now being concentrated in Camden under the direction of Dr. Zworykin, the General Electric group led by Dr. Alexanderson decided to publicize their research efforts with a demonstration of large screen television. This took place on May 22, 1930, in Schenectady, New York.

Dr. Alexanderson's group had developed a large screen television projector using the Kerr cell originally devised by Dr. August Karolus of Telefunken. This equipment was moved to Proctor's Theater (RKO) in Schenectady. With the assistance of Ray Kell and Merrill Trainer, they were able to present television images on a six-foot-square screen. The picture was about half as bright as that of the regular motion picture with good shading up to the limits of illumination. The projector was a standard 175-ampere motion picture machine.

The scene was picked up in the television studio at Schenectady by a regular 48-hole disc using the "flying spot" method. The picture was transmitted by a 140-meter transmitter to an antenna on top of the theater. The 48-line, 16 frames/sec picture showed many defects, including a slight swaying of the image. However, the large size of the screen proved startling. The picture was accompanied by the sound from a pair of loudspeakers transmitted on 92 meters. The program consisted of an announcement by Mr. Trainer, a series of vaudeville acts, and a finale, an orchestra number with the conductor directing from the television studio a mile away.[23]

At this time, the unification of RCA was underway. In essence Westinghouse Electric and the General Electric Company were reduced to partners, having large stock ownership and powerful representation on the board of directors of RCA. But David Sarnoff's desire for complete independence came unexpectedly with the aid of the United States government.

On May 13, 1930, it was announced that the Department of Justice had filed an antitrust suit against RCA, the General Electric Company, Westinghouse Electric, and the American Telephone and Telegraph Company. It wanted the new agreement scrapped, the patent pool disassembled and all exclusive contracts (both home and abroad) made nonexclusive; further, the Justice Department required that the four corporations compete with each other in the production and sales of radio and other electrical equipment.

Coming at this time, as the depression was deepening, could have been fatal to the Radio Corporation of America. For RCA to agree to the terms of divestment and the changes in the patent structure would have been a disaster. But largely through the efforts of David Sarnoff, a satisfactory agreement was reached with the Justice Department.[24]

On June 14, 1930, Philo Farnsworth applied for his first patent on a cathode ray receiving tube. This was to be known as the "Oscillite." It was to be used for both oscillographic and television use. Farnsworth planned to focus the electron beam by means of a long magnetic coil that extended the length of the tube. The tube had a concentration electrode that caused an electrostatic field to accelerate the beam in such a manner that it passed through an aperture, although slightly convergent. Then it was planned to focus the beam sharply as it struck the screen by means of the long magnetic coil.[25]

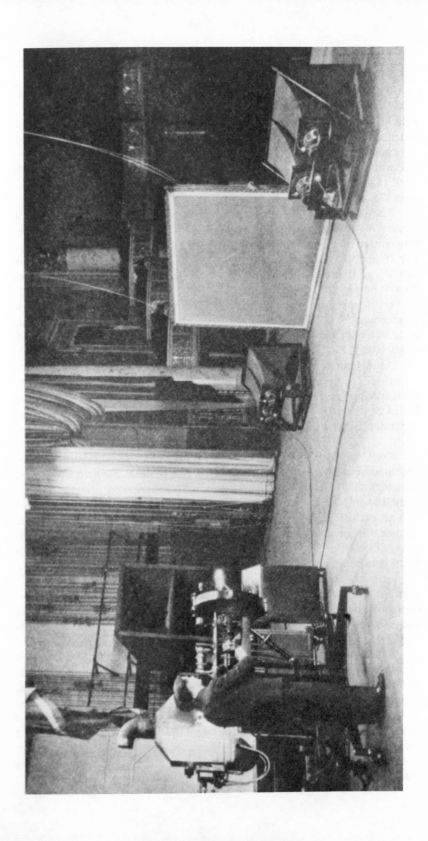

Philo Farnsworth also applied for a patent for an electron image amplifier on June 14, 1930. He described an advanced dissector tube in which he formed an electron image, dissected its image into steps of elementary width and applied the strips of said electron image charge to control the intensity distribution of space current of elongated cross-section to form successive partial images of greater intensity.[26]

Starting in June 1930, Philo Farnsworth made several attempts at transmitting his television pictures by both wire and radio. He tried to send television signals of 300 kc bandwidth on a 1000 kc carrier over an ordinary telephone line. He also tried to transmit signals on a four-meter radio link. Neither test was very successful, with the radio signal showing severe multiple reflections. However, this was the first transmission of an all-electric television signal by radio. Due to costs, no further tests were made after August 1930.[27]

On July 7, 1930, the Technical and Test Laboratory of RCA turned over the operation of the RCA television transmitter at 411 Fifth Avenue to NBC. It went on the air on July 30, 1930, and at this time the test laboratory under Dr. Alfred Goldsmith was dissolved.[28]

There was much dissension at the new Zworykin Television Research Laboratory in Camden, New Jersey. It seems that the two groups, General Electric and Westinghouse, could not agree as to which path to follow. The Westinghouse Group was for electric television. The General Electric people still insisted that mechanical scanning had merit.

It was decided to evaluate the two systems at a test house in Collingswood, New Jersey. This evaluation took place around July 15, 1930. According to Bucher, Zworykin's group had developed a complete telecasting system based on 80-line scanning and the use of the Zworykin cathode ray picture tube for reproduction. There was a television film transmitter using a Nipkow disc. A mechanical impulse generator was used to keep the transmitter and receivers in synchronization.

Elmer Bucher also claimed that there was a "camera" developed for studio pickups. But there is no record of such. It is assumed that the flying spot setup was the "camera" referred to by Bucher. (The best information available is that the Zworykin Group was using the two-sided experimental camera tubes for slides and film only. These tubes simply did not have enough sensitivity for "live" pickups at this time. Of course, they did have the Wilson "image dissector," which was operating quite well, but it is known that it also did not have enough sensitivity to be used in a studio. There was to be no studio camera for at least another year.) The General Electric Group relied on its flying spot scanner and the projection system of Alexanderson/Karolus.

Both systems were shown and evaluated, and the cathode ray system of Dr. Zworykin was shown to be far superior. Yet the General Electric

Opposite: General Electric's large screen demonstration, RKO Theater, Schenectady, N.Y., May 22, 1930. Ray Kell is running the projector.

Manfred von Ardenne (right) and John L. Baird, Berlin, 1930.

people insisted that their method had merit. It was finally decided to allocate 90 percent of the funds to the Zworykin television system and 10 percent to the General Electric system. It was decided to abandon mechanical scanning at the transmitter as soon as the Zworykin camera tube attained a higher degree of perfection.

The results obtained with his equipment were so superior to those of any other or prior system that some enthusiastic observers declared the system ready for public service. But the conclusion was overly optimistic; a larger and more detailed picture was deemed essential for a telecasting service to the home.[29]

On July 14, 1930, Baird Television gave its first demonstration of a large screen television system. It was some five by two feet. Baird had returned to his very first patent and developed a large screen consisting of 2100 tiny metal filament lamps set in a cubicle covered with ground glass. Each of the 2100 lamps was connected to a commutator, which contacted each lamp in its proper time sequence. A 30-line picture was projected some 12½ times/sec. It was claimed that the inertia in each lamp helped to create an image that had greater brilliance and less flicker.

This screen was demonstrated on July 14, at Long Acre, as Baird Television presented its first television play, "The Man with a Flower in his Mouth." The reviewer watched the large screen and claimed that "the image greatly and rapidly varied." This large screen was made portable and was first shown at the London Coliseum on July 28, 1930. It was then transported to Berlin where it was demonstrated at the Scala Theatre on the week of September 18, 1930. It was also shown at the Olympia Cinema in Paris and the Röda Kvarn Cinema in Stockholm.[30]

On July 17, 1930, V.K. Zworykin applied for his first television patent for RCA Victor. It was a slightly advanced version of his May 1, 1930, patent for Westinghouse Electric. It was for a camera tube with a target structure consisting of a plurality of conducting plugs having a light-sensitive head element extending through insulating apertures. Two fine mesh screens enclosed the conducting plugs. Since each of these elements formed a condenser, they were continuously charged by the electron emission from the light-sensitive plug. Much was made of the fact that the condensers continually charged until they were discharged by the cathode ray beam.

It was planned to employ 6400 elements in evenly spaced parallel rows of 80 evenly spaced elements. The rays from the cathode ray beam reach the positive screen at a velocity corresponding to the potential difference between this screen and the cathode. Part of these electrons are absorbed by the screen and pass or leak to ground by way of a battery and a conductor. Those electrons which pass through the openings of the screen strike directly a spot on the exposed side of the composite anode, the remainder striking the surface portion of an electrode immediately adjacent to or above this anode.

The target worked in the following manner. When all of the light-sensitive elements are uncharged, the same number of electrons strike each of the surface portions of the electrode for all positions of the cathode ray beam with respect to the composite anode. This causes a direct current to flow through the resistance by way of the battery and ground to cathode. But when the value of the charges on the conducting plugs varies, a corresponding current from the electrode goes through the resistance to an amplifier which becomes the picture signal. Other methods of fabricating the mesh cathode and the composite anode were mentioned. Several of these tubes were built and operated.

On July 30, 1930, Major Edward Howard Armstrong filed for the first of three new patents on a system of wide-band frequency modulation (FM). Armstrong had invented four of radio's most important developments: the regenerative or feedback circuit in 1914, the heterodyne in 1917–18, the super-regenerative circuit in 1921 and the super-heterodyne in 1922.

On August 5, 1930, Telehor Akt-Ges of Berlin, Germany, applied for a patent for television receivers. It was to use a rotating mirror system in which the mirrors were in strips corresponding to the width of the picture. The mirrors mounted on a spindle, which was rotated by a phonic drum. Since there were more strips than picture lines, it was planned to secure a phase relationship by moving the mirror system axially. Although a similar mirror system could be used for scanning at the transmitter, it did not appear in the specification.

V.K. Zworykin of the Radio Corporation applied for a patent for a new type of light valve on August 15, 1930. Basically, the invention called for the use of a local light source of constant intensity which was modulated by the action of a special screen in its path. The screen was to be constructed with a series of apertures and cooperating plates so that as it was struck by the modulated cathode ray beam, it would vary the amount of light transmitted by the screen to develop a picture. This appears to be the first patent covering the use of a cathode ray beam to modulate a special screen to produce large screen television images.[34]

The 1930 Berlin Radio Exhibition was held during the week of August 21–31. It featured the Fernseh A.G. transmitter built for the German Post Office. It also showed a standard televisor developed by Fernseh using the patents of the Baird Company. The only other equipment was that of the Telehor Company which was featuring receivers, both finished and in kit form. Telefunken did not exhibit the apparatus of Dr. Karolus at this time.[35]

On September 19, 1930, Alda V. Bedford of the General Electric Company applied for a patent covering the generation of pulses at the end of each scanning line, which would substantially correct any imbalance in light and dark portions of the line. By this time, Alda Bedford, Ray Kell, Merrill Trainer and several other General Electric engineers had been transferred from General Electric to RCA Victor and were working under W.A. (Doc) Tolson in a new division called the Development Television Test Section.[36]

On October 4, 1930, Dr. Herbert E. Ives of the Bell Telephone Laboratories applied for a patent covering the use of the new Kodacolor lenticular film for a color television system. In this process, the film was covered with a series of ridges (lenticules) in such a manner as to separate the three colors by means of an objective lens provided with a plurality of different contiguous color filters. This created a group of striations that represented the various colors. This was done with ordinary black and white emulsion.

To get color on playback, another special lens similar to the taking lens with a set of color filters now reproduced the picture in full color. In the television system the light was divided by mirrors and sent to three photocells. Their output became the color television signal.[37]

Dr. Ives delivered a paper on this system for the transmission of images in color from motion picture film on October 7, 1930. He mentioned the relative ease of transmitting images from motion picture film, while admitting that the practical simultaneity of an event was lost when film was used. However, the advantages to be gained over the material transportation of film especially in the home were considerable.

But considering the cost of Technicolor film, he proposed the use of the relatively new Kodacolor film in which the images were produced in black and white on lenticular film. This produced a triple linear mosaic which represented the three colors. By projecting this film through a lens with three apertures, covered by red, green, and blue filters (similar to those used in recording), the picture would be reproduced in full color.[38]

On October 20, 1930, G.W. Walton of London applied for a patent on a nonvisual television recording system. The inventor called it the Stixograph process. The recording was to be made by continuously impressing

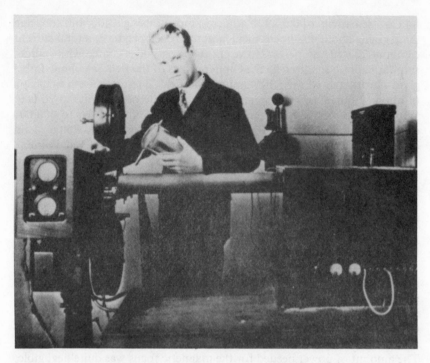

Philo Farnsworth and his 1930 television apparatus.

the photographic exposure on a moving recording surface. It could be made photographically on a film strip, in spiral form on a disc, or on a cylinder in the form of a helix. The record material could be either opaque or transparent. Playback seems to be with the use of a suitable optical system as described in a previous patent. This seems to be the first non-visual television recording process using photography similar to a motion picture sound track.[39]

E. Hudec of Berlin applied for a patent covering an electric scanning generator in which synchronizing pulses were sent at the end of each line on November 11, 1930. The patent also covered an electric scanning generator for cathode ray television scanning.[40]

In November 1930 Philo Farnsworth described his all-electric television system in detail for the first time. It consisted of an "Image Dissector" tube, which converted light into electrical impulses; a wide-band amplifier flat to 600 kilocycles; synchronization of two alternating currents of sawtooth form, which also turned off the beam on its return path; and a picture tube, which was a modified Braun oscillograph or "Oscillite" (also called the Oscillight) which was magnetically focused and deflected. The horizontal frequency was some 3000 cycles, and the vertical frequency was 15 cycles, so that 200-line images were produced.

The dissectors had cathodes coated with potassium hydride, which had low sensitivity of 0.5×10^{-6} amperes/lumen; using a 400-watt tungsten lamp giving about 40 lumens incidental to the cell produces a total current of about 20×10^{-6} amperes. However, using cathodes coated with sodium sulphur vapor (sensitized by the Olpin process of the Bell Telephone Labs) gives sensitivities of 6.5×10^{-6} amperes/lumen. These require a light flux of about 2 lumens when the aperture-to-cathode ratio is one to 20,000. With an amplifier having a gain of 50,000, an amplifier flat to 400,000 cycles will handle a target current of 2×10^{-10} amps or allow a voltage gain of 250,000. Therefore a light flux of 0.4 lumen was considered ample.

Farnsworth claimed that a 1500-watt tungsten lamp at a foot from a face with a lens opening of $F/2$ approaches the needs for direct scanning. However, using the photo surfaces of Zworykin (cesium-magnesium) with a sensitivity of 25×10^{-6} amperes/lumen would permit "direct scanning" with illumination that would not be too bright to be used with animate objects. However, Farnsworth admitted that dissectors having this sensitivity had not been built as yet.

The Oscillite picture tube was not quite so successful. It would function only when secondary electrons were emitted from the fluorescent screen. But although it was admitted that an unstable condition existed with the screen assuming either a large negative or positive potential, it was claimed that the effect was not bothersome at all. Also the deflection coil system used for the picture tube was exactly the same as for the dissector. The amount of power needed for the magnetic focus was quite negligible. Farnsworth ended his article by stating that means other than the extremely wide bandwidth to transmit television pictures would be forthcoming.[41]

On December 1, 1930, Dr. Lewis Koller of the General Electric Company described his methods of preparing thin films of cesium. These were divided into two classes: (1) where a thin film of cesium is absorbed on a layer of oxygen, and (2) where a thin film of cesium is absorbed on a layer of suboxide of cesium. Surfaces of the latter type were prepared by coating a cathode with metallic cesium and then admitting oxygen in very small quantities. The measurements showed that the most sensitive surfaces were obtained when the cesium had taken up sufficient oxygen to form a suboxide rather than the normal oxide Cs_2O. These films owe their properties to the arrangements of the molecules near the surface. When deposited on silver these become known as the Cs-CsO-Ag surface. It appears that this surface was sensitive enough to produce fairly strong picture signals. Certainly, Dr. Zworykin at Camden was the first to use these new surfaces in his camera tubes, including the modified Farnsworth dissectors that RCA/Westinghouse was building.[42]

On December 3, 1930, Philo Farnsworth appeared before the Federal Radio Commission. He delivered a paper stating that he had developed a method to reduce the television bandwidth to about 10 kc. This entailed the use of an "image compressor" which was to suppress part of the wide picture frequency band so that the width transmitted was only some 7 kc wide, the suppressed part of the signal to be replaced at the receiver. Thus a 15 kc telephone line could have both picture and sound on it. (This was similar to a single-side band-carrier eliminated transmission.) It appears that Farnsworth's calculations had been checked and approved by the Naval Research Laboratories but had turned out to be inoperative. This paper caused a great deal of harm to his reputation among radio engineers.[43]

A patent covering this scheme was applied for on December 4, 1930. Farnsworth claimed that he could filter out the high frequency components at the transmitter to reduce the bandwidth required. At the receiver he would form square-fronted waves to be combined with the transmitted currents to restore the components lost in the filtering. Farnsworth claimed that pictures transmitted by this system had a slight increase in contrast as well as bringing out the angles and planes in sharp relief.[44]

On December 27, 1930, Kenjiro Takayanagi of Japan applied for a patent on an "accumulating system." This was for a television camera tube consisting of a series of photocells connected to a series of condensers. They were to be discharged by some sort of rotating commutator.[45]

A similar scheme was applied for by A. Konstantinov on December 28, 1930, when he applied for a Russian patent for a television camera tube. Basically it consisted of a series of condensers and cells of photo elements that were to discharge through a switch, which might be the beam of a cathode ray tube.[46]

By this time, the idea of a charge storage device was quite common. The problem was how actually to make such a device. That Zworykin had actually reduced this principle to practice at this time was not to be known for several more years. In fact it wasn't too long before the problems of such a camera tube were thought by certain authorities to be insolvable.

During the first week of January 1931, the Physical and Optical Society's Twenty-First Annual Exhibition was held at the Imperial College of Science, South Kensington. A feature of this Exhibition was a demonstration of television by the H.M.V. Gramophone Company, Ltd. It was not well known that the Gramophone Company, which had been the English relative of the Victor Talking Machine Company, was now affiliated with RCA Victor. The exhibition was the result of a limited research program that had been started in March 1929. As an affiliate of RCA Victor, the Gramophone Company had been receiving the television patents of RCA. However, the television system shown had been developed solely by the engineers of the Gramophone Company.

At this time it was made quite clear that the Gramophone Company had no intention of producing this apparatus on a commercial basis. The work had been undertaken as an advanced laboratory experiment in the course of which might be expected to emerge information of direct value to the company's principal business of sound reproduction.

The demonstration was under the direction of C.O. Browne, who had developed the system with R.B. Morgan, J. Hardwick and W.D. Wright.

Wright, who had been employed at Westinghouse in East Pittsburgh from March 1929 to March 1930, had worked with Dr. Zworykin on his earliest experiments with camera tubes. Due to personal problems, he had left Westinghouse in March 1930 and returned to England. Here he had gone to work part-time for the H.M.V. Gramophone Company when he was not teaching at Imperial College. In his position at Westinghouse, he had had full access to all of Dr. Zworykin's early work on the Kinescope and the early camera tubes.[47]

The demonstration seemed to have come as a surprise to the Baird Television Company, which immediately filed suit. Until this time, the Baird Television Company had had a complete monopoly on research and development of television in Great Britain. One result of the lawsuit was intensive research by the Gramophone Company into television patents and methods. The main objection turned out to be over the use of the word "Televisor," to which Baird Television laid claim. However, nothing came of the suit.

The demonstration used a film projector as a source of 150-line signals. Actually the image was divided into 5 sections or zones of 30 lines each. A lens drum was used to traverse a section of images over 5 scanning apertures at 12.5 frames/sec. The 10-inch lens drum carried a spiral of 40 lenses. A prism placed in front of the projector bent the rays of light at right angles and through the lenses of the drum. The light from the lenses fell on a row of photoelectric cells of the cesium/copper type (high vacuum) with a sensitivity of some 48.3 microamperes/lumen, each with its own individual amplifier.

At the receiver, light from an ordinary arc lamp was sent through 5 individual Kerr cells. There the beams were focused on a 10-inch mirror drum with 30 mirrors (the blank spaces produced black). The light then went to a ground glass screen some 20 by 24 inches. Outside of some bad flicker and general inequality of the zones, the detail was good and the brilliancy about the same as an ordinary home movie projector.[48]

About this time (January 1931) the Bell System reported on a three-channel television system that it had built and tested. Since the pictures that were capable of being transmitted by the existing system of about 4500 elements were already straining the limits of both the electrical and mechanical elements of the system, it was difficult to propose that a system capable of transmitting some 350,000 elements with a bandpass of some 3.5 million cycles would be necessary. So it was decided to build a three-channel system for film only, due to the scanning requirements. The results were not too promising, for the need to balance the three channels was of first priority and the hardest to achieve. Obviously, some means other than mechanical scanning was necessary to solve the problem.[49]

The General Electric Company reported that it had successfully transmitted television pictures from Schenectady, New York, to Leipzig, Germany, on February 13, 1931. They also claimed that they had recorded television images on motion picture film. Several hundred feet of 35mm film had been shot, and the results were equally as good or better than the television image itself. It was hoped that they could be used for "news reel display."[50]

In February 1931, RCA completed construction and installation of a 2.5 kw VHF transmitter at the Camden plant and a receiving station at Collingswood, New Jersey. In July 1931, a similar transmitter was installed at the Empire State Building, where RCA was in the process of building a complete television installation. The scanning rate was raised from 80 to 120 lines at 24 frames/sec. The picture was to be transmitted at 44 megacycles and the sound on 61 megacycles. It appears that Elmer W. Engstrom was to be in charge of the Empire State television installation, which went into operation on October 30, 1931.[51]

Meanwhile, in Dr. Zworykin's Camden lab, many new patents were being applied for. Among the applicants: Arthur Vance, for an improved mechanical scanning generator; Randall Ballard, for a system of blanking pulses; W.A. Tolson, for a picture framing generator; Ralph Batchelor and V.K. Zworykin, for improved picture tubes; and Ray Kell, for generating sync pulses.[52]

Dr. Zworykin's greatest problem at this time was with his two-sided camera tubes. Not only were they difficult to construct and operate, but as a result of RCA's policy of secrecy (RCA was loath to show its system to anyone outside of its patent structure), they were thought to be inoperative. To dispel this idea, RCA invited United States Patent Examiner C.J. Spencer to visit Camden on February 20, 1931, for a demonstration. There are no details available, but it was reported that he was shown a two-sided camera tube constructed in accordance with the disclosure of the July 17, 1930, Zworykin patent application.[53]

While details of the RCA television system were being kept a secret, much information about the Farnsworth television system was being printed in England, Germany, and the United States. There was an article in *Fernsehen* for February 1931, and two by Dinsdale in *Wireless World* for March 1931 and *Science and Invention* in May 1931. Dinsdale reported that he had not yet seen a demonstration but stated "that independent and reliable witnesses reported that the images are better than the 72 line images produced by the Bell Telephone Labs two-way system which are unquestionably the best images produced to date by mechanical means." There were two articles in *Radio News* as well as an article by Mitchell in the *Journal of the Royal Society of Arts* for May 1931. The author praised Farnsworth by stating, "He is about the only important worker making use of strictly electrical methods for transmission."[54]

On March 27, 1931, Manfred von Ardenne applied for a patent for a television system using cathode ray tubes for both transmitter and receiver. This patent described the use of a Braun tube to produce a flying spot of light so that a transparency could be scanned in systematic fashion. It also called for the use of a Braun tube at the receiver. Von Ardenne claimed that he had his flying spot system working by December 14, 1930, and would demonstrate it in August 1931.

According to the patent application, von Ardenne stated that sinewave scanning caused severe problems in the image: the irregular speed caused variations in the detail of the center of the picture where the beam was traveling fastest, displacement of the images due to phasing, and in the light and dark areas in the picture. He therefore recommended a "tilting" or jump scan (sawtooth) for both the horizontal and vertical movements. Scanning was accomplished by a traversing bright spot on the screen of the Braun tube. Behind the tube was a photoelectric cell (with a diffusing sheet between, to even out the signal) followed by the necessary amplifier. Von Ardenne also described the use of a Braun tube as a flying spot scanner for "live" images if enough light could be produced.[55]

Von Ardenne indicated in an article in *Fernsehen* in April 1931 that the cathode ray tube was clearly the solution to the problem of getting the 8000/ 10,000 elements needed to render television worthwhile. He stated, however, that "of all the patented schemes, only the one due to Zworykin, using special tubes, seems to have met with any successful development — at any rate on the transmitting side." No mention was made of the Farnsworth Image Dissector tube, which was working quite well at the moment.[56]

It is of interest to note where von Ardenne got his information about the Zworykin camera tube. It is known that RCA had started to furnish all of its licensees and affiliates with vital information about the development of television in the Camden Laboratories. Von Ardenne had been trading patents with RCA since 1926 and obviously was also being kept well informed; he later claimed that he had been in personal correspondence with Dr. Zworykin himself. Similar information was being sent to the newly formed EMI in Great Britain as well as Telefunken in Germany. Von Ardenne had developed a Braun tube capable of high brightness and was now going ahead with a television system without the necessity of building a special camera tube.[57]

In April 1931, some four months after the television demonstration by H.M.V. Gramophone Company, a new holding company, Electric and Musical Industries, Ltd. (EMI) was formed by merging the H.M.V. Gramophone Company with Columbia Graphophone Company, Ltd. The depression was now worldwide and was affecting the entertainment industry, especially phonographs and radio receivers. It had been decided that by joining forces, the two competing record companies could enjoy certain economies. As a result, they were unified and became part of EMI Ltd., and for several years existed alongside it.

Another partner was the Radio Corporation of America. RCA, which had acquired a substantial interest in the Gramophone Company through its acquisition of the Victor Talking Machine Company, owned approximately 27 percent of the new company. David Sarnoff, who had sat on the Board of Directors of the Gramophone Company since March 1929, took his place on the EMI board of directors in April 1931.

From the Gramophone Company came C.O. Browne, G.E. Condliff, W.F. Tedham and W.D. Wright. From Columbia Graphophone came Isaac Schoenberg, Allan Blumlein, P.W. Willans, E.C. Cork, H.E. Holman and others. The first television project was to perfect a system for the transmission of films based on the Zworykin/RCA Kinescope. A 120-line system at 24 frames/sec was planned using a mirror drum film scanner. In fact, it was the same film scanner used in the H.M.V. Gramophone Company's January 1931 demonstration. William F. Tedham, the chemist who had been working on photocells for the Gramophone Company, was put in charge of the project and was to be assisted by H. Neal and J.W. Strange, with H.G.M. Spratt in charge of receiver design.[58]

Early in the spring of 1931, RCA sent EMI several of their new Kinescopes, and D.W. Wright attempted to build a receiver and pick up the Baird television signal with it. The results were minimal. However, EMI was pleased with the new bright, picture tubes, and according to C.O. Browne, "television images 6 inches square" were "formed by means of these tubes and very good illumination" was obtained.[59]

The Third Annual Exhibition of the Television Society was held in University College, London, on April 15, 1931. Capt. Wilson and A.A. Waters presented a prismatic drum receiver. Mr. F.H. Haskell showed a sample of a double-drum receiver, and H.J. Peachy demonstrated an "All Mains Receiver for Sound and Vision." The transmitter and receiver of C.E.C. Roberts were again shown and were still not working. E.H. Traub showed a model of a universal scanning disc comprising four superimposed discs.[60]

On April 24, 1931, Lee De Forest applied for a patent on a television receiving method and apparatus. This was for recording television signals on motion picture film. It included a rotating head with a number of discharge points which were to electrically etch the incoming signal on the emulsion thereby forming visible images to be quickly projected onto a large screen.

A modification of this patent was applied for on September 22, 1931. This apparatus consisted of a revolving wheel with a series of needle points. These points were electrically connected to the receiver and had the picture signal impressed on them. These points passed over a strip of 35mm film coated with pure metallic silver. As the impulses varied, so did the etching action of the needle points as they passed over the film. Thus the dark and light parts of the picture were to be reproduced as modulated lines on the film. Owing to many difficulties, this method was soon abandoned as impractical. De Forest claimed that he worked on this idea from 1930 till 1933 and actually built this device. He claimed that most difficulties were overcome but that "cathode ray beam progress was such to consign to limbo all mechanical systems be they ever so clever."[61]

On May 8, 1931, Baird Television used its new outdoor television equipment, which was housed in a caravan (a movable wagon), to televise

Randall Ballard (left) and Les Flory, members of RCA's Zworykin group, on the roof at the RCA labs in Camden with an RCA Image Dissector camera, 1931. They are checking the outdoor performance of the equipment.

an outdoor scene from his Long Acre Studios. In order to produce daylight television, Baird had arranged a large mirror to reflect the light from the scene to a two-foot mirror drum of the Weiller type. It had 30 mirrors set at an angle that reflected the scanned image to a photocell.

On June 3, 1931, Baird Television took this same caravan to Epsom Downs to televise the Derby and placed it opposite the grandstand and winning post. The signals were sent by land line to the control room at Long Acre, from there to Savoy Hill, and then to the Brookmans Park transmitter, where it was broadcast on 261 meters. The sound was sent on 356 meters. It was reported that the pictures were received as far as 120 miles away. This caravan was later moved to Savoy Hill itself and from October 1931 on a weekly program was transmitted from this vehicle.[62]

At the RCA laboratories in Camden, the Zworykin group was having very great success with its version of the Farnsworth Image Dissector. According to several sources, early in 1931 the tube had been made so sensitive that it was possible to get pictures outdoors by "direct vision" in bright sunlight. Ballard had designed a dissector tube in April 16, 1931. Leslie Flory's first job at RCA was evaluating the dissector tube. Thus the first "direct vision" pictures ever produced came from an RCA Image Dissector;

Farnsworth himself was not able to accomplish such pictures until August 1933.[63]

On the other hand, the Zworykin group at RCA was having very little success with its two-sided camera tubes. Around May 14, 1931, Dr. Zworykin decided to investigate a single-sided target. According to his notebook, by June 12, 1931, several tubes had been built that were giving quite promising results, and it was decided to procede along these lines.[64]

Harley Iams had come back to work for Dr. Zworykin at RCA on April 24, 1931. He was assigned to the new single-sided camera tube project along with Gregory N. Ogloblinsky, Leslie E. Flory, and Sanford Essig, the RCA chemist. Arthur Vance and Randall Ballard were continuing work on scanning and synchronizing generators.

According to all reports, these early single-sided camera tubes had a target consisting of a mica surface on which silver was deposited. There were several methods used to make a mosaic of the silver deposit: (1) by means of a ruling machine; (2) by etching the silver; (3) by use of a fine-mesh screen which was used as a mask and the silver deposited over it; and (4) by a method in which a layer of silver dust was settled slowly on the mica.

None of these methods produced a satisfactory mosaic. A real breakthrough came when Essig was baking one of the silver-covered mica targets in an oven and accidentally left it in too long. When it came out he found that the silver had broken into a beautiful uniform mosaic of insulated silver globules.

An elaborate exhausting and baking schedule was then followed. The backside of the mica had a thin layer of metal applied to it. After the silver mosaic had been baked, it was oxidized by admitting oxygen into the tube and ionized by a high frequency current. Cesium was admitted and deposited on top of the silver oxide. The electron gun assembly was heated by radio frequency currents to keep the cesium off of it. Finally, the tube was exhausted and baked to get rid of all of the gases. However, much experimentation was required to perfect this process.[65]

It appears that at this time in 1931, the television laboratories of Philo Farnsworth were still in desperate need of new financing. Most of the staff had been laid off, and new sources of money were being sought. An appeal for funds resulted in a contract with the Philadelphia Storage Battery Company of Philadelphia (Philco).

The Philco Corporation was the largest manufacturer of radio sets in the United States. As such it was very dependent on the RCA patent structure. It was very anxious to break away from its subservient position to RCA in the new field of television.

As the Farnsworth electrical television system was the only alternative to the RCA/Zworykin system at the time, Philco offered to support his work. They proposed to pay his research expenditures, which were to be credited as prepaid royalties, leaving Farnsworth in control of his inventions. Philo Farnsworth was to come to Philadelphia, where a research laboratory was to be set up atop the Philco Plant.

Word that the Farnsworth Laboratories were for sale also reached RCA. During the week of May 18, 1931, David Sarnoff himself went to visit the Green Street laboratories in San Francisco. He had several reasons for coming: (1) to see firsthand what Philo had accomplished; (2) perhaps to buy up his work to insure that RCA had possession of a viable camera tube (he certainly was aware of the problems Zworykin was having with his tubes); and (3) perhaps to buy it up so that no one else could do so.

However, he was too late. He arrived at the Green Street laboratories while Philo Farnsworth was in Philadelphia with Jesse McCarger negotiating the contract with Philco. Sarnoff was shown through the labs by George Everson, who later claimed that Sarnoff seemed quite impressed with what he had seen but indicated that he felt the Zworykin receiver avoided any of the Farnsworth patents.

However, David Sarnoff certainly had an interest in the "Image Dissector" camera tube. He offered some $100,000 for the enterprise, including the services of Farnsworth himself. (At the depth of the depression, this was quite a generous offer.) Sarnoff was assured that such a deal was not possible, and with that he left, stating, "There's nothing here we'll need." From this time forward, the rivalry between RCA and Farnsworth became quite intense.[66]

The agreement between Philco and Farnsworth was signed in June 1931, and Farnsworth made plans to move his laboratory to Philadelphia. He kept the Green Street laboratory open with one or two employees and moved his equipment (amidst great secrecy) to a penthouse laboratory in Philadelphia. By December 1931, it was reported that the Philco Corporation was applying for a license for a television station.[67]

On May 30, 1931, Siemens Akt.-Ges in Germany applied for a patent for improvements in cathode ray tubes. The patent described how cathode ray beams could be converged or diverged by means of electrostatically charged diaphragms in the form of flat rings symmetrically surrounding the axis of the beam. It stated that negatively charged diaphragms produced convergence and positively charged diaphragms caused divergence. The patent claimed that an image-amplifying devide corresponding to the microscope could be produced by a combination of the diaphragms. This was the first patent covering an electron microscope.[68]

In May 1931 Westinghouse Electric described a new cathode ray oscilloscope using the high vacuum tube designed by Dr. Zworykin in 1928/29. It was $9'' \times 19'' \times 21''$ and was self-contained. It appears to be the first portable cathode ray oscillograph ever designed and built. Both Westinghouse and General Electric continued to build and improve the new Zworykin Kinescope for uses other than television.[69]

G.B. Banks of Baird Television Ltd. applied for a patent for a method of modulating an arc lamp on June 2, 1931. This method would make possible the direct projection of large-screen television images without resorting to the use of either a Kerr cell or similar light-valve schemes.[70]

On July 14, 1931, Philo Farnsworth applied for a patent for a scanning and synchronizing system. The most important feature of this patent was the method of supplying the high voltage to the anode of the cathode ray tube. This was done by generating an alternating current, utilizing a part of this current to move the cathode ray beam, rectifying a portion of the current cycle, and utilizing the rectified current to energize the anode of the cathode ray reproducer. This was accomplished by using the pulses to charge a condenser to a high value. This condenser was connected to the anode of the picture tube, thus furnishing the anode current for its operation. This was quite a revolutionary feature. It is the process which is used in most modern day receivers.[71]

Also on July 14, 1931, Philo Farnsworth applied for a patent for a Projecting Oscilight. In this patent, Farnsworth proposed to project the electron beam onto the fluorescent screen and project the light reflected from it through a lens onto a screen. The fluorescent screen, which was obliquely mounted on a metal plate, was connected to an anode to carry off the electric charges that otherwise accumulated on the screen.

It appears that the Farnsworth Oscillite was plagued by the fact that after a short period of operation, a large negative charge would gather on the screen and slow down the approaching electrons, decreasing the brilliancy of the picture. Only when the electron beam knocked out secondary electrons would the screen operate normally with a positive charge. This is the first patent in which the picture was viewed from the same side of the screen as was struck by the electron beam. It was claimed that pictures projected up to two feet square could be viewed in a darkened room.[72]

The Columbia Broadcasting System (CBS) inaugurated its new television station W2XAB in New York City on July 21, 1931. It was claimed that this was the first occasion of an American network to inaugurate a regular schedule of sound and visual programs. Amid a gala ball on the twenty-first floor, guests were shown images on "Standard" Jenkins and Shortwave and Television receivers. Mayor Jimmy Walker of New York City was the honored guest. The images were easily recognizable, but at times they would become distorted. Scanning was the RCA standard of 60 lines at 20 frames/sec. The sound was transmitted by WABC (the New York CBS station) and the entire Columbia Radio network.

After the inauguration, the sound was transmitted by station W2XE, the CBS shortwave station. The station was on the air for some 7 hours a day, 2 to 6 P.M. and 8 to 11 P.M. This schedule continued until February 25, 1933, when CBS halted all television transmission until "better equipment becomes available."[73]

On July 24, 1931, it was reported that television images from several television stations along the Eastern Seaboard were successfully received aboard the USS *Leviathan* while at sea. The test had been arranged by

Shortwave and Television Corporation Pictures and were received from CBS and NBC in New York, 3XK in Washington and W1XAV and W1XAU in Boston.[74]

The Berlin Radio Show was held in August 1931 and featured the new cathode ray television system of Manfred von Ardenne. It was claimed that his exhibit drew the biggest crowds. It was a flying spot system using von Ardenne cathode ray tubes at both the transmitter and receiver.

The transmitter had a motion picture projector that used an endless loop of film running at a rate of 5 to 8 frames/sec. This could either be hand-cranked or motor-driven. The system was troubled with severe flicker although the detail and intensity were good. A moving commutator was used to trigger the line pulses. Synchronization of the film-drive Maltese Cross and the time-base discharge was made by a contact on the film drive that triggered the time-base. The light from the film was projected through a lens of some 7.5 cm or more focal length onto a photoelectric cell. Picture and synchronizing potentials were applied to a common carrier. The picture was received on a Braun tube within a cabinet. With an electrical potential of 4000 volts, a stop brightness of two to three candlepower was claimed.[75]

Manfred von Ardenne was first to publicly demonstrate a television system using cathode ray tubes for transmission and reception. Since neither Philo Farnsworth nor Dr. Zworykin had as yet given any *public* demonstrations of their equipment, von Ardenne gets the priority. (However, it is to be noted that von Ardenne did not have a "camera tube" as such, nor did he have much interest in producing one. This he left to Dr. Zworykin.)

At this exhibit, Loewe Radio was sponsoring the von Ardenne system. The German Post Office showed two receivers that were in operation. Fernseh A.G. also showed several working mechanical receivers as well as a cathode ray receiver that was not working. Another big attraction was the introduction of the "Tekade-Telehor" mirror-screw system. This consisted of a pile of mirrors (one for each line) helically arranged as a spiral staircase. It was claimed that this new arrangement had the advantage of simplicity, with no special lenses needed. Tekade also had a cathode ray tube on display.[76]

In August 1931 General Radio Company of Boston offered a cathode ray oscillograph for sale. This was a two-piece unit with the von Ardenne cathode ray tube in a separate housing. The two-foot-long, gas-filled tube was supplied by Leyboldt in Germany. This appears to be the first cathode ray oscillograph for sale in the United States. Both Westinghouse and General Electric were building cathode ray oscillographs using their version of the Zworykin tube, but there is no record of these being on the market.[77]

On September 2, 1931, Roscoe H. George and Howard J. Heim applied for a patent for a television system. Basically this patent was concerned with a system of synchronizing signals to be sent during the time interval between one pictorial element and the beginning of a succeeding pictorial element. It was planned to transmit synchronizing pulses during the period of discontinuity of picture currents and a special synchronizing pulse of greater amplitude than the picture impulses during the interval between the end of one frame and the beginning of the new frame.[78]

George and Heim, along with C.F. Harding of Purdue University at Lafayette, Indiana, had been working on a television system since May 7, 1929. They had been funded by the Grigsby-Grunow Company, which manufactured Majestic radio receivers. Their television system was designed around a cathode ray tube designed by R.H. George. It was a high vacuum tube using electrostatic focus with the second anode in the form of a disc. A complete television system using a film projector with a Nipkow scanning disc and a cathode ray receiver was completed by December 1931. A radio transmitter, W9XG, had been built and was in regular operation by March 29, 1932.[79]

On September 10, 1931, Max Knoll and E. Ruska presented a mathematical explanation of the new field of electron optics. It appears that in order to compare the analogy of light with an electron beam, they had constructed tubes with mesh screens of different sizes and shapes, which influenced the action of an electron beam as it passed through the different fields. There were several diagrams showing the effects of the varying fields on the electron beam.[80]

On September 16, 1931, Dr. Frank Gray of the Bell Telephone Labs applied for a patent on a form of DC restoration. Gray planned this restoration either by scanning a black strip beside an object or by making an aperture smaller than the two apertures in the scanning disc. At the receiver, a special circuit rectified the signal, and a condenser was charged to reduce the potential applied to the grid of a valve whose plate circuit was supplied with corresponding direct current. The resistance allowed the charge on the condenser to leak away so that the condenser was recharged by the next signal produced by scanning the black strip.[81]

C.N. Kataiev applied for a Russian patent for a television camera tube on September 23, 1931. This was essentially a two-sided camera tube using a target of rivets or pins stuck through a plate. A "Fig. 2" was more interesting. It described a single-sided target in which the light from the subject passed through the signal plate (which would have to be semitransparent) and struck the photoelectric material, where it set up a charge pattern. There was a grid for collecting the charges, and the signal was developed through a resistance. The electron beam had to go through the collecting grid in order to discharge the photoelectric material.[82]

A report on progress in television in the Soviet Union in 1931 disclosed that very little creative work was being done. It revealed that most of the research was similar to the work of the Baird Company in London, with very few original ideas. Most of the schemes were rather primitive, using 30-line scanning at 12.5 frames/sec with positive synchronization. It was planned to use horizontal scanning for cinema films and vertical scanning for "live" pickups.[83]

On September 24, 1931, the Baird Television Company demonstrated its "modulated arc" projector before the British Association Meeting in the section devoted to "Mechanical Aids to Learning." It was claimed that the image was of intense brilliancy with good detail and definition, but no more was ever heard of this device.[84]

In September 1931 Capt. A.G.D. West of the Gramophone Company Research and Design Department visited the RCA Zworykin laboratory in Camden, New Jersey, and was shown the latest results of RCA Victor. Capt. West had formerly been chief research engineer of the BBC in London. He reported that "television is on the verge of being a commercial proposition. They [RCA] intend to erect a transmitter on top of a New York skyscraper and if all is well, to market their receiving apparatus in the autumn of 1932."

He indicated that the picture was some six inches square and the quality similar to that of an ordinary cinema from the back of a large theater. It was planned to sell receivers at about £100 ($470), and they were to be self-contained in a single cabinet.

As a result of his visit, the board of directors of EMI on October 28, 1931, authorized the purchase of the complete Victor transmitting equipment at a cost of £13,000 ($50,000) plus £2000 ($9,400) for installation.[85]

However, this purchase was adamantly opposed by Isaac Shoenberg, now head of the EMI Patent Department, for several reasons. First, he did not wish EMI to become dependent on RCA. Second, Marconi's Wireless Telegraph, being the recipient of the RCA patents in England (through its basic agreement), was in possession of all of the RCA television patents, which could present problems to EMI. (There were also rumors that Marconi's Wireless Telegraph was eager to join forces with Baird Television as they were both engaged in research into mechanical television.) Third, Shoenberg knew of the expertise that Marconi had in radio transmitters. Finally, being an ex–Marconi employee, he saw a chance to bring his former company into the television picture as a partner.

Enquiries to the Marconi Company disclosed that they had a transmitter available that could be suitably modified for television use. The Marconi transmitter was a 9.74 meter, low power SWB-type Tx used for experimental transmission between Rome and Sardinia. It was to be modified for 6- to 8-meter transmission. This Marconi transmitter was delivered to EMI at Hayes, Middlesex on January 25, 1932.[86]

On October 6, 1931, Manfred von Ardenne applied for a patent in which he described the use of variable velocity scanning at both the transmitter and receiver. Since the scanning ray was of constant velocity, it was necessary to use the signal coming from a photoelectric cell to modulate the sawtoothed currents used to drive the scanning circuits in the tube. Frequencies lower than the picture frequencies were cut off, and the resulting signal was sent to a special resistance-capacitance network.[87]

Von Ardenne was keenly aware of the problems of using gas-filled tubes for television, but they were excellent performers as long as the beam did not have to be rapidly modulated. The use of variable velocity scanning was one solution to the problem. One of his tubes was on display in London at the November 1931 meeting of the Television Society at University College. It appears that von Ardenne's tubes were so reliable and bright that Sir Robert A. Watson Watt was using them in his early radar research in England.[88]

The Zworykin research group at Camden was making excellent progress with its new single-sided camera tube. It appears that the project was being headed by Gregory N. Ogloblinsky. A new, larger glass envelope was designed to accommodate a bigger (4-by-4-inch) mosaic. The new tube was working; how, no one knew for sure. It had very low efficiency and produced great amounts of spurious signals. This was due to the copious amount of secondary emission caused by the impact of the high velocity electron scanning beam. But Dr. Zworykin's gamble had paid off. He had never wavered in his determination to build a practical camera tube using storage. At last, he had an answer to the Farnsworth "Image Dissector."

On October 8, 1931, Dr. Zworykin added a new claim to his still-pending December 1923 patent application. This was the claim of "a photo-electric layer over which said electron stream is deflected is adapted to pass and upon which the picture is adapted to be focused, and a circuit connecting the photo-electric layer and cathode."[89]

The design of the new single-sided camera tube was finalized and on October 23, 1931, it was named the Iconoscope. Many tubes had been built and operated, but according to Garret and Mumford, the first really successful tube was built and tested in the Zworykin laboratory on November 9, 1931. According to Harley Iams, this was probably tube number 16, which was the first Iconoscope to give a reasonably good picture.[90]

On November 13, 1931, V.K. Zworykin applied for a patent for a "Method of and Apparatus for Producing Images of Objects." This was Dr. Zworykin's first patent application showing his new camera tube in which the target was single-sided and therefore both the light from the scene and the scanning electron beam impinged on the same surface.

The patent stated that the screen structure was of the same general type and operated on the same principle as copending applications, serial no. 448,834 (May 1, 1930) and serial no. 468,610 (July 17, 1930). The patent showed a "Fig. 2" with a single-sided target. It had a thin sheet of mica deposited with a thin film of platinum on the back side. The front surface consisted of individual photo-sensitive elements made by placing a suitable mask against this side and (in vacuum) evaporating cadmium to cause the individual elements to be deposited through the openings.

As an alternative, a continuous film of cadmium might be applied to the mica sheet and scratched through by a ruling machine. Instead of cadmium, uranium, thorium, cerium or other materials sensitive to ultraviolet

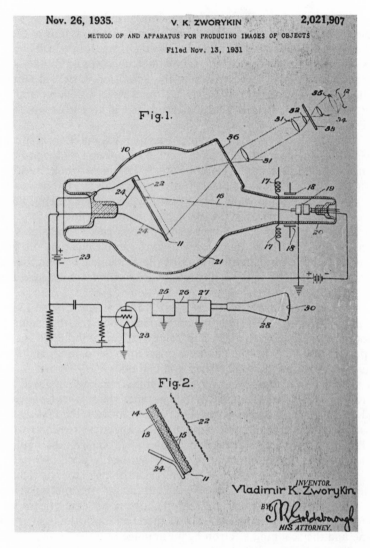

Diagram from V.K. Zworykin's Iconoscope patent (filed in 1931).

light might be used. Also alkalis such as lithium or sodium might be used, in either pure form or similar to the cesium-oxide photocell.

The positive charges cause corresponding impulses or picture signals to be developed in the grid circuit of a suitable amplifier tube for which the platinum film is connected to this circuit by way of one of the wire supports carrying the screen structure. No mention was made of the storage principle or of anything except observing a gas discharge, electric sparks, secondary emission under ultraviolet and X-ray radiation.[91]

Four of the original claims of this patent were taken out of this application and given to Kolomon Tihany. Tihany's patents were certainly ingenious and deserving of great credit. As a result, there have even been claims that Tihany "invented" the Iconoscope. However, there is no evidence that he ever built or operated a tube of this kind, and we must give Dr. Zworykin and his research team at Camden the credit they so richly deserved.[92]

Dr. Zworykin's research group designed, built, and operated the first camera tubes in the world using high velocity electron beams. Even though their first two-sided tubes were crude and had limited success, they gave the group much important data to later create more practical camera tubes.

The May 1, 1930, patent application of Zworykin (serial no. 448,834) ran into an interference (#62,721) on November 27, 1931, with Harry J. Round and Charles F. Jenkins. Round, of the British Marconi Wireless Company, had applied for a reissue of his United States patent no. 1,759,594, which had been issued May 20, 1930.

Three interferences were declared by the Patent Office between Round, Zworykin, and others. On November 9, 1933, Zworykin moved to substitute for the May 1, 1930, patent application, his earlier application, serial no. 683,337, filed December 29, 1923, in order to get an earlier priority.

Dr. Zworykin (through the RCA Patent Department) repeated this motion in each of the three interferences. The examiner of interferences denied his motion in each interference, on the grounds that the 1923 Zworykin application as filed did not disclose the inventions of the claims in issue. This motion was also denied on the grounds that Zworykin's claims in his 1923 application depended on certain amendments which had been made to the specifications but which the examiner held to be departures therefrom.

In the matter of priority, Round relied upon the filing date of his British patent, dated May 21, 1926. Zworykin stood on his 1923 filing date. The board of appeals affirmed the actions of the examiner of interferences. Round won by default and on June 28, 1935, was awarded the interferences, as confirmed by the board of appeals on February 26, 1936.[93]

In order to reinforce the claims made in the Zworykin 1923 patent application, the RCA Patent Department instructed Harley Iams to build several models of the "1923" tube according to the original specification. Late in 1931, Iams built four tubes. The first was simply the sensitizing of an aluminum oxide surface that was supported by aluminum foil on the opposite side of the aluminum oxide surface to be sensitized. The second version included the collecting grid positioned between the photosensitive surface and the source of light. These tubes used cesium as a photoelectric surface. The third tube used potassium as mentioned in the patent specification. Finally, a tube was constructed that used potassium supported by the aluminum oxide surface and was constructed exactly in accordance with the patent specifications. According to a sworn affidavit by

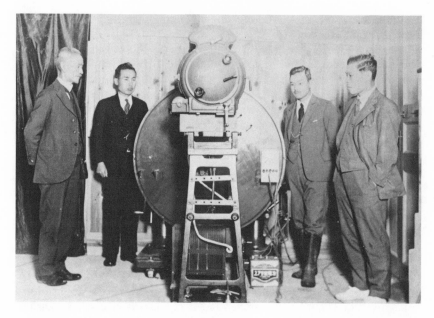

Kenjiro Takayanagi's flying spot apparatus, 1931. Takanayagi is second from left.

Harley Iams, this tube "produced an electro-optical image which was a reasonable likeness of the light image falling upon the transmitting unit."[94]

On October 21, 1931, Ulises A. Sanabria demonstrated a large screen television system at the B.S. Moss Broadway Theater. Sanabria was still using his 45-hole disc with triple interlace. He projected a picture some ten feet in size. It was claimed that pictures were "pretty good," although the illumination was not particularly bright.[95]

John L. Baird was visiting the United States in October 1931 and was reported to have visited the laboratories of Dr. Alexanderson at the General Electric Company and those of the Bell Telephone Company. However, Baird did not seem impressed with what he had seen. On October 25, 1931, he was quoted as saying that he saw "no hope for television by means of cathode ray bulbs." He also did not believe in the utilization of shortwaves and was "very skeptical about their success in television because they cover a very limited area." Baird's short-sightedness in these two areas was to cause him much grief in the future.[96]

It was reported that in Japan, professors Kenjiro Takayanagi and Tomomasa Nakashima of the Hamamatsu Technical College had been transmitting television pictures from the radio station JOAK in Tokyo since November 1, 1931. They were transmitting pictures of 10,000 elements (80 lines) at 20 frames/sec on a frequency of 84.5 meters. It was planned to demonstrate this equipment at the Fourth Exhibition of Invention in Tokyo to be held from March 20 to May 10, 1932.[97]

T. Thorne Baker applied for a patent relating to a system of color television on November 2, 1931. The color was to be separated by the use of a scanning disc made up of three different transparent sectors of colored portions. A similar disc was to be used at the receiver in order to reconstruct the picture in color.[98]

On November 5, 1931, Fernseh A.G. of Berlin applied for a patent for a method of intermediate film recording. In this system for the television transmission of a moving or continuously varying scene using an intermediate photographic record, the sensitive layer was scanned before being fixed or after a preliminary fixing process within a short time of the actual photographic exposure. When the scanning to be affected was before the film was being fixed, the sensitive coating might be blue-sensitive and a scanning beam of a different color, red for instance, might be used.[99]

Fernseh, of course, had no information as to what had been done in the Bell Telephone Labs with this process. However, Fernseh had decided that it was the only feasible method of picking up a "live" or outdoor image at the time. As costly and cumbersome as it was to be, they were now developing equipment that would substitute for the lack of a suitable television camera tube.

Robert Harding, Jr., of the National Television Corporation, applied for a patent on November 7, 1931, for a system of recording television pictures on either motion picture film or sensitized paper. The system used transverse scanning across a moving strip. The signals were recorded on the emulsion by either normal photography or by a special pen with India ink.[100]

On November 19, 1931, Electric and Musical Industries Ltd. (EMI) of Hayes, Middlesex, applied for its first television patent. It was for an improved method of forming a fluorescent screen on the large end of the cathode ray bulb. Its purpose was to form a screen without the use of binders that created problems with the high vacuum in the tube. Also they intended to provide a screen that would conduct the electrons from the screen back to the anode to prevent accumulation of electrons on the screen.

This patent, which was communicated from the RCA Victor Company of Camden, New Jersey, was of immense value to the newly formed EMI, as it made it possible for them to manufacture their own cathode ray tubes for television use. RCA, which had provided them with picture tubes, now was giving them the "know-how" as well. This was the first of many patents furnished to EMI by RCA in order to develop a practical television system.[101]

Joseph Dwyer McGee was hired by EMI on January 1, 1932. He had been a research student at the Cavendish laboratory under such men as Lord Ernest Rutherford and Sir James Chadwick. He became associated with William F. Tedham, who was hard at work on the development of the (RCA) high vacuum, electrostatically focused cathode ray tube. Tedham was also building photocells of the silver–silver oxide cesium type that had been disclosed by Dr. Koller of the General Electric Company. These cells were required by C.O. Browne, who was developing a mirror-drum film system using 120 lines. McGee found that Tedham had advanced remarkably well, "considering the resources at hand," and had the "hard" electrostatic focus tubes operating very well. Tedham's research into the cathode ray tube was assisted by Alan D. Blumlein, C.O. Browne, and M.B. Manifold, who were developing much of the needed circuitry such as amplifiers, high-voltage supplies, scanning circuits, etc. McGee found that Tedham was familiar with the literature of the entire field of television and "especially with the proposals of Campbell Swinton."[102]

It was apparent that W.F. Tedham was not only receiving all of the RCA patent applications, but was also in touch with Sanford Essig, the RCA chemist, or at least they knew of each other's work. According to Keith Geddes, "EMI had access to the work that was being carried out in the RCA Laboratories on a revolutionary new tube, the 'Iconoscope.'" While this has often been denied, it is true that Tedham knew of Dr. Zworykin's work, although it is possible that he may not have known of all of the fine details.[103]

In January 1932 Baird Television Ltd. was sold to Isadore Ostrer, President of Gaumont-British Films. Isadore and his brother Murray had bought out the stock of Sydney Moseley when Baird Television Ltd. had gone into voluntary liquidation. This purchase saved Baird Television from complete financial collapse. Moseley was soon to become a director of the new company.[104]

On January 6, 1932, Randall C. Ballard of the Radio Corporation applied for a patent for an all-electric synchronization generator. Basically this patent was for a method for maintaining a fixed relationship between the horizontal and vertical deflection frequencies. Using 180-line pictures required a horizontal scanning frequency of about 4320 cycles, which was divided down to 720 cycles, then down to 120 cycles and finally to 24 cycles. This division required the use of so-called "blocking oscillators," which developed impulses at a definite submultiple of those developed by the preceeding blocking oscillators.

This patent was the second to show the new single-sided configuration of the Iconoscope with a grid in front of the target. The use of 24 cycles was to conform with the speed of sound film. Because of its lack of sensitivity it was expected that the first use of the Iconoscope would be to transmit motion picture film. The camera tube was described as the same general type as Zworykin's serial no. 48,610 (July 17, 1930) and serial no. 574,772 (Nov. 13, 1931), even though the former was a two-sided target and the latter was single-sided. This new synchronizing generator was being developed at Camden. The Empire State television transmitter was still using a version of Arthur Vance's mechanical sync generator for its experimental transmissions.[105]

On February 24, 1932, Sanford Essig of the Radio Corporation applied for a patent for a new method of making a mosaic for an Iconoscope. Specifically this was a patent for making an insulated supporting plate to which were applied or which carried individual, minute, photosensitive, electrically conductive elements insulated from each other and spaced uniformly apart.

According to the patent application, a fine layer of silver was applied to a thin sheet of mica and then baked for about 15 seconds at 800 degrees. This caused silver to separate into minute, individual globules. Then the silver surface was oxidized and photosensitized by means of a cesium pellet which covered the silver-oxide surface. Methods were mentioned to remove any surplus cesium that may have accumulated between the individual silver globules.

In operation, the object to be transmitted was projected onto the photosensitive surface of the mosaic structure. Electric emission then took place from the individual elements in varying degrees proportional to the amount of light striking the elements.[106]

This patent was followed by Sanford Essig's application for another patent, which was filed on July 30, 1932. This was for a method of oxidizing the electrode structure by applying a high frequency field externally and independently of the structure and of varying the intensity of the field with respect to the different parts of the structure. The field might be produced by an electrode on an insulating handle connected to a source of high frequency voltage oscillations. The field ionized the oxygen, and the electrode was moved about until even oxidation of the screen produced an even color change thereon. The oxygen was finally evacuated and the screen was photosensitized with cesium.[107]

Another important patent was applied for by RCA at this time. This application was for improvements in the Farnsworth transmitting tube by V.K. Zworykin and G.N. Ogloblinsky on March 10, 1932. This patent related to the application of a variable focus of the individual rays to a point substantially at the opening of the anode aperture. This was to be done by superimposing a corrective wave form on the electromagnetic focusing field. Thus the ray would always be in focus at the scanning aperture. This patent application indicated how important the dissector camera tube was to RCA Victor at the time. It became the subject of two patent interferences, #69,636 and #73,812, which were both won by Philo Farnsworth on April 26, 1938.[108]

There would be another major attempt by the RCA Patent Department to gain control of the dissector. On May 28, 1932, a patent interference (#64,027) was declared between Zworykin's still-pending December 29, 1923, patent application (serial no. 683,337) and that of Farnsworth's USA patent no. 1,773,980 (filed 7 January 1927) issued August 16, 1930. There was only one claim in issue: the forming and function of an "electrical image." RCA tried to prove that the transmitting apparatus of Zworykin formed and used an "electric image" in a manner similar to the dissector. The attorneys for Farnsworth proved that only a tube of the dissector type could produce an "electrical image" that was scanned to produce the television signals. The interference proved that the two types of transmitter tubes operated differently and that RCA had no right to make such a claim. This was a great victory for Farnsworth and gave him complete control of the dissector. However, it also gave RCA added impetus to improve the Iconoscope and eliminate its many deficiencies.[109]

The RCA television system had now progressed to the point where a demonstration was in order. As the Iconoscope was not yet quite ready, mechanical scanning was used at the transmitting end. However, the Kinescope was capable of displaying fairly good pictures. So on May 17, 1932, RCA demonstrated its system to a group of its licensees and manufacturers' representatives. The press was excluded.

The meeting was held at 153 East Twenty-Fourth Street and was addressed by David Sarnoff from the Empire State Building transmitter. This transmitter had been operating since March 1932 with video being sent on W2XF at 41 megacycles (6.28 meters) and the sound on W2XK at 61 megacyles (4.9 meters). The picture transmission was 120 lines at 24 frames/sec. There were both "live" and film pickups, the "live" pickup by means of a flying spot scanner, and the 35mm motion picture film by means of the unidirectional film scanner, both using a mechanical sync generator.

The picture was received on cathode ray receivers with a picture about five inches square and was claimed to be "fairly clear." It was reported that viewers were "surprised at the clarity of the film transmission." The "live" images were inferior to the film. RCA stated that the system was not quite ready to leave the laboratories and that much work remained to be done. This demonstration was the first to show the new Zworykin Kinescope and, for reasons which are not clear, was not shown to either the press or the public.[110]

However, by this time it was clear that Sarnoff's dream of having an operating television system on the air by the Autumn of 1932 was dead, for this was to be the last demonstration of the RCA television system until April 24, 1936.

The introduction of television in 1932, as the United States was at the bottom of the Great Depression, could only have hurt the radio industry, which had weathered the depression with a minimum of financial damage. At any rate, from this point on, RCA was to slow down the field tests from the Empire State Building and send television back to the laboratories in Camden for several more years.

On May 21, 1932, Don Lee Television in Los Angeles, California, gave a demonstration of a self-synchronized receiver. Don Lee Television had been formed when Harry Lubcke had left the Farnsworth Laboratories on June 30, 1930, and had interested Thomas A. Lee (son of Don Lee) in building a television station in Los Angeles.

Research had begun in November 1930, and by May 10, 1931, an image from motion picture film had been transmitted across the room in the laboratory. On September 11, 1931, a construction permit had been granted for station W6XAO, and by December 1931 the station was on the air on 44.5 megacycles. By May 1932, a self-synchronized cathode ray receiver of Harry Lubcke's design was completed, and it was decided to test its self-synchronizing abilities in an airplane. It seems that the parts for the receiver came from Gilfillan Brothers, Inc., in Los Angeles, who were radio manufacturers. Lubcke states that he built his own picture tubes as well as purchasing tubes from von Ardenne and RCA.[111]

All television transmission was from motion picture film, there being no "live" pickup. Three types of film scanners were experimented with: sine-wave scanning with an oscillating mirror (similar to the first Zworykin/Westinghouse system), a "flying spot" scanner (using a cathode ray tube), and finally a simple Nipkow disc scanner.

On May 21, 1932, a television receiver with the proper power supplies was taken aboard a tri-engine Fokker of Western Air Express with seven passengers. Four flights of about ten minutes' duration were undertaken. It was claimed that the image of a motion picture star (Loretta Young) on film could be seen clearly. The Don Lee transmitter was operating on a frequency of 44.5 megacycles with 150 watts of power and transmitted an 80-line picture at 15 frames/sec. A field strength contour map of the area was made. No sound was transmitted. This appears to be the first report of television reception by a cathode ray receiver in an airplane.[112]

In May 1932 Manfred von Ardenne revealed details of the variable scanning velocity system of R. Thun that he had been experimenting with. It was claimed that von Ardenne had overcome the various difficulties so successfully that he could already transmit and receive 10,000-element pictures by this sytem. In this system, the scanning speed of the transmitter was changed by the output of the photocells (i.e., it sped up when brighter and slowed down when darker) and was employed to modulate the discharge voltage of the line-time base.

One of the peculiarities of this system was that the picture being transmitted appeared on the end of the transmitting cathode ray tube. Otherwise, it used the same elements, projector, and cathode ray tubes as the system displayed in August 1931 at the Berlin Radio Exhibition.[113]

At this time in the United States, much progress was being made on the Zworykin high vacuum Kinescope. In May 1932 G.F. Metcalf of General Electric described a new cathode ray oscillograph tube. It was a high vacuum tube employing electrostatic focus with a hot cathode. It had a grid to be used to cut off the beam for photographic work, to aid in focusing and to protect the cathode from high fields. Focusing was done by adjusting the potential on the cylinder. It had internal deflection plates although it was claimed that magnetic coils could be used externally. It had response as high as 500,000 cycles and had a life expectancy of approximately 1000 hours. Metcalf had been working on tubes of this kind since late in 1929, when he sent one of his first "television" tubes to Ray Kell for experimentation. Metcalf was careful to give credit for the electrostatic focusing method to both V.K. Zworykin and R.H. George.[114]

Another important article was published in May 1932 by Allen B. Dumont of Upper Montclair, N.J. DuMont had left De Forest Radio Company, where he had been vice president and chief engineer, and was experimenting with the manufacture of cathode ray tubes. He reported that a high vacuum tube with dual accelerating electrodes with an additional anode of silver coated on the funnel-shaped portion of the bulb would give a spot that would remain of constant diameter as the modulating electrode voltage was varied.

This tube was operated with a small negative bias, and drew no current in the modulating circuit. A signal of several volts would modulate the spot from minimum to maximum brightness, and the variable control constant of the tube would cause greater changes in the light intensity at the high intensities for a given change in modulating electrode voltage.

DuMont mentioned the greatest difference between tubes made for television reception and those made for oscillograph work was the ability to vary the intensity of the spot without changing its diameter. This was no problem with oscilloscope tubes, for once the brightness was set, it could be left that way until the test was completed. But television presented a unique problem in that the proper modulation of the beam at high brightness was the most important feature of the tube. This was never successfully accomplished with gas-filled tubes.[115]

On June 1, 1932, Baird Television had taken their caravan to Epsom Downs, where it was stationed outside the Grand Stand and next to the winning post. Inside, a huge mirror drum with 30 mirrors was placed so that it could see the finish line. There were three sets of photocells and amplifiers so that three sets of signals were transmitted. One set, the center one, was sent to the BBC, where it was transmitted on a wave-length of 261 meters for home consumption. The three feeds from Epsom Downs were sent separately to the Metropole Theater, where the three-zone, special arc projectors were fed the three signals, which were combined at a mirror drum synchronized with the transmitter to be projected onto a large screen some 10 feet wide and 8 feet high.[116]

Kenjiro Takayanagi applied for a Japanese patent on June 13, 1932, for an "electron beam scanning device." The patent showed three forms of camera tubes. The first was simply a circular photoelectric plate with a collecting screen, which was scanned from the rear of the tube. The second disclosed a single row of photoelectric cells, also scanned from the rear. And the third appeared to have a full screen plate. In each of these tubes the photoelectric cell was connected to a condenser.[117]

On July 7, 1932, John C. Wilson of Baird Television, London, applied for a patent for a television transmitting device. It comprised a rotary scanning device (mirror drum) mounted on a rigid structure. It was the device used by Baird Television at Broadcast House for telecasts by the BBC.

V.K. Zworykin seen on the television screen, 1932.

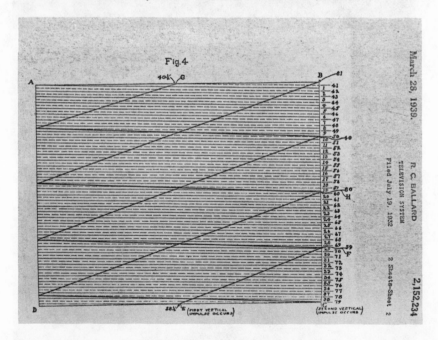

Diagram from Randall C. Ballard's intermeshed (interlaced) scanning patent (filed in 1932).

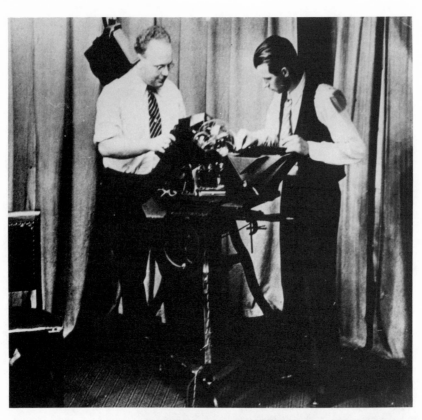

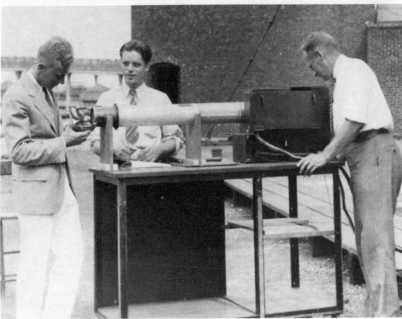

The Wilson device acted in the manner of an optical camera in that the operator could move the device in a vertical direction and/or swivel it horizontally. It was to be used with either the floodlight or spotlight ("flying spot") methods of television.

On July 19, 1932, Randall C. Ballard of the Radio Corporation applied for a television system using what was called intermeshed (now called interlaced) scanning. This system was to do two important things; first, it would eliminate or minimize picture flicker, and second, it would allow an increased number of scanning lines without increasing the width of the frequency channel.

By this time Dr. Zworykin's Kinescope was capable of high brightness. Even though the latest Iconoscopes were finally able to be taken out of doors and produce "direct vision" they were still transmitting slides and film with the Nipkow disc. It was imperative to run motion picture film at the normal sound speed of 24 frames/sec in order to be able to use it for broadcasting.

In motion picture techniques, it is possible to eliminate flicker by means of a multi-bladed shutter, which gives an effective frame rate as high as 72 frames/sec. But this was not possible in a television system. The idea of interlacing a picture, say for stereoscopic or color television, using mechanical discs was also quite old by this time. Both Schröter (of Telefunken) and von Ardenne had previously applied for patents for interlaced scanning using cathode ray tubes. But Ballard's was the first patent that introduced a practical method for interlacing using an odd-line scanning sequence and the means to accomplish it.

Ballard described a method of using a Nipkow disc to scan motion picture film with an odd number of holes (in this case, 81). Choosing an odd number of lines gave two sets of frames, which coincided or meshed with each other. As the beam swept line 38.5, an impulse caused the vertical sweep generator to move the beam back to the top of the frame. It would arrive there in the middle of line 40, causing the next line to be intermeshed between line 1 and line 2. This would continue until line 79, at which point another impulse would cause the beam again to go to the top of the frame, this time to the start of line 1. Then the process repeated itself.

The Ballard intermesh patent became basic to both the RCA Victor and EMI patent structure. However, as ingenious as this patent was, several problems soon appeared. One was that even 48 frames/sec was not high enough to eliminate flicker; also, the 60-cycle power standard in the United States caused ripple effects in the picture. Finally, a new

Opposite, top: Merrill Trainer, left, and Ray Kell of RCA installing an Iconoscope tube in a television camera at Camden, 1932. Bottom: Gregory Ogloblinsky, left, Richard Campbell, center, and V.K. Zworykin taking pictures of the total eclipse of the sun, August 31, 1932. This was a demonstration of how the Iconoscope could produce "direct vision" in outdoor transmissions.

phenomenon, "interline" flicker, appeared, caused by neighboring lines differing in time relationship by one half of a frame period. This phenomenon was due to the limited number of lines in use at the time. One result was that the number of lines was raised from 120 to 180 late in 1932.[119]

It appears that EMI also tried intermeshed scanning late in 1932. All of EMI's experiments with intermeshed scan were made on a special adjustable mirror drum. However, EMI was still using vertical scanning throughout 1932, and the experiments failed. The picture proved to be nothing more than "a number of lines moving across the screen, in the direction at right angles to the scanning lines." It is interesting to note that while both RCA and EMI used the same number of lines, their research was being done independently. The two different approaches — with EMI using vertical scanning and RCA using horizontal scanning — constitute a good example.[120]

Fernseh A.G. was not privy to the RCA patent information. There is no evidence that they were even trying to devise a "live" camera at this time. They had turned to the use of motion picture film to solve their problems of the "live" or outdoor pickup for television. They had come to the same conclusion that Dr. Ives of the Bell Telephone Labs had come to in 1925 — since the television scanning of film was an accomplished fact, why not use motion picture film as the prime source of television signals?

Fernseh had designed and built such a system. It was first described in July 1932 and shown at the Berlin Radio Exhibition in August 1932. The system had a film camera, which had a film magazine. After exposure, the film was led through a light-tight tunnel to a light-tight cabinet containing the photographic solutions, where it was developed and fixed as a negative. It then passed to the television scanning apparatus, where a photocell behind a scanning disc converted the light from the film into electrical impulses, which went to an amplifier and to the transmitter. It was claimed that the whole photographic process was reduced to some 10 seconds. The equipment used a 90-hole Nipkow disc revolving at 1500 rpm.

The projector was of the continuous drive type (not intermittent) for two reasons: first, to avoid subjecting the still-moist film to violent stresses; and second, to avoid the splattering of the thin layer of water that covered the film. The sound track was recorded in the usual manner on the side of the film so that the 10-15 second delay was of no consequence. It was planned to make the apparatus portable so that it could be put into a truck.[121]

CBS, which had been telecasting for two hours a day except for Saturday and Sunday, announced in July 1932 that they were able to transmit both picture and sound on a single channel. William B. Lodge, chief engineer for CBS, stated that the process involved double modulation. A carrier beam of 45 kc was modulated by the sound, while the picture consisted of frequencies up to 40 kc. A filter was required at the receiver to keep the 45 kc signal out of the picture. The overall bandwidth was 2.750

mc to 2.851 mc. The transmitter of 500 watts used the 60-line, 20-frame standard. The fundamental carrier was 2800 kc.[122]

On August 5, 1932, V.K. Zworykin of the Radio Corporation applied for a patent for an electrical method of stereoscopic television. The transmitter consisted of two cathode ray tubes, to be used to scan the scene alternately. At the receiver, both sets of lines were reproduced on the same screen and viewed through a grating.

A different scheme was to use either a Nipkow disc with mirrors to alternately scan the two images, or one camera tube divided into two sections separated with a nonsensitive strip to permit the interpolation of a synchronization signal.[123]

Marconi's Wireless Telegraph Company announced a new system for the commercial transmission of news by television on August 5, 1932. Essentially it consisted of a unique tape on which characters were printed by a special typewriter. Light from a 1000-watt source passed through a lens system, onto a reflecting mirror through a system of lenses mounted in a spiral on the drum. There were 15 lenses on the drum, and the repetition rate was some 20 pictures/sec.

The apparatus consisted of a photocell and amplifier, a synchronous motor controlled by a tuning fork that turned the lens drum, and finally a special synchronizing circuit to send out a signal for the purpose of keeping the receiver scanning motor in step. It was being readied for a demonstration in September 1932.[124]

About this time in 1932, an excellent survey of the state of the art of television was published. This was the *Handbuch der Bildtelegraphie und des Fernsehens* edited by Fritz Schröter. It included all of the existing mechanical systems. However, the section by F. Schröter and F. Banneitz was quite critical of the efforts of Schoults, Seguin, Zworykin, Sabbah, von Codelli, and Tihany in their expositions of electrical scanning methods.

Since Fritz Schröter was director of research for Telefunken GmbH at the time, and it is known that Telefunken was receiving the RCA patent applications and licensee bulletins along with Marconi and EMI, it is presumed that he was also being kept informed about the Zworykin camera tube project.

His pessimism was obvious when F. Schröter set out to prove these electrical scanning proposals were "not free from electrical and quantum-theoretical objections." Schröter stated:

> The common thought to all these proposals was to project the image as a whole onto the photoelectric screen and there to convert it into a uniform distribution of electrical quantities such as conductivity or charge potential. These variations in conductivity or potential are sampled point by point by the scanning electron beam and converted into internal resistance fluctuations which are used after amplification to modulate a carrier frequency.

Schröter continued:

None of the above described cathode ray scanning devices had the chance of being realized in the foreseeable future because the vacuum technology difficulties are very great and the tools for their being overcome have not yet been developed. Neither the potassium or selenium rasters can be produced with the high amount of individual cells with homogenious [sic] inherant [sic] sensitivity. Nor can they be produced because of the technical complications or lack of physical research on the basic premise. We can however, justify or occupy ourselves with these proposals by considering a possibility of extreme importance those devices which permit accumulation of charge by photo-effect by the use of individual cells, might be the only solution for the future for transmission of normal brightness with a fine raster.

Schröter mentioned the "opposing systems" of Max Dieckmann, C.E.C. Roberts and Philo Farnsworth in which the systems would need amplification by secondary emission because of their low outputs.[125]

Schröter's pessimism at this time is not hard to understand. Publicly, the record showed that only Philo Farnsworth had even attempted to build and operate an electric camera tube. If Schröter was being informed of Dr. Zworykin's progress, then it can only be assumed that he just did not believe the reports. However, the Farnsworth device had been in operation for over four years, its method of operation public knowledge, and photographs had been shown of its results. Perhaps it is possible that Schröter could not believe that Farnsworth had succeeded where Dieckmann had failed!

Even though Schröter, of the Telefunken Company, described the futility of ever producing a practical camera tube, the attitude at EMI was exactly the opposite. W.F. Tedham and J.D. McGee, knowing of the work being done at Camden, were anxious to try out the new scheme for a single-sided camera tube.

As a result, two things happened. First was the filing of a patent application on August 25, 1932, by W.F. Tedham and J.D. McGee of EMI. This was for "improvements in or relating to Cathode Ray tubes and the like." According to the specification, it stated that "television systems are already known in which at the transmitting station, scanning is affected with the aid of a cathode ray tube. In such systems, an image of the object to be transmitted is optically projected upon a photo-electrically active anode of a cathode-ray tube, the anode being scanned by the cathode beam. The anode may consist of a glass sheet coated on one side with a uniformly conductive material and on the other side with a 'mosaic' of small, insulated, elemental areas of oxidized silver having a coating of photo-electric material such as caesium."

Essentially, this patent was for a method of depositing a substance through a wire mesh in order to obtain a great number of insulated photoelectric elements. A unique feature of this patent was a photoelectric ring around the mosaic and formed the same way, but so connected that it could be used for testing the sensitivity of the tube.[126]

Second was the decision to build such a tube to test the theory. It appears that EMI's agreement with RCA forbade it from engaging in the field of communications. EMI was using a mirror-drum film scanner as a source of picture signals, and presumably all work on an electric camera tube was to be done in Camden. Therefore, a tube was built by Tedham and McGee rather surreptitiously, that is, without official sanction.

A special glass envelope was blown to enclose the many elements. An aluminum disc target and a special mesh screen were inserted into the tube. The screen had a mesh of 50 meshes/inch to form the target. After completion of the silver evaporation on the target, the stencil mesh was removed and an electron gun used for electrostatic focus (similar to those used in Tedham's picture tubes) was inserted into the neck of the tube. After proper treating of the glass and metal parts, cesium vapor was admitted into the tube while it was being baked at 180°C. The tube was then pumped and sealed off.

Then Tedham and McGee borrowed a signal amplifier from C.O. Browne and drove the scanning coils on the neck of the tube in parallel with those of a picture tube from the same scanning generator. After a few minor adjustments a picture appeared, "as if by magic." The definition was as good as one could expect from such a coarse mosaic. There was little image lag and it seemed reasonably sensitive. Dr. McGee states they were so overtaken by this event that they neither took photographs of the apparatus nor of the transmitted picture.

Soon the picture began to fade, as the gas from the electron gun anode was too much for the photocathode. Nothing more was done except the tube was put away and somehow survived. According to McGee, no more tubes were built until September 1933, and to this day he categorically denies any knowledge of the Zworykin/RCA project.[127]

Isaac Shoenberg had become director of research on August 22, 1932, and since what they had done was against company policy, Tedham and McGee did not tell him of their experiment. G.E. Condliff headed the Advanced Development Division, with A.W. Whitaker in charge of Advanced Research Development and Design Division. Capt. A.G.D. West had left EMI to join Ealing Studios as the chief sound engineer.[128]

RCA was keeping their research at Camden quite a secret. However, there were many rumors as to what was going on in Camden. On August 26, 1932, W.E.W. Mitchell, secretary of the Television Society, wrote Dr. Zworykin in Camden asking for a paper covering the results of his laboratory research. Zworykin replied on September 20, 1932, stating, "Our Company still does not consider it advisable to release for publication the results of laboratory research before this development has reached the commercial stage. The business depression is largely responsible for the delay in commercialization."[129]

This letter seemed to be the reason for an article in the *Journal of the*

Television Society by A. Dinsdale in which he stated that for "some years past, television engineers from the G.E.C., Westinghouse Company and RCA have been concentrating at the RCA Victor plant in Camden, N.J. where they have been reputedly busily engaged in secret on a cathode-ray system of television. No information on this work has been officially released, unless, unknown to me at the time of preparing this paper, Dr. Zworykin who is in charge of this work had forwarded a paper to the Society, as I know he had been asked to do."[130]

Dinsdale never revealed where he got his information. But it is known that at least three men in Great Britain were aware of Dr. Zworykin's work: A.W. Whitaker, W.D. Wright and Capt. A.D.G. West had seen it personally. Others such as Tedham, Shoenberg and personnel in the Patent departments at both EMI and Marconi as well as HMV were also getting all of the RCA television patent applications.

In spite of all these rumors, the "secrets of Camden" were well kept. There had been an article that commented that both RCA Victor and the Philco Corporation were said to be working on home televisors of the cathode ray type. However, the writer was very pessimistic over the future of cathode ray television. It seems that he had never seen a demonstration and based his observations on past reports.[131]

The Berlin Radio Exhibition was held in August 1932. The "intermediate film" system of Fernseh was on display. Also, Fernseh exhibited a 90-line spot-light scanner and a Fernseh 90-line mirror screw receiver. Telefunken showed both a mechanical and a 90-line cathode ray receiver. Tekade displayed a 90-line mirror screw receiver in three different sizes.

Loewe Radio was showing its latest cathode ray receiver designed by Kurt Schlesinger, who had formerly worked for Manfred von Ardenne. It had a tube showing pictures some 9 by 12 centimeters. Loewe also displayed a large cathode ray tube with an image size of 18 by 24 centimeters, which was not working.[132]

On September 1, 1932, Marconi's Wireless Telegraph Company gave a demonstration of its television news system. The signals were sent some 180 miles, from the Marconi plant in Chelmsford to St. Peters School, York. The messages appeared on a ground glass screen at 60 words per minute. The television news receiver consisted of a ground glass screen some 25 inches by 3 inches with a sodium tube of the dumbbell type mounted close to an aperture. The modulated light was projected onto the screen by means of a mirror wheel, which was driven by the synchronous motor at 1200 rpm and gave horizontal scanning. The picture was transmitted on 1000 meters.

For the first time a 50-line Marconi television transmitter of the flying spot type was described. A 50-line, 15 frames/sec receiver projected pictures of some 8 inches by 8 inches onto a ground glass screen. A sodium tube was used, the light being projected onto the screen by means of a mirror wheel driven at 900 rpm with 15 frames/sec. Synchronization was effected by the same amplifier as was used for the news machine. In addition, there was a 50-line "projection receiver" using an arc lamp modulated by a Kerr cell and projected onto the screen by a mirror wheel, similar to the other two machines.[133]

Later in September, Marconi's Wireless Telegraph Company revealed that it would develop television apparatus suitable for entertainment purposes. Thus Shoenberg of EMI had been correct in enlisting the aid of the Marconi Company, for it was not about to sit idle and do nothing to develop a television system.[134]

On September 30, 1932, the Bell Telephone Labs reported that they had received a new cathode ray tube: type FT-53, from the General Electric Company, at a cost of $210. It had been ordered sometime in June to give them an idea of outside progress on such tubes. The tube was tested and found to give a good spot of illumination but soon became defective.[135]

On October 4, 1932, an article by M. Knoll and E. Ruska described a magnetic electron microscope with a cold cathode. Several microphotographs were shown, and suitable systems for picture-taking with the "ionic microscope" were shown.[136]

W.D. Wright of EMI applied for a patent on October 12, 1932, for overcoming the keystone distortion of a cathode ray tube. Wright planned to project the image upon the side of the anode facing the cathode ray by means of a simple optical system that would be tilted in such a manner as to produce an image larger at the top than the bottom, thus correcting the keystone distortion. Similar patents were applied for by Arthur Vance, Richard Campbell and Alva Bedford of RCA at this time, although their solutions to the problem differed.[137]

On November 15, 1932, Fernseh A.G. of Berlin applied for a patent for an improvement in intermediate film transmission. In this case, the system used an endless band of film in which a light-sensitive layer was continuously applied to the film, exposed in the camera, developed, eventually removed by a brush or similar device and then reprocessed.[138]

EMI by this time was ready to demonstrate its new film transmitter and cathode ray receiver. On November 29, 1932, it approached the BBC to ask representatives to witness a demonstration of "high-definition" television. This was done on December 6, 1932, with a "200"-line picture. (It actually was 130 lines, although the EMI standard at the time was 180 lines.)

This demonstration was publicized in a magazine and infuriated the Baird Company in regard to the RCA/EMI links. Isaac Shoenberg was also offended and ordered all further publicity halted. However, EMI was invited to move its equipment to Broadcast House (the headquarters of the BBC in London) and planned to do so early in 1933. This was the beginning of a long, bitter battle between Baird and EMI that was not resolved until 1937.[139]

On November 31, 1932, RCA announced that it had agreed to a consent decree in the antitrust suit that the Department of Justice had filed against it and the other big electrical companies in May 1930. It was a victory for RCA as it kept everything it had gained through unification while winning complete freedom from the other corporations, General Electric and Westinghouse. However, General Electric's influence was still strong as most of the executives and managers had come from GE. It was claimed that as the Empire State television project was being shut down that Elmer W. Engstrom was moved to Camden, where he was to take charge of the Zworykin television research project.[140]

It was later claimed that the Philco television station, W3XE, started transmitting 240-line pictures by "an electronic method" sometime in 1932. This was done in collaboration with Philo T. Farnsworth.[141] Very little has ever been disclosed about the activities of Farnsworth while he was with Philco. However, it is known that neither Philco nor Farnsworth was happy with the arrangement and it was about to be terminated.

Chapter 9

The Iconoscope: 1933–1935

During the early part of 1933, RCA built and operated a complete television system at Camden, N.J. The system used the new camera tube of Zworykin as a pickup device. Scanning was 240 lines sequential at 24 frames/sec. The picture and sound were sent out by two transmitters, on 49 mc for the picture and 50 mc for the sound. A mechanical synchronizing generator was used during this period; otherwise the system was all-electric.

Experiments were carried out using a remote camera about one mile from the studio, relayed to the transmitter by radio. The tests were made under conditions likely to occur in a regular television service. The greatest praise went to the new camera tube of Zworykin, for it permitted transmission of greater detail, wider areas of coverage in the studio and of course, outdoor pickup or "direct vision." It was claimed that the tube had removed the last major technical obstacle to television broadcasting.[1]

There were many important patents applied for in January 1933 by the RCA engineering staff at Camden. Among the applicants: Gregory N. Ogloblinsky, for means for maintaining the picture signal level; Ray D. Kell, for a method of film projection in which scanning is effected during nine-tenths of the cycle of operations, with one-tenth of the cycle for projection of the image onto the mosaic; Alva V. Bedford, for projecting film where certain film frames may be scanned a certain number of times and other film frames a smaller number of times to develop picture signals; and Richard L. Campbell, for a synchronizing generator with return blanking and other features.[2]

Dr. V.K. Zworykin was quite busy at this time. In February 1933 he delivered a paper, "On Electron Optics," before the Optical Society of America. In it he discussed the concentration of an electron beam by the use of ionized gas in low vacuum, and magnetic focusing and electrostatic focusing in high vacuum. He described the use of wire mesh electrodes or the use of concentric cylinders or coaxial diaphragms. He also mentioned the use of the "electron microscope" described by Bruche and Johanson.[3]

On March 5, 1933, it was reported that Dr. Zworykin had developed an "electro-magnetic lens" that would cause the electron beam rays to converge to a point of intense brilliancy. This lens was based on the use of a thin coil of wire using magnetic rather than electrostatic focus, which gave sharper pictures and was eventually to supplant Zworykin's earlier method.[4]

CBS Television had gone off the air in March 1933 after deciding to wait for better transmitting apparatus. Also NBC had discontinued its regular television transmissions from the Empire State Building and was now conducting tests in secret. The only stations in the United States to remain on the air with some regularity were Don Lee's in Los Angeles and that of Purdue University, which continued to transmit programs although on a limited basis.[5]

Harley Ambrose Iams of the Radio Corporation applied for a patent on March 30, 1933, for a method and apparatus for television. The patent was for a special form of Iconoscope in which the call-letters or other information may be either scratched on the screen, or by the use of a mask, or by having the target have different electrical characteristics. This was the first camera tube to impart information irrespective of conditions of illumination of the entire screen. It was called the Monoscope.

On that same day, Harley Iams also applied for a patent for producing a mosaic screen by the use of a ruling machine or other method for ruling the mosaic as to create parallel rows of spaced, conductive parallelograms.[6]

Philo Farnsworth applied for a patent for a scanning oscillator on April 3, 1933. It was for a linear time-base generator using an iron-cored choke in the circuit. This patent presented many advantages.[7]

On April 8, 1933, V.K. Zworykin applied for a patent for a secret method of television whereby the audio was sent in the picture portion of the signal. On April 19, 1933, the U.S. Patent Office examiner of interferences made several important decisions in Dr. Zworykin's favor.[8]

Early in 1933, EMI proposed to the British Post Office that EMI go ahead with a television service, but the company would not cooperate with Baird Television. EMI suggested that with some minor changes in the BBC's ultra-shortwave transmitters and with equipment supplied from HMV (a part of the EMI complex), it could go ahead and produce receiving sets by the autumn of 1933.

The British Post Office sent engineers to EMI at Hayes in February 1933. The engineers reported that the picture was good and the film was easy to follow. But the Post Office decided not to let EMI transmit from Broadcast House until further demonstrations of the Baird system had taken place.

The Baird Company was quite upset over the progress that EMI had made and stated that the progress violated the agreement between Baird and the BBC. It immediately brought up the argument that "dealing with EMI...would be dealing a heavy blow at British industry and directly assisting an American concern." This became the battle cry of Baird Television for the next three years.

The British Post Office suggested that both Baird and EMI give demonstrations of shortwave television. This took place on April 18, 1933, from Long Acre (Baird) and April 19, 1933, from Hayes (EMI). Again it was agreed that the EMI transmissions and equipment were far superior to those of Baird. However, the Post Office still refused to let EMI use Broadcast House as it might prejudice Baird's case. The result of these demonstrations was a major change in policy of Baird Television in regard to cathode ray television.[9]

The Fourth Exhibition of the Television Society was held April 5 and 6, 1933, at the Imperial College of Science, London. Among the exhibits was a demonstration of the 30-line Baird system onto a large screen 3 feet high by 1 foot, 3 inches wide. The picture was transmitted from Broadcast House on 7.75 meters (38 mc) while the sound came over a land line. The receiver used a Kerr cell with a 30-segment mirror drum; the 30-line definition was only good for closeups. Marconi's Wireless Company showed its new "News" system whereby printed letters were projected onto a screen. This "news" was sent between rooms. Marconi also demonstrated a 50-line picture projected on an 8 inch screen at 20 frames/sec. It used horizontal scanning and the picture quality was considered to be good.[10]

During this period, the engineers at EMI were applying for many patents of importance. On April 13, 1933, P. Willans applied for a patent for the reinsertion of the DC component. On May 5, 1933, J.D. McGee applied for a patent for a two-sided camera tube with the use of short aluminum wires with a thin insulating coating of aluminum oxide covered by a conducting film of silver. An earthed grid collected the emission from the screen and a collector behind the screen collected the secondary emission and was applied to an amplifier. Two more important patent applications were filed by Alan Blumlein on June 16, 1933, for impedence networks for low frequency compensation. C.O. Browne, A.D. Blumlein and J. Hardwick on July 11, 1933, applied for an improved form of DC restoration.[11]

The directors of Baird Television had decided that it was time to start a research program into cathode ray television. The first step was the hiring of Capt. A.G.D. West as the technical director of Baird Television in May 1933. Capt. West, of course, had full knowledge of the entire EMI research program, including the development of the Kinescope and early work on the Zworykin camera tube. By July 1933, Capt. West wrote Noel Ashbridge, chief engineer of the BBC, that Baird Television was actively pursuing experiments on a 120-line cathode ray system.[12]

Also at this time in 1933, the Philco Corporation decided to sever its relationship with Philo Farnsworth. It had become apparent that Philo's aim at establishing a broad patent structure through research was not identical with the production program of Philco.

The Philco Corporation, as a licensee of RCA, knew of the television research being done in Camden. So in May 1933, the Philco Corporation hired Albert F. Murray, who had been director of the Advanced Develop-

Capt. A.G.D. West, hired as technical director of Baird Television in May 1933, brought to his new position his complete knowledge of the EMI research program.

ment Division at RCA Victor. As such he had full knowledge of all of the work being done by the Zworykin research group, including camera and receiving tubes and their associated circuitry. Albert Murray became engineer in charge of the Philco Television Research Department and brought with him a half-dozen key RCA people from Camden.[13]

Philo Farnsworth filed for a very important patent application on April 26, 1933, while still with the Philco Corporation. It was for an "Image Dissector," which was a very misleading title. For it was not an Image Dissector at all (i.e., it was not a cold cathode tube in which the entire electron image passed in front of a scanning aperture to create the picture signal), but a very advanced storage-type camera tube that used a low velocity electron scanning beam from a hot cathode. This was the very first patent to describe this highly important feature.

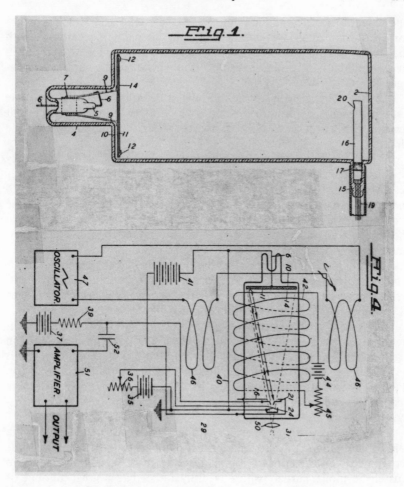

Diagrams from patent for Philo Farnsworth's low-velocity scanning camera tube (filed in 1933). This was the first patent to feature a tube using a low-velocity scanning beam.

It employed a cathode ray beam that explored a photosensitive screen or target made up of a large number of insulated areas or "islands" of photoelectrically active material. The screen was so positioned that it permitted an optical image of the view to be projected thereon. Means were provided to deflect the beam so that it scanned the entire target.

The potentials were so adjusted that the cathode ray stream decelerated as it approached the plate, the velocity of the electrons actually reaching the plate being extremely small. Since each of the insulated areas constantly lost electrons in proportion to the light intensity of the image falling on them, the electron beam was substantially constant and the number of electrons absorbed from the screen was equal to the total lost due to photoelectric emission since it was last scanned. Thus the unabsorbed portion of the beam varied with the intensity in accordance with the illumination of the portion of the screen it was scanning, thereby effectively modulating the unabsorbed portion with a picture current component.

It was planned to have the modulated beam return along the same path by the magnetic field to an anode, where it passed through the output resistor (39) and thence back to the cathode, thereby completing the circuit.

There are many items of interest in this patent. First, the target may be constructed through the use of a fine wire gauze, or by the use of silver set on a rough surface of powdered willamite. The usual activation with cesium and oxygen was to follow. Second, there was an emphasis on the arriving electron stream being slowed to almost zero velocity as it neared the screen, this velocity depending on the potential of the particular photosensitive island to which it was directed. Finally, Farnsworth claimed that the photoelectrons themselves did not enter into the picture current, which was negative in sign in comparison to a direct photoelectric current; that no physical conduction occurred to the back plate, which was to be at cathode potential; and that ionization is rigorously avoided.

It was claimed that a tube of this type was remarkably stable. The entire photoemission during the entire time was effectively used, resulting in a gain in efficiency of some 100,000 times with a 320-line picture. There is no evidence that Farnsworth actually built such a tube in his laboratory. But this patent was the progenitor of all future low velocity scanning beam, storage camera tubes. Another important patent from Philo Farnsworth![14]

After Farnsworth left Philco, he decided to remain in the Philadelphia area rather than return to San Francisco. Farnsworth Television was reorganized, and it appears that it received much new financing from Russell Seymour Turner, whose wealthy father had a great amount of Farnsworth Television stock.[15]

About this time in 1933, a television signal was sent from the Empire State Building transmitter (on 120 lines) by radio to an intermediate point (Mt. Arney, New Jersey) and then retransmitted to a receiver at the RCA laboratories in Camden.[16]

With the departure of Albert Murray to Philco, it was apparent that the "secrets of Camden" were a secret only to the public at large. So it was decided to reveal the Iconoscope at the Eighth Annual Convention of the Institute of Radio Engineers in Chicago, Illinois, during the Century of Progress Exposition.

On Monday, June 26, 1933, Dr. V.K. Zworykin presented a paper, "The Iconoscope—A New Version of the Electric Eye." Zworykin described a short history of television up to this time, describing how the use of mechanical scanners could not get enough light to produce an outdoor picture. A description of how the Iconoscope works indicated that it was capable of storing energy between scans, by means of each individual photocell storing its charge until discharged by the scanning beam. Each photocell rose in potential depending on the amount of brightness and was discharged in a constant scanning sequence, its output being proportional to the brightness of this part of the picture.

However, it was admitted that there were problems: the beam not only neutralized the positive charge of the photoelement but also charged it negatively; the light from the scene charged the entire mosaic and caused a current that moved across the mosaic.

It was claimed that the mosaic sensitivity was of the same order as a high vacuum cesium-oxide photocell and had the same spectral sensitivity. (This was no problem at first, but later was to cause much concern due to its lack of red response, which caused faces to look very unnatural). Sensitivity was supposed to be the same as photographic film using the same optical system. It was also claimed that some tubes were good up to 500 lines with good margin for improvement. Dr. Zworykin gave credit to Gregory N. Ogloblinsky, Sanford F. Essig, Harley Iams, and Lesly E. Flory, who did much of the theoretical and experimental work on this development.[17]

All authorities agree that this disclosure was of major importance. For all intents and purposes, the disclosure of the Iconoscope marks the beginning of the age of electric television. Zworykin now had a complete system (only an electric time-base and blanking generator were missing) with a practical camera tube to complement his picture tube, the Kinescope.[18]

Dr. Frank Gray of the Bell Telephone Labs wrote a report on July 6, 1933, about Dr. Zworykin's new Iconoscope. The report reflected a cautious attitude. Since there had been no demonstration in Chicago, Gray stated that he had no way of judging how well the Iconoscope worked in practice, but he also stated there was no reason why successful results could not ultimately be obtained.

Dr. H. Ives and O.E. Buckley of the Bell Telephone Labs felt at first that while the Iconoscope was an important step in the right direction, it really hadn't changed the basic problem of television, which was to provide a receiving apparatus that would be simple, cheap, long-lived and capable of quantity production.[19]

The Bell Telephone Labs had finally realized by February 1933 that their 72-line, two-way television system was not "the most advanced state of the art." The tremendous lead that the Bell Labs had had since 1925 had finally been dissipated. The lack of a suitable cathode ray receiver had diluted all of their early experimental successes. Zworykin at RCA, as well as Farnsworth and most of the British, German and Japanese television laboratories, had long since passed up the Bell Labs in terms of the number of lines and quality of images.

By July 20, 1933, the disclosure of the Iconoscope by Dr. Zworykin convinced the Bell Telephone Labs that mechanical television was no longer viable, and Dr. Ives stated that "we would do well to start some work along these lines [of the Iconoscope]." On July 31, 1933, Dr. Gray suggested that they build an Iconoscope and learn as they went along. This was the start of an active program by both Frank Gray and John Hofele to build a practical camera tube of their own design.[20]

What about the prior efforts of Philo Farnsworth? He certainly had had an all-electric television system in his laboratory since July 1929. But he lacked a bright, large cathode ray display tube, and his efforts were soon overshadowed by the disclosure of the storage-type camera tube, the Iconoscope. Philo Farnsworth's Image Dissector, with its limited sensitivity, bore the seeds of its own destruction. And of course, RCA made every effort to discredit nonstorage devices, whether mechanical (Nipkow discs) or electrical (the Image Dissector). But one thing must be made clear: the early Iconoscope was never as sensitive as it was claimed to be; nor, conversely, was the Image Dissector as insensitive as RCA and others claimed it to be.

The importance of the Iconoscope was that it *did* work, and its many built-in deficiencies led RCA and other laboratories into further research that ultimately led to the modern camera tubes of today.

It is ironic that the introduction of the Iconoscope in 1933, which made a practical television system possible, also marked the end of a television service in the United States. It appears that David Sarnoff had decided not to start a television service in the United States, as it would have hurt the thriving radio industry. The RCA television system would not be allowed to come out of the laboratory for several more years.

There is no question that the Iconoscope, while adequate for laboratory experiments, needed much work before it could be used on an everyday basis. RCA still did not have an electric scanning and pulse generator. Finally, there was much work to be done on receivers and transmitting apparatus. A systematic research and development program was initiated by Elmer W. Engstrom, who was now heading the RCA television project.[21]

In July 1933 Dr. Zworykin went to London, where he visited the laboratories of EMI. In September 1933, Isaac Shoenberg set up a laboratory at EMI to build English Iconoscopes under the direction of Dr. J.D. McGee. W.F. Tedham was to remain with picture tube research, which he did not relish. Within a short while, Dr. Leonard Broadway took over the project from Tedham, who had gotten quite ill. EMI had modified its agreement with RCA and was now going into the communications business. Their television system was still operating at 180 lines at 25 frames/sec with vertical scanning.[22]

On July 15, 1933, U.A. Sanabria gave a large screen demonstration at Macy's Department Store in New York City. Sanabria was still using a 45-hole disc. He was now using a new carbon dioxide lamp, which was claimed to be larger and brighter than before with a life of some 300 hours. Sanabria, who had demonstrated his first television system at a convention in Chicago in June 1928, was still using the same basic system some six years later. This seems to be the last demonstration of large screen mechanical television given in the United States.[23]

On August 8, 1933, W.S. Percival, C.O. Browne and E.C.L. White of EMI applied for a patent for a method of forming frame pulses to prevent "hooking" at the top of the picture. This was the last British patent for several years in which the company name of EMI was used along with the inventor's name. The American patents, which took longer to process, still used the name EMI, however, and were applied for by Grover and Oppenheimer, the RCA patent attorneys.[24]

On August 9, 1933, the first newspaper photograph of an Image Dissector being used for "direct vision" was published. It showed George Everson in front of a Farnsworth television camera being operated by Arch Brolly. Brolly had remained at the Green Street laboratory in San Francisco and was now running the Farnsworth Television Laboratories there. With a minimal staff, Brolly had been building improved dissector tubes while Philo Farnsworth was in Philadelphia.

Later in September 1933, a photograph of the same camera being used for the first "outdoors shot" ever tried on the Pacific Coast was published. The sensitivity of the dissector with new improved photo-cathode surfaces was more than adequate in bright sunlight.[25] RCA, of course, never revealed that they had used the dissector for "direct vision" some two years earlier!

On August 12, 1933, J.C. Wilson of Baird Television applied for a patent for a special form of television transmitter. The image was to be formed on a luminescent screen scanned by radiation, and then scanned by a cathode ray tube of sufficient brightness to produce saturation of the fluorescent material. The change in the amount of light, picked up by photocells, is proportional to the change in the luminosity of the screen and corresponds to the elemental areas.[26]

The Berlin Radio Exhibition was held in August 1933. There were exhibits by Fernseh, Tekade, Loewe Radio, the German Post Office, von Ardenne and the Heinrich Hertz Institute. Tekade demonstrated two 90-line mirror-screw receivers with some of the best 90-line images shown. Telefunken showed a 180-line system featuring a cathode ray tube of the gas-filled type. It also showed an intermediate film transmitter, developed for Agfa by Prof. August Karolus, which worked extremely well. It was claimed that film was produced in some 15 seconds with good quality.

Fernseh did not show its 1932 intermediate film transmitter but did show for the first time a large screen intermediate film receiver. Images were fed by a 120-line disc to a Kerr cell of special construction, where they were photographed on a continuous loop of film. The film was developed, giving a positive copy where it passed through a standard cinema film projector onto a screen some six by eight feet. The results were not very good, the image being "thin" and marred by splashes and bubbles on the film.

However, it was regarded as one answer to the large screen projection problem.

Loewe Radio had a 180-line transmitter with a cathode ray receiver on display. It was claimed that the receiver, which was designed by Dr. Kurt Schlesinger, presented the best images at the exhibition. Manfred von Ardenne demonstrated his variable speed scanning system to the public for the first time. The transmitter was the usual flying spot cathode ray tube. At the receiver, the electron beam was of constant brightness (it was unmodulated) but was sped up for darker sections and slowed down for brighter portions. The limitations of such a system were only too apparent. It was announced that the German Post Office planned to standardize on 180 lines at 25 frames/sec as soon as certain changes were made at the transmitter.[27]

On September 4, 1933, L.H. Bedford and O.S. Puckle of Cossor, Ltd., applied for a patent for a method of television using variable velocity scanning.[28]

The rivalry between EMI and the Baird Television Company continued to become more intense. By this time, Baird Television had a cathode ray system operating. The first public demonstration was given to the British Association on September 12, 1933. Pictures some eight inches square were shown on cathode ray receivers. Baird was transmitting 120-line pictures at 25 frames/sec. Both films and cartoons were shown. It was announced that the Baird Company had acquired a lease on the South Tower of the Crystal Palace for several years. Transmissions were to be on 6.05 meters for picture and 6.2 meters for sound.[29]

On September 13, 1933, V.K. Zworykin applied for the first patent employing cathode ray tubes for stereoscopic television. At the transmitter, two transmitting tubes (Iconoscopes), spaced about 2½ inches apart, viewed the scene with each tube scanning alternate lines. With appropriate circuitry, only the proper left and right views were sent to a picture tube. At the receiver, the picture was to be viewed through a horizontal grating which would act as the optical separator, permitting each eye to see only the picture intended for it. Thus pictures would be presented to the viewer in stereoscopic relief.[30]

It was claimed that Baird Television gave demonstrations of 180-line television from the Crystal Palace in October 1933. The reception was on cathode ray receivers located at Film House, Wardour Street, in London. Both film and "live" pictures were transmitted.[31]

On October 13, 1933, the BBC stated that a series of tests of "high-definition" television would be carried out through its ultra-shortwave transmitter at Broadcast House. The first series would be by Baird Television until the end of 1933. A second series of tests would begin in January 1934 with equipment installed by Electric and Musical Industries, Ltd. (EMI).

The General Post Office announced that the Baird 30-line transmissions would be continued until March 31, 1934. No decision had been made to a further series of transmissions after that date. This appears to be the first official announcement that the BBC had finally decided to settle the issue between Baird and EMI by a series of competitive tests.[32]

On October 11, 1933, it was reported that Guglielmo Marconi had visited the laboratories of RCA Victor at Camden and had been given a demonstration of the RCA television system by Dr. Zworykin. It was claimed that he expressed "amazement" at the advanced stage of television in the USA.[33]

In November 1933 RCA set up a laboratory at Harrison, New Jersey, to build Iconoscope tubes. Harley Iams had been put in charge of this project.[34]

About this time, W.D. Wright of EMI visited the RCA laboratories in Camden. He was surprised to find that Dr. Zworykin was now transmitting 243-line interlaced pictures at 24 frames/sec using his Iconoscope and Kinescope. Wright was impressed at the effectiveness of this method since EMI's prior efforts at interlace had ended in failure. It appears that EMI's use of vertical scanning had been the biggest part of the problem, and as a result it was decided to change to horizontal scan with interlace at the earliest possible date.[35]

On November 14, 1933, the Compagnie pour la Fabrication des Compteurs et Matériel d'Usines à Gaz applied for a patent for a television receiver using a cathode ray beam and a rotating mirror. The beam was to be modulated by means of electrostatic plates that would vary the area of the spot.[36]

It was announced that on November 17, 1933, Prime Minister James Ramsey McDonald had visited EMI at Hayes for a demonstration of television.[37]

On December 6, 1933, W.F. Tedham (of EMI) applied for a patent for a television transmitting tube. This important patent by Tedham used the light derived from a cathode ray tube (flying spot) to discharge a mosaic instead of an electron beam. The scanning beam caused saturation emission of electrons from each element, which pass to an anode, bringing each element to the potential of the anode (about 20 volts). When the element is illuminated by the light from the object only, the electron emission decreases, and the electrons leak through a semiconducting layer to a plate. This produces a current through resistance, which becomes the picture signal.

It was claimed that this invention avoided the hazard of gas emission from the oxide-coated cathode of the electron gun. It would also prevent the great amount of secondary emission caused by the high velocity scanning beam. It differed from the Henroteau patent of May 29, 1929 (see page 135), whereby the mosaic was discharged by a light beam scanned by mechanical means.[38]

On December 12, 1933, Telefunken GmbH applied for a patent for a television transmitter. It was a form of Iconoscope tube with only a single row of photoelectric elements arranged either in a line or in a spiral. The vertical movement was by means of a mirror drum. This seems to be the first Telefunken patent for an electric camera tube patterned after the Zworykin Iconoscope. The patent mentions a previous but unpublished invention similar to the above. (Zworykin's patent application of May 1, 1930, serial number 448,834, described a single line tube with a revolving mirror and was not issued until June 17, 1941.) Of course, this tube followed Schröter's idea for a camera tube as mentioned in his 1932 book.[39]

Major Edwin Armstrong received four patents on his new "wideband FM" system on December 26, 1933. He had built a breadboard model of his transmitter and receiver at his Columbia University laboratories. He then invited his old friend David Sarnoff to witness a demonstration of his latest invention. Sarnoff was greatly impressed and invited Armstrong to use the facilities of RCA for further experiments.[40]

On January 31, 1934, the Compagnie pour la Fabrication des Compteurs et Matériel d'Usines à Gaz, of Montrouge, France, applied for a patent on what was to be known as "spot wobble." This was a method of oscillating the horizontal scan of the beam of a receiver tube just enough to fill in dark spaces between lines.[41]

EMI continued to improve its television system. In January 1934 representatives of the BBC saw a further demonstration at EMI in Hayes in which the results were "extremely good." Dr. McGee, who was in charge of the EMI camera tube project, reported that the first presentable pictures from an electronic camera were made on January 24, 1934, to the company chairman, Alfred Clark, and to Isaac Shoenberg on January 29, 1934. The first tubes were made by a ruling process; however, by tube number 12, they were using the silver aggregation process of Essig, which gave much better sensitivity and picture quality.[42]

Sir Louis Sterling, managing director of EMI, returned from America on March 23, 1934, and stated that "television is years off." This obviously came from David Sarnoff, who had told Sir John Reith, director-general of the BBC, that he was not going to start a regular television service until both competitive pressure and technological experience had increased. EMI by this time had developed a "hard" cathode ray tube with a life of some 1700 hours, which made a home receiver a viable item. Dr. McGee's camera tubes were getting more sensitive, and the first outdoor pictures were taken on April 5, 1934, when a camera was pointed out a window. With the availability of an electronic camera tube, EMI went to 243 lines interlaced at 25 frames/sec.[43]

On February 24, 1934, V.K. Zworykin described a new television "super-microscope" to the American Physical Society. It was claimed that this new electric microscope would allow scientists to explore the realms of ultraviolet and infrared wavelengths. It used a special Iconoscope with a quartz window as a pickup device.[44]

In February 1934 L.H. Bedford and O.S. Puckle of Cossor, Ltd. described their velocity modulation system of television. It was a system rather similar to that demonstrated in May 1932 by Manfred von Ardenne. However, the Cossor system combined both velocity and intensity modulation of the scanning beam. It was able to reduce the scanning beam current only in the black areas of the picture. This was supposed to permit high values of contrast while not reducing the brightness characteristic.[45]

However, this system was impractical due to its many complications, and it was admitted that this system would be restricted to the use of motion picture film, although it was conceivable that it could be used with either the Zworykin or Farnsworth scanning ray methods.

On March 3, 1934, J.H. Jeffree of Scophony, Ltd., London, applied for a patent for an electro-optical light valve. It was comprised of a medium traversed by high frequency mechanical waves so that the medium acted as a diffraction grating upon reflected or transmitted light.

The mechanical waves could be generated by a piezoelectric crystal. A line of light passed through the light valve and was reflected from a mirror drum onto a screen. The mechanical waves moved with a finite velocity and the drum was rotated so that all parts of the line appeared stationary and were simultaneously reproduced. Another mirror drum produced the vertical scan.[46]

Scophony, Ltd., had been formed in 1930 by Solomon Sagall. Sagall had been interested in the work of von Mihály and others as far back as 1929. His main interests were in novel methods of optical-mechanical television as a means of producing large screen images. Other stockholders in Scophony included Gaumont-British, Ferranti Electric, and Oscar Deutsch of the Odeon Theatre Chain.[47]

In March 1934, Major Edwin Armstrong was invited to set up his equipment in the Empire State Building and use the RCA 44 mc television transmitter. David Sarnoff ordered all future television transmission from the Empire State Building cancelled and turned the transmitter over to Armstrong for actual tests.

On June 16, 1934, Armstrong made his first successful FM radio transmission from the Empire State transmitter. His experiments continued throughout 1934. This move by David Sarnoff solved two problems. First, it gave his friend and RCA shareholder, Major Armstrong, a suitable laboratory to prove what his new system could do. Second, it gave Sarnoff the opportunity to stop any further television activity from the Empire State transmitter for the time being.[48]

On March 12, 1934, Baird Television gave a demonstration to the BBC, but it was not as good as that of EMI. However, it was noted that all of EMI's demonstrations had been of motion picture film. On March 21, 1934, Sir Harry Greer, chairman of the board of Baird Television, addressed the stockholders of the company by means of ultra-shortwave television. He delivered his address from the Crystal Palace to receivers at Film House, Wardour Street. On March 28, 1934, Baird Television gave a demonstration to some 40 members of Parliament. During this period

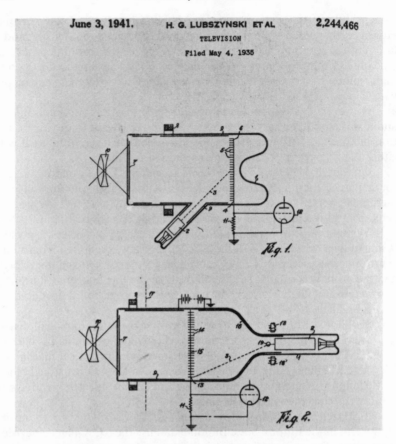

June 3, 1941.   H. G. LUBSZYNSKI ET AL   2,244,466
                        TELEVISION
                    Filed May 4, 1935

Hans G. Lubszynski and Sidney Rodda's Image Iconoscope patent (applied for in 1934 in Great Britain).

the BBC had sent a notice to Baird Television to terminate existing arrangements for experimental broadcasts by March 31, 1934.[49]

Hans Gerhard Lubszynski and Sidney Rodda of EMI applied for a patent for a camera tube on May 12, 1934. It combined the image section of the Farnsworth dissector with the storage plate of Zworykin. The optical image is projected onto a photoelectric surface (7), the electrons being accelerated en masse towards and focused upon a mosaic electrode (6) which was scanned by a cathode ray beam (3). The photoelectric surface may consist of either a semitransparent covering on the interior surface of the tube (1) of cesium on an oxidized coating of silver, or a wire mesh coated with photoelectric material. The electrons are preferably focused by a magnetic solenoid (8) and accelerated by an electrode (9).

The mosaic electrode may consist of a sheet of mica or comprise silver particles on a mica sheet backed with aluminum, each silver particle forming a condenser, which is discharged through the resistance (11) by the cathode ray beam. The electrons are accelerated to such a speed that they produce secondary emission from the electrode (6), leaving each element positively charged.

A variation was described using a two-sided electrode of silver plugs set in a mesh of insulated wires. This was the first patent application for a tube of the kind to be known as the Image Iconoscope.[50]

The rivalry between EMI and Baird Television led the BBC and the General Post Office to consider setting up a committee to finally settle the matter. This was formed under the direction of Lord Selsdon, Sir William Mitchell-Thomson, who was to advise the postmaster-general, Sir Kingsley Wood, on questions concerning television and "to report on the relative merits of the several systems." This committee was set up May 16, 1934, and met for the first time on June 7, 1934.[51]

On May 22, 1934, the Marconi Wireless Telegraph Company, Ltd., joined forces with EMI to form Marconi-EMI, Ltd. This powerful alliance now left Baird Television with the General Electric Company of Britain (not connected with GE in the USA), who was furnishing its cathode ray tubes, and Fernseh A.G. in Germany as its only allies. It was claimed that Fernseh was doing research into "hard" cathode ray tubes and that Loewe Radio had the rights to the von Ardenne television patents as well.[52]

EMI at this time was spending some £100,000 a year on research alone. This coalition coordinated the expertise of Marconi in wideband VHF transmission (as well as their control of the RCA patents) with EMI's experience in television receivers and transmitters and developmental electronic camera tubes.[53]

On May 24, 1934, Arthur W. Vance and Harry Branson of RCA Victor applied for a patent for a method of adding a polarizing potential to the cathode of a transmitting tube. This was to be done by means of flooding the target with low velocity electrons, which increased the number of redistributed electrons, thus increasing the sensitivity of the tube.[54]

The RCA television system was described in glowing terms at the Ninth Annual IRE Convention on May 28, 29 and 30, 1934. It was claimed that the detail was as good as "8mm home movies." However, no demonstration was given. Dr. W.R.G. Baker, vice president and general manager of RCA Victor, discussed the tremendous costs involved in setting up a television system in the United States and declared that he could not expect advertisers to bear the costs while the system was starting up.[55]

The Selsdon Committee started taking testimony on June 7, 1934, and on June 8 Isaac Shoenberg appeared before it. He stressed that the EMI system was based on three prime components: (1) the use of the DC component (Br. Pat. No. 422,906 of Willans); (2) sending sync with the picture (Br. Pat. No. 425,220 of Percival, Browne and White); and (3) interlaced scan (Br. Pat. No. 420,391 of R.C. Ballard).

The Baird television system was based on four patents. They were Br. Pat. No. 269,658 (the flying spot) and three patents concerning sync methods: Br. Pat. No. 269,834 and 275,318 and 336,655.

Baird Television again accused EMI of being a subsidiary of RCA, which was a non-British Company. EMI's answer was that every bit of equipment used in the EMI system, including cathode ray tubes, "everything down to the last screw was home manufactured." This of course was true; EMI was capable of creating all of its own hardware and was doing so. Its dependence on RCA was now limited to a few key patents (the most important one being the Ballard patent on interlaced scan that was simple in concept though difficult to put into practice).[56]

As far as the Iconoscope was concerned, Isaac Shoenberg claimed that EMI had never been provided with a method of making a mosaic. This was strange, for the two patents of Sanford Essig (see pages 178-179) certainly gave the details for producing mosaics using the latest techniques. Obviously, the actual details of making such mosaics had to be learned as they went along. EMI has never admitted that such details were given them![57]

Other laboratories besides RCA and EMI were building developmental Iconoscopes at this time. The Philco Radio and Television Corporation, under the direction of Albert Murray, was making excellent progress and had a workable Iconoscope by the summer of 1934. The Bell Telephone Laboratories' first developmental Iconoscope was tested on July 31, 1934, by J.R. Hofele, who claimed that "shadowgraphs were clearly recognizable." It was claimed that Telefunken in Germany built its first Iconoscope at this time. (As the German RCA licensee, they certainly had received the Essig patents as well as other important information.) There was also a report of an Iconoscope built in Russia by a scientist named Krusser.[58]

In July 1934 Pierre Mertz and Frank Gray of the Bell Telephone Labs published an article which was based on the research done by Gray and Hofele in 1928/29. It indicated that by the use of two-dimensional Fourier analysis, a theory of television scanning had been developed. It stated that "a television signal leaves certain parts of the frequency range relatively empty of current components. Certain considerations indicated that a large part of the energy of the signal might be located at multiples of the frequency of line scanning." This important article indicated that as a result, much more information could be fitted into the television signal with no visible effects on the received picture.[59]

Baird Television under Capt. West's direction had turned to cathode ray television for reception, but still depended on the flying spot scanner for "live" pickups. Since this of course was limited to a very small area, another method was needed for studio and outdoor scenes. The first choice was that of the Fernseh intermediate film system, which had been in use in Germany since August 1932. While cumbersome, it did offer a method of picking up studio action, boxing matches, plays and, even more important, outdoor scenes.

However, the need for an electronic camera tube was imperative. Control of the Iconoscope was in the hands of RCA, EMI and Telefunken.

The only other device was the "Image Dissector" of Philo Farnsworth. Sometime in June 1934, contact was made with Farnsworth to bring a demonstration unit to London. This was planned for the fall of 1934.[60]

In August 1934 the first report on the new 120-line Scophony projection system was given. The picture size was some 14 by 18 inches. The scanning device was said to be extremely small, about two inches in diameter and three inches in length. It was claimed that an apparatus capable of projecting pictures seven feet by six feet had been completed.

A demonstration of the Scophony Stixograph principle of nonvisual recording was also given. This was an optical method of resolving a picture into a straight line. The whole picture was to be instantly presented as a succession of joined-up strips. The speed of the film was about one millimeter/sec and a four-minute program would occupy a piece of film only a couple of inches in length.[61]

On August 3, 1934, A.D. Blumlein and J.D. McGee of EMI applied for a patent for a camera tube with cathode potential stabilization. The individual elements of the screen were to be brought to approximately the potential of the cathode. This was supposed to prevent the scattering of the secondary electrons over the mosaic and to stop the irregular action of the beam at the end of the scanning cycle. There were means to fully discharge the elements when sudden changes in the illumination of subject occurred. Tubes of this kind could be used with either single- or two-sided targets.[62]

In the summer of 1934 the Franklin Institute of Philadelphia invited Philo Farnsworth to give a demonstration of his television equipment. Starting on August 25, 1934, and for ten days, Television Laboratories, Ltd., gave daily exhibitions of their equipment to the public. This was the first public demonstration of a complete electronic television system ever given. (The earlier 1931 demonstration by von Ardenne did not include a camera tube; it had no light-to-electricity transducer; it used an unmodulated cathode ray tube as a form of flying spot transmission; and it used a rotating commutator to produce scanning pulses.) So Philo Farnsworth is given credit for this most important advancement.

Both the camera and receiver were compact and mobile, which was quite an achievement. An improvised studio was set-up in the Frankin Institute with the camera on the roof. The receiving set was some 12 by 13 inches to provide a view for some 200 people.

The programs were of 15-minute duration, starting at 10 o'clock in the morning, and they ran all day long. The entertainment consisted of such vaudeville talent as could be found, athletic events such as tennis and the appearances of various politicians.[63]

An article on the Farnsworth system appeared in August 1934 by A.H. Brolly, who was the chief engineer of Television Laboratories, Ltd. This was a rather complete description of the system. It is of interest that Brolly admitted that the dissector had rather poor sensitivity, the output being some 0.504×10^{16} coulombs or 317 electrons! This presented no problem with the transmission of motion picture film where there was adequate light, and Brolly claimed that the use of an electron multiplier made possible outdoor scenes, or scenes from life, with moderate light.[64]

The Berlin Radio Exhibition was held in August 1934. Fernseh displayed both a spot-light transmitter and a film transmitter using a 45-hole disc running in a vacuum. The receiver was cathode ray with a 10 by 10-inch picture. Their mechanical intermediate film projector was also demonstrated on 180 lines but with poor results. Tekade showed its mirror screw system on 90, 120 and 180 lines. They also had a cathode ray receiver on display that was not working.

Telefunken demonstrated an eight- by ten-inch cathode ray receiver with the best pictures in the show, except for the intense flicker, which made it hard to watch. It also showed Dr. August Karolus' big screen four-channel projection system. The Loewe company was using high vacuum cathode ray tubes for the first time. Finally, the German Broadcasting Company displayed an intermediate film transmitting van which was made by Fernseh A.G. This vehicle was in daily operation.

Von Ardenne showed his new high vacuum cathode ray tube. Although it was an advance over his old tubes it did poorly. It had a reddish color and the "handkerchief effect" was visible. However, it did exhibit good detail.[65]

An important visitor at the Berlin Radio Exhibition was Prof. Kenjiro Takayanagi from Japan. Takayanagi had visited Dr. Zworykin in Camden, New Jersey, in the summer of 1934 and was shown the RCA television system using the Iconoscope. It was indicated that they were hard to build and had a short life. He was quite impressed with it and was determined to build such a tube when arrived home.

He also visited the laboratories of Philo Farnsworth in Philadelphia as well as the laboratories of Bell, General Electric and Westinghouse but saw nothing on television. He then went to England and visited the Baird Laboratories, where Capt. A.D. West showed him a variety of receivers with some good 180-line pictures. He then went on to Berlin but was allowed only to see the television exhibits at the Berlin Radio Exhibition. He decided that the best pictures he had seen were from a Fernseh receiver.

When Takayanagi arrived home in Japan he wrote several lengthy reports about his visit. As a result he was able to enlist the aid of NHK (Japan Broadcasting Company) and Nippon Electric Company, Tokyo. This culminated in the building and testing of the first Japanese Iconoscope in November 1935. This 1934 trip by Kenjiro Takayanagi was the start of an organized effort by the Japanese government to devise and develop television systems of their own design.[66]

On August 31, 1934, Alda Bedford and Ray D. Kell of the Radio Corporation applied for a patent for an Iconoscope transmitter, including an electrode which was made relatively positive during periods of projection to increase the sensitivity of the tube.[67]

Interestingly enough, EMI was still applying for patents on mechanical interlaced scanning generators as late as August 31, 1934. On September 18, 1934, C.O. Browne, F. Blythen and A.D. Blumlein applied for a patent for an important method of DC restoration by the "clamp method." Another camera tube patent was filed by J.D. McGee and L. Klatzow on September 20, 1934. This patent was for a method of projecting the light from an image through a screen onto a double-sided mosaic. With all of this laboratory work, it was still reported by "mid 1934 the camera tubes of McGee had not yet been developed to a stage where they could be used on a commercial basis, but promising results had been made in the laboratory."[68]

On September 29, 1934, Alda V. Bedford of the Radio Corporation applied for the first American patent on a camera tube incorporating the image section of Farnsworth with the storage plate of Zworykin. This was basically the same tube (the image Iconoscope) as that of Lubszynski and Rodda. It also stated that the mosaic need not be photosensitized, thus avoiding the problem of leakage between adjacent particles on the mosaic.[69]

This patent application became the subject of interference #74,655, which was won by Alda Bedford. It appears that he was able to prove an earlier conception date and was awarded the priority. When it came to patents and interferences, RCA recognized no one, including an ally such as EMI![70]

Alda V. Bedford of RCA applied for a patent for a "shading generator" on October 26, 1934. In experimental use, it was found that the Iconoscope when used with sufficient lighting for "direct vision" was a quite satisfactory pickup tube. But when used to project motion picture film, the Iconoscope was found to have severe problems, especially with film that had adjacent scenes in which the lighting contrast was quite different.

The shading generator of Bedford was designed so that it could compensate for the shifting electron charge pattern across the face of the Iconoscope mosaic due to rapid changes in lighting. This charge pattern became known as "tilt and bend," or in England as "black spot." By injecting various sine, parabolic, or sawtooth currents or combinations thereof onto the picture it was possible to neutralize these effects and get reasonable pictures from the Iconoscope.[71]

Philo Farnsworth published a complete technical article on the Farnsworth television system in October 1934. It featured an Image Dissector tube with a built-in electron multiplier with a transparent film of cesium-silver-oxide for a target. It was claimed that "sensitivity was now adequate for outdoor scanning even when there is no direct sunlight." It was not necessary to have a particularly sensitive image cathode. Good images had been transmitted direct from the subject with sensitivity considerably less than a microampere/lumen. The use of interlaced scanning was discussed as a means of eliminating flicker. Farnsworth had been using a method of even-line interlacing since March 1934 and filed for a patent in November 1934.

The receiving tube (oscillite) was a hard tube using magnetic focus with a short coil. Deflection was also magnetic, with the horizontal deflection by means of specially shaped pole pieces. The deflection angle was 15° or less. Post-acceleration of the electron beam was not mentioned, although the walls of the tube were silvered to provide means for draining the electrons from the screen. It finally stated that motion picture projection was by means of continuously moving film.[72]

The magazine *Electronics* made a survey in October 1934 of present-day systems of television. It compared the systems of (1) RCA Victor; (2) Philco Radio and Television; (3) Television Labs, P.T. Farnsworth; (4) J.V.L. Hogan; (5) International Television, W.H. Priess; and (6) Peck Television, W.H. Peck.

The most interesting part of the article was the disclosure that Philco was using their version of the Iconoscope as a "cathode ray" camera tube. It also revealed that Philco was operating at the same number of lines (240–360) and frames (24–60) as RCA Victor.[73]

At this time RCA was operating on 343 lines at 30 frames interlaced two-to-one. In spite of the advantages of a 24 frame rate (to be compatible with film) RCA had found that 48 half-frames (or fields) was not quite high enough to eliminate picture flicker at the brightness levels then available with the Kinescope. It was decided that, since there was a 60-cycle power source in the United States, going to 60 fields would eliminate several problems. The most troublesome was that of ripple patterns moving across the picture. The choice of 60 fields solved both the ripple and flicker problems.

EMI was using 243 lines interlaced two-to-one late in 1934. However, they decided to stay with 50 fields (25 frames) due to the 50-cycle power supply in England. Thus their flicker threshold was lower than that in the United States. This was the beginning of the division of standards—25 frames (50 fields) in Europe and 30 frames (60 fields) in the United States—that prevails to this day.[74]

Lord Selsdon and three members of his committee, F.W. Phillips, Col. A.S. Angwin and Noel Ashbridge, arrived in the United States on October 29, 1934. They held a meeting with members of the FCC in Washington, D.C. They then visited Camden, N.J., where they were shown the television research laboratories of V.K. Zworykin at RCA, and Philadelphia, where they visited the laboratories of Philco Radio and Television Corporation as well as the Television Laboratories, Ltd., of Farnsworth.

Their reports on RCA and Philco (no mention of Farnsworth was made) were quite good. At RCA Victor they were shown 343-line, 30-frame pictures. There were both indoor and outdoor demonstrations. "Very good reproductions were obtained," with superior absence of flicker. They claimed that the Philco standards were comparable to RCA's and were sufficient to give clear, defined images on the receiver.[75]

Four representatives of the Selsdon Committee went to Berlin on November 5, 1934, and visited the television laboratories of the German Post Office, the television department of Reichs-Rundfunk-Gesellschaft, and various German firms developing television. They reported that Telefunken was able to present pictures with exceptional brightness, but with noticeable flicker. Fernseh demonstrated an intermediate film pickup with a time-lag of 75 seconds, and also an intermediate film receiver that had been used successfully. Loewe Radio showed a cathode-ray receiver that could be used for interlaced pictures.[76]

The Selsdon Committee had also been investigating the state of television in England. It was reported that late in 1934 the Baird Company had received a Farnsworth Image Dissector camera and set it up in the Baird Laboratories in the Crystal Palace. A demonstration was set up on December 6, 1934. It was claimed that the images were "a somewhat crude representation of a studio scene." Baird's only good studio pictures came from the intermediate film method.

Even though the Selsdon Committee never saw the Farnsworth equipment, George Everson claimed that these demonstrations were an important factor in the Selsdon Committee's choice of Baird and EMI as the two suppliers of equipment to the BBC.[77]

It was ironic that Baird Television, which had complained so bitterly about the connection between EMI and RCA, should now have to go to an American television company, Television Laboratories, Ltd., in Philadelphia, to provide them with an electronic camera tube so that they could have a competitive electronic system!

On November 6, 1934, D.M. Johnstone of Baird Television applied for a patent for an electron camera tube that could be discharged by either a light beam or an electronic beam. This was the first of many patents applied for by engineers of the Baird Company in order to compete with Marconi-EMI. Also as a result of the collaboration of Baird Television with Farnsworth, Fernseh in Germany started to build its first dissector tubes.[78]

On November 19, 1934, C.O. Browne, F. Blythen, J. Hardwick and E.C.L. White (of EMI) applied for a patent for an electronic scanning generator with associated waveforms. On November 23, 1934, a patent for a photosensitive device with a leaking insulating material was applied for by W.F. Tedham.[79]

There was a report on November 29, 1934, of a recent demonstration of Edison Bell, Ltd. of a recording system called the "Visiogram." Ordinary motion picture film was used to record television signals by the variable density method familiar to film sound recording techniques. By means of a simple attachment, the film signals were translated back into visual images on an ordinary television receiver. The demonstration given was extremely poor.[80]

On December 12, 1934, Rolf Möller of Fernseh A.G. of Berlin applied for a method of recording television images on film from a cathode ray tube. This appears to be the earliest patent of this kind.[81]

W. Hickok of the Radio Corporation applied for a patent for a photoelectric device on December 21, 1934. This patent stated that a wire mesh screen such as was described by Kolman Tihany in a co-pending application (serial number 369,598, for a camera tube using a single-sided target) was the type usually constructed. However, Hickok proposed to use a similar wire mesh for a two-sided mosaic. He then described a method for producing such a wire mesh screen. By this time RCA was in the process of buying up all patents that pertained to the Iconoscope.[82]

On January 14, 1935, the Television Committee of Lord Selsdon published its report and recommendations. It stated that delegations had been dispatched to the United States and Germany. They reported that they had inspected the facilities of Baird, Cossor, Marconi-EMI and the Scophony Company, who had provided demonstrations. They had received evidence from Feranti, General Electric, Plew Television, the BBC, Newspaper Proprietors Association, the Radio Manufacturers Association, and the Television Society. In addition, they had examined some 38 witnesses and had come to the following conclusions:

(1) A high definition service should be established in London.
(2) Two systems, Baird Television, Ltd., and Marconi-EMI Television Company, Ltd., should be given the opportunity to supply the necessary apparatus. Transmission from both companies should be able to be received on the same receivers.
(3) The definition should not be inferior to a standard of 240 lines and 24 pictures per second.
(4) It is recommended that the British Broadcasting Corporation should exercise control over the television service.

The report was signed by Lord Selsdon and the members of his committee.[83]

Baird Television gave a large number of demonstrations in January and February 1935. Both indoor and outdoor transmission were made by the intermediate film process. The Baird flying spot scanner was used for close-ups of lecturers and announcers.

It was also claimed that a demonstration of the Farnsworth "electron camera" was given to the press in February 1935. Talking pictures were transmitted from one room to another with picture definition of 700 lines. Other reports in March 1935 indicated that Baird's electron camera (the Farnsworth Image Dissector) was capable of taking indoor or outdoor scenes with any degree of definition from 100 to 500 lines.

Baird Television was also using two types of film projectors, one a disc scanner giving 180-line definition and the other an electron scanner with a definition of from 100 to 500 lines (at the turn of a knob) with no moving parts. All transmission by radio was from the Crystal Palace on 180 lines, 25 frames/sec on a frequency of 7 meters for picture and 8.5 meters for audio. The radiated power was some 2 kw.[84]

At this time, Baird Television described the first complete cathode ray tube film recording device for television reproduction in cinemas. The picture on the cathode ray tube was to be photographed onto a continuously moving film by a special camera containing two drums which rotated at a constant speed. The film, having been exposed to both sound and vision, was developed for 20 seconds, washed for 5, fixed for 20, washed for a further 15, and dried for about 60 seconds. Thus in a total of less than two minutes it passed into a cinematograph projector, which projected it onto the large screen. It was stated that this equipment was to be installed in December 1935 at the Dominion Theatre in London for projection on a 24-foot screen.[85]

Much important research was going on at the EMI laboratories in Hayes. On February 9, 1935, H.G. Lubszynski and J.D. McGee applied for a patent on a camera tube in which the electron gun was normal (perpendicular) to the screen. It had a mosaic of mutually insulated conductive elements coated with a photoelectric material to which light penetrated through the mica and the conducting layer. This was an early attempt to produce an Iconoscope-type tube in which the beam and the light impinged on the same side but without the problems of keystone distortion and the odd shape of the normal Iconoscope. Unfortunately, because tubes of this type lost much sensitivity when the light went through the mica before striking the mosaic, they never became practical.[86]

On March 20, 1935, A.D. Blumlein applied for a patent for circuitry for producing "blacker than black" pulses. This was an important part of the newly developed EMI transmission waveform. Also on March 20, 1935, Leonard Klatzow of EMI applied for a patent for an improvement in an Iconoscope mosaic. Klatzow had found that a very thin layer of silver deposited on top of the silver cesium photosensitive layer had two desired characteristics. First, it increased the apparent sensitivity of the mosaic from about 7.5 microamps per lumen to about 25 microamps per lumen. Second, it was found that it also gave very good response to visible light but very little beyond a wavelength of 700 nm.[87]

Although Marconi-EMI had won the bid to provide a service and equipment to the BBC on the basis of a 240-line, 25 frame/sec system, Isaac Shoenberg had other plans in mind. He decided to stretch his system to the limit and offer neither a 240- nor a 243-line system (the latter of which EMI was now using and RCA had abandoned) but to pass up RCA, now using 343 lines interlaced at 30 frames, and go to the next step—405 lines.

By this time both RCA and EMI were using synchronizing systems, which used a method of electronic division by means of vacuum tubes. The number of lines (243 and 405) were chosen as being multiples of small odd integers, which facilitated the electrical interlocking of the line and frame frequencies required for interlacing. The number of integers for 243 lines was $9 \times 9 \times 3$ (RCA was using $7 \times 7 \times 7$ for 343 lines). EMI changed the integers to $9 \times 9 \times 5$, which gave 405 lines.[88]

Once the number of lines was chosen, it was easy to generate a

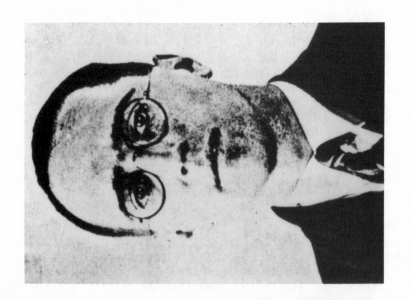

frequency that was the result of the number of lines times the number of frames. Multiplying 405×25 gave 10,125. This was generated by an oscillator and then divided in steps; by 9 to equal 1125, by 9 to equal 125, and finally by 5 to equal 25. Each field consisted of 202.5 lines, which was 405 divided by 2.

Going to 405 lines meant a 65 percent increase in the scanning rate, a threefold increase in picture signal bandwidth, and a fivefold decrease in signal/noise ratio in signal amplifiers. The use of interlace was imperative, for it was only too apparent that all the 25-frame television systems had intolerable flicker in them.

EMI claims that Shoenberg offered a 405-line service to the BBC as early as February 25, 1935. This was a tremendous gamble. Not only did EMI have to produce an electronic camera tube capable of 405-line capability, but the radio transmitter had to have a modulator of some 2.5 mc bandwidth to make 405 lines meaningful. The easy thing to do would have been to stay with 240 lines or, even better, 243 lines interlaced. But Shoenberg had confidence that his laboratory under Alan Blumlein could and would build the system in time for the competition with Baird Television. By the week of April 10–15, 1935, EMI was able to demonstrate a 405-line picture to Gerald Cock, director of the BBC Television Service, and it was claimed that "he was very impressed."[89]

On March 22, 1935, the German Post Office opened a "regular" public television service from Berlin. This was on a 180-line standard at 25 frames/sec. The transmission was on less than 8 meters (37 Mh) with vision on 6.77 meters and sound on 7.05 meters. It was stated that the German Post Office had been telecasting daily on 7 meters since about September 1934. It was claimed that suitable receivers would be on sale to the general public by August 1935.

All broadcasts were from motion picture film. There was a Nipkow disc television film scanner as well as the use of the "television pickup car," which was Telefunken's intermediate film system. It was claimed that two kinds of receiving sets were in use: the mirror-screw device and the cathode ray receiver. However, there is no evidence that any sets were manufactured or sold at this time.[90]

Around the same time, Manfred von Ardenne described a superheterodyne receiver for 700–800 kc reception using single side band reception. This appears to be the first description of a television receiver using this important feature. He also discussed the importance of the transmission of the DC component for high quality pictures. Von Ardenne, who had done much research on high vacuum cathode ray tubes, stated that only those kind of tubes would be used in television.

While the German Television Service was claimed to be "high definition" it suffered from two major defects: low image detail and very bad

Opposite, left: Isaac Shoenberg, director of research at EMI. Right: Alan Blumlein of the EMI research group.

picture flicker. So, despite many claims to the contrary, it was a medium definition service at best. It lasted only until August 19, 1935, when a disastrous fire put it off the air.[91]

On April 3, 1935, it was announced that the first television station in England would be built at the Alexandra Palace on the north side of London. On June 7, 1935, the line standards were revealed for the first time, i.e., that Baird Television was to go ahead with 240 lines at 25 frames/sec sequential and that Marconi-EMI was to use 405 lines interlaced at 25 frames/sec.[92]

The announcement of this very high standard by Marconi-EMI met with quite stern opposition from just about every expert. Von Ardenne commented that the use of such a wide frequency band was quite impractical and that although interlacing was capable of eliminating flicker completely, a new phenomenon, "interline flicker," would be visible. Von Ardenne said that he would settle for 240 lines operating at 50 images/sec, or even 180 lines would be adequate. E.H. Traub believed that 180 lines at 50 frames would be as good as, say, 360 lines interlaced at 25 frames/sec. T.C.M. Lance saw no need for interlacing. E. Wikkenhauser suggested that 405 lines was much too high and that a 240-line picture would be ample for home use.[93]

It was reported that the French P.T.T. (Postes, Télégraphes et Téléphones) had started an experimental 60-line, 25 frames/sec service on April 26, 1935, on a 175-meter channel. It used the apparatus of Rene Barthelemy of the Compagnie pour la Fabrication des Compteurs et Matériel d'Usines à Gaz. It appears that most of the early French television pioneers such as E. Belin, A. Dauvillier and F. Holweck had left the field of television research. P. Chevallier had joined Rene Barthelemy, and Georges Valensi continued working in television as did M. Marc Chauvierre and M. Henry De France.[94]

In April 1935, Rene Barthelemy gave a demonstration of his television system at L'Exposition Universelle et Internationale held in Brussels. It was a low definition system of 60 lines at 25 frames/sec. Although it used cathode ray tubes for reception, the "cameras" were of the Nipkow disc type. Each was on a tripod and therefore movable and had an enclosed rotating disc in a mechanism with a very sensitive photoelectric cell.

Motion picture film was also shown from a special 35mm film projector. A "live" studio was provided with several "cameras" and banks of bright lights. Barthelemy's method of synchronization was used as well as the new method of filling in the spaces between the lines of the receiving tube by oscillating the beam vertically.[95]

The promised setting up of a high definition television service in London did not go unheeded in the United States. On May 7, 1935, David Sarnoff announced plans for an extensive field test program by RCA. Some of the goals were (1) to establish the first modern transmitting station in the United States, (2) to manufacture and distribute a limited number of receiving sets and (3) to build studio facilities to develop the necessary

Rene Barthelemy (1935).

studio technique. These goals were supposed to take from twelve to fifteen months to complete.[96]

Some of the newest patents from the RCA laboratories included the last patent application of Gregory N. Ogloblinsky on February 28, 1935, for a special camera tube with a screen in two parts. (Ogloblinsky had been killed in a high speed automobile accident in France late in 1934.) J.P. Smith of RCA applied for a patent on an electronic sync generator on February 28, 1935. There was also an even-line interlacing system applied for by R.D. Kell and A.V. Bedford on March 26, 1935.[97]

David Sarnoff was still in no hurry to launch a television service in the United States. He certainly could benefit from the lessons learned in setting up the London Television Service. Two steps were being taken. First, the research in the RCA Laboratories in Camden, N.J., was sped up. Second, Sarnoff politely asked Major Edwin Armstrong to remove his experimental FM radio equipment from the Empire State Building in order to make way for the resumption of television experiments.

Major Armstrong's experiments from the Empire State transmitter had been quite successful. So successful, in fact, that he had tried to convince David Sarnoff that the whole AM system of radio be scrapped in favor of his new FM system. While Sarnoff could agree that FM had certain advantages in noise-free radio reception, he could not and would not jeopardize the existing profitable AM radio system. As a result, the FM transmissions ceased in October 1935, and the two old friends soon became deadly enemies. Armstrong's ouster from the Empire State Building was the beginning of a long personal feud between Sarnoff and Armstrong.[98]

On May 9, 1935, V. Zeitline, A. Zeitline and V. Kliatchko applied for several patents for camera tubes. They were assigned to the Gaz Company of Montrouge. Among the most interesting was that for a combination camera and receiving tube in the same envelope. It had a screen having both fluorescent and photosensitive properties. By means of switches, it was possible to change its function from a camera to a receiving tube.[99]

On May 15, 1935, Mr. F. Plew gave a demonstration of "Gramovision" at Selfridges Department Store. The playback was from wax disc records. The detail was low, consisting of 30-line pictures as broadcast by the BBC.[100]

At this time Philo Farnsworth was applying for many important patents on both storage and nonstorage camera tubes. On July 6, 1935, he applied for a patent for a special charge storage electrode in which the side coated with photoelectric material received the optical image. It was also impinged by a high velocity electron stream from an electron gun. The beam was modulated by the charge image and passed through to the insulated side. Here it was to be amplified and collected by an anode to become the television signal. There were other variations, in which the electron beam after passing through the charge storage electrode was scanned en masse as in the regular Image Dissector.[101]

On the afternoon of July 26, 1935, John Hofele of the Bell Telephone Labs demonstrated a 72-line photoconducting television transmitting tube to several high-ranking members of the Bell Labs. The surface was made of a film of red mercuric iodide cooled by solid CO_2. It was claimed that the cooling allowed low vapor pressure of the red HgI_2 film stable, thereby permitting working conditions over long period of time. The transmitter contained an electron gun designed by Frank Gray. The images were received on a 72-line tube of Mr. Davisson. It was claimed that "in view of the excellent images obtained, it was decided to try immediately a 240-line transmitter for its usefulness in the coaxial demonstration." Two 240-line scanning circuits were promised by September 1, 1935. This appears to be the first demonstration ever given of a photoconductive camera tube.[102]

On July 30, 1935, Philo Farnsworth gave a demonstration of his system to an audience of members of the Press and Radio Editors. It was presented from his Television Laboratories, Ltd., at Chestnut Hill, Philadelphia, by A.H. Brolly, chief engineer, and George Everson, secretary of Television Laboratories. Both "live" and film presentations

A demonstration of Philo Farnsworth's 1935 Image Dissector camera. Farnsworth at far right.

were made by wire and radio. The pictures were sent at 240 lines at 24 frames/sec. The wire demonstration used a direct circuit with a frequency band of 2 megacycles and was sent to a receiver with a 14-inch picture tube. The radio demonstration was from a 15-watt transmitter on approximately 40 megacycles over a distance of 50 feet to a standard receiver with a 7-inch picture tube.

It was claimed that the pictures were presented with a "clarity and sharpness of definition that surprised many of the observers." It was also claimed that the film pickup in particular was "of a very high order of excellence and was equal to the average home-movie in detail, brilliance and contrast." Although the demonstration was on 240 lines, it was claimed that it was intended to increase the number of lines to 360 or 400 and that interlacing was to be introduced at 48 frames.

Farnsworth confirmed his ties with Baird in England and Fernseh A.G. in Germany. He stated that he was building a transmitter in San Francisco; another was to be built in Philadelphia and, later on, a third one in New York City. He stated that he thought television had advanced to the point of having real entertainment value and that he didn't intend to upset the radio industry, but to make contributions to it.[103]

The Berlin Radio Exhibition was held in August 1935. The intermediate film projection system of Fernseh A.G. was demonstrated again. However, by this time Fernseh had dispensed with the mechanical scanning disc and Kerr cell in favor of the cathode ray tube. This marks the beginning of the era of cathode ray television film recording. The system was on display by the Berlin Broadcasting Company (Reichs-Rundfunk-Gesellschaft) and the results were "rather a little disappointing." Fernseh also showed a 320-line film projector using a Nipkow disc running in a vacuum. This produced the best pictures in the show although there was a certain amount of flicker. Fernseh also showed 180-line interlaced pictures.

Telefunken showed pictures of 180 lines using both sequential and interlaced scanning systems. Prof. August Karolus also demonstrated a large "lamp screen." It was 2 meters square and had a brilliance of some 1,000 lux. It contained at least 10,000 lamps and was run at 50 pictures/sec with absolutely no flicker. Teckade presented the only mechanical system, its mirror-screw receiver. Loewe featured a receiver that could operate at four standards at the flip of a switch; 180 lines both sequential and interlaced, and 240 lines sequential or interlaced. All of the even-line interlaced systems seemed to have a very pronounced "interline" flicker.[104]

There were no television demonstrations of any kind at the Wireless Exhibition at Olympia in August 1935. It appears that the sale of radios had slumped in Great Britain with the announcement of the start of a television service in the London area. The British Radio Manufacturers Association had announced that no television receivers or kits of parts would be allowed to be displayed.[105]

There was a report on the activities of Prof. Kenjiro Takayanagi of the Institute of Technology of Tokyo in August 1935. In it was described his work on a combination Nipkow disc scanner in the studio and a cathode ray tube for an image reproducer. The equipment was working on 80 lines at 25 frames/sec. A further report by the Television Engineers of Japan showed that they had made considerable progress in their laboratories. They were experimenting with all aspects of television research. They had, in addition to the Takayanagi system, intermediate film systems, receivers using mirror-screws and camera tubes of both the Image Dissector type of Farnsworth and the Iconoscope of Zworykin. Their cathode ray receivers featured the high voltage, electrostatically focused tube. It appears that all research was concentrated in Tokyo under the auspices of the Japanese Government. Takayanagi had created the core of the future Japanese television industry with his vision and ingenuity.[106]

On August 5, 1935, Fritz Schröter of Telefunken applied for a patent on a camera tube. It was a form of image iconoscope. However, it was unique in that the electron image was focused on only one strip of photocells. This one strip was then scanned by the electron beam and caused the picture signal. Then the electron image was moved down to the next line and scanned again. This pattern was repeated for the entire picture.[107]

On September 7, 1935, Philo T. Farnsworth applied for a patent for a camera tube of the storage type. It comprised a cathode ray tube with an envelope containing an apertured control electrode having a sensitive face and an opposing insulating face, a cathode and anode cooperating when energized to direct an electron beam of elemental cross section against said photoelectric face and a collecting anode adjacent said insulating face. The main feature appeared to be that there was no mosaic as such (discrete islands of photoelectric material) but a continuous surface on which the charges were fixed.[108]

The low definition television service of the BBC was finally ended on September 15, 1935, in anticipation of the coming "high definition" television system. All of the 30-line, 12½ frame Baird "Televisors" were now obsolete. It appears that not many were in actual use and very few objections were raised. (A postcard survey got no results.) But the Baird experiment had lasted some six years and provided the BBC with a wealth of experience in the operation (as primitive as it was) of a practical television system.[109]

The scientists at EMI continued their research into advanced camera tubes. In September 1935, H. Miller applied for two patents pertaining to camera tubes. The first, on September 10, related to a mosaic screen utilizing the photovoltaic effect. The screen consisted of a semiconducting layer capacitively associated with a conducting electrode and separated from it by a "blocking layer" of high resistance. When the junction between the semiconductor and the blocking layer was illuminated by the image to be transmitted, electrons flowed from the semiconductor to the conducting electrode. Either electrode might be made mosaic (islands of material) and the scanning caused by electron or light beam.

The second patent application by Miller, on September 24, 1935, concerned a transmitting tube with a photoconductive screen. The screen might consist of mica coated with platinum, liquid silver, or some other material, and zinc selenide. The screen might be transparent and its thickness less than the diameter of the scanning spot.

Another variation filed by Miller on October 29, 1935, stated that the photoconductive material, which should be a better secondary electron emitter than the material itself, may be a sulphide or oxide of lead, thallium, mercury, cadmium or silver, or a halogen compound of lead or thallium, or a crystalline form of selenium, sulphur, phosphorous, or iodine.[110]

On September 24, 1935, Hans G. Lubszynski of EMI applied for a patent for a camera tube with a transparent two-sided photoelectrode which would be discharged by either an electron beam or the light from a cathode ray tube.[111]

David Sarnoff returned from Europe in October 1935 after a ten-week stay. He denied that there were any changes in the RCA/EMI relationship. But this was not true. He had gone abroad in July to negotiate the separation of the two companies. By this time EMI neither desired nor needed any assistance from RCA to provide a television service. Shoenberg's desire to be free of any domination from RCA was now finalized. RCA had sold its EMI stock for some $10,225,917 in cash. No longer could Baird Television Ltd. insinuate that EMI was dependent on RCA or anyone else.

EMI was now free to enter the competition with Baird Television with no suggestion that it was foreign owned and operated.[112]

In October 1935 complete details of Baird Television and Marconi-EMI systems were revealed for the first time. The Baird signal was rather simple: it transmitted 240 lines sequentially at 25 pictures/second. A picture ratio of 4 to 3 was maintained. Amplitude modulation of the picture was used, with the picture carrier increasing towards white. Line and frames signals were in the opposite direction. The maximum picture frequency was 2 megacycles with no DC component being transmitted.[113]

Up to now only the barest details of Marconi-EMI's system had been publicly revealed. Although it was claimed that Isaac Shoenberg had submitted a fully detailed specification to the Television Committee early in 1935, it had been cloaked in secrecy. No one outside of a few key individuals had seen a demonstration. Of the two rivals, Marconi-EMI had been the most closemouthed.

The details revealed a very advanced, highly sophisticated set of specifications, one that turned out to be the standard for Great Britain for almost 50 years with few modifications. (It was finally phased out on January 2, 1985.) The basics were a 405-line, interlaced 2:1 system at 25 frames/sec. It used rectangular horizontal pulses, and a serrated vertical pulse (no equalizing pulses as the later American standard would). Modulation was white in a positive direction; polarization was vertical, and the picture bandwidth was some 2.5 megacycles (actually 2 megacycles at first) involving the use of double side-band modulation. The DC component was transmitted.[114]

In October 1935 both Western Electric and RCA refused to allow the telecasting of motion picture film licensed by them in Great Britain. Sir John Reith appealed to David Sarnoff, who waived prohibition until further notice. Western Electric also agreed as long as television had not passed out of the experimental into a commercial stage.[115]

The Baird Company gave its first demonstration of 240-line pictures from the Crystal Palace on November 8, 1935. It was received at the Press Club in London. It was claimed to be entirely successful. Pictures of several artists and parts of talking films were shown.[116]

In December 1935 Baird Television again announced that a demonstration of a full size television screen would be made at the Dominion Theater in London. It was planned to use the intermediate film system that Baird (and Fernseh) had "perfected." However, because of many problems, the planned demonstration was cancelled. Baird Television was to go to another system in order to demonstrate large screen television.[117]

Eric C.L. White of EMI applied for a patent for a pulse-operated thermionic valve apparatus on December 4, 1935. It was to be used for frequency division, electrical counting circuits and the like. It proved to be a superior means for generating pulses for a television sync generator.[118]

On December 31, 1935, Philo Farnsworth applied for a patent for an electrostatic lens method. It was planned to concentrate the electron image, thus reducing its size, in order to use less current in the magnetic scanning coils.[119]

The end of 1935 found Marconi-EMI with the most advanced television system in the world. By this time, they had passed up every other company, including RCA. Baird Television Ltd. was desperately trying to catch up in technology but had started too late. Even with the able assistance of Philo Farnsworth and its German ally, Fernseh A.G., the Baird Company's efforts were to be in vain.

Chapter 10
The London Television
Service: 1936–1939

On January 15, 1936, H.G. Lubszynski of EMI applied for three important patents. One was for an image iconoscope with added secondary emission. Another was for a camera tube that used several target electrodes. But his most important patent disclosed means for having the electron beam approach the screen to be scanned substantially "normally," i.e., at an angle of 15 degrees or less. It had been found that the current collected from a screen was dependent not only on its potential but very much upon the angle of incidence of the beam. It was recommended that the electrons be traveling at a comparatively low speed in order not to gain too high a lateral velocity.

By this time, efforts to produce a low velocity electron beam had shown that perpendicular landing of the beam was a necessity in order to have a flat field. It appears that as the angle of the beam increased, the beam lost much of its power and caused gradual fading of the image. Lubszynski's patent was very important, for it was the first step taken to produce a camera tube using a low velocity electron beam in order to eliminate the various harmful effects of a high velocity beam striking a target. These included "tilt and bend" (the uneven shading over the surface of the mosaic) and the copious secondary emission from the high velocity scanning beam.[1]

The work of Arturo Castellani was described in January 1936. Mr. Castellani was director of SAFAR (Societa Anomina Fabbricazione Apparecchi Radiofonici) in Italy. He had developed a television camera using his new camera tube, called the Telepantoscope.

Basically it was a form of Iconoscope with an electron beam that scanned a photoelectric mosaic. However, the electron beam scanned only a single line horizontally. A rotating mirror drum was used for the vertical movement of picture. The mirror drum had a synchronizing disc on it to ensure perfect synchronization. For film transmission, the mirror drum was dispensed with, using the continuous movement of the film for the vertical component.

226

The tube was small enough to be installed in a camera about the same size as an ordinary movie camera. It was claimed that Mr. Castellani had first displayed television equipment at the Radio Show in Milan in 1930.[2]

In February 1936 Dr. Zworykin gave a lecture on electron multipliers. He described his work on a new "electron image" tube. This tube could be used to produce a visible image from both the ultraviolet and infrared portions of the light spectrum. It operated by having a translucent photocathode made of a microscopic layer of platinum sputtered on a glass or quartz plate. A thin layer of oxidized silver would be reacted with cesium vapor, forming a sensitive photosensitive surface. Light from the scene would strike this layer and would cause electrons to be emitted from the other side. These would be concentrated by means of several electrical anodes which would focus the electrons onto a fluorescent screen. By means of this tube, examination of living specimens under infrared light was made possible. Or, it was claimed, it could be used to see through fog, smoke or darkness. A demonstration of the tube with motion pictures was given at the lecture.[3]

At this time in 1936 there were many difficulties in setting up the London Television Service. Relations between Baird Television and Marconi-EMI were very strained. Neither company would allow the other to know what it was doing. Terence C. Macnamara was in charge of planning the new station. Douglas C. Birkenshaw, engineer in charge at the Alexandra Palace, had the difficult task of keeping peace between the companies. They had come to no agreement regarding a standard form of license regarding their television patents.[4]

The early plans of the Baird Company included (1) the spot-light process, (2) the electron (Farnsworth) camera, (3) the use of the intermediate film process and (4) a mechanical film scanner using a Nipkow disc similar to that of the intermediate film process.

The Spotlight Studio used a disc scanner running at 6,000 rpm and having four spirals, each of 60 holes. Each spiral was brought into use by means of a further shutter disc revolving at 15,000 rpm. The large disc, which was enclosed in a vacuum, was rotated by means of a 100-cycle, 3-phase synchronous motor of ½ horsepower. The small disc was driven by a 1/20-horsepower, 50-cycle, 3-phase motor.

The light source was a large arc consuming 120 amperes. Owing to the intense heat generated by an arc of this power, the scanning gate was water-cooled. The reflected light was picked up by 4 large photocells of the multiplier type whose positions were adjustable. A cathode ray monitor was provided in the spotlight projection room.

The electron camera studio was equipped with two experimental electron cameras whose associated apparatus was housed in a further adjacently situated subcontrol room. One of the cameras was mounted on a movable run truck and the other on a tripod. The scanning currents and other supplies for these cameras were all generated in the subcontrol room

and sent to each camera by a composite cable. The camera outputs were amplified in head amplifiers and the output passed back along a composite cable to the subcontrol room. Intercamera fading was carried out in this control room, and the single output passed to the central control room.

The intermediate film process had a special camera using 17.5mm film (half of 35mm) which after being photographed was quickly developed, washed, fixed, and washed again. The film was scanned while still wet. The film was run through an underwater gate through which was directed a beam of light from a 60-ampere arc. The disc was driven by a ½-horsepower, 3-phase motor, with the disc being enclosed in a vacuum. It ran at 6,000 rpm and contained 60 holes arranged on the circumference of a circle. The light from the disc was sent to a photocell of the multiplier type and then passed through a series of amplifiers to the central control room. The sound was recorded on the film so that it was in sync with the picture when it was projected some 65 seconds later.

Two identical sets of Telecine equipment were installed for the transmission of 35mm motion picture film. The film was driven under continuous motion by a modified film projector and after illumination by a 60-ampere lamp was scanned by a disc unit similar to that of the intermediate film apparatus. There were means for a rapid changeover of both sound and vision from the output of one projector to another. Each of these picture sources was connected to the central control room, where they were all monitored and sent to the transmitter via a concentric cable. Transmission was the Baird standard of 240 lines sequential at 25 frames/sec.[5]

The Marconi-EMI system was built around the "Emitron" camera tube. This was Marconi-EMI's trade name for its version of the Iconoscope. There were six cameras all told. Four of the cameras were built into the Marconi-EMI studio. Camera 1 was usually in the center of the studio on a mobile truck. Cameras 2 and 3 might cover the scene from alternative viewpoints, while camera 4 was usually reserved for announcers or captions. The other two cameras were fed motion picture film from conventional 35mm film projectors. Sound was picked up by a moving coil microphone suspended from a boom, while an orchestra was covered by a ribbon microphone, and two other microphones were available as needed.

The Emitron cameras included an Emitron camera tube, an optical lens system and viewfinders, and a head amplifier. The optical system consisted of a matched pair of lenses, either 6.5 inch f/3 for normal use, or 12-inch focal length lenses at f/4.5, the width of the mosaic being some 4.75 inches. Automatic compensation for parallax was provided at all distances.

The signals from the various cameras were sent to a "fading and monitoring mixer," where any signal could be sent out for transmission

Opposite: Arturo Castellani and his Telepantoscope camera tube.

over the air, or sent to a second channel where it could be previewed before being used. There was even a third channel, used as either a spare or a means for transmitting film signals while rehearsing a live program. There was no instantaneous switching of pictures, only a means for slowly mixing from one channel to another (which did allow superimpositions).

An elaborate system of correcting the "tilt and bend" signals were incorporated in the system as well as the necessary controls for controlling the focusing beam and its electrical gain and adjusting the size of the picture. Picture transmission was on the Marconi-EMI standard of 405 lines interlaced two-to-one at 25 frames. This was the most advanced television system in the world at the time.[6]

On April 9, 1936, John L. Baird of Baird Television Ltd. applied for a patent for a color television method. It was a simple method of setting a rotating color wheel with three filters (red, green and blue) in front of a cathode ray tube so that each filter was viewed when its color was being transmitted. The use of only two filters was mentioned as well as the projection of the images through the filters onto a viewing screen.[7]

During the months of April and May of 1936, V. Jones of Baird Television Ltd. applied for several patents on various forms of electronic camera tubes. Baird Television was doing much research into electronic camera tubes in order to offset the advantage that Marconi-EMI had. Much effort was made to improve the Farnsworth Electron Camera. In spite of the fact that it was working quite well in the United States, Baird Television had very bad luck with it. For reasons which have never been explained, it never could produce reasonable pictures for Baird in England. As a result, it was sparingly used in the demonstrations at the Alexandra Palace according to Tony Bridgewater.[8]

The promise of a high definition service in England spurred much activity in the United States. RCA gave a demonstration of its system to the press on April 24, 1936, from Camden, N.J. This was the first demonstration given by RCA since May 17, 1932. It was of a 343-line, 30-frame interlaced system. The Empire State transmitter went back on the air on June 29, 1936. It was also a 343-line picture. However, it was not until July 7, 1939, that the pictures were considered "worth showing." This was the occasion of a demonstration of the RCA television system at Radio City for an assembly of RCA licensees. It was revealed that three receiving sets were in operation in the area but that within a short time more than 100 sets would be distributed at scattered outposts.[9]

In Los Angeles, the Don Lee Broadcasting System under Harry Lubcke had completed the design and construction of a high definition system. It was a 300-line, 24-frame sequential system. There was no interlacing due to the fact that the Los Angeles area was served by both 50- and 60-cycle power. Public demonstrations were held daily beginning on June 4, 1936.[10]

On June 15, 1936, a new set of television standards was presented to the Federal Communications Commission by the Television Committee of the RMA. They recommended a channel width of 6 mc, the use of between 440 and 450 lines at 60 fields interlaced, with spacing of the picture and sound carriers of approximately 3.25 mc. The use of negative picture polarity, with the sound carrier above the picture carrier was recommended, as was space to provide for seven channels between 42 mc and 90 mc. Three items were left for future discussion: (1) the use of vertical or horizontal polarization of transmission, (2) transmission of the DC component, and (3) maximum percentage of modulation.[11]

The Philco Radio and Television Corporation had also carried out a series of tests on 345-line, 30-frame interlaced pictures with sound on 54.25 mc and vision on 51 mc. Picture modulation was 2.5 mc and it was claimed that a special type of modulator had been developed. Philco was asking for a 6 mc total channel width.

On June 18, 1936, Philco started a series of "regular" programs, and a special demonstration was given to the press on August 11, 1936. The test of both film and "live" television (a mock prize fight from the roof of the plant) was staged under the direction of Albert F. Murray. It was noted that there was little difference in the pictures off the air or from concentric cable.[12]

Farnsworth Television had also improved its equipment. A new experimental television studio had been equipped with several Farnsworth cameras, for both "live" and film use. By this time, the "live" camera was quite compact, weighing some 75 pounds, being only $10 \times 12 \times 15$ inches wide. It even included a lens disc mounted with 4 lenses for varying focus. It was claimed that the overall sensitivity of camera was such that 40 foot-candles was sufficient for satisfactory television pictures!

Farnsworth Television was transmitting on 343 lines at 30 frames interlaced. It was announced that a new television station was being built in North Philadelphia. It intended to operate with the picture at 62.75 mc and the sound at 68 mc with a 2.5 mc bandwidth.[13]

On June 25, 1936, L. Klatzow of EMI applied for a patent for a method of coating the mosaic screen of an Iconoscope with silver after it has been assembled in the tube. Means were described so that the screen could be tested until satisfactory performance was achieved.[14]

Dr. C.B. Joliffe of RCA mentioned in June 1936 the possibility that for television transmission a portion of one side-band could be eliminated and more space be available for broadcasting. Until this time, most television broadcasting had been accomplished as double side-band with two symmetrical sides, it being obvious that the second side-band was redundant.[15]

It had long since been found that the received television picture was improved when the receiver had been slightly detuned. Von Ardenne had reported on this phenomenon earlier, and RCA stated that they, too, had noticed its results but claimed that at a modulation frequency of some 500 kc doubling the bandwidth did not make a great deal of difference.

However, with the greater bandwidths now being used, experiments were being made to take advantage of this feature. There were no difficulties when the carrier was one edge of the overall selectivity curve. This method also reduced the number of stages in the i-f system of the receiver. It also stated that if one side-band could be suppressed at the transmitter, it would result in considerable savings in channel bandwidth requirements. It was reported on November 29, 1936, that field tests were being pursued by W.J. Poch and D.W. Epstein of the RCA Laboratories.[16]

There was a report of a private demonstration of the new Scophony television system in July 1936. A "Junior" receiver was demonstrated with a picture some 8 inches by 10 inches on 240 lines at 25 pictures/sec. It was claimed that the definition was remarkably good. Another demonstration was given of a picture some 5 feet by 5 feet, while a third screen of some 13 feet by 10 feet was in the process of being set up.

More details of the new Scophony system were released. It used a new method of "light control" beam convertor and "split focus." The light control was a method of simultaneous projection whereby as many as fifty or one hundred apertures were operating at one time. This resulted in increased brightness. There was mention of supersonic waves in a liquid column which were modulated and caused to stand still by the use of a rotating mirror drum. The use of "split focus" was an optical arrangement of crossed cylindrical lenses which caused a beam of light to be focused in two separate planes, thus producing more light with reduced size of the moving parts.[17]

The Eleventh Olympic Games were held in Berlin, Germany, in July/August 1936. This was covered by television for the first time in history. The coverage was by the German Post Office (DRP), which was using Iconoscope cameras furnished by Telefunken. The Post Office had three Iconoscope cameras, two covering the main areas and the third at the swimming pool. One of the cameras was equipped with lenses of 250 mm (10 inches), 900 mm (35.5 inches) and 1600 mm (63 inches) in order to cover all of the events. The Post Office was also using several intermediate film trucks.

Fernseh also provided equipment for the games. They had a Farnsworth electron camera which "delivered very sharp signals, free from interference components, but only in very bright weather." Fernseh also furnished an outside broadcast van using the intermediate film system, which had the advantage of mobility and could take pictures in almost any weather.

The games were transmitted to Berlin, where they were viewed mainly in some 25 "television parlors" and theaters, as well as in the Olympic Village. Transmission was on 180 lines at 25 pictures/sec. Unfortunately, it was reported that the reception was rather poor, the whole screen shook and "the eye strain being considerable ... many didn't stay for the remainder of the afternoon events."[18]

Radio Olympia opened in London on Wednesday, August 26, 1936.

It featured television transmissions for the first time. Television broadcasting from the Alexandra Palace was scheduled daily from noon to 1:30 and from 4:30 to 6:00. Three brands of receivers were displayed: Bush Radio (manufactured for Baird Television Ltd.), the Marconiphone Company, and H.M.V. combined sound and vision receivers. All sets were to operate on both the Baird and Marconi-EMI standards.

Baird Television won the toss of a coin and started the first day's transmissions. There were many "live" pickups, but the bulk of programming seems to have been excerpts of motion pictures and newsreels of the day. There were many breakdowns of equipment and it was even claimed that there were overt acts of sabotage. Baird Television staged another of its "firsts" by taking a Baird television receiver up in an airplane and receiving pictures from the Alexandra Palace.

However, it was agreed that the show was successful and that it did whet public interest in receivers and a demand for the same. At the end of the show, it was announced that the programs from the Alexandra Palace would be suspended for some four or five weeks until a regular service would begin.[19]

The 1936 Berlin Radio Exhibition was held after the Olympic Games from August 28 to September 6, 1936. While the official German television standard was 180 lines at 25 frames/sequential, most of the exhibits were being exhibited on a 375-line standard at 50 fields/interlaced scanning.

Fernseh showed an electron camera of the Farnsworth type that had been used at the Olympic Games. This camera was operating at 180 lines and the "pictures were very pleasant." Fernseh also displayed a 375-line film transmitter using a Nipkow disc. It was claimed that the best pictures at the exhibition came from this apparatus. Fernseh had just delivered a second intermediate film transmitter to the German Post Office and had supplied a spot-light transmitter to be used in a two-way television system.

Telefunken was using Iconoscope camera tubes for all their equipment including film projection. They displayed a 7 by 9-inch television receiver. They also had a small theater where they projected pictures some 3 by 3½ feet. Loewe Radio showed a regular receiver as well as a projection type with a picture size of 16 by 20 inches on a ground glass screen. Lorenz displayed a receiver with a 7 by 9-inch picture.

Tekade showed the only mechanical receiver, which had a double mirror screw with a lens drum and an arc lamp modulated by a Kerr cell. The pictures were reasonably good with fair brightness.

Missing from this exhibit was the intermediate film receiver of Fernseh. (According to one source, it was in London and was going to be used by Baird Television for a large screen demonstration at the Dominion Theatre. This demonstration never took place.) Also missing were the Karolus large screen lamp bulb screens and any of the television equipment of Manfred von Ardenne. A demonstration of the Berlin-Leipzig Television Telephone was given in the Exhibition Hall.[20]

In Japan, it was reported that the Japan Broadcasting Corporation (NHK) was going to do extensive research in television in order to make possible direct viewing of the 1940 Olympic Games, which were to be held in Tokyo, Japan. The experiments were to be directed by Dr. K. Takayanagi of the Hamamatsu Engineering College, who had been released from his duties at that Institution.[21]

The opening of the London Television Service was scheduled for November 2, 1936. A coin was tossed to see which system would open the service, and Baird Television won. At 3:30 the service was started with speeches by R.C. Norman, chairman of the BBC; Major Tryon, the postmaster-general; Lord Selsdon; and Sir Harry Greer, the chairman of Baird Television. The speeches were followed by some light entertainment. It was reported that John Logie Baird was present but was not invited to take part in the ceremonies.

A half-hour later, the program was repeated on the Marconi-EMI Television system with a speech by Alfred Clark, the chairman of Marconi-EMI. The trials were on. One comment on the opening day was that the EMI transmission was "faultless," a portent of things to come. The television service started that day was to continue (with a few minor interruptions) for the next few years. Only World War II could bring it to a halt.

However, the Baird system was in trouble from the beginning. It was apparent that it could not hold out for long. The spot-light studio, operating in near darkness, was hopelessly out of date; the intermediate film system was very dependent on a huge supply of water, sometimes running out of it and halting operations. The Farnsworth electron camera, still in a developmental state in England, was presenting problems. It was used for a few programs but, due to low sensitivity (noise) and poor geometry, was soon withdrawn.[22]

The final blow to the Baird Company was a disastrous fire at the Crystal Palace on November 30, 1936, which destroyed its research laboratories.[23] That the Baird system was to be soundly defeated was soon apparent. This defeat was preordained, but circumstances were such that since Baird Television had a powerful press behind it and EMI had been so secretive about its work, a government decision in EMI's behalf would have provoked a row of immense proportions. However, the trials continued until the end of 1936.

On November 5, 1936, Alda V. Bedford and Knut J. Magnusson of the Radio Corporation applied for a patent for a television camera apparatus. It was for a complete camera including double optics for the operator and camera tube. It also included a pedestal on wheels for mobility and means for raising and lowering the camera head. It was the prototype for the television camera used by RCA for the next 5 to 7 years.

In November 1936 the Research Laboratory of N.V. Philips, Gloeilampenfabrieken, Eindhoven, Holland, described a complete Iconoscope camera system. As it was experimental, it could be used on a great variety of line frequencies from 90 lines at 50 frames sequential to 405 lines at 25 frames/interlaced. In addition to the "live" camera, a complete film chain using an Iconoscope was displayed. This marks the beginning of the Philips interest in electronic television.[25]

On December 7, 1936, Baird Television gave a demonstration of large screen television at the Dominion Theatre in London. It was a mechanical system that produced a picture some 8 feet by 6 feet with a minimum of flicker. (This same system was again demonstrated on January 4, 1937). It was later revealed that this system used spot-light scanning with a mirror drum in conjunction with a slotted disk. The pictures were of 120 lines at 17 frames/sec. It used a form of interlaced scanning to reduce flicker. The transmitter was on the third floor of the theatre and all transmission was closed-circuit. At the receiver, the light from a high intensity lamp was modulated by a Kerr cell. A mirror drum with a slotted disc reconstituted the picture.[26]

The trials between Baird Television and Marconi-EMI were coming to an end some three months after they had begun. On February 4, 1937, the BBC announced that they had chosen the Marconi-EMI system over that of Baird Television, Ltd.

From February 8, 1937, on, the 405-line standard only would be telecast from the Alexandra Palace. Three reasons were given for this choice: (1) the superior quality due to the high definition, (2) much less flicker due to interlacing and (3) the greater scope for development offered by the Emitron camera. It was promised that these standards would not be substantially altered before the end of 1938. Actually, the victory of Marconi-EMI gave the London Television Service a set of standards that would serve them well for almost fifty years.[27]

In January 1937, both Farnsworth Television and RCA promised that they would soon be using the new unofficial RMA 441-line standard. However, the first demonstration on 441 lines in the United States was given by the Philco Radio and Television Corporation on February 11, 1937. It was claimed that the pictures offered 30 percent more clarity than comparable 345-line pictures. In addition, Philco claimed that it was introducing high fidelity television as it was using a modulation frequency of 4.5 mc, which meant that Philco was transmitting over 680 picture elements per line — and only 588 elements were necessary to create equal horizontal to vertical resolution. Details of a new transmitter modulator were not revealed except to state that one side-band was attenuated. At the receiver, a "quasi-single side-band" reception system was used. The head end circuits were "detuned" so that the i-f band-pass region was centered over the unattenuated sideband.[28]

On March 31, 1937, Standard Telephone & Cables, Ltd., applied for a patent for a video recorder using magnetized tape. The magnetic tape passed through a gap in a yoke surrounding a cathode ray tube. Inside this tube an electron beam modulated by the television signal was made to pass between a gap, which then transferred its signal to the yoke through which the magnetic tape was traveling.

For playback, when the tape passed through the gap, it caused variations in the circuit, which then entered the tube, causing the electron beam to be modulated. This beam then struck a target, which caused variations in the output current of the device.[29]

The new Farnsworth Studios in Wyndmoor, Pennsylvania, were operating in May 1937. Both film and live pickups were shown. In fact, the "live" studios using Farnsworth cameras seemed to be using about the same amount of lighting as those using Iconoscope cameras. It appeared that the Farnsworth cameras needed about 150/170 footcandles for studio lighting, while the Iconoscope cameras used about 100 footcandles. In either case, this was quite bright and made for very hot television studios.

Motion picture film projection was able to provide some 200 footcandles, which was more than adequate for both camera tubes. But whereas the Image Dissector was able to project clear, distinct pictures, the Iconoscope film projection was bothered with shading problems that produced smudgy, blotched pictures. As a result, there was renewed interest into film projection using dissectors or Nipkow discs.[30]

It was reported in May 1937 that television equipment built by RCA Victor was expected to reach Moscow that month for use in a television center erected in Moscow. Other centers were to be constructed in Leningrad and Kiev and use equipment built in Soviet factories.[31]

On May 12, 1937, at the Twelfth Annual I.R.E. Convention in New York City, RCA demonstrated a new method of large screen television using a tube developed by Dr. R.R. Law of the RCA Harrison, N.J., laboratories. The tube, called a projection kinescope, was some 18 inches long and projected an image some 1½ inches by 2¼ inches onto its fluorescent screen. It was able to project an image as large as 3 by 4 feet. While the demonstration was impressive, it was claimed that it was not for home use, but would be confined to the laboratory.[32]

Also at this convention, a paper was read on the "Theory and Performance of the Iconoscope." It was proven that as a storage device, the Iconoscope had very low efficiency, between 5 to 10 percent. This low efficiency was caused by the redistribution of secondary electrons produced by the beam and the fact that small fields draw away the photoelectrons from the mosaic. A phenomenon known as "line sensitivity" was discussed. It referred to the fact that the line ahead of the scanning beam was subject to a strong positive field and consequently had high photoelectric efficiency.

The article mentioned two methods for increasing the sensitivity of the Iconoscope. The first was by the use of secondary emission signal multipliers and a low capacitance mosaic. The second made use of secondary emission image intensification, which could be accomplished by allowing an electron image produced in some form of image tube to fall on a mosaic constructed in such a way that the elements extend through the mosaic. This was one technique employed in the new "image iconoscope."[33]

Also on May 12, 1937, the BBC telecast the coronation of George VI from a position in Hyde Park Corner in London. This was the first outside broadcast using the newly adopted Marconi-EMI television system. Three cameras fed their pictures to a van, from which they were sent by a special coaxial cable to the Alexandra Palace.[34]

The 1937 Television Exhibition in London opened on June 10 at the Science Museum. The exhibition featured a Cossor film scanner, which provided television signals when the Alexandra Palace was off the air. It used a cathode ray tube to produce an unmodulated raster. The film was run between it and a photocell to produce the video signal. This signal was amplified and mixed with sync pulses and fed to the various receivers. This system was similar to the 1931 von Ardenne film projector.

Baird Television Ltd. demonstrated a version of their old 30-line television system and showed the latest model of the Farnsworth electron image camera. Other exhibits included those of Scophony and its large screen mechanical scanners. There were samples of coaxial cable from Standard Telephone & Cables, Ltd., similar to that installed between London and Birmingham in 1936.

EMI displayed one of its outside broadcast vehicles as well as the latest type of Emitron camera. The vehicle, which really was a traveling control room, was rather large, being some 27 feet long, 7 feet wide and over 10 feet high and weighing some 9 tons. Inside the vehicle was all of the equipment required to operate three Emitron cameras and the necessary sound equipment. Each camera had 1,000 feet of multi-core cable to allow it to operate away from the vehicle. There was complete control room scanning and amplifying equipment including the use of a fader as well as two visual monitors. Up to six microphones could be fed to an audio mixer, where an audio signal could be sent by land-line to the Alexandra Palace.

This van was to be accompanied by a second similar vehicle with an ultra-shortwave vision transmitter built into it. It operated in the region of 64 mc and delivered a power of 1,000 watts at peak picture white modulation to a special antenna. Finally, there was a third vehicle that supplied the electric power for both the other units. This complete outside broadcast unit was the prototype for all future remote trucks.

In addition, EMI displayed a "working" model of the television camera of Campbell Swinton, which had been built in the EMI laboratories. Unfortunately, there is no information available as how it was constructed or operated. Only a photograph is available. This exhibit was in line with EMI's contention that the Emitron camera tube was based on the writings of Campbell Swinton and not necessarily those of Dr. Zworykin.[35]

EMI also displayed a working model of a photoconductive tube by H.

Miller and J.W. Strange. In a later paper, Miller and Strange described their efforts to produce a practical camera tube using the photoconductive effect. Several patents had been taken out, but they disclosed that up to now no one had succeeded in producing a transmitter using the photoconductive effect. (Obviously, they were not yet aware of the progress being made in the Bell Telephone Laboratories by Hofele and Gray.)

After extensive experiments, zinc selenide had turned out to be the most sensitive material tested, and a tube was constructed using it. It produced sharp pictures, the conductivity along the surface being negligible. Miller and Strange mentioned that similar work on photoconductive tubes was being done by Harley Iams and Albert Rose of RCA and Max Knoll and Fritz Schröter of Telefunken.[36]

In July 1937, the tennis matches at Wimbledon were televised by means of the mobile outside broadcast unit of the BBC. The games were transmitted on ultra-shortwaves twelve miles to the Alexandra Palace. This was the first time that any outside event had been televised without a cable link. Another first for the London Television Service![37]

On July 22, 1937, Farnsworth Television and the American Telephone and Telegraph Company signed an agreement whereby each had the privilege of using the other's patents. This was quite a feather in Farnsworth's cap. It meant that AT&T had finally recognized the value of his work in television. This agreement had taken place after some four months of examination by the Bell Telephone Laboratories to analyze the 150 Farnsworth patents and submit a formal report. The agreement was nonexclusive; both were free to license other parties.[38]

Harley Iams had been joined by Dr. Albert Rose in the laboratories of the RCA Manufacturing Company at Harrison, N.J. They reported on their work on camera tubes in August 1937. It included research on tubes with light sensitive targets such as the Iconoscope, which were photoemissive; on targets made of cuprous oxide on copper, which were photovoltaic; and on targets made of aluminum oxide (Al_2O_3) or zirconium oxide (ZrO_2), which were photoconductive. Targets made of selenium were also tried but with rather poor results.

They had found the most sensitive targets were those in which an electron picture was focused upon a scanned, secondary electron emissive target. The scanning and picture projection might be separated by using a two-sided target. Coupling between the two sides was obtained by conducting plugs through the target. This was a two-sided form of the image Iconoscope. It was noted that work on this kind of tube had begun in 1933 coincident with that of Hans Lubszynski of EMI. Iams and Rose claimed that this general design offered considerable hope for the future as the operating sensitivity was high and the optical arrangement convenient.[39]

The Berlin Radio Exhibition was held from July 30 to August 8, 1937. Fernseh A.G. did not display the Farnsworth Image Dissector at this time. It was claimed that in spite of secondary electron multiplication, it was not sufficiently sensitive for general work. However, Fernseh displayed two types of Iconoscope cameras. One was a large camera for studio work with the viewfinder lenses mounted over the taking lenses as in the RCA camera. It had lenses of f/1.8 with a focal length of 18 cm. The other was a smaller camera with f/1.5 lenses side by side similar to the Emitron camera. The pictures had good definition, and the halftone values were very good.

All of the demonstrations were on 441 lines at 50 fields/interlaced. Fernseh displayed its intermediate film transmitter, which did use the Farnsworth Image Dissector as a film scanner. Fernseh also showed a Nipkow disc film transmitter running in a vacuum. It was claimed that this last equipment produced the best pictures at the show. It appears that there had been complaints that pictures from motion picture film from the Alexandra Palace were marred by dark and light patches.

Telefunken had on display two Iconoscope cameras set up in a studio. It also demonstrated a television "public address system" using a cathode ray spot-light transmitter. This system used a high brightness cathode ray tube as a light source and projected its picture on a large 5 by 6-foot screen, which was also produced by cathode ray projection. It operated on 147 lines, interlaced scanning. It was claimed that the amount of flood light on the speaker required in order to televise with an electron camera was very many times in excess of the illumination projected on the speaker when using spot-light transmission.

The German Post Office also had a demonstration studio with Iconoscope cameras and a mechanical film transmitter of the Nipkow disc type that transmitted extremely good pictures. Both Loewe Radio and Lorenz demonstrated 441-line Nipkow disc film transmitters. It was reported that the German government was in no hurry to start an extensive program service and that it was probable that no developments would take place on the commercial side for the next two years.[40]

Radio Olympia was held from August 25 to September 4, 1937, and consisted mostly of displays of home television receivers. There were 14 small theatres displaying sets from 14 manufacturers. Most were regular direct-viewing screens except for H.M.V., which had a 10 by 8-inch reflected picture, and Philips, which had a projected 20 by 16-inch picture. It was reported that the performance of the sets varied from "very good, outstanding brilliance" for a Baird T12 receiver, to "poor definition" for a Pye 4045, Major 1 receiver.

Scophony Ltd. did not give a demonstration, claiming that because of the considerable amount of irregular timing and phase shifting of the television signal from the Alexandra Palace, it was quite difficult for receivers (of the Scophony type) that possessed mechanical inertia to operate satisfactorily.[41]

However, that was a very minor criticism of the London Television Service. Arriving in a constant stream, visitors from the United States were astounded by (1) the uniform high quality of the pictures, (2) the regularly scheduled programs and (3) the coverage of outside events. Some of the comments made at the time were "an operative system giving good stable pictures of acceptable detail, brilliance and interest"; "stability, freedom from faulty sync and a wide contrast range"; and "of remarkable contrast and detail; exactly like a movie." A real tribute to Isaac Shoenberg and the engineers of Marconi-EMI.

The programming was variable, ranging from short dramatic skits to comedy, lectures, newsreels and of course film cartoons. The major criticism was for the film transmissions from the Emitron cameras with their "shading" problems.[42]

Receiving sets were on sale for a very high price at the time, from $300 to $800, and as a result only a very limited number of sets (fewer than 3,000) found their way into homes around London.

The Columbia Broadcasting System announced that it was going to build studios in Grand Central Terminal in New York City. They claimed that they were experimenting with 441-line pictures using a film scanner with continuous motion projected onto a Farnsworth Image Dissector tube with a 9-stage electron multiplier.[43]

In September 1937 Dr. Peter Goldmark, the chief television engineer for the Columbia Broadcasting System, reported that the BBC was already using a new "electric camera," which had been rendered panchromatic to a fair degree. EMI was now using Emitron camera tubes, using the new Klatzow method of finalizing treatment of the mosaic with silver to get rid of the excessive infrared response that was so typical of the cesium-silver-oxide mosaics being used at the time.

In addition, Dr. Goldmark reported on a new television camera about ten times more sensitive than any in use. He was referring to the new "Super Emitron" camera tube of Hans Lubszynski and Sidney Rodda, which was used for the first time in November 1937. This was an advanced form of image Iconoscope.[44]

The Super Emitron tube worked in the following manner: the scene to be televised was optically focused onto a continuous transparent photocathode surface, and the electron image so generated resembled that obtained with the Image Dissector tube. This electron image was electrostatically accelerated towards the secondary emission mosaic (which was not photosensitive) and at the same time was electromagnetically focused by a coil.

The charges stored in this manner on the mosaic were greater than in the ordinary Iconoscope for two reasons: (1) the continuous photocathode was more sensitive than a regular mosaic and (2) five or more electrons left the mosaic for every primary electron incidental on it. Hence it was as much as ten times more sensitive than the ordinary Iconoscope. In addition to the increased photosensitivity, the size of the optical picture on the photocathode surface was smaller than the ordinary mosaic, and shorter focal length lenses could be used for more depth of focus.

At first, this new tube suffered from some serious electrical and optical distortions. Among them were curvature of field, pincushion and "S" distortion. However, these problems were slowly solved, while the tube's increased sensitivity was an important asset for covering outdoor events. The first use of the new Super Emitron camera was the coverage of the "Cenotaph" ceremony in London on November 11, 1937.[45]

The Bell Telephone Company had long been working on a coaxial cable system, and on November 9, 1937, it transmitted the first television pictures between New York City and Philadelphia. It used a 1 mc wide, coaxial system. The pictures were originated from a 6-foot steel mechanical disc scanner operating on 240 lines at 24 frames/sec. The image from the motion picture film passed continuously in front of 240 high speed lenses set in a circle on the disc.

The light from the film went to a phototube containing an electron multiplier. The output of the multiplier was applied to a double modulator, which raised the entire spectrum about 100 kc. Thus the region between 0 and 100 kc was available for the sound channel and sync pulses. Sync pulses were obtained optically from special holes drilled in the scanning disc and were transmitted on a separate channel. The picture signal was equalized and corrected for phase distortion by means of repeaters every ten miles over the coaxial line.

The pictures were reproduced on a conventional cathode ray receiver using a green screen. It was claimed that the pictures were comparable in quality to the 441-line interlaced pictures being shown in New York and Philadelphia.[46]

RCA was projecting motion picture film using an Iconoscope. The use of interlacing at 60 fields/sec complicated the process. The projector had a special intermittent with a ratio of 3:2 that allowed the first frame to be scanned three times at 1/20 second while the second frame was scanned two times at 1/30 second, thus averaging 1/24 second each. A special shutter admitted light only during the vertical blanking period, which created a charge-picture on the mosaic that remained until scanned. While this solved the film speed problem, it appears that the picture quality was not as good as that produced by the Image Dissector or Nipkow disc.[47]

On November 9, 1937, the Philco Television Corporation announced that it was using a new transmitter modulator developed by W.N. Parker with a range of nearly 5 mc using one side-band. Reception was by use of a quasi-single side-band receiver.[48]

The new large screen Scophony system was demonstrated in London at British Industries House on December 8, 1937. It was claimed that "the pictures were crisp, flickerless and bright enough to be seen in comfort by everyone." Certain adjustments had been made to the television signal from the Alexandra Palace that allowed the Scophony receiver to follow its signal with no difficulty. A picture was projected onto a large screen (six feet by five feet) as well as a home receiver providing a two-foot-square picture.[49]

Also on December 8, 1937, a large screen television demonstration was given at the Palais Theatre in Kent by Baird Television. The picture, some eight feet by six feet, was of a regular program of the BBC from the

Alexandra Palace. However, Baird Television stated that it planned to provide its own programming from the Crystal Palace.

The projection equipment consisted of a special picture tube that formed a small bright picture some two inches square, which was then projected by a lens of large aperture onto the screen. It was announced that Gaumont-British Pictures Corporation intended to equip some fifteen theatres in the London area with large screen television equipment.[50]

It was reported on December 12, 1937, that the first mobile unit for NBC Television was presented to Radio City. It consisted of two motor vans. The first one consisted of the complete pickup apparatus including cameras, sync generators, rectifiers, amplifiers for blanking and deflection and line amplifiers. This van carried two Iconoscope cameras, which were connected by several hundred feet of coaxial cable. The sound equipment included several parabolic microphones.

The second van, connected by 500 feet of coaxial cable, contained a complete microwave relay transmitter. The vision transmitter operated on 177,000 kc and was connected to a special directional aerial. It was expected to have a range of some 25 miles and to be in operation early in 1938.[51]

Allen B. DuMont applied for a patent for a system of communication on January 11, 1938, whereby the transmitter (camera) and receiver (viewing screen) were in the same glass envelope. It was planned to have a single beam sweep across a photosensitive surface and then a fluorescent screen. By means of electronic switching, it would be possible to both send and receive pictures from the same apparatus.[52]

On January 17, 1938 (also on April 30 and June 1), Georges Valensi applied for a patent for a color system using a single channel. He described means for combining signals (both monochrome and color) into a single channel so that a reduction in bandwidth was accomplished.[53]

The work of G. Krawinkel, W. Kronjager and H. Salow of Berlin-Templehof on a storage television pickup tube with a semiconducting dielectric was reported in January 1938. They discussed the possible replacement of a nonconducting target layer (such as mica) by a semiconducting one (i.e., slightly conducting glass) which should give higher field strengths at the target.[54]

G. Braude (in Russia) applied for a patent for a camera tube using a semiconducting two-sided target on February 3, 1938. The patent called for a thin dielectric plate that had a certain amount of leakage. An image was to be projected onto the photosensitive side of the plate through a transparent electrode "A" (mesh screen) and was to be scanned on the back side of the plate by an electron beam. The light from the scene produced photoelectrons on the photosensitive side of the mosaic element, which were transferred to the mesh screen, which could be placed on the directive plate. This would be discharged by the action of the electron beam scanning the back of the plate and become the picture signal.

It was possible to use an electron image (such as in the image

Iconoscope) that passed through the mesh screen to a semitransparent mosaic, which was not photosensitive. It was later claimed that such a mosaic was realized and tested. This use of a thin dielectric plate with controlled leakage was an important step forward toward the goal of a practical two-sided target.[55]

On February 4, 1938, John L. Baird gave a demonstration of color television at the Dominion Theatre in London. The television transmission was by wireless from the South Tower of the Crystal Palace. The picture was 120 lines. Transmission and reception were by means of a mirror drum with 20 mirrors revolving at 6,000 rpm. These mirrors reflect the scene to be transmitted through a lens with 12 concentric slots at different distances from its periphery. By this means the field given by the 20-line drum is interlaced six times to give a 120-line picture repeated twice for each revolution of the disc. Each of the slots was covered with a light filter, blue-green and red being used alternately, the effect of this being to transmit lines of the picture corresponding to a blue-green image and a red image. Light from a high intensity arc lamp was concentrated on the moving aperture in the disc and yielded sufficient light to fill a screen 12 feet by 9 feet. Results indicated that the picture was still experimental and one should not be critical of its "imperfections." This appears to be the first demonstration of large screen color television by wireless. Another Baird first. The program consisted of live pickups, colored slides and a colored cartoon.[56]

In February 1938 the Allen B. DuMont Laboratories announced that they had developed a television system which could transmit pictures without synchronizing signals. By reducing the number of frames to 15 per second, they claimed they could cut the television bandwidth in half. As a result, they were transmitting 441-line pictures at 15 frames/sec interlaced 4:1.

It was planned to use double sawtooth scanning: from left to right and right to left horizontally, and at the same time from top to bottom and bottom to top vertically, to eliminate the need for synchronizing signals. The waveforms of the vertical and horizontal scanning voltages were used as modulating signals on an auxiliary carrier. After demodulation and amplification at the receiver, the waveform was then used directly as a sweep voltage for the receiving cathode ray tube.

It was asserted that a flickerless, 441-line image was produced, even though only 15 frames/sec were being transmitted. The audio was sent on a subcarrier of 25,000 cycles with a channel some 266 kc wide. It was claimed that this method saved some 2 megacycles in bandwidth.[57]

On March 29, 1938, the Farnsworth Company announced a new motion picture projector for television using a continuous movement devised by Harry S. Bamford. It used two lens discs, each carrying a total of 24 lenses and rotating in opposite directions. The projector was so synchronized with the scanning system of the dissector tube, that alternate frames were scanned two and three times respectively, providing an interlaced picture. It was claimed that the pictures had "unusually good contrast and definition."[58]

In April 1938 there was a report on high definition pictures from Fernseh A.G., using a film projector with a Farnsworth Image Dissector tube incorporating an electron-multiplier type of phototube. These were 441-line images interlaced 2:1 at 50 fields/sec. Pictures from this projector were thrown onto a screen some 6½ feet wide (2 meters) by a special projection-type cathode ray tube.[59]

On May 28, 1938, Peter Goldmark of CBS applied for a patent for a motion picture film projector with a plurality of lenses so that only one at a time was used to project an image onto an Image Dissector tube.[60]

Philo Farnsworth described a storage type of camera tube in May 1938. In this tube, it was claimed, the image was amplified before scanning. The tube consisted of an image grid, a signal screen and a cathode ray gun within the tube. The image grid was made up of a thin sheet of suitable metal, perforated with approximately 160,000 holes to the square inch. On the side towards the window of the tube was deposited an insulating substance, and upon this insulator were deposited numberless small islands of photoelectrically active material. The signal screen was a comparatively fine mesh of wire in front of the image grid.

Due to the action of the light from the scene, an electrostatic charge image was set up on the image grid. The electron gun projected a fine high velocity beam of electrons on the metal side of the image grid, and secondary electrons were produced at the point of impact of the beam. These electrons were drawn through the holes in the screen by the positive action of the photo islands on the opposite side. This resulted in amplification since far more electrons were produced per picture element. Almost all of the electrons were collected by an anode, although a small amount might be collected by the photoislands. A tube of this type was introduced by Philo Farnsworth in November 1938 at the fall meeting of the IRE. It was later claimed that this Farnsworth image amplifier tube had been operated in the laboratory with scenes having only 2 or 3 candles/square foot.

It was mentioned that this principle could also be used as a normal dissector tube. In this case, the back of the storage screen was coated with photosensitive material, which if flooded from a uniform light source produced photoelectrons. These photoelectrons were subject to the same triode action. However, in this case an amplified electron image was formed, which was scanned across an aperture as in the standard dissector tube.[61]

The Television Committee of the RMA, under acting chairman Albert F. Murray, approved a new set of American television standards on June 3, 1938. This included a 441-line frequency so that the synchronizing generator could be simplified ($3 \times 3 \times 7 \times 7$ as integers) at 60 fields interlaced. Other specifications included a 4:3 aspect ratio, negative picture modulation, horizontal polarization, a constant black (DC) level and the adoption of the serrated type of vertical sync pulses with additional equalizing pulses.

The advent of single side-band operation led to a separation of some

4.5 mc between picture and sound, rather than 3.25 mc, for greater picture detail. It was claimed that the Philco experimental television transmitter W3XE in Philadelphia was already transmitting signals according to the new proposed RMA standards in July 1938.[62]

Baird Television had installed a large screen cathode ray projection unit in the Tatler Theatre, Charing Cross Road. The device was used to project pictures some six feet by eight feet across. A public demonstration was given on June 9, 1938, of the "Trooping of the Colours."[63]

In London, the London Television Service was telecasting three times daily. There were transmissions at 12 noon, 3:00 P.M. and at 9:00 in the evening. In addition, the outside broadcast units were covering a wide variety of outdoor events, including boxing in April, the Whitney Cup Polo Match and Chelsea Flower Show in May, "Trooping of the Colours" from Whitehall, the Lords Test Match and the Derby in June, Wimbledon and cricket in July of 1938.[64]

In spite of the artistic and technical success of the London Television Service the sale of sets was quite low. It was decided that Radio Olympia, to be held on August 24–September 3, 1938, would have at least 20 set manufacturers with television as the main attraction. Alexandra Palace would be broadcasting some five or six hours daily during the exhibition. There was a statement that unless there was a boost in the sales of sets, the second television transmitter at either Birmingham or Manchester would not likely be built.[65]

At the Thirteenth Annual Convention of the IRE, held in New York City from June 16–18, 1938, many papers of interest were presented. They ranged from papers on single side-band transmission, multi-stage electron multipliers, to "The Image Iconoscope" by Harley Iams, George Morton and V.K. Zworykin. These latter three reported that their work had been parallel with that of EMI and others and their tube operated on the same principles. It was claimed that the Image Iconoscope was some six to ten times more sensitive than the Iconoscope which needed at least 1,000 to 2,000 footcandles for good operation.[66]

However, RCA was not really interested in the Image Iconoscope in spite of its advantages over the Iconoscope. Harley Iams and Albert Rose were hard at work in the RCA Laboratories on a camera tube using low velocity electron beam scanning. Iams had applied for a patent on May 31, 1938, in which the target transferred its pattern to a photoelectric screen by means of a magnetic field. This target was discharged by the action of a flying spot cathode ray tube. Thus, since only low velocity electrons were discharged, no "dark spot" signals were produced.

On July 30, 1938, Albert Rose of RCA applied for a patent that proposed to use a low velocity electron beam for scanning a translucent mosaic target. The electrons not reaching the target were returned by a different path to a collecting electrode in front of the electron gun. The television signal could be taken either from the signal plate or from the electrode, where it could be amplified by an electron multiplier. The entire tube was immersed in a magnetic field from a coil, and scanning was by a magnetic coil for vertical deflection and electrostatic plates for horizontal deflection.[67]

On September 12, 1938, Albert Rose and Harley Iams of RCA described their work on low velocity scanning beam tubes. The article mentioned the importance of a uniform axial magnetic field which would keep the beam well focused and substantially in its normal path as it approached the target.

It also mentioned that it was desirable to have the low velocity beam approach the target at a consistent angle of incidence for improved operations. Another requisite was relatively high beam currents (about two microamperes).

A description of two tubes using the relatively simple photoelectric beam (flying spot scanning from a cathode ray tube) was given. The first used a two-sided target (as described in the September 23, 1937, application of Rose and of the application of Iams of May 31, 1938) using a photocathode and a single-sided mosaic at right angles.

Photos of the experimental tubes were shown. The first type used a two-sided target and cathode ray tube scanning. This tube demonstrated the improvements to be expected in signal strength, operating efficiency and dark spot control from low velocity scanning. In the other tube, photoelectrons released from the mosaic were collected by the scanning electrode instead of a separate collector electrode.

In addition, and of more importance, two tubes using "thermionic-beam" scanning were described. Two tubes were built, one using electrostatic horizontal and vertical deflection and the other using electrostatic horizontal but magnetic vertical deflection. A one-sided, photosensitive mosaic with a translucent signal plate was used, the optical image being projected on the mosaic through the signal plate.

It was claimed that both tubes were able to resolve at least 100 lines per inch on the mosaic, the transmitted picture having very little spurious shading and relatively high signal strength. An operating efficiency of 71 percent was calculated. The article concluded that while many problems had been solved, much additional work remained for the purpose of determining optimum designs.[68] The Iconoscope continued to be the "standard" studio tube both in the United States and Europe, with the Super Emitron (Image Iconoscope) being used out-of-doors by the BBC in London.

On July 12, 1938, Dr. Werner Flechsig of Fernseh GmbH applied for a patent on a color picture tube. This tube proposed to use three beams (each representing a basic color) which deflected simultaneously to a screen containing color producing phosphors. In front of the screen and between the electron guns was situated a grid screen that allowed each beam to reach only its own color. Thus it would be possible to project a simultaneous color picture using the grid as a means of color separation.[69]

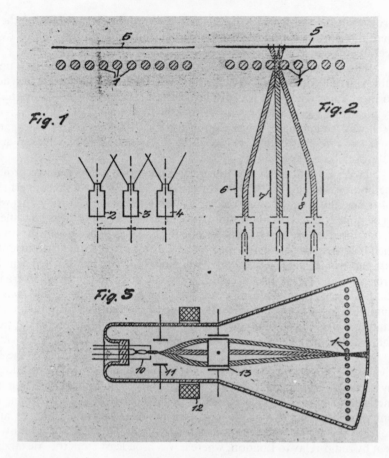

Diagram from Werner Flechsig's color picture tube patent (applied for, 1938; issued 1943).

The Berlin Radio Exhibition opened August 5, 1938. All demonstrations were given on the new 441-line standard. Fernseh demonstrated a large screen projector, 10 by 12 feet, and a home receiver with a picture some 8 by 9½ inches to cost about £35 or £40 on October 1, 1938. An upright set with a 16-inch tube was displayed as well as a home-type projection receiver with a picture 14 by 16 inches. Fernseh had both a mechanical 441-line disc transmitter and a film transmitter using Image Dissector tubes which gave excellent pictures, quite free from shading errors.

Telefunken was now using an Arcadia (made by Mechau) type of motion film projector. This used optical compensation in the form of a series of moving mirrors with continuous film movement. It was being used with either the Iconoscope camera tube or the flying spot (cathode ray tube) scanner. They demonstrated a 2-foot picture tube, which gave quite a brilliant black and white image. In addition, they also displayed a projection-type set with a 16 by 20-inch screen for home use. Finally, there were three projectors in the exhibition hall showing pictures some 5 by 6 feet in size.

The German Post Office had a complete television station in a portable van that could transmit pictures while in motion. In addition, a crude form of color television was displayed from special motion picture film, by means of a projector having two color components. The tube screen itself was red and blue. It was demonstrated at 180 lines at 25 frames, and as there were two colors with a color disc, there was bad flicker at a 12½-cycle rate.[70]

D.W. Epstein of RCA applied for a patent on a television recording method on September 30, 1938. It was for a device that would convert the 24-frame film speed so as to record 30-frame television pictures. This was to be done with a special intermittent which would record field 1 and field 2, and lose the first part of field 3 while the film was pulled down. It would then record all of field 4 and the first part of field 5. It would then lose the last part of field 5 while the shutter was closed for film pulldown. Then the process would repeat itself. Thus it would be possible to record 30-frame (60-field) television pictures onto 24-frame motion picture film was a minimum loss of information. The timing of the shutter was quite important, and a major difficulty was in the joining of two different fields, i.e., the last line of field 3 with the first line of field 5.[71]

On September 30, 1938, the London Television Service covered the arrival of British prime minister Neville Chamberlain's return from Munich by means of its outside broadcast unit. Chamberlain brought with him his message of "Peace in Our Time!" The Marconi-EMI outside broadcast unit was there with three cameras and the necessary microphones and covered the arrival and ceremonies following it. The "live" program was sent by radio-relay to London, where it was broadcast from the Alexandra Palace.

This coverage was called "the most striking of all" by the *London Times*, which stated that it had "a quality of history in the making which no other outside broadcast has equalled." The *Times* continued, "To see these events as they take place is something different in kind from a newsreel after the event; it has a particular thrill and would alone make the possession of a set worth while." This broadcast appears to have been the first actual broadcast by television of a major news event as it was actually happening. It was one of the highlights of the 1938 season of the London Television Service and would not be equalled for many years.[72]

RCA announced on November 6, 1938, that it had come to an agreement with Harry R. Lubcke, director of television for the Don Lee Television System. RCA had purchased certain patents and methods of Mr. Lubcke pertaining to synchronization methods and apparatus.[73]

It was reported on December 21, 1938, that Dr. V.K. Zworykin had been granted his patent, USA 2,141,059, after some 15 years in the Patent Office. This occurred after the Patent Office tribunals had decided against him; a District of Columbia court of appeals had finally reversed them. This patent, originally filed on December 29, 1923, was involved in no fewer than 11 interferences between the original application and the final version. It had twice been before the United States court of appeals and had been in litigation for some 12 years.[74]

Actually Dr. Zworykin's 1925 patent application, USA Patent No. 1,691,324 (issued in 1928), would have given him the priority he wished, as it had more promise; it mentioned both the use of discrete globules and the use of a fine mesh screen in place of aluminum foil. But the patent departments at both Westinghouse Electric and RCA insisted that the 1923 application be given the earliest priority.

The case before the court of appeals was to be decided on only one issue: the construction of the photocell. If the 1923 filing showed an application disclosing a photosensitive plate of a specific construction, then Zworykin was entitled to the award of priority. This was the argument of Zworykin's lawyers.

The only question in controversy was whether the potassium of the photoelectric element was in the form of elemental areas and whether it was new matter in the 1923 application. If it was, Zworykin was entitled to make the claims in his 1923 application, and Zworykin was the first inventor. On November 2, 1938, the court of appeals ruled to grant Zworykin his patent. It was issued to Westinghouse Electric and Manufacturing Company.[75]

Having won this case, Dr. Zworykin applied for another patent on November 26, 1938, which was essentially the same as the December 29, 1923, application but included a new "Fig. 6." This figure showed a typical single-sided front surface Iconoscope. There were only two claims, and they referred to the action of an electrical condenser being connected to an electrical circuit in series with a second insulating gap, with an electrical circuit being adapted to effectively utilize a discharge from said condenser. This patent was also assigned to Westinghouse Electric and Manufacturing Company of East Pittsburgh.[76]

In addition, Dr. Zworykin reapplied for another patent on December 20, 1938, that had been originally filed on May 1, 1930, and had not yet been granted. It, too, added a new figure, which showed a typical single-sided front surface Iconoscope. The claims primarily concerned an image screen consisting of a plurality of insulation-supported conductive elements having electrically separated surfaces responsive to radiant energy, and means for deflecting a beam and causing it to scan said conductive elements. This patent was also issued to Westinghouse. This series of patents thus gave Dr. Zworykin and Westinghouse complete control of the Iconoscope.[77]

On December 30, 1938, RCA applied for a patent for an optical projection system using a cathode ray tube. It applied Schmidt optics in the form of a large convex spherical mirror facing the tube. This mirror acted to converge and reduce the spherical aberration and coma of the image.

It was claimed that it provided an optical system with an aperture ratio of f/0.6 or greater.[78]

The RMA Television Committee made a decision concerning Standard T-115 regarding single side-band transmission on January 19, 1939. In this standard, both side-bands were generated and one side-band removed by filters in the antenna transmission line. This was a very important advance as it allowed a maximum of picture detail while conserving broadcast bandwidth. It was too late for the BBC in London to adopt single side-band transmission, as their standards had been set in 1936, and they had to continue use of double side-band modulation.[79]

RCA reported in February 1939 that it had been recording, from the face of a cathode ray tube, television pictures of images transmitted by the BBC in London. RCA showed a four-minute film of images received at Riverhead, N.Y., by their film recording equipment. The images were unsteady and not sharp, although at times they were clear enough that one could recognize the announcer as Jasmine Bligh. As far as is known, this is the first American recording of images from the face of a cathode ray tube, and it certainly sets a record for the long-distance recording of television images.[80]

On February 14, 1939, RCA gave a demonstration of their large screen television projector at the Waldorf-Astoria in New York City. Pictures some four by six feet were shown.[81]

The Boon-Danaher prizefight was telecast on February 29, 1939, to two theatres in London and proved to be a huge success. As a result, Gaumont-British (the Ostrer company that owned Baird Television) announced that they were going to install theatre television equipment in some 350 theatres. At this time, the large screen television system of Baird Television Ltd. was being demonstrated on a 9 by 12-foot screen at the Gaumont-British office in New York City.[82]

On May 24, 1939, EMI gave a demonstration of its new large screen television projector at its theatre in Hayes, Middlesex, England. The image, as seen on a 15 by 12½-foot screen, was "comparable with ordinary film standards." The occasion was the annual running of the Derby.[83]

Philco Radio and Television Corporation gave a demonstration of its new "portable" television transmitter to a group of radio dealers in New York City on March 7, 1939. It was self-contained, with a camera, mounted on top of a box, that weighed some 420 pounds. It had a complete transmitter operating on RMA standards with a power of less than 1 watt that had a range of some 175 feet. It was not for sale but was being used for further research and study.[84]

Also in March 1939 General Electric stated that it planned to operate a television relay station in the Helderberg Mountains around Schenectady, N.Y. General Electric had not been very active in the field of television since its divorce from RCA in late 1932. However, with the advent of commercial television in the United States, General Electric had embarked on a development program and was going to build a television transmitter,

David Sarnoff at the New York World's Fair, April 20, 1939, speaking before an NBC Iconoscope camera. His image was sent to the Empire State transmitter and rebroadcast.

television receivers and especially television cameras of its own design. General Electric was planning to transmit television signals from Schenectady to Troy and Albany, N.Y.[85]

The RCA/NBC television transmitter in the Empire State Building was being overhauled to conform with the newly adopted RMA standards, including a single side-band filter. It was being readied for the opening of the World's Fair in New York City in the spring of 1939.

Six American manufacturers announced plans to have television receivers on sale by May 1, 1939. They were the American Television Corporation, Andrea Radio Corporation, Allen B. DuMont Laboratories, General Electric, Philco Radio and Television Corporation and the RCA Manufacturing Company of Camden, N.J. Farnsworth Television and Radio Corporation stated that they were going to raise several million dollars so as to be able to manufacture television receivers. Andrea Radio claimed that it was the first to put television sets on sale using the new 441-line standards.[86]

David Sarnoff appeared before an NBC Iconoscope camera on April 20, 1939 (prior to the opening of the World's Fair) and dedicated the RCA exhibit. This was claimed to be the first time that pictures from the TeleMobile (RCA's portable van) were sent to the Empire State transmitter and rebroadcast. The RCA exhibit included a large screen projector and a "flask" receiver, which had a large picture tube (some 18 by 24 inches) with front viewing and had a brightness of highlights of 40 candles/square foot. It also contained a complete 16mm film projection chain and provided space for the TeleMobile.[87]

For David Sarnoff, this was the realization of some eleven years of planning. His original idea, late in 1928, to have a television system operating in the United States by 1932 had long been delayed. A five-year plan had turned into an eleven-year reality. Very few people in 1928 had foreseen the depression or how long it would last. In fact, in 1939 the world was still suffering from its effects.

Television in the United States made its formal debut on Sunday, April 30, 1939, with the telecasting of a speech by President Franklin D. Roosevelt at the opening of the World's Fair in New York City. The images were sent to receivers placed at strategic locations. It was claimed that the pictures were clear and steady.[88]

The time seemed to be ripe for a commercial television system in the United States. The introduction of the new television system did not seem to hurt the sale of radio sets at all. However, the sales of new television sets were very slow and disappointing. Following the lead of the BBC in London, RCA/NBC now embarked on a long series of special events in order to stimulate interest in the new medium. There were outside broadcasts of the Columbia/Princeton baseball game on May 17, 1939; the Six-Day bike race on May 16–22, 1939; the Baer-Nova prizefight on June 1, 1939; and the parade in honor of King George VI and Queen Elizabeth on June 11, 1939. All of these events were covered with a single camera.[89]

On June 1, 1939, a new high quality mechanical film scanner was described by the General Electric Company of England. It had an apertured (Nipkow) disc running in a vacuum. It used continuously moving film illuminated by a split optical system to eliminate flicker, with a mechanism to compensate for film shrinkage. Synchronizing signals were also produced by holes in the disc. This was another solution to the problem of poor film transmission by the Iconoscope.[90]

Harley Iams and Albert Rose of RCA Manufacturing Company publicly revealed details of their new low velocity scanning beam camera tube to the New York section of the IRE on June 7, 1939. This pickup tube was called the Orthicon, an abbreviation of Orthiconoscope. The name was derived from the fact that the curve between input light and output current was a straight line. It was claimed that no shading problems were present.

The tube was described as being some 20 inches long and 4 inches in diameter. The image plate was some 2 by 2½ inches wide. Picture resolution was claimed to be some 400 to 700 lines. Sensitivity was supposed to be some 10 to 20 times that of the Iconoscope. On July 23, 1939, it was reported that the Orthicon was in the final stage of development and would be ready for broadcast by the first of next year.[91]

On July 27, 1939, John L. Baird gave the first demonstration of a color television system using a cathode ray tube. The pictures were transmitted from the South Tower of the Crystal Palace, a distance of two miles to Mr. Baird's home and laboratories in Crescent Wood Road in Sydenham.

The scanning device was a revolving drum with 34 facets in conjunction with a color disk which caused the spot of light to be interlaced three times so as to give a complete picture of 102 lines. This was completed 16⅔ times a second, each line of light being passed to a photocell which translated the light into electrical impulses. A flying spot system projected its light through a stationary slit, behind which revolved a scanning disc. Each slot in the scanning disc was covered with a color filter, the first slot red, the next blue-green and so forth. The mirror drum revolved at 6,000 rpm while the scanning disc revolved at 500 rpm.

At the receiver, a color filter was rotated in front of the cathode ray tube in a manner that presented the proper blue-green or red filter in synchronization with the transmitter, producing a full-color picture. The image was projected through a lens onto a three-foot white paper screen. It was reported that "flesh tints came through well, blue and red brightest, but scarlet tended to have an orange tint. Definition was not as good as in black and white television."[92]

The Sixteenth (and last) Berlin Radio Exhibition opened on July 28, 1939. (The next show was to be in Cologne in 1940.) The main feature of the exhibition was a "standard" television receiver designed as a joint effort of Fernseh A.G., Telefunken, Lorenz, Loewe, and TeKaDe. It was a rather small table model with a picture some 19.5 cm by 22.5 cm in size. It was to be available for some £ 32.10s ($137). It featured a new, square, flat-faced picture tube and had only some 15 valves.

There were supposed to be exhibits of large screen television by Dr. Karolus and Telefunken. However, the Karolus projector developed problems and was never shown, and the Telefunken projector was on display for two days only and was withdrawn.[93]

In July 1939, the *Journal of Applied Physics* published an issue devoted to television. It included articles by David Sarnoff, Knox McIlwain, Pierre Mertz, Peter Goldmark, and E.W. Engstrom. The article by McIlwain, a "Survey of Television Pick-up Devices," was quite revealing. It indicated that a study of the sensitivities of the two competing camera tubes, the Iconoscope and Image Dissector, were not as far apart as had been indicated. The Iconoscope needed at least 100 candles/square foot and could transmit a usable picture at 10–15 candles/square foot. The image dissector needed 150–170 candles/square foot as a minimum and could give a recognizable picture with an average illumination of 4 footcandles! However, it was conceded that the Image Dissector was useful for outdoor pickup under only the most favorable conditions.[94]

The annual Radio Exhibition at Olympia was opened on August 23, 1939, with a speech from the Alexandra Palace by Sir Stephen Tallents, the public relations officer of the BBC. This was the first time an exhibition was opened by television. Again there was heavy emphasis on television, with models from HMV, Baird Television Company, GEC, Scophony and Ferranti. As a result, it was announced that some 500 sets a week were being sold in the London area.[95]

But this success was to be short-lived, for with the beginning of World War II in Europe, the BBC television station at the Alexandra Palace was closed down on September 1, 1939 — one of the first casualties of the war. The station had been ordered shut down at noon with no advance warning. Some 23,000 television sets had been sold since the station's opening in November 1936, and they were now rendered useless for the duration of the war. It was rumored that the high cost of operating the London Television Service was the primary reason for the early closing of the Alexandra Palace![96]

The television system in the United States continued to improve. As a great portion of the technical research had been done by the Radio Corporation, it was important for RCA to come to terms with its competitors. RCA had been buying up most of the important patents concerning camera and receiving tubes. In addition, there were certain circuits that were necessary in a television system. Many of these were owned by Philo Farnsworth. As a result, RCA had to come to an agreement with him.

Philo Farnsworth had signed agreements with Philco (1931), Baird and Fernseh (1934), and the American Telephone & Telegraph Company (1937). In September 1939 an agreement was reached between Farnsworth and RCA. It was signed by Otto Schairer of the Radio Corporation of America and E.A. Nicholas of the Farnsworth Television and Radio Corporation. Nicholas was the former head of the Licensing Division of RCA. It was the first time that RCA had a contract to pay continuing royalties for the use of patents. The agreement was announced on October 2, 1939. This agreement was a tremendous victory for Philo Farnsworth and represented full recognition of his valuable contributions to the field of television.[97]

In Los Angeles, the Don Lee television station W6XAO, which had been operating at 300 lines sequential at 24 frames on frequencies of 45 megacycles for vision and 49.75 megacycles for sound, was shut down during the summer of 1939 in order to convert over to the new RMA 441-line, single side-band operation. Early in November 1939, W6XAO went back on the air. At this time, RCA, General Electric, Gilfillan Brothers and Stewart-Warner placed television receivers on the market in the Los Angeles area. It was announced that Don Lee Television had ordered portable television field equipment from RCA to be delivered by mid–December.[98]

On October 17, 1939, the Radio Corporation was celebrating the twentieth anniversary of its founding. A special program was sent from the Empire State television transmitter to an aircraft equipped with a receiver. The end of the telecast showed the plane landing at North Beach Airport, so that observers in the plane could see themselves landing.[99]

Farnsworth Television, which did not have an exhibit at the World's

Fair in New York City, did have a traveling exhibit that was in Seattle, Washington, during the first week of November 1939. The unit featured a "live" Farnsworth electron camera which was used in demonstrations.[100]

On November 8, 1939, the Ges. zur Forderung der Forschung auf dem Gebiete der Technischen Physik and der Eidgenoissischen Technichen Hochschule (the Swiss Institute of Technology) of Zurich, Switzerland, filed for a patent for a large screen television projector. It had a light-modulating screen that was to be locally deformed by the cathode ray beam. This mosaic screen was to be a layer of oil, or a mixture of gum and oil, or gum, gelatine, synthetic resin, etc.

Light from an independent source was to go through a series of lenses, a reflector and a lens to a modulating screen. Light reflected from the back of undeformed parts of the modulating screen was shut off by a reflector; but light affected by the deformed parts of the modulating screen passed the reflector and was directed by a lens system to form an image on a screen. This device was planned to project television pictures with sufficient light intensity to fill a large screen.[101]

The FCC adopted new rules regulating broadcasting on November 29, 1939. Two classes of stations were set up: Class 1, broadcasting on an unscheduled experimental basis, and Class 2, to offer a scheduled public program service using limited commercial operation. The FCC refused to set up any standards for transmission, mistakenly inferring that each manufacturer would use the standard it liked best. It was apparent that there was much dissension among the smaller manufacturers, and on December 22, 1939, the FCC decided to call a hearing on standards and related matters early in 1940.[102]

In December 1939 Scophony described for the first time a new camera tube called the Diavisor. It used principles patented by A. Rosenthal. The camera tube encased an image screen consisting of an alkali halide crystal mounted on a signal plate. A cathode ray beam scanned the surface of the crystal. The luminous energy of the image served as an exciting radiation, the crystal having been previously prepared to produce color centers. The cathode ray beam served as the quenching radiation.

The crystal stored an amount of energy corresponding to the intensity of the light upon it. This energy was freed by the action of the scanning beam when most of the quenching radiation freed electrons from the volume element of the crystal. This energy went to a resistance across which the picture signals were developed. A camera tube using an electron image was also described as using a light beam that was deflected by mechanical means.[103]

During this period, television had progressed from a purely experimental medium to a full-fledged commercial venture. The London Television Service, which had opened in 1936, had set a standard of excellence that was not to be matched anywhere for many years.

Television systems were getting more reliable, with better (more sensitive) cameras, and receivers with larger and brighter screens. It appeared that a commercial television service in the United States would be introduced in 1939 as soon as certain problems could be solved. However, there was much unhappiness among the smaller manufacturers and the FCC was loathe to set standards. Elsewhere throughout the world, television was being given low priority as the nations prepared to go to war.

Chapter 11
The First NTSC: 1940–41

On January 1, 1940, the Don Lee television station in Los Angeles, California, telecast the Rose Bowl Parade from Pasadena. This was accomplished using the two new portable television cameras recently acquired from RCA. The weather was overcast with considerable rain. The television signal was relayed nine miles from Pasadena to W6XAO, where it was transmitted to the Los Angeles area.[1]

Public hearings by the FCC beginning on January 15, 1940, indicated a break in the ranks of the television industry in regards to the standards (or lack thereof) in the United States. Both the Philco Corporation and DuMont Television sought to make changes. Philco wished to go to 605 lines at 24 frames/sec. DuMont desired a flexible system using 625 lines at 15 frames/sec. The Zenith Radio Corporation claimed that television was not ready for the public. In addition, Major Edwin Armstrong put forth the case for FM broadcasting, charging that RCA was trying to block the growth of his invention by all possible means. This shocked the new FCC chairman, James L. Fly, who ruled that the matter of permanent allocation would have to be held up until FM's needs were met.[2]

Members of the FCC, led by Chairman Fly, inspected the television station of RCA/NBC in New York and the new General Electric station W2XB in Schenectady, N.Y. They then visited the Allen B. DuMont Laboratories and were given demonstrations of television on both the RMA and DuMont standards.[3]

On February 5, 1940, they visited the RCA manufacturing plant in Camden, N.J., and were shown several new Iconoscope camera tubes. They witnessed a demonstration of large-screen television as well as a comparative test of 24-frame vs. 30-frame television.

They were also given a "demonstration" of color television. According to one source, it was a "simulated" three-color system utilizing three separate transmission channels using a system of mirrors for composition of the aggregate image. Another source claimed that it was a two-color flying spot system combined optically on a single screen. At any rate, it was the first indication that RCA was engaging in research into color television.[4]

The FCC members finally visited the Philco Corporation in Philadelphia and were given a demonstration of the Philco 605-line, 24-frame system. Philco claimed this resulted in 35 percent better picture quality.[5]

On February 28, 1940, the FCC stated that a sponsored program service was to be permitted on or after September 1, 1940. Two classes of stations were again set up. This time, Class 1 was to carry forward technical investigations and might have more than one channel. Class 2 was to experiment in program production and technique and to operate on one channel only.

RCA then announced a great sale of television receivers on March 15, 1940, at reduced prices, hoping to sell 25,000 receivers before the end of the year. This announcement upset the FCC, as it regarded as an action tending to freeze standards on which they were operating. As a result, further hearings were set on April 8, 1940, to discover whether the research and experimentation and the achievement of higher standards for television were being unduly retarded by RCA.[6]

In February 1940 Scophony Ltd. described a new development called the Skiatron method of large screen television projection. It was based on a tube with the principle of "electron opacity." Certain ionic crystals would have an opaque deposit, which could be dissolved by the correct combination of maintaining the crystals in an electrical field at a suitable temperature.

When the deposit was drawn toward the positive pole, it disappeared, leaving the crystal substantially transparent. The modulated cathode ray beam produced in the crystal an opaque deposit of a density proportional to the instantaneous intensity of the beam.

In operation, a screen built of certain crystal materials would have storage capabilities. It was planned that the image was to be presented for the full "frame" time rather than on a single line basis. The electron beam would trace a new picture so that motion was possible, but essentially the plate was to present an image equal to the frame scanning frequency. The screen would remain constant until the electron beam struck the area on the next scan, when it would immediately adjust itself to the new value.

Using this new storage principle, it was claimed that there were many advantages to the system. No interlacing (to reduce flicker) would be necessary. There could be considerable savings in bandwidth; or conversely a much higher definition would be possible. The system could be well adapted to a subtractive method of color television by using three Skiatron tubes, each having a screen of a given alkali halide crystal having deposits of the colors necessary to produce the proper colors. These would be bluish-green (minus red), magenta (minus green), and yellow (minus blue) in proper registration. This was Scophony's first nonmechanical large screen device.[7]

EMI Laboratories reported in March 1940 that they were experimenting with a method for photographing television images on motion picture film by means of a continuous film camera. There was a mirror drum which moved relative to the motion picture film so as to present a stationary image relative to it and the film. This eliminated the difficulties caused by the interlaced television picture. Either a positive or negative picture could be displayed on the cathode ray tube so that either a negative or positive image could be developed.

It was reported as "conceivable that motion picture studios will one day replace their cameras by Emitrons and photograph their films from a monitor tube in a way similar to that which has been described. Higher standards of definition would be required, of course, but this involves no insuperable technical problems, and [would result in] increased flexibility ... from the fading and superimposition facilities, particularly in regards to trick shots and shots involving expensive sets."

This of course, seems to be the very first reference to the making of motion pictures by electronic means, quite a revolutionary concept. EMI was not content merely to give television a memory (the film recording process) but was proposing to allow the motion picture or cinema to take advantage of television production techniques. Since all television broadcasting was barred in England due to the war, this could have been a way to put the dormant Emitron cameras to work for a purpose quite apart from that which they were originally intended. A very prophetic statement at the time.[8]

This process was augmented by the fact that EMI at the same time reported that work was being done to provide a cathode ray viewfinder for the Emitron camera. Admitting that the optical viewfinder was quite satisfactory in most cases, it was thought that certain circumstances would benefit from the provision of a cathode ray viewfinder either on the camera or at remote location.

However, at the time it was admitted that there were serious difficulties in placing such a monitor on a camera. It was planned to use many of the electrical connections to the Emitron tube to the viewfinder so as to cut down the amount of wiring as well as the extra weight involved. Although a diagram of the proposed cathode ray viewfinder was shown, there was no word as to whether or not such a device had been built.[9] (V.K. Zworykin had first proposed the idea for an electronic viewfinder in his lab notes of July 13, 1931, but this fact was never made public until 1981.)[10]

The electronic viewfinder would prove to be the most important addition ever made to the television camera. It would allow the television cameraman to actually see what he was shooting at the very moment, in contrast to the optical finder used in motion picture production, which only gave the cameraman an approximation of what was actually being recorded on film.

In spite of the war in Europe, EMI was still continuing research into camera tubes. Patents were filed by W.S. Brown for camera tubes with perpendicular electron beam scanning and photoconductive surfaces including an image section. Patents were also filed by J.D. McGee, H. Miller, and G.S.P. Freeman for the use of stop electrodes to intercept electrons with large radial velocities, and by J.D. McGee and H.G. Lubszynski for an electron image tube.[11]

Work on an Iconoscope type of camera and a large screen television projector was reported by the British Thomson-Houston Company. The former would be the first television camera in England not built by either EMI or Baird Television.[12]

RCA gave the first demonstration of a telecast from an airplane in flight on March 6, 1940. A new, lightweight, two-camera television chain weighing some 700 pounds was installed in a United Airlines Boeing 247-D. The pictures were transmitted to the RCA building, where they were relayed to the Empire State Building for broadcast to home receivers. It was claimed that the pictures were "fine at times" although most of the images were dim and distorted. However, the experiment was hailed as a great success.[13]

On March 23, 1940, the FCC rescinded its offer of limited operations for Class 2 stations. The FCC claimed that research and experimentation with systems based on other standards would be hindered because of the RCA campaign to sell a large amount of television receivers. It was agreed that flexible standards (such as those the DuMont Laboratories had proposed) could be achieved, but it was not agreed that such flexibility was worth the cost. Therefore a reappraisal of the whole situation was mandatory.[14]

In April 1940 there was also a hearing of the Senate Interstate Commerce Committee of Senator Ernest Lundeen to consider the desirability of investigating the FCC itself. Senator Burton K. Wheeler invited both James L. Fly, chairman of the FCC, and David Sarnoff, president of RCA, to air their views. Senator Wheeler suggested that they settle their differences peaceably. This goal was finally accomplished.

Interestingly enough, during this session David Sarnoff gave high praise to his former opponent Philo Farnsworth, referring to him as "an American inventor who I think has contributed, outside RCA itself, more to television than anybody else in the United States.... He had made significant inventions!" Of course, by this time, RCA had come to terms with Farnsworth, and Sarnoff could afford to be lavish in his praise.[15]

At the rehearings, the Philco Corporation and the DuMont Laboratories as well as U.A. Sanabria and Lee De Forest agreed that the RCA action had frozen the television standards and curtailed research. The FCC announced that it would set standards as soon as engineering opinion of the industry was prepared to approve any one of the competing systems of broadcasting as the standard system. It was stated that only then would the commission "consider the authorization of full commercialization."[16]

On April 28, 1940, RCA announced to the American Radio Relay League that a new amateur Iconoscope (1847) would be introduced. It had a mosaic less than 2 inches in diameter. It was capable of generating a 120-line picture at 30 pictures/sec. It was only 7 7/16 inches long. The mosaic was perpendicular to the axis of the tube.

In operation, the light from the scene passed through a transparent conductive signal electrode. On the other side of the electrode (facing the beam) was a mosaic consisting of a large amount of particles deposited on the back side of the signal electrode. An enormous amount of light was lost passing through the transparent electrode and there was no mention of the sensitivity of the tube. This was the first commercial camera tube of this configuration to be manufactured and sold. The cost was about $25. This new tube was demonstrated to the press on June 3, 1940.[17]

RCA demonstrated a new system of large screen television to its stockholders in one of its NBC studios on May 7, 1940. The images, some 4½ by 6 feet in size, were supposed to be comparable to home television quality.

The new RCA system incorporated projection optics of extremely wide aperture. The image on the face of the Kinescope, which measured only 2.4 by 3.2 inches, did not face the screen but was thrown onto a concave mirror 16 inches in diameter. This mirror collected the light and magnified the image some 22 times and was projected through a glass lens surrounding the neck of the tube. This image was projected some 20 feet onto the screen. (This appears to be the first application of Schmidt optics to large screen television.) The picture tube had some 56,000 volts applied to it.[18]

At this time, David Sarnoff's old rival, Major Edwin Armstrong, was awarded a tremendous victory. On May 22, 1940, the FCC issued Order no. 67, designating 40 FM channels, each 200 kilocycles wide, in the band from 42 to 50 mc. This included Television Channel 1 (44–50 mc), which belonged to RCA/NBC in the New York City area, the Don Lee station in Los Angeles and the new Zenith station in Chicago. They were all forced to shut down and have their transmitters converted to a different frequency (50–56 mc) on a new Channel 1. RCA was also in favor of an FM system by this time, although it was a narrow band system in contrast to Major Armstrong's wideband FM method.[19]

During the week of June 25 to 28, 1940, NBC televised the Republican National Convention in Philadelphia. Scenes of the floor activities were picked up by both Iconoscope and Orthicon cameras and transmitted 104 miles by coaxial cable to New York City, where they were telecast by the Empire State transmitter. It was claimed that there were some 4,000 receivers in use in New York.

The NBC signal from New York was received by the General Electric Company relay station in the Helderberg Mountains and rebroadcast by the GE television transmitter W2XB to the Schenectady area.[20]

The Philco Corporation also had a television unit at the convention and telecast it to the Philadelphia area over W3XE. It was a joint effort with the Mututal Broadcasting System. It was claimed that there were some 5,000 sets in the Philadelphia area at the time.[21]

In the United States, it had become obvious that the problems of television standards had to be worked out before a successful commercial system could prevail. Taking its cue from the success of the Lord Selsdon Committee in 1935/36, the Radio Manufacturers Association (RMA) decided to set up a committee comprising representatives of all companies and organizations interested in television to formulate acceptable standards. This seems to have been decided at a meeting between Dr. W.R.G. Baker, director of engineering for the RMA, and Chairman James L. Fly of the FCC.

It was decided to open the deliberations to all members of the industry whether they were members of the RMA or not. The RMA sponsored a new National Television Standards Committee (NTSC) in cooperation with the FCC. It was decided to set up panels of experts, and a parliamentary procedure was agreed upon. Appointment of Dr. W.R.G. Baker as chairman of the new NTSC was announced on July 17, 1940. The organization of committee members was completed and the first meeting held on July 31, 1940.

The following companies were asked to send one representative each to the NTSC: Bell Telephone Labs, Columbia Broadcasting System, Don Lee Broadcasting System, DuMont Labs Inc., Farnsworth Television and Radio Corporation, General Electric Company, Hazeltine Service Corporation, John V.L. Hogan, Hughes Tool Company, IRE, Philco Corporation, Radio Corporation of America, Stromberg-Carlson Telephone Mfg. Company, Television Productions, and the Zenith Radio Corporation.

Nine subcommittees were set up. They were Systems Analysis, P.C. Goldmark, CBS; Subjective Aspects, A.N. Goldsmith, IRE; Television Spectra, J.E. Brown, Zenith; Transmitter Power, E.W. Engstrom, RCA; Transmitter Characteristics, P.T. Farnsworth; Transmitter-Receiver Coordination, I.J. Kaar, General Electric; Picture Resolution, D.E. Harnett, Hazeltine; Synchronization, T.T. Goldsmith, DuMont; Radiation Polarization, D.B. Smith, Philco.[22]

On August 25, 1940, it was reported that the Don Lee station in Los Angeles had stepped up its definition from 441 to 525 lines. They stated that they were on the air some 14½ hours per week and claimed that some 500 home television sets were in operation.[23]

The Columbia Broadcasting System announced on August 29, 1940, that it had perfected a color television system that would be ready by January 1, 1941. A private test had been viewed on August 28, 1940, by FCC chairman James L. Fly, who stated "that if we can start television off as a color proposition, instead of a black and white show, it will have a greater acceptance with the public." CBS claimed that it was capable of being broadcast on a 6 megacycle channel and that "existing receivers need not suffer radical changes to adapt them to three colors instead of mere black and white."[24]

Then on September 4, 1940, Dr. Peter Goldmark of CBS gave a

Dr. Peter Goldmark of CBS with his color film projector, August, 1940. In September of that year, Goldmark gave a demonstration of color film and slides.

demonstration of color film and slides only. The color film used a standard Farnsworth Image Dissector tube with a continuous motion projector. The 16mm film was run at 60 frames/sec, although it was claimed that 24-frame projection could be used with mechanical and optical alterations. A filter disc of 7.5 inches with 6 filter segments (2 sets of red, green and blue) were placed in front of the dissector tube. The use of the nonstorage Image Dissector made it possible to simply filter that part of the image being scanned. The disc was driven at 1200 rpm, which produced two color progressions of 1/40th second each, covering three fields of 1/120 second with interlacing. Thus 60 complete frames were sent each second. This gave a decided improvement in the representation of movement, and overall flicker was reduced.

At the receiver, a disc of about 20 inches was used with a 9-inch cathode ray tube. The number of lines was 343, with a 4.25 mc bandwidth. The reduced number of lines was more than compensated by the effective realism. It was claimed that "the results were impressive."

It was stated that experiments had been made with storage-type tubes such as the Iconoscope and Orthicon. Some major alterations were necessary to produce "live" pictures, such as the use of an optical method of interlacing. This entailed the use of optically flat inclined glass plates attached to the filter disc, one plate after every second filter element. This optical method of producing interlace avoided the storage of charge between successive fields while retaining the high sensitivity of the storage tube.[25]

On September 7, 1940, Dr. Goldmark applied for several patents covering this color system. CBS claimed on November 12, 1940, that direct pickup of color television had been achieved in the CBS Labs. But it was understood that it was still a laboratory process.[26]

The introduction of a color system by CBS at this time was highly significant. CBS, which had had an experimental television transmitter since late 1938, had never really gone on the air. CBS was obviously in no hurry to get started in television. The CBS Radio system was very prosperous and they did not have the stake in television that RCA had.[27]

The company's decision to demonstrate a workable color television system was to have far-reaching consequences for CBS and the television industry in general. Perhaps it was hoped that the introduction of a color system at this time would delay television from going commercial until the color system could be perfected. At any rate, CBS and RCA/NBC, who had been great rivals in the program field, were now to become competitors in the technical field as well.

The invention of the Orthicon camera tube by Albert Rose and Harley Iams of RCA in 1938 had confirmed that a tube could be built and operated with low velocity electron beam scanning. The important principle of orthogonal scanning (perpendicular beam landing) while immersed in a longitudinal magnetic field had been proven.

However, the Orthicon had many faults when operated in the field or studio. Due to its linear output, it had a tendency to "charge up" whenever the target was overloaded by scenes with high light intensities or when sudden bursts of light occurred such as when flashbulbs were discharged. There was a lack of details in the low lights due to the linear output and scenes had a lower range of intermediate grays. Thus it was quite unsatisfactory under conditions of high peak brightness and high scene contrast.[28]

RCA had been seeking means to improve this tube. One technique would be to use a different type of two-sided target. On September 20, 1940, Albert Rose of the RCA Research Laboratories, Harrison, N.J., applied for a patent covering this important feature. It incorporated a semiconducting glass target. This of course allowed for two-sided operation. (In the United States, this patent application, serial no. 357,543, was forfeited after it was classified Top Secret. All such patents were confiscated in the United States after December 7, 1941, as a result of the war.)[29]

The search for a practical two-sided target had begun with Harold McCreary in 1924 (see p. 67) and Camille Sabbah in 1925 (see p. 76). Dr. Zworykin had built his first really successful tube in July

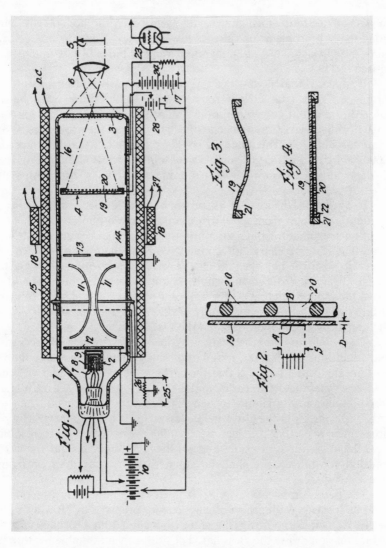

Diagram from Albert Rose's patent for a two-sided glass target (filed in 1940; no patent was granted, as the material was classified Top Secret during the war years).

1929 using a simple two-sided target (see pp. 138–139). All of his efforts to produce a practical camera tube in 1930/31 were frustrated by the difficulties in constructing practical two-sided targets that were free from surface blemishes, had a uniform surface, and were easy and economical to manufacture. These difficulties, of course, led Dr. Zworykin to the use of the single-sided target in his successful Iconoscope starting in July 1931.

However, the Iconoscope was far from perfect. Even the addition of an "image" section, which gave it more sensitivity, did not solve its enormous shading problems or raise its low efficiency. The new low velocity tube, the Orthicon, was a great improvement but still left much to be desired.

It appeared that a two-sided target would improve the Orthicon's performance. Such a target was found by Dr. Albert Rose when he discovered that a thin glass membrane similar to ordinary window glass, or what Corning Glass Company classified "G-B," had the properties he had been searching for. This material could be formed into a thin (less than 0.0002″ with a resistance of some 5×10^{10} ohm-centimeters) uniform sheet of glass. Situated close to this membrane would be a wire mesh signal screen.

In operation, the image was formed on one side of the glass either by secondary emission from an electron image from a photocathode, or by direct photoemission from a discontinuous coating of cesium on the glass sheet. The positive charge at a point "B" made the opposite "A" of the sheet also positive, and when the charge on "A" was neutralized by the low velocity beam, it reduced the whole region to cathode potential and released the induced charge on the adjacent part of the grid so as to give a picture signal. During the remainder of the frame, the charges on "A" and "B" united by conduction between the two faces.

The conductivity and thickness of the sheet were selected to satisfy four conditions: (1) that the period of discharge between the faces shall be less than the frame time; (2) that the capacity between "A" and "B" shall be several times that between "B" and the signal screen to give a useful fraction of conversion of charge to signal; (3) that the thickness of the sheet and its spacing from the grid shall be less than half the diameter of a picture element to confine the electrostatic influence of "B" to the corresponding element on the other side; and (4) that the time constant for lateral diffusion for the charge shall be equal to or greater than the frame time.

The patent application went on to describe how such a membrane could be formed. A thin sheet of glass may be prepared by blowing a bubble onto a metal supporting ring and then heating it in a furnace until the surface tension draws the glass flat. The grid is then assembled within the ring at the correct spacing by means of a slip ring. Dr. Rose claimed that he had built tubes using such a glass target as early as May 10, 1940. It was claimed that using this new and improved target gave sensitivities of from 3 to 10 times more than the Orthicon and some 30 to 500 times greater than the sensitivity of the Iconoscope.[30]

In October 1940 it was reported that the Gaumont-British Picture Corporation had finally dropped the name of Baird Television and was now calling itself Cinema Television. This was in keeping with their policy of adapting television to the use of theatre television.[31]

Dr. E.F.W. Alexanderson, consultant to General Electric, gave a demonstration of color television to several members of the NTSC at his home in Schenectady on November 20, 1940. It was a two-color system using orange-red and greenish-blue filters in front of the picture tube. These filters were mounted in a 24-inch disc rotating at 1800 rpm, set about a foot in front of a standard television receiver. It was claimed that a similar disc was mounted in front of the television camera at the studio and that all else was the same as a regular television transmission.[32]

On December 10, 1940, E. Crosby of the Radio Corporation applied for a patent for a color television system incorporating a single camera tube with special filters built into the tube in order to transmit a color signal. A similar set of colors was to be incorporated in the receiving tube to reconstitute the color picture.[33]

During the week of December 21, 1940, John L. Baird described a new version of his cathode ray color system. Baird claimed that he was now transmitting and receiving 600-line pictures at 25 frames/sec. Baird was using a two-color disc of blue-green and red revolving in front of a cathode ray tube. At the transmitter, a method of flying spot scanning was used with a cathode ray tube behind a rotating disc fitted with filters. The light from the cathode ray tube was then projected onto the scene and picked up by three large photocells. The signals from the cells were to be transmitted by wireless, or, as the war now made that impossible, to be sent over a land line.

At the receiver, a picture was produced on a cathode ray tube that had a disc similar to that of the transmitter. It was kept in synchronization by means of a special signal in the picture. The colored pictures were sent by a lens to a screen some 2½ by 2 feet. An article describing this device included a color photograph of the picture on the screen of the receiver. This seems to be the first published color photograph taken of a color television image.[34]

On January 9, 1941, CBS gave the first public demonstration of a direct camera pickup in color to members of the IRE in New York City. The live color pictures were sent from the CBS Laboratories and transmitted by wire to the new CBS studio building several blocks away. Three receivers were used, including a table model.[35]

The Bell Telephone Labs reported on January 11, 1941, their television research using a film scanner. The Image Dissector had been chosen as the pickup device as it was free of spurious signals and had a linear voltage output. To demonstrate their system, the Bell Telephone Labs used specially printed 35mm motion picture film in a 60-frame format. This solved the interlace problem.

This scanner was used in the January 1941 meeting of the IRE in New York. A demonstration was given of motion picture film transmitted from the Bell Telephone Labs in New York City over the coaxial cable to Philadelphia and back. This was a distance of some 190 miles. It was claimed that observers could not distinguish between the local and the long distance signals.[36]

John L. Baird applied for a patent for his color television transmitter on January 13, 1941. It described a revolving filter wheel so shaped that each color was sharply defined on the mosaic of a pickup tube. The filter was to be external to the tube. On January 14, 1941, Baird gave a public demonstration of this new "high definition" color system. Mr. Baird had been perfecting this system at his laboratory in his home in Sydenham, England.[37]

Scophony Ltd. presented its first demonstration of its large screen projector at its headquarters in New York City on January 15, 1941. Television images were projected onto a 12- by 9-foot screen by a projector behind the screen. It was reported that the images were of "good general quality" but that a little more light on the screen would have helped.[38]

On January 27, 1941, the National Television Systems Committee submitted its report on television standards to the Federal Communications Commission. The committee produced reports and minutes totaling 600,000 words, devoting 4,000 man-hours to meetings and an equal time to travel and witnessing 25 demonstrations of technical matters.

The NTSC recommended the following television standards: (1) there shall be a television channel six megacycles wide, with the picture carrier 4.5 megacycles lower in frequency than the sound carrier; (2) the number of scanning lines shall be 441 with a frame frequency of 30/sec and a field frequency of 60/sec; (3) the aspect ratio shall be 4 units horizontally and 3 units vertically; (4) AM shall be used for both picture and synchronizing signals; (5) a decrease in light intensity shall cause an increase in radiated power; (6) the black level (DC constant) shall be represented by a definite carrier level, at 75 percent of the peak carrier amplitude; (7) the sound portion shall use FM, with a preemphasis of 100 microseconds and the maximum deviation of plus or minus 75 kiloscyles/sec; and (8) it shall be standard to radiate horizontally polarized waves. A precise method of producing the interlaced synchronizing signals was also specified.[39]

Two major changes in these standards were made on March 20, 1941. There was the recommendation of the alternate use of frequency or amplitude modulation for the synchronizing signals, and the adoption of the 525-line standard. The last was on the recommendation of the Bell Telephone Laboratories, which claimed that the effect on picture quality in the vertical and horizontal dimensions would be small and that the larger number of lines would produce a more uniform field of illumination in the reproduced picture.[40]

The television transmitter of the Alexandra Palace had been turned off on Sepember 1, 1939, with the declaration of war between Germany and Great Britain. However, in 1941, it was again operating in great secrecy against the German Luftwaffe.

The German air force was operating a directional beam system called "Y-Gerat" aimed at the London area. It sent out two separate transmissions to fix the aircraft's bearing and range from the beacon. It was transmitted on frequencies between 42 and 48 megacycles. A clever scheme was devised by Dr. R.V. Jones, Head of Scientific Intelligence on Britain's

Air Staff, in which the beam was intercepted by a receiver at Highgate and sent by land line to the Alexandra Palace, where its powerful transmitter reradiated the "echo" on the frequency of the German ground station. The effect on "Y-Gerat" was catastrophic, and the system of range measurement was completely ruined.

The Jones method was code-named "Domino." The first jammer went on the air the middle of February 1941 and the second at Beacon Hill a few weeks later. Between these two stations, the "Y-Gerat" apparatus was rendered useless, and by the end of May 1941 was just about given up. As far as is known, the Alexandra Palace then remained dormant for the remainder of the war.[41]

NBC gave a demonstration of its new color system to the press on May 1, 1941. It was very similar to the CBS system, using 120 fields giving 20 interlaced frames/sec. It used three-color discs at both the transmitter and receiver. The demonstration was closed-circuit, although it was claimed that it had previously been transmitted over the air for some 40 miles. O.B. Hanson, NBC chief engineer, stated that while this was the simplest method of producing a color system, the ultimate answer should be all-electronic, comparable to the present black and white system.[42]

The FCC announced on May 2, 1941, that the NTSC standards had been adopted officially and that commercial television would be permitted on or after July 1, 1941. The NTSC kept open the question of color television, realizing that while it was not now ready for commercial utilization, its future potential required other testing, and that it could coexist with monochrome television.[43]

RCA demonstrated its new large screen television system on May 9, 1941. This demonstration was at the New Yorker Theater, which presented the Soose-Overlin prize fight from Madison Square Garden. Prior demonstrations had been given to the press and the FCC on January 24 and April 4, 1941.[44]

RCA was using its new large screen projector using Schmidt optics. In order to get the required brightness (some 5 footlamberts) a special cathode ray tube was used which was some 14 inches long with a diameter of 7 inches. The face of the tube pointed away from the screen, and the end of its neck pierced a small hole in the center of the correcting plate of the optical system. A concave reflecting mirror, some 30 inches in diameter, was mounted a few inches in front of the tube. The image was picked up and passed through the correcting lens with a magnification of 45 times. Some 60 to 70 kilovolts were used to drive the cathode ray tube and some 400 candlepower were delivered. The use of a 5-to-1 directional screen resulted in the highlight brightness of some 5 footlamberts. The optical system had a speed rating of f/0.7 and was a variation of the Schmidt astronomical camera.[45]

The Allen B. DuMont Laboratories of Passaic, New Jersey, had long been engaged in a variety of television research. This had included a television transmission system using variable scanning frequencies, and the manufacture of oscilloscopes, picture tubes, and television receivers. On June 23, 1941, the DuMont Laboratories introduced a new television camera. It used an 1850 Iconoscope (made by RCA) and had provision for interchanging lenses with focal lengths from 6½ inches at f/2.5 to 16 inches at f/3.5. However, the most important part of this new camera was that of a cathode ray, or electronic, viewfinder mounted on the left side of the camera.

As we have noted, this was an old idea. However, no one had actually built a commercial television camera with this important feature on it. Until this time, all television cameras had used either the image from the reflection of the camera tube mosaic, a dual-lens system, or a simple wire frame finder. The idea of affixing an electronic viewfinder was tantamount to affixing a television receiver to the side or top of the camera.

The DuMont electronic viewfinder consisted of a high intensity, 5-inch, electrostatic-type cathode ray tube which was sweep-driven from signals to the camera. Controls were provided for adjustment of brightness, contrast and electrical focus. The device weighed 14 pounds and had seven tubes. The electronic viewfinder was chosen by DuMont so that the television cameraman had the instantaneously developed picture before him at all times. Until this time the television cameraman was operating as blindly as his counterpart, the motion picture film cameraman. This one feature now gave the television camera an advantage over the film camera that was to have far-reaching consequences. The rest of the camera's electrical components were so distributed that the elements could be contained on a simple dolly for quick setup and operation.[46]

RCA introduced its new portable Orthicon Television Camera on June 25, 1941. It had the advantage of the Orthicon camera tube for unfavorable lighting conditions. The camera itself was in two pieces. The bottom section, weighing 54 pounds, included the camera tube and associated circuits. The upper section contained the amplifiers and optical viewfinder. This necessitated the use of twin lenses in operation, one for the pickup tube and the other for the operator.[47]

On June 25, 1941, Dr. Albert Rose of the research laboratories of RCA Manufacturing Company delivered the first paper to attempt to compare the eye with photographic film and the television process. His purpose was to "obtain expression for or estimates of 'true sensitivities' of the three imaging systems." Dr. Rose stated that film, the human eye and some pickup tubes have in common formal properties that can be clarified by first considering an ideal reproducing device. Rose came to the following conclusions: (1) The eye surpasses both film and pickup tubes in versatility and operating sensitivity. (2) Film and pickup tubes may record scenes at about the same levels of scene brightness. Film has the possibility of hundredfold improvement in operating sensitivity. (3) Pickup tubes at 441 lines have a still-unrealized improvement in operating sensitivity over 100,000-fold.[48]

July 1, 1941, was to be the start of commercial telecasting in the United

States. Some 22 stations across the USA were supposed to begin on this date. Only WNBT (NBC) in New York had paid programming. This included a test-pattern clock with the Bulova Watch logo, a news broadcast sponsored by Sun Oil, a television version of a radio show for Lever Bros., and a quiz show for Proctor and Gamble. They also televised (unsponsored) a Dodgers-Phillies baseball game and a USO program in the evening. An excellent beginning.

CBS (WCBW) telecast a dance lesson, a newscast and an art exhibit in the evening. DuMont (W2XWV) transmitted both "live" and film programs in the evening. With fewer than 4,000 (the number was probably closer to 2,000) television sets in the New York area, sponsored television was not very practical. CBS announced that it would go commercial starting in September 1941.[49]

On July 11, 1941, John L. Baird applied for a patent for a system of three-dimensional color television. The apparatus used a frame frequency of 1/150 sec and a scanning field of 100 lines interlaced five times to give a 500-line picture. Successive 100-line frames were colored green, red and blue for true color effect. A cathode ray tube, working as a flying spot scanner, provided the light for the photocells. In front of the projecting lens, a device consisting of mirrors at right angles split the emerging light into two paths separated by the space equal to the separation of the human eyes. By means of a revolving shutter, the scene was scanned by each beam alternately, so that images corresponding to the right and left eye were transmitted in rapid sequence. Another disc with red, green and blue filters separated the image into its color components.

At the receiver, the colored pairs of pictures were reproduced in sequence and projected onto a field lens, alternate halves of the lens projecting so that the observer's left and right eyes were presented alternately with left and right images. The combined effect was a stereoscopic image in full color.

A demonstration was given to the press on December 18, 1941. It was claimed that "the original scene is reproduced with depth and had the appearance of solidity — as though it were being watched through a window." Only one person at a time could view the picture, and any movement to one side would destroy the illusion. Baird stated that he was working on means to throw the picture onto a large screen.[50]

CBS described its first "live" color television camera on September 2, 1941. It was designed around a specially modified Orthicon tube with lower mosaic capacitance. This permitted the voltage on the mosaic to build up to higher levels for a given illumination. This tube was developed with the cooperation of the RCA Radiotron Division. It was claimed that this camera gave very acceptable color pictures with incident light of 150 foot-candles on the subject.

The camera consisted of a filter drum driven by a synchronous motor that separated the color images to the Orthicon tube. The black level was established at the camera by applying blanking pulses to the grid of the

Orthicon. The color camera, which had a twin lens system, was mounted in a square container with the electronic components inside of a cylindrical housing. Signals were fed by a single, multi-wire cable, and it could be mounted on a standard motion picture tripod. This appears to be the first "live" color television camera ever built and operated. For film pickup, the Image Dissector tube was still being used. CBS claimed that it had inaugurated a field-test period of its new color system on June 1, 1941.[51]

In October 1941 an article appeared describing the Scophony large-screen television system. This included a description of the "Skiatron" method of large-screen television. The "Skiatron" used a cathode-ray tube with a crystalline screen which was exposed and modulated by a cathode ray beam. The screen exhibited the property of electron opacity, which meant that it could be rendered opaque when scanned by an electron beam. By scanning with a suitable beam and the proper temperature, it was possible to cause the opacity to remain constant for substantially the whole frame period and to disappear quickly when the beam returned to produce the opacity for the following frame. The article also mentioned the combination of the supersonic light control with electronic scanning. It included a photograph and diagram of the new "Skiatron" tube.[52]

The American television industry was off to a slow start after the new NTSC standards had been adopted. The sales of sets were sluggish, and only a few television transmitters were in actual operation. Furthermore, the infant television industry was now concerned with the United States defense program, which was diverting certain strategic materials and demanding that skilled personnel be used for electronic research. On May 27, 1941, President Franklin D. Roosevelt had declared a state of unlimited national emergency. Neither raw materials nor production capacity could be diverted to television. RCA's television receiver production line had been closed for over a year, and other companies had been forced to drop their work on television in favor of research for national defense.[53]

Programming was at a minimum and only a few stations were actually telecasting in December 1941. They included NBC, CBS, and DuMont in New York City, General Electric in Schenectady, Philco in Philadelphia, Don Lee in Los Angeles, and station WBKB in Chicago. The bombing of Pearl Harbor on December 7, 1941, quickly ended most of the television broadcast activities in the United States.

American television, which had finally reached a goal of technical excellence, was suddenly given the lowest priority. The only television research and manufacturing was that in conjunction with the war effort. No one knew or could even forecast how long the war would last. The enemy was formidable, and the United States was straining to get its defense industry into high gear. The infant television industry, which had suffered many false starts in the past, was once again put under wraps to await a brighter tomorrow.

Notes

1. Archaeology and Prehistory of Television: 1671-1879

1. C.W. Ceram, *Archaeology of the Cinema* (New York: Harcourt, Brace & World, 1965).
2. Henry D. Hubbard, "The Motion Picture of Tomorrow," *Transactions of the Society of Motion Picture Engineers* no. 12 (1921): pp. 159-167.
3. Linda Grant, "Sony Unveils New 4.4 Pound Videotape Home Movie Camera," *Los Angeles Times*, 2 July 1980, p. 2.
4. Albert Abramson, *Electronic Motion Pictures* (Berkeley: University of California Press, 1955).
5. This has been hinted at in about a dozen or so photographic magazines. See for instance: E.G. Glazer, "Forecast 1984," *Technical Photography* 16 (Feb. 1984): pp. 11-13. Kodak announced its entree into the field of video on January 5, 1984. It stated that it would offer "Kodavision," an 8mm videotape system being perfected in Japan by Matsushita Electronic Ind. Co. of Japan (makers of Panasonic television equipment). In April 1984 Kodak announced that it was going to market a complete line of videotapes. These were to be made in Japan at first until Kodak had set up its own facilities.
6. This material comes from three good sources: Josef Maria Eder, *History of Photography* (New York: Dover, 1932, revised edition); Martin Quigley, Jr., *Magic Shadows, The Story of the Origin of Motion Pictures* (New York: Harcourt, Brace & World, 1965); and Ceram, *op. cit.*
7. John C. Patterson, *America's Greatest Inventors* (New York: Thomas Y. Crowell, 1943).
8. Alexander Bain, Br. Pat. No. 9745 (1843). Applied 27 May 1843; issued 27 Nov. 1843.
9. Alexander Bain, Br. Pat. No. 11,480 (1846). Applied 12 Dec. 1846; issued 12 June 1847.
10. Frederick C. Bakewell, Br. Pat. No. 12,352 (AD1848). Applied 2 Dec. 1848; issued 2 June 1849.
11. Giovanni Caselli, Br. Pat. No. 2532 (AD1855). Applied 10 May 1855; issued 10 Nov. 1855.
12. Giovanni Caselli, Br. Pat. No. 2395 (AD1861). Applied 25 Sept. 1861; issued 19 Nov. 1861.
13. L. d'Arlincourt, Br. Pat. No. 1920 (1869). Applied 23 June 1869; issued 10 Dec. 1869.
14. Alexander Graham Bell, U.S. Pat. No. 174,465. Applied 14 Feb. 1876; issued 7 Mar. 1876. Elisha Gray filed a caveat on 14 Feb. 1876 for a telephone also, but this was not for a patent.

273

15. Jons J. Berzelius, "On Selenium Crystals and the Preparation of Selenium," *Annalen der Physik* (Leipzig) **7** (1826): pp. 242–243.

16. H. Schulze-Manitius, "Chronik der Nachrichtentechnik, 1858," *Radio und Fernsehen* no. 1 (1955): p. 33.

17. Edmond Becqueral, "Studies of the Effect of Actinic Radiation of Sunlight by Means of Electric Currents," *Comptes Rendus des Séances de l'Academie* **9** (1839): pp. 145–149.

18. Michael Faraday, "Rotation of plane of polarization," *Diary* 13 Sept. 1845 [*Philosphical Translations 1846.*]

19. Willoughby Smith, *Journal of the Society of Telegraph Engineers* **5** (1873): pp. 183–184.

20. John Kerr, *Philosophical Magazine* **5** (1875): p. 337.

21. John Kerr, *Philosophical Magazine* **5** (1877): p. 321.

22. Julius Plucker, *Annalen der Physik* (Leipzig) **107** (1859): p. 77; H. Schulze-Manitius, "Chronik der Nachrichtentechnik, 1858," *Radio und Fernsehen* no. 6 (1955): p. 152.

23. Wilhelm Hittorf, *Annalen der Physik* (Leipzig) **136** (1869): p. 8.

24. E. Goldstein, *Berl. Monat,* **1876**: p. 284.

25. William Crooks, *Philosophical Translations, Royal Society* **170** (1879): p. 135.

26. L. Figuier, "Le téléctroscope, ou appareil pour transmettre à distance les images," *L' Année Scientifique et Industrialle* **21**, no. 6 (1877): pp. 80–81.

27. Thomas A. Edison, U.S. Pat. No. 200,521. Applied 24 Dec. 1877; issued 19 Feb. 1878. It was announced in the *Scientific American* **37** (17 Nov. 1877): p. 304. A diagram was shown in *Scientific American* **37** (22 Dec. 1877): p. 384.

28. Wordsworth Donisthorpe, "Talking Photographs," *Nature* **18** (24 Jan. 1878): p. 242.

29. Adriano de Paiva, "A telephonia, a telegraphia, e a telescopia," *O Instituto* **25** (20 Feb. 1878): pp. 414–421.

30. "The Telectroscope," *English Mechanic* **28** (31 Jan. 1879): p. 509.

31. "Punch's Almanac for 1879," *Punch* **75** (9 Dec. 1878): p. 11.

32. Denis D. Redmond, "An Electric Telescope," *English Mechanic* **28** (7 Feb 1879): p. 540.

33. C.M. Perosino, "Su du'n telegrafo ad un solo filo." *Atti della R. Acad. delle Science di Torino* **14** (March 1879): p. 4a.

34. "The Telectroscope," *Scientific American* **40** (17 May 1879): p. 309.

35. A. de Paiva, "O telescopio," *O Commercio do Porto* no. 241 (10 July 1879). This comes from two good sources: G. Goebels, "From the History of Television—The First Fifty Years," *Bosch Technische Berichte* **6**, no. 5/6, (25 May 1979), p. 4; and G. Shiers, "Historical Notes on Television before 1900," *Journal of the Society of Motion Picture and Television Engineers* **86** (March 1977): p. 131. I have not been able to get the original article.

36. Gordon Hendricks, *Eadweard Muybridge, The Father of the Motion Picture* (New York: Grossman/Viking Press, 1975), pp. 114–115.

2. Early Schemes and Inventions: 1880–1899

1. Catherine Mackenzie, *Alexander Graham Bell: The Man Who Conquered Space* (Boston and New York: Houghton Mifflin, 1928), p. 227.

2. W.E. Ayrton and J.J. Perry, "Seeing by Electricity," *Nature* **21** (21 Apr. 1880): p. 589.

3. "Seeing by Telegraph," *English Mechanic* **31** (30 Apr. 1880): pp. 177–178.

4. "Seeing by Electricity," *Scientific American* **42** (5 June 1880): p. 355. Later on Carey was to make an earlier claim of 1875, but since this cannot be substantiated, we will go by the 1880 date which is still very early.

5. William E. Sawyer, "Seeing by Electricity," *Scientific American* **42** (12 June 1880): p. 373.

6. Alexander Graham Bell, "Production of Sound by Radiant Energy," *American Journal of Science* **20** (1880): p. 305; Alexander Graham Bell, "Selenium and the Photophone," *Nature* **22** (23 Sept. 1880): pp. 500–503.

7. Maurice LeBlanc, "Etude sur la transmission electrique des impressions lumineuses," *La Lumière Electrique* **2** (1880): pp. 477–481.

8. A. de Paiva, *La téléscopie électrique basée sur l'emploi du selenium* (Porto: A.J. da Sylva, 1880). This is from G. Goebel, "From the History of Television—The First Fifty Years," *Bosch Technische Berichte* **6**, no. 5/6 (25 May 1979): p. 4.

9. C. Senlecq, "The Telectroscope," *English Mechanic* **32** (11 Feb. 1881): pp. 534–535.

10. "Tele-Photography," *Telegraph Journal* **10** (1 Mar. 1881): pp. 82–84. There was supposed to be a demonstration before the British Royal Institute, but I can find only a paper read before the Physical Society. Often the press will report a "demonstration" when only a paper was read. In any event, it is claimed that a slightly different version of this equipment is still in existence in the Science Museum in London.

11. William Lucas, "The Telectroscope, or Seeing by Electricity," *English Mechanic* **35** (21 Apr. 1882): pp. 151–152. According to Shiers, Lucas became dismayed and never built this apparatus. See Shiers, *op. cit.*, p. 32.

12. Paul Nipkow, DRP Pat. No. 30105. Applied 6 Jan. 1884; issued 15 Jan. 1885.

13. P.I. Bakmet'yev, "The New Telephotograph," *Elektrichestro* no. 1 (1885): pp. 1–7.

14. S. Bidwell, *La Lumière Électrique* **18** (1885). (From J. Blondin, "Le téléphote," *La Lumière Electrique*, 1893: p. 261.)

15. Sumner Tainter, U.S. Pat. No. 341,287. Applied 29 Aug. 1885; issued 4 May 1886.

16. Oberlin Smith, "Some Possible Forms of Phonograph," *Electrical World* **12** (Sept. 1888): pp. 116–117.

17. Written by H.W. "Sur la vision à distance par l'électricité par L. Weiller." *Lum. Elec.* **34** (16 Nov. 1889): pp. 334–336. (From *Le Genie Civil Revue Générale des Techniques* **15** (1889): p. 570.)

18. Written by E.R. "Les problèmes de la téléphonie d'après M. Henri Sutton," *La Lumière Electrique* **38** (1890): pp. 538–541; H. Sutton, "Telephotography," *Telegraph Journal & Electrical Review* **37** (6 Nov. 1890): pp. 549–551; H. Sutton, "TelePhotography. A System of Transmitting Optical Images Electrically," *Scientific American Supplement* **70** (3 Sept. 1910): p. 151.

19. Quigley, Jr., *op. cit.*, pp. 122–123.

20. Eder, *op. cit.*, pp. 512–513.

21. "Anschutz's Motion Pictures and the Stroboscopic Disc," *The Philadelphia Photographer*, 19 Nov. 1887, pp. 328–330.

22. Hannibal Goodwin, U.S. Pat. No. 610,861. Applied 2 May 1887; issued 13 Sept. 1898.

23. Quigley, Jr., *op. cit.*, p. 126.

24. *Ibid.*, p. 128.

25. Gordon Hendricks, *The Edison Motion Picture Myth* (Berkeley and Los Angeles: University of California Press, 1961), p. 191. This is the most accurate and

objective book covering this fascinating era. The other is by Terry Ramsaye, *A Million and One Nights: A History of the Motion Picture* (New York: Simon and Schuster, 1926). Ramsaye gives this date as 1886: p. 44. See also Julius Pfragner, *Eye of History* (Chicago, New York and San Francisco: Rand, McNally, 1964), p. 122; David Robinson, *The History of World Cinema* (New York: Stein and Day, 1973), p. 15; and Kenneth McGowan, *Behind the Screen* (New York: Delacorte, 1965), p. 69.

26. The author does not wish to get involved in the Edison/Dickson controversy and the reader is advised to read Hendricks and Ramsaye, *op. cit.* It appears, however, that Ramsaye was awed by Edison and may not be reliable at times.

27. Thomas A. Edison, U.S. Pat. No. 589,168. Applied 24 Aug. 1891; issued 31 Aug. 1897. Thomas A. Edison, U.S. Pat. No. 493,426. Applied 24 Aug. 1891; issued 14 Mar. 1893.

28. Ducos du Hauron, Fr. Pat. No. 61,976. Applied 5 July 1864; issued 1 Mar. 1866; Wordsworth Donisthorpe, Br. Pat. No. 4344/1876. 9 Nov. 1876. Prov. protection only; Augustin Le Prince, U.S. Pat. No. 376,247. Applied 2 Nov. 1886; issued 10 Jan. 1888.

29. William Friese-Green, Br. Pat. No. 10,131. Applied 1 June 1889; issued 10 Jan. 1888.

30. Ramsaye, *op. cit.*, pp. 88, 166.

31. Thomas A. Edison, U.S. Pat. No. 307,031. Applied 15 Nov. 1883; issued 21 Oct. 1884.

32. Heinrich Hertz, "Ultra-Violet Light and Electric Discharge," *Annalen der Physik* (Leipzig) **31** (1887): pp. 983–1000.

33. W. Hallwachs, "On the Effect of Light on Electrostatically Charged Bodies," *Annalen der Physik* (Leipzig) **33** (1888): pp. 301–312.

34. Julius Elster and Hans Geitel, "The Use of Sodium Amalgam in Photoelectric Experiments," *Annalen der Physik* (Leipzig) **41** (1890): pp. 161–165.

35. A. Stoletow, "On Photoelectric Currents in Rarefied Air," *Journal of Physics* (USSR) **9** (1890): pp. 468–473.

36. J.J. Fahie, *A History of Wireless Telegraphy* (Edinburgh and London: Blackwood and Sons, 1901), pp. 292–304.

37. Noah S. Amstutz, Br. Pat. No. 4715/AD1891. Applied 17 Mar. 1891; issued 2 May 1891; C. Francis Jenkins, *Vision by Radio* (Washington, 1925), p. 73.

38. A. Blondel, *La Lumière Electrique* **41** (1891): pp. 407, 507; W. Duddell, *Electrician* **39** (1897): p. 636. The latter comes from J.T. MacGregor Morris and R. Mines, "Measurements in Electrical Engineering by Means of Cathode Rays," *Journal of the Institute of Electrical Engineers* (London) **63** (Nov. 1925): pp. 1056–1107.

39. M. Brillouin, "La photographie des objets à tres grande distance," *Révue Générale de Sciences* **2** (30 Jan. 1891): pp. 33–38.

40. Leon Le Pontois, "The Telectroscope," *Scientific American Supplement* **35** (10 June 1893): pp. 14546–14547.

41. Q. Majorano, *Electricista* **3** (1894): p. 3. From J.C. Wilson, *Television Engineering* (London: Sir Isaac Pitman & Sons, 1937), p. 460. Also in Shiers, *op. cit.*, p. 134.

42. C. Francis Jenkins, "Transmitting Pictures by Electricity," *Electrical Engineer* **18** (25 July 1894): pp. 62–63. See also C.F. Jenkins, *Animated Pictures* (Washington, D.C.: H.L.M. McQueen, 1898). Jenkins participated in the birth of the motion picture as well as that of television, some 28 years later.

43. Carl Nystrom, DRP Pat. No. 94,306. Applied 11 Jan. 1895; issued 11 Oct. 1897.

44. Guglielmo Marconi, Br. Pat. No. 12,039. Applied 2 June 1896; issued 2 July 1897. W.P. Jolly, *Marconi* (New York: Stein and Day, 1972), p. 35. For consistency, in this volume we shall call Alan Archibald Campbell Swinton by the name Campbell Swinton, although there have been many references to him as A.A.C. Swinton.

45. J.T. MacGregor Morris, "Ambrose Fleming: His Life and Early Researches," *Journal of the Television Society* 4 (1945): pp. 266–273; Sir William Crooks, *Phil. Transactions of the Royal Society* 170 (1879): p. 135; J.J. Thomson, "On the Masses of the Ions in Gases at Low Pressures," *Phil. Mag.* 48 (1899): pp. 547–567.

46. Ferdinand Braun, "Uber ein Vehrfahren zur Demonstration und zum Studium des zeitlichen Verlaufes variabler Strome," *Annalen der Physik* (Leipzig) 60 (1897): pp. 552–559; H. Ebert, "Das Verhalten der Kathodenstrahlen in electrischen Wechselfeldern," *Annalen der Physik und Chemie* 64 (1897): pp. 240–261.

47. Jan Szczepanik and Ludwig Kleinberg, Br. Pat. No. 5031. Applied 24 Feb. 1897; issued 24 Feb. 1898. Also Dan. pat. No. 2231. Applied 13 Jan. 1898; issued 3 May 1899.

48. J. Armengaud, "The Dussaud Teleoscope," *Scientific American Supplement* 46, no. 1174 (2 July 1898): p. 18793.

49. M. Wolfke, Russ. Pat. No. 4498. Applied 24 Nov. 1898; issued 30 Nov. 1900.

50. A.A. Polumordvinov, Russ. Pat. No. 10738. Applied 23 Dec. 1899. (This is from Shiers, *op. cit.*, p. 135.)

51. Vlademar Poulsen, Dan. Pat. No. 2653. Applied 1 Dec. 1898; issued 31 Oct. 1899. Also U.S. Pat. No. 661,619. Applied 8 July 1899; issued 13 Nov. 1900. There is also a Brit. Pat. No. 8961 (AD1899).

3. The First Devices: 1900–1911

1. "The International Electricity Congress," Constantin Perskyi, "Television," *Electrician* 45 (2 Sept. 1900), pp. 820–822.

2. V. Poulsen, "The Telegraphone," *Annalen der Physik* (Leipzig) 3 (1900): pp. 754–760; V. Poulsen, "The Telegraphone," *Electrician* 46 (30 Nov. 1900): pp. 208–210; Vlademar Poulsen, "The Telegraphone — A Magnetic Speech Recorder," *Scientific American Supplement* 51, no. 1307 (19 Jan. 1901): pp. 20944–20945.

3. E. Ruhmer, "The Photographone," *Sci. Amer. Supp.* 52, no. 1336 (10 Aug. 1901): p. 21420.

4. Otto von Bronk, DRP Pat. No. 155,528. Applied 12 June 1902; issued 22 Oct. 1904.

5. J.H. Coblyn, "La vision à distance par l'électricité." *Comptes Rendus des Séances de l'Academie* 135 (27 Oct. 1902): pp. 684–685.

6. Edouard and Marcel Belin, Fr. Pat. No. 339,212. Applied 8 Dec. 1903; issued 10 Jan. 1905. There were three additions to this patent, which all became part of the original patent (a feature of the French Patent system): No. 4248 of 8 June 1904, No. 4044 of 8 June 1904 and No. 4403 of 30 Jan. 1905.

7. H.J. Ryan, "The Cathode Ray Alternating Current Wave Indicator." *American Institute of Electrical Engineers* 22 (2 July 1903): pp. 539–552.

8. "La vision à distance par l'électricité." *Electro* 11 (Oct. 1903): pp. 153–154.

9. Werner von Jaworski and A. Frankenstein, DRP Pat. No. 172,376. Applied 20 Aug. 1904; issued 21 June 1906.

10. Paul Ribbe, Br. Pat. No. 29428. Applied 31 Dec. 1904; issued 2 Feb. 1905. Paul Ribbe, Br. Pat. No. 29429. Applied 31 Dec. 1904; issued 23 Feb. 1905. Paul Ribbe, DRP Pat. No. 160,813. Applied 19 May 1904; issued 19 May 1905.

11. A. Wehnelt, *Phys. Zeit.* **6**, no. 22 (1905): pp. 732–733; A. Wehnelt, DRP Pat. No. 157,945. Applied 15 Jan. 1904; issued 13 Jan. 1905.

12. J.A. Fleming, Br. Pat. No. 24850. Applied 16 Nov. 1904; issued 21 Sept. 1905.

13. Lee De Forest, U.S. Pat. No. 836,070. Applied 18 Jan. 1906, refiled 19 May 1906; issued 13 Nov. 1906. Lee De Forest. U.S. Pat. No. 841,387. Applied 25 Oct. 1906; issued 15 Jan. 1907. Lee De Forest. U.S. Pat. No. 879,532. Applied 29 Jan. 1907; issued 18 Feb. 1908.

14. Robert von Lieben, DRP Pat. No. 179,807. Applied 4 Mar. 1906; issued 19 Nov. 1906.

15. Georges P.E. Rignoux, Fr. Pat. No. 364,189. Applied 10 Feb. 1906; issued 16 Aug. 1906. See also G.P.E. Rignoux, Fr. Pat. No. 382,535. Applied 10 Dec. 1906; issued 10 Feb. 1908.

16. Max Dieckmann and Gustav Glage, DRP Pat. No. 190,102. Applied 12 Sept. 1906; issued 9 Sept. 1907. Max Dieckmann and Gustav Glage, DRP Pat. No. 184,710. Applied 10 Oct. 1906; issued 2 Apr. 1907.

17. Friedrich Lux, *Bayerischesten Industries und Gewererbeblatt* Bl. 38 13, 1906. This description comes from Arthur Korn and Bruno Glatzel, *Handbuch der Phototelegraphie und Telautographie* (Leipzig: Otto Nenmich, 1911), pp. 474–476. There is some doubt that the machine described is the same one pictured. The original article is unobtainable at this time.

18. R.T. Haines, J. St. Vincent Pletts and E.A. Lauste, Br. Pat. No. 18057/1906. Applied 11 Aug. 1906; issued 10 Aug. 1907. Lauste is said to have spent some time with E. Ruhmer. He visited America in 1911 and gave the first actual sound-on-film demonstration made in the United States. He recorded the sound continuously ahead of the picture. It was claimed that Lauste recorded both sound and picture in perfect synchronization. His machine, called the "Photocinematophone," was demonstrated several times in London.

19. Boris Rosing, Russ. Pat. No. 18076. Applied 25 July 1907; issued 30 Oct. 1910. See also Boris Rosing, DRP Pat. No. 209,320. Applied 26 Nov. 1907; issued 24 Apr. 1909. See also Boris Rosing, Br. Pat. No. 27570/1907. Applied 13 Dec. 1907; issued 25 June 1908. It is interesting to note that the British patent, which was applied for last, was the earliest to be issued.

20. S. Bidwell, "Practical Telephotography," *Nature* **76**, no. 1974 (29 Aug. 1907): pp. 444–445.

21. S. Bidwell, "Telegraphic Photography and Electric Vision," *Nature* **78**, no. 2014; 105–106, (4 June 1908): pp. 105–106.

22. C.F. Jenkins, U.S. Pat. No. 909,421. Applied 7 Feb. 1908; issued 12 Jan. 1909.

23. J. Adamian, Brit. Pat. No. 7219/AD1908. Applied 1 Apr. 1908; issued 28 May 1908. There is also an earlier Russian Patent No. 17912. Applied 5 Mar. 1908; issued 20 Sept. 1910.

24. G.P.E. Rignoux, Fr. Pat. No. 390,435. Applied 20 May 1908; issued 5 Oct. 1908.

25. S. Bidwell, "Telegraphic Photography," *op. cit.*, p. 105.

26. A.A. Campbell Swinton. "Distant Electric Vision," *Nature* **78**, no. 2016 (18 June 1908): p. 151.

27. Gilbert Sellers, U.S. Pat. No. 939,338. Applied 18 July 1908; issued 9 Nov. 1909.

28. A.C. Anderson and L.S. Anderson, Brit. Pat. No. 30,188. Conv. date 24 Dec. 1908; issued 22 Sept. 1910.

29. Max Dieckmann. "Fernubertragungseinrichtungen hoher Mannigfaltigkeit," *Prometheus* **20**, no. 1010 (3 March 1909): pp. 337–341. See also Max

Dieckmann, "The Problem of TeleVision—A Partial Solution," *Sci. Amer. Supp.* **68**, no. 1751 (24 July 1909): pp. 61–62 and B. von Czudrochowski, "Das Problem des Fernsehens," *Zeitschrift für Physik und Chemie* **4** (July 1909): pp. 261–265.

30. "Das elektrische Fernsehen," *Zeitschrift für Schwachstromtechnik* **15** (1909): pp. 393–395; see also A. Gradenwitz, "Un appareil de télévision," *La Nature* **38** (29 Jan. 1910): pp. 142–143.

31. H.D. Varigny, "La vision à distance," *L'Illustration* no. 3485 (11 Dec. 1909): p. 451.

32. A. Ekstrom, Swed. Pat. no. 32,220. Applied 24 Jan. 1910; issued 3 Feb. 1912.

33. Michel Schmierer, DRP Pat. No. 234,583. Applied 10 Apr. 1910; issued 15 May 1911. See also Michel Schmierer, DRP Pat. No. 229,916. Applied 30 Apr. 1910; issued 4 Jan. 1911; and Michel Schmierer, DRP Pat. No. 264,275 (taken from 229,916). Applied 3 Nov. 1912; issued 24 Sept. 1913 but delayed until 29 Apr. 1925.

34. Gustav H. Hoglund, U.S. Pat. No. 1,030,240. Applied 18 Apr. 1910; issued 18 June 1912.

35. Alf Sinding-Larsen, Br. Pat. No. 14,503/AD1911. Conv. date 20 June 1910; issued 21 Mar. 1912. Alf Sinding-Larsen, DRP Pat. No. 260,901. Applied 14 June 1911; issued 13 June 1913.

36. J. Elster and H. Geitel. "Uber gefarbte Hydride der Alkalimetalle und ihre photoelektrische Empfindlichkeit." *Physikalische Zeitschrift* **11** (1 Apr. 1910): pp. 257–263.

37. Boris Rosing, DRP Pat. No. 255,746. Applied 2 Mar. 1911; issued 19 Mar. 1912. Boris Rosing, Br. Pat. No. 5259/AD1911. Applied 2 Mar. 1911; issued 30 Nov. 1911. Boris Rosing, Br. Pat. No. 5486/AD1911. Applied 4 Mar. 1911; issued 29 Feb. 1912. Boris Rosing, U.S. Pat. No. 1,161,734. Applied 5 Apr. 1911; issued 23 Nov. 1915. Boris Rosing, U.S. Pat. No. 1,135,624. Applied 5 Apr. 1911; issued 13 Apr. 1915.

38. P.K. Gorokhov, *Boris L'vovich Rozing* (Moscow: 1964), p. 54. There are pictures of the apparatus on p. 55.

39. E. Ruhmer, "Rosing's System of Telephoty." *Zeitschrift für Schwachstromtechnik* **5** (April 1911): pp. 172–173. See also E. Ruhmer, "Der Rosingsche Fernseher," *Die Umschau,* 1911, pp. 508–510. This article has the first drawings of the transmitter and receiver of Rosing's television apparatus. See also Robert Grimshaw, "The Telegraphic Eye," *Scientific American* **104** (1 Apr. 1911): pp. 335–336. This article has actual pictures of both the receiver and the transmitter on page 335. It also has a diagram of the system similar to the patent application. See also "Prof. Rosing's 'Electric Eye'—A New Apparatus for Television," *Scientific American Supplement* **71**, no. 1850 (17 June 1911): p. 384; and "An Important Step in the Problem of Television," *Scientific American* **105** (23 Dec. 1911): p. 574. Note that there is no mention of Boris Rosing in the index of the *Great Soviet Encyclopedia* (New York: Macmillan, 1973, 1978, 1983) under the heading "Television." They mention Adamian, Kataev, Konstantinov, Shmakov and Zworykin. However, in the section "Pulse Engineering," Rosing was cited as "the first to use crt for tv reception of video signals, thus beginning the development of tv" (p. 572, vol. 10). There was a decided change in the 1983 edition. Under the heading of "Rozing, Boris L'Vovich," he is quoted as having proposed a plan in 1907 for generating television pictures using a cathode-ray tube, and in 1911 for demonstrating television transmission and reception of simple geometric figures. It stated that Rosing died in 1933 in Arkhangel'sk, where he had been since 1931. There is no hint as to why Rosing's great achievements have been thus played down by the Soviet regime.

4. *"Distant Electric Vision"*: 1911–1921

1. "Distant Electric Vision," *London Times*, Nov. 15, 1911, p. 24b.
2. A.A. Campbell Swinton, "Presidential Address," *Journal of the Röntgen Society* **8**, no. 30 (Jan. 1912): pp. 1–13.
3. Korn and Glatzel, *op. cit.* The author in October 1986 finally found a copy in the British Library of R. Ed. Liesegang, *Beitage zum Problem des Electrischen Fernsehens* (Dusseldorf: R. Ed. Liesegang, 1891) which has a section, pp. 89–120, that was also devoted to this subject. Thus it predates Korn and Glatzel by some 20 years!
4. Irving Langmuir, U.S. Pat. No. 1,558,436. Applied 16 Oct. 1913; issued 25 Oct. 1925. See also Irving Langmuir, U.S. Pat. No. 1,219,961. Applied 20 July 1914; issued 20 Mar. 1917, for a high vacuum cathode ray tube. See also Irving Langmuir, "The Effect of Space Charge and Residual Gases on the Thermionic Current in High Vacuum," *Physical Review*, 2d ser. **2** (Nov. 1913): pp. 402–403, 450–486.
5. W.D. Coolidge, "A Powerful Röntgen Ray Tube with a Pure Electron Discharge," *Physical Review*, 2d ser. **2** (Dec. 1913): pp. 409–430, and *Gen. Elec. Rev.* **17** (1914): p. 104.
6. Samuel Lavington Hart, Br. Pat. No. 15,270/AD1914. Applied 25 June 1914; issued 25 June 1915.
7. M. Lippmann, "Dispositif pour la vision à distance de M. Georges Rignoux," *Comptes Rendus des Séances de l'Academie* **159** (27 July 1914): pp. 301–304. Presented 13 July 1914. R. Arapu, "The Telephotographic Apparatus of Georges Rignoux," *Scientific American Supplement* **79** (22 May 1915): p. 331.
8. Andre Volgre, Fr. Pat. No. 478,361. Applied 1 Apr. 1915; issued 8 Dec. 1915.
9. Marcus J. Martin, "Television, When Shall We See as Well as Hear by Wireless?" *Wireless World* **3** (June 1915): p. 193; Marcus J. Martin, "The Wireless Transmission of Photographs," *Wireless World* **3**: article 1, pp. 57–60, April 1915; Article 2, pp. 102–107, May 1915. Article 3, pp. 162–165, June 1915. Article 4, pp. 228–232, July 1915. See also Marcus J. Martin, *Wireless Transmission of Photographs* (London WC2: Wireless Press, 1916).
10. H. Winfield Secor, "Television, or the Projection of Pictures over a Wire," *Electrical Experimenter* **3**, no. 4 (Aug. 1915): pp. 131–132, 172–174).
11. Alexandre Dauvillier, Fr. Pat. No. 521,746. Applied 20 Aug. 1915; issued 19 July 1921.
12. D. McFarlan Moore, U.S. Pat. No. 1,316,967. Applied 30 Nov. 1917; issued 23 Sept. 1919.
13. Alexander M. Nicolson, U.S. Pat. No. 1,470,696. Applied 7 Dec. 1917; issued 16 Oct. 1923. Later this patent was covered by two British patents filed on 7 Sept. 1923: Br. Pat. No. 228,961 and Br. Pat. No. 230,401.
14. Jakob Kunz, U.S. Pat. No. 1,381,474. Applied 24 Aug. 1918; issued 14 June 1921.
15. This material comes from a variety of sources. The best are G.L. Archer, *History of Radio to 1926* (New York: American Historical, 1938), and G.L. Archer, *Big Business and Radio* (New York: American Historical, 1939). Also E. Lyons, *David Sarnoff* (New York: Harper & Row, 1966); E. Barnouw, *A Tower in Babel* (New York: Oxford University Press, 1966); G.F.J. Tyne, *Saga of the Vacuum Tube* (Indianapolis: Howard W. Sams, 1977).
16. Dionys von Mihály, Fr. Pat. No. 546,714. Conv. date 18 Feb. 1919; issued 22 Nov. 1922. Also Br. Pat. No. 174,606, issued 25 May 1923. Dionys von Mihály, Br. Pat. No. 174,607. Conv. date 9 Dec. 1920; issued 25 April 1923. DRP Pat. No.

348,295. Applied 6 Nov. 1920; issued 6 Feb. 1922. It was claimed that in 1920, von Mihály had built a system that transmitted letters on a mosaic screen similar to the 1909 Rignoux and Fournier scheme. It had a mosaic of selenium cells, each connected to a solenoid. When energized these solenoids would induce a potential in another coil, which was rapidly rotated behind the mosaic to scan the bank of solenoids. A similar device in the receiver would operate a bank of lamps through relays. The scanners were synchronized by a pendulum movement driven through a worm gear. This is from Dionys von Mihály, *Das electrische Fernsehen und das Telehor* (Berlin: M. Krayn, 1923). This is the first book dedicated to television. According to Gerhart Goebels, this machine never did work, and pictures of it may be spurious. (Letter from G. Goebel of 10 June 1982).

17. "Piezo-Electricity and Its Applications," *Engineering* (London) **107** (25 Apr. 1919): pp. 543–544. See also D. Keys, "A Piezoelectric Method of Measuring Explosion Pressures," *Philosophical Magazine* **42** (Oct. 1921): pp. 473–484.

18. H.K. Sandell, U.S. Pat. No. 1,423,737. Applied 10 Sept. 1919; issued 25 July 1922. Also covered by Br. Pat. No. 200,643. Filed 16 May 1922; issued 5 Sept. 1923. Issued to Mills Novelty Co.

19. C.F. Jenkins, U.S. Pat. No. 1,385,325. Applied 23 Oct. 1919; issued 19 July 1921. High speed motion picture machine. C.F. Jenkins, U.S. Pat. No. 1,681,009. Applied 5 Feb. 1921; issued 15 Feb. 1927. C.F. Jenkins, "Continuous motion picture machines," *Transactions of the Society of Motion Picture Engineers* no. 10 (1920): pp. 97–102.

20. Franz Skaupy, DRP Pat. No. 349,838. Applied 28 Nov. 1919; issued 10 Mar. 1922. Skaupy has sometimes been given credit for the first hot cathode television picture tube, as his patent was issued before Nicolson's. However, application date has priority over issue date in this history. When a patent is filed is of more importance than when it is issued, as the length of time in the patent office depends on a combination of legal and technical factors. Priority is given to the inventor who first reveals his idea for outside scrutiny with proof that can sustain it.

21. H.J. van der Bijl, U.S. Pat. No. 1,565,873. Applied 10 Aug. 1920; issued 15 Dec. 1925. J.B. Johnson, U.S. Pat. No. 1,565,855. Applied 26 Nov. 1920; issued 15 Dec. 1925. J.B. Johnson, "A Low Voltage Cathode Ray Oscillograph," *Physical Review* **17** (1921): pp. 420–421; J.B. Johnson, "A Low Voltage Cathode Ray Oscillograph," *Bell System Technical Journal* **1** (July 1922): pp. 142–151.

22. S.N. Kakourine, Russ. Pat. No. 144. Applied 18 Aug. 1920; issued 31 Mar. 1925.

23. H.C. Egerton, U.S. Pat. No. 1,605,930. Applied 24 Aug. 1920; issued 9 Nov. 1926.

24. E.F. Seiler, "Color-Sensitiveness of Photoelectric Cells," *Astrophysics Journal* **52** (1920): pp. 129–153.

25. T.W. Case, "Thalofide Cell—A New Photo-Electric Substance," *Physical Review* **15** no. 4 (1920): pp. 289–292; T.W. Case, "A Photoelectric Effect in Audion Bulbs of the Oxide-Coated Filament Type," *Transactions of the Electrochemical Society* **39** (1921): pp. 423–428.

26. For an early article describing this situation see John B. Brady, "The Radio Patent Situation," *Radio News* **4** (Nov. 1922): pp. 850, 882–903. See also Lawrence Lessing, *Man of High Fidelity* (New York: Bantam, 1969), pp. 103–104; Archer, *History of Radio, op. cit.*, pp. 191–204.

27. Archer, *History of Radio, op. cit.*, pp. 207–211. Also, Archer, *Big Business and Radio, op. cit.*, p. 19.

28. Archer, *History of Radio, op. cit.*, pp. 112–113, 189.

5. The Early Camera Tubes: 1921–1924

1. Archer, *Big Business and Radio, op. cit.*, p. 8.

2. E.L. James, "Radio Reproduces Note Across Ocean," *New York Times*, 5 Aug. 1921, p. 1. For a more detailed description see, Jaques Boyer, "La transmission électrique des images," *La Nature* 50, no. 2501 (11 March 1922): pp. 151–157; E. Belin, "Telegraphic Transmission of Photographs," *Comptes Rendus des Séances de l'Academie* 174 (6 Mar. 1922): pp. 678–680. It was claimed that two Englishmen, H.G. Bartholmew and M.L.D. MacFarlane, transmitted photographs over the Western Union cables between London and New York in 1920. They used a complicated method of punching the perforated tape in order to transmit and receive their pictures. From C.R. Jones, *Facsimile* (New York: Murray Hill, 1949), pp. 19–20.

3. Edvard-Gustav Schoultz, Fr. Pat. No. 539,613. Applied 23 Aug. 1921; issued 28 June 1922.

4. Marcus J. Martin, *The Electrical Transmission of Photographs* (London: Sir Isaac Pitman, 1921).

5. C.F. Jenkins, "Prismatic Rings," *Transactions of the Society of Motion Picture Engineers* no. 14 (May 1922): pp. 65–71. See also C.H. Claudy, "Motion Pictures by Radio," *Scientific American* 127 (Nov. 1922): p. 320. C.F. Jenkins, U.S. Pat. No. 1,544,156. Applied 13 Mar. 1922; issued 30 June 1925. Jenkins applied for 11 television patents in the year 1922.

6. Boris Rtcheouloff, Russ. Pat. No. 3803. Applied 27 June 1922; issued 31 Oct. 1927.

7. Nicolas Langer, "A Development in the Problem of Television," *Wireless World and Radio Review* 11 (11 Nov. 1922): pp. 197–201.

8. "Belin Shows Tele-Vision," *New York Times*, 2 Dec. 1922, p. 1; "Tele-Vision," *London Times*, 9 Dec. 1922, p. 9f; "Une réalisation experimentale de la television," *Annales des Postes Télégraphes et Téléphones* 12 (Apr. 1923): p. 517; Robert E. Lacault, "The Belin Radio-Television Scheme," *Science and Invention* 10, no. 12 (Apr. 1923): pp. 1166–1217.

9. Alfred Gradenwitz, "Radio Telegraphy," *Radio News* 4 (Aug. 1922): pp. 226–227.

10. Arthur Benington, "Transmission of Photographs by Radio," *Radio News* 4 (August 1922): pp. 230, 369–372.

11. Edouard Belin, Fr. Pat. No. 571,785. Applied 27 Dec. 1922; issued 23 May 1924. See also Br. Pat. no. 209,049. Conv. date 27 Dec. 1922; issued 16 Feb. 1925.

12. Georges Valensi, Fr. Pat. No. 577,762. Applied 29 Dec. 1922; issued 10 Sept. 1924. See also U.S. Pat. No. 1,664,798. Conv. date 7 Sept. 1923; issued 3 Apr. 1928. This is a combination of the 1922/23 patents except that Valensi was not allowed to include a modulated and deflected cathode ray tube (due to the Nicolson patent?) and therefore he disclosed a cathode ray tube which was a pure light valve, varying in brightness but not being deflected. Fr. Pat. No. 572,716. Applied 3 Jan. 1923; issued 12 June 1924 with the addition, No. 28,926, applied 9 Apr. 1923; issued 9 May 1925.

13. Dionys von Mihály, DRP Pat. No. 422,995. Applied 2 Jan. 1923; issued 21 Dec. 1925. Also Br. Pat. No. 209,406. Conv. date 18 Dec. 1923; issued 27 Nov. 1924. Von Mihály, *Das Electrische Fernsehen und das Telehor, op. cit.*; Nicolas Langer, "Radio Television, The Mihály Telehor Machine," *Radio News* 5 (May 1924): pp. 1570–1571, 1686–1690. This appears to be the first television device built after the war.

14. "De Forest Demonstration of Phonofilm," *New York Times*, 13 Mar. 1923, p. 12:2. Lee De Forest, "The Motion Picture Speaks," *Popular Radio* 3 (Mar.

1923): pp. 159–169. Lee De Forest, "The Phonofilm," *Transactions of the Society of Motion Picture Engineers* no. 16 (May 1923): pp. 61–75.

15. W.S. Stephenson and G.W. Walton, Br. Pat. No. 218,766. Applied 18 Apr. 1923; issued 17 July 1924.

16. S.R. Winters, "The Transmission of Photographs by Radio," *Radio News* 4 (Apr. 1923): pp. 1772–1773; W. Davis, "Seeing by Radio," *Popular Radio* 3 (Apr. 1923): pp. 266, 275.

17. C.F. Jenkins, "Recent Progress in the Transmission of Motion Pictures by Radio," *Transactions of the Society of Motion Picture Engineers* no. 17 (Oct. 1923): pp. 81–85; O. Wilson, "Wireless Transmission of Photographs," *Wireless Age* 10 (July 1923): pp. 67–68; C. Francis Jenkins, *Vision by Radio, Radio Photographs, Radio Photograms* (Washington, D.C.: Jenkins Laboratories, 1925), p. 119. It could have been either a slide or photograph, not necessarily a living person.

18. J.L. Baird, "Television," *Journal of Scientific Instruments* 4 (Feb. 1927): pp. 138–143; "Seeing by Wireless," *London Times*, 27 June 1923, p. 1c; J.L. Baird and Wilfred E.L. Day, Br. Pat. No. 222,604. Applied 26 July 1923; issued 9 Oct. 1924.

19. John H. Hammond, Jr., U.S. Pat. No. 1,725,710. Applied 15 Aug. 1923; issued 20 Aug. 1929.

20. J.E. Gardner and H.D. Hineline, Br. Pat. No. 225,553. Conv. date 28 Nov. 1923; issued 28 May 1925. A convention date implies that a patent was applied for in the United States; I have never been able to find one. J.E. Gardner was one of the witnesses on the U.S. Pat. No. 2,141,059, which was filed by V.K. Zworykin, also of Westinghouse, on 29 Dec. 1923.

21. Alexandre Dauvillier, Fr. Pat. No. 592,162. Applied 29 Nov. 1923; issued 28 July 1925. See also Br. Pat. No. 225,516. Conv. date 10 Sept. 1924; issued 10 Dec. 1925. U.S. Pat. No. 1,661,603. Conv. date 22 Aug. 1924; issued 6 Mar. 1928. DRP Pat. No. 515,397. Conv. date 31 Aug. 1924; issued 5 Jan. 1931.

22. Louis de Broglie, "A Tentative Theory of Light Quanta," *Philosophical Magazine* 47 (Feb. 1924): pp. 446–458. Presented 1 Oct. 1923.

23. W. Rogowski and W. Grosser, DRP Pat. No. 431,220. Applied 21 Dec. 1923; issued 4 Feb. 1927. See also W. Rogowski and W. Grosser, U.S. Pat. No. 1,605,781. Conv. date 7 Nov. 1925; issued 2 Nov. 1926.

24. V.K. Zworykin, U.S. Pat. No. 2,141,059. Applied 29 Dec. 1923; issued 20 Dec. 1938. The many reasons this patent took some 15 years to go through the U.S. Patent Office will be explained as we come to them. The original patent application is available and is of interest as it reveals how this patent took its final form.

25. A.G. Jensen, "The Evolution of Modern Television," *Journal of the Society of Motion Picture and Television Engineers* 63 (Nov. 1954): p. 181. Its operation was questioned in many interferences. See, for example, interference #64207 (against Farnsworth), which we will deal with later.

26. V.K. Zworykin, "The Early Days: Some Recollections," *Television Quarterly* 1, no. 4 (Nov. 1962): pp. 69–72.

27. H. Gernsback, "Radio Vision," *Radio News* 5 (Dec. 1923): pp. 681, 824. Gernsback was the reputable editor of *Radio News* and was very unlikely to have been taken in by a publicity stunt. He indicates that he witnessed an actual demonstration of the apparatus, and there are pictures of the transmitter and receiver. This was also reported by W. Davis, "The New Radio Movies," *Popular Radio* 4 (Dec. 1923): pp. 436–443. The author has decided from this evidence that Jenkins did have a working television machine sometime early in 1923 and was the first inventor to actually send and receive television (moving) images by radio.

28. Edouard Belin, Fr. Pat. No. 571,785. Addition no. 29,259. Applied 5 Jan.

1924; issued 10 July 1925. "Television Promised by French Inventor," *New York Times*, 14 Jan. 1924; p. 1; Lucien Fournier, "Television by the Belin System," *Practical Electrics* 3 (Mar. 1924): pp. 244–246.

29. Edmund E.F. d'Albe. Br. Pat. no. 233,746. Applied 15 Jan. 1924; issued 15 May 1925.

30. A.A. Tschernischeff, Russ. Pat. No. 769. Applied 26 Jan. 1924; issued 31 Oct. 1925.

31. Laurent Seguin and Augustin Seguin, Fr. Pat. No. 577,530. Applied 8 Feb. 1924; issued 6 Sept. 1924.

32. George J. Blake and Henry J. Spooner, Br. Pat. No. 234,882. Applied 28 Feb. 1924; issued 28 May 1925.

33. V.K. Zworykin, U.S. Pat. No. 2,017,883. Applied 17 Mar. 1924 (renewed 27 June 1931); issued 22 Oct. 1935, which allowed Zworykin to make certain changes in it to conform with his *amended* 29 Dec. 1923 patent application. As far as can be determined at this time, Zworykin made no reference to globules until Oct. 2, 1925, when he tried to amend his 29 Dec. 1923 application. See page 79.

34. V.K. Zworykin, U.S. Pat. No. 1,709,647. Applied 17 Mar. 1924; issued 16 Apr. 1929.

35. N. Langer, "Television, An Account of the Work of D. Mihály," *Wireless World and Radio Review* 13 (19 Mar. 1924): pp. 760–764, and (26 Mar. 1924): pp. 794–796.

36. Apollinar Zeitlin and Wladislavus Zeitlin, DRP No. 503,899. Applied 18 Mar. 1924; issued 31 Mar. 1932.

37. H.J. McCreary, U.S. Pat. No. 2,013,162. Applied 10 Apr. 1924; issued 3 Sept. 1935.

38. Charles F. Jenkins, U.S. Pat. No. 1,530,463. Applied 23 Apr. 1924; issued 17 Mar. 1925.

39. A.A. Campbell Swinton, "The Possibilities of Television with Wire and Wireless," *Wireless World and Radio Review* 14 (9 Apr. 1924): pp. 51–56; (16 Apr. 1924): pp. 82–84; (23 Apr. 1924): pp. 114–118. Presented 26 Mar. 1924.

40. J.L. Baird, "An Account of Some Experiments in Television," *Wireless World and Radio Review* 14 (7 May 1924): pp. 153–155.

41. D.E. Howes, U.S. Pat. No. 1,810,018. Applied 28 May 1924; issued 16 June 1931.

42. August Karolus, DRP Pat. No. 471,720. Applied 21 June 1924; issued 18 Feb. 1929. See also U.S. Pat. No. 1,885,604. Applied 2 June 1925; issued 1 Nov. 1932. Karolus eventually produced the most practical Kerr cell for television use.

43. J. Strachan, "The Early History of Television," *Wireless World and Radio Review* 14 (11 June 1924): pp. 305–307.

44. Karl C. Randall, U.S. Pat. No. 1,660,886. Applied 11 July 1924; issued 28 Feb. 1928.

45. This information comes from Dr. Ernst Alexanderson's own personal records. They are stored at Schaffer Library, Union College, Schenectady, N.Y. This collection of Alexanderson's papers, correspondence, lab notes, drawings, etc. is vast. As the chief engineer of General Electric and RCA, Alexanderson was responsible for many of the achievements of these companies. I have of course concentrated on his efforts to produce a workable television system from 1924 through 1931. This material is used with the kind permission of the Library at Union College (which must be commended for taking excellent care of it and for having patience with me in my search for relevant material). It will be henceforth cited as the *Alexanderson/G.E. File*. The information on Hoxie came from Archer, *Big Business and Radio, op. cit.*, pp. 323–324.

46. Max Dieckmann, DRP Pat. No. 420,567. Applied 29 Aug. 1924; issued 26 Oct. 1925.

47. This material came from a personal interview with Kenjiro Takayanagi at the headquarters of JVC in Tokyo, Japan, on 9 Nov. 1981. I conducted an oral interview with him through a translator, and received several summaries of his accomplishments. This will be henceforth cited as the *Takayanagi File.*

48. Charles A. Hoxie, Br. Pat. No. 240,463. Conv. date 23 Sept. 1924. Applied 23 Sept. 1925; issued 25 Nov. 1926.

49. L.T. Jones and H.G. Tasker, "A Thermionic Braun Tube with Electrostatic Focusing," *Journal of the Optical Society of America* 9 (Oct. 1924): pp. 471–478.

50. "Pictures by Radio Sent from London Here in 20 Minutes," *New York Times,* 1 Dec. 1924, p. 1.

51. "Picture of Message is Sent by Wireless Using a New Process," *New York Times,* 4 Dec. 1924, p. 1; "New Radio Picture Blurred by Static," *New York Times,* 5 Dec. 1924, p. 6.

6. The Mechanical Era Begins: 1925–1927

1. J.L. Baird, "Television. A Description of the Baird System by Its Inventor," *Wireless World and Radio Review* 15 (21 Jan. 1925): pp. 533–535; J.L. Baird, "Television or Seeing by Wireless," *Discovery* 6 (Apr. 1925): pp. 142–143.

2. Herbert E. Ives, "Television: 20th Anniversary," *Bell Laboratory Record* 25 (May 1947): pp. 190–193. This information comes from the archives of the Bell Laboratories in Short Hills, N.J. It is Case 33089 for a "System of Television." This is a report from H.E. Ives to H.D. Arnold dated 23 Jan. 1925. Henceforth it will be cited as *Bell Labs, 33089.* See also *Bell Labs, 33089,* memorandum from J.G. Roberts, dated 14 May 1925.

3. A. Dauvillier, Fr. Pat. No. 592,162. Second addition No. 30,642. Applied 11 Feb. 1925; issued 20 July 1926.

4. Max Dieckmann and Rudolf Hell. DRP Pat. No. 450,187. Applied 5 Apr. 1925; issued 3 Oct. 1927.

5. Rudolph Hell made this claim in an interview with Gerhart Goebel on 1 Aug. 1951. See Gerhart Goebel, "Das Fernsehen in Deutschland bis zum Jahre 1945," *Archiv Post-und Fernmeldewesen* 21, no. 230 (Aug. 1953): p. 279. This has been an invaluable source of information to me. So has Mr. Goebel, whom I consider the ranking German television historian.

6. *Nature* 115 (4 Apr. 1925): pp. 505–506.

7. "D'Albe Demonstration," *London Times,* 18 Apr. 1925, p. 12c. See also *Nature* 115 (25 Apr. 1925): p. 613.

8. Camille A. Sabbah, U.S. Pat. No. 1,694,982. Applied 27 May 1925; issued 11 Dec. 1928. U.S. Pat. No. 1,706,185, issued 19 Mar. 1929. U.S. Pat. No. 1,747,988, issued 18 Feb. 1930. These were all combined in Br. Pat. No. 252,696, issued 28 Apr. 1927. Sabbah lost Patent Interferences nos. 54,922, 54,923, and 55,448 to Zworykin of Westinghouse. Although GE and Westinghouse owned RCA, their rivalry was deep and often bitter. This was especially true when it came to any kind of electrical patent.

9. "Jenkins Shows Far Off Objects in Motion," *New York Times,* 14 June 1925, p. 1:4; "Jenkins Test of 'Talking Movie' Radio Set," *New York Times,* 12 Aug. 1925, p. 3:2; "Movies over the Air," *New York Times,* 13 Sept. 1925, p. 3:6. See also C.F. Jenkins, *Radiomovies, Radiovision, Television,* (Washington, D.C.: Jenkins Laboratories, 1929); C.A. Herndon, "'Motion Pictures' by Ether Waves,"

Popular Radio **8** (Aug. 1925): pp. 107–113; W.B. Arvin, "See With Your Radio," *Radio News* **7** (Sept. 1925): pp. 278, 384–387; C.F. Jenkins, "Radio Movies," *Journal of the Society of Motion Picture Engineers* no. 21 (May 18–21, 1925): pp. 7–11.

10. This is from the engineering notebook of Frank Gray, 15 June 1926. The notebook is in the archives of the Bell Laboratories at Short Hills, N.J. It is book number 1413. It will be henceforth cited as *Eng. Notes, F. Gray*. See also *Bell Labs, 33089*, letter from Gray to Ives, dated 26 June 1925.

11. Boris L. Rosing, Russ. Pat. No. 3425. Applied 25 June 1925. Issue date unknown. This is from Boris L. Rosing, "La participation des savants russes au développement de la télévision électrique," *Revue Générale de L'Electricité*, 6 Apr. 1932, pp. 507–515. This is a French translation of the original article that appeared in *Electritvhestvo*, Numero Special (May 1930): pp. 47–57.

12. *Bell Labs, 33089*, memorandum by Ives, dated 10 July 1925; progress report by Gray, dated 28 July 1925.

13. V.K. Zworykin, U.S. Pat. No. 1,691,324. Applied 13 July 1925; issued 13 Nov. 1928. Br. Pat. No. 255,057, issued 31 March 1927. Campbell Swinton was so pleased with this patent that he wrote a letter to Dr. Alexanderson of GE about it, dated 20 April 1927. I have a copy of this letter from the Alexanderson records.

14. This information comes from the original patent application no. 683,337 that Zworykin filed on 29 Dec. 1923. The file shows the progress of the patent through the U.S. Patent Office. It has all of the rejections, interferences, correspondence, etc., until the patent was finally granted on 10 Nov. 1938. This file will henceforth be cited as the *Zworykin File*. See page B 1625 of the *Zworykin File*, dated 2 Oct 1925. This was in the form of an amendment. See *Zworykin File*, page 100R, dated 18 June 1936.

15. This is from the *Zworykin File*, page 34, dated 2 Oct. 1925. The 13 July 1925 patent application indicated that a certain amount of work had actually been done to produce a satisfactory photoelectric plate. Certainly by this time Zworykin had found that a layer of film produced few or no results. The change to a porous screen and globules would have eliminated many serious problems. Zworykin indicated to Garratt and Mumford (see n.8:90) that he had started work on an electronic television system in 1925. But I could not get hold of their notes to confirm this. He also makes the claim of building tubes in *Institution of Electrical Engineers (London)* **73** (Oct. 1933): p. 438, and in *L'Onde Electrique* **12** (Nov. 1933): p. 507.

16. This comes from the archives of the Westinghouse Labs in East Pittsburgh. This was in the form of a *Westinghouse Research Report R429A* (marked "Confidential"), dated June 25, 1926, written by V. Zworykin. This report indicated that some form of research project had been funded and worked on. It indicated that both camera and receiving tubes had been built. The difficulties in making camera tubes were noted. The project was to be temporarily discontinued in order to work on a mechanical method that was still in progress. It was planned to continue the work on new orders 6-4520 and 6-4522 (which I have not been able to find). This agrees with the decision by management to have Zworykin work on something more practical. It is to be noted that Zworykin did not participate in any of the future Westinghouse television projects. (See Westinghouse television demonstration of August 1928 on pp. 121–122.) They were all headed by Dr. Frank Conrad.

17. Zworykin has made several claims to have built and operated a television system as early as 1923. He wrote me this in a letter dated 14 Feb. 1952. But because he offered no proof, I must reject this claim. In other patent applications it was claimed that a tube or tubes were built between Jan. 1924 and 2 June 1924. Also it was claimed that a "tube had been built and tested" before 2 Oct. 1925. This is from the *Zworykin File*, page 34, dated Oct. 1925. Knowing how long it takes to

design and build such a complicated device, I would say that a tube or tubes were built and operated sometime between the middle of 1924 and the end of 1925.

18. *Westinghouse Research Report R429A, op. cit.*

19. As far as the camera tube itself is concerned, it was described several times by witnesses who supposedly had seen it in operation. It is easy to understand Zworykin's and Westinghouse's reluctance to produce it in evidence when there is the possibility that (a) it may have not been operating at the time, or (b) that perhaps, its construction and mode of operation were different from what was claimed in the patent application. But the tube itself exists; in fact, there are at least two different tubes from the pictures that have been produced. In 1931, Harley Iams built four tubes in order to prove that the original 1923 patent application did operate. I asked him if the tube on display had been built by him and he gave me an emphatic "no." In fact, he wrote me that later Zworykin was trying to give the name "Iconoscope" to a 1926 tube! Also, Les Flory, who had come to work for RCA in 1930, stated that he had seen a tube of this type in Zworykin's office. Based on all of this evidence, I must conclude that Zworykin did build and operate the first camera tubes in the world sometime between the middle of 1924 and late 1925.

20. This comes from two different sources. Pictures of the equipment and a description are shown in Dr. Gustav Eichhorn, *Wetterfunk Bildfunk Television* (Leipzig: B.G. Teubner, 1926), pp. 75–82. A short description was given by G. Goebel, *op. cit.*, p. 279. He quotes *Munchener Neueste Nachrichten* **21**, no. 230 (Aug. 1925): pp. 5, 21. This indicates that the equipment was on exhibit, but no claims were made that it was actually operating.

21. T.W. Case, U.S. Pat. No. 1,790,898. Filed 25 Aug. 1925; issued 3 Feb. 1931.

22. *Alexanderson/GE File*, memoranda dated 23 Oct. 1925 and 31 Oct. 1925.

23. *Eng. Notes, F. Gray*, 2 Nov. 1925. This insertion of the DC component is something that Baird never did!

24. *Bell Labs, 33089*, memorandum from Gray to Ives, dated 30 Nov. 1925. Ives, *op. cit.*, p. 191.

25. Grabovski, Popoff, and Piskounoff, Russ. Pat. No. 5592. Applied 9 Nov. 1925; issued 30 June 1928. A.A. Tschernisheff, Russ. Pat. No. 3511. Applied 28 Nov. 1925; issued 31 Aug. 1927. He also received Russ. Pat. No. 3510 for a camera tube. None of these patents is available from either the Washington or London patent offices.

26. W. Rogowski and W. Grosser, "Kathode-ray Oscillograph," *Archiv für Elektrotechnik* **15** (5 Dec. 1925): pp. 377–384.

27. "Reports 'Television' an Accomplished Fact," *New York Times*, 19 Dec. 1925; p. 10:2; L. Fournier, "The Latest Advance Toward Television," *Radio News* **8**)July 1926): pp. 36–37, 84.

28. J.L. Baird, Br. Pat. No. 269,658. Applied 20 Jan. 1926; issued 20 Apr. 1927.

29. It was claimed that Baird's breakthrough came on 2 Oct. 1925 in the form of an "exotic circuit" (such as introducing a transformer) that magically gave a real image with details and gradations of light and shade. See R.W. Burns, "The First Demonstration of Television," *Electronics & Power* **21** (Oct. 1975): p. 955. A letter to Dr. Burns asking for details of this valuable circuit met with no reply. There was a circuit patent applied for by Baird on 21 Oct. 1925 (Br. Pat. No. 270,222), which supposedly reduced the inertia of selenium cells. But an analysis of it shows that it could not work practically, otherwise it would have been one of the most important patents in television history! The proof that it did not work is that it was never heard of again. This story was also related in M. Baird, *Television Baird* (Cape Town: Haum, 1973). Also Wadell, Smith and Sanderson, "J. Baird and the Falkirk

Transmitter," *Wireless World* **82** (Jan. 1976): pp. 43–46 suggests that Baird distorted details of his work to hide progress from his competitors. So I am forced to the conclusion that it was the discovery of the "flying spot" scanner that was the real breakthrough. Why this is denied to this day remains a mystery to me. Also, none of the biographical books on Baird, such as Ronald F. Tiltman, *Baird of Television* (London: Seeley Service, 1933) or Sydney Moseley, *John Baird: The Romance and Tragedy of the Pioneer of Television* (Long Acre: Odhams Press, 1952) or John Rowland, *The Television Man* (New York: Roy, 1966), sheds any light on the subject!

30. "Television Perfected Asserts London Paper," *New York Times*, 23 Jan 1926, p. 10:5. See also "The 'Televisor'," *London Times*, 28 Jan. 1926, p. 9c.

31. See Maurice Exwood, *John Logie Baird: 50 Years of Television*, IERE History of Technology Monograph (London: Institution of Electrical and Radio Engineers, Jan. 1976), p. 14. The "visual purple" story is related in J.L. Baird, "Television," *Experimental Wireless* **4** (Dec. 1926): p. 736. The claim for a secret photocell "of the colloidal type, that is, made up of extremely finely divided selenium held in a suspension in a liquid," comes from A. Dinsdale, "And Now, We See By Radio!" *Radio Broadcast* **10**, no. 2 (Dec. 1926): p. 141. The covering of the Baird apparatus was related by W.C. Fox in George Shiers, "Television 50 Years Ago," *Journal of Broadcasting* **19**, no. 4 (fall 1975): p. 394. It is also related in a recently discovered report by F.G. Stewart in April 1926, who was ordered to report on the Baird apparatus. He states that "the instruments were entirely enclosed except for input lens and the screen. The inventor declined to show me the interior of the apparatus as he had definitely decided to give a minimum of information upon the details of construction and operation to anyone." See F.G. Stewart, "Television," unpublished manuscript (kindly lent me by T. Bridgewater), Apr. 1926.

32. R.W. Burns, "Early Admiralty and Air Ministry Interest in Television," unpublished monograph, 1984.

33. Reginald S. Clay, Br. Pat. No. 273,227. Applied 9 Feb. 1926; issued 9 June 1927. U.S. Pat. No. 1,719,756. Conv. date 3 Feb. 1927; issued 2 July 1929.

34. *Eng. Notes, F. Gray*, 10 Feb. 1926. The patent was filed with the U.S. Patent Office on 26 May 1926 and given serial number 111,731. It was never issued. I can only presume that by this time a patent covering the basic flying spot scanner could not be granted.

35. *Bell Labs, 33089*, letter from Gray to Ives, dated 2 March 1926.

36. Marius Latour, Br. Pat. No. 267,513. Applied 9 Mar. 1926; Conv. date 8 Mar. 1927; issued 24 Nov. 1927.

37. *Bell Labs, 33089*, memorandum from R.C. Mathes, dated 8 May 1926.

38. Henry J. Round, Br. Pat. No. 276,084. Applied 21 May 1926; issued 22 Aug. 1927. See U.S. Pat. No. 1,759,594. Conv. date 11 May 1927; issued 20 May 1930. In an interference no. 62,721 between Round and Zworykin, Round won. It seems that although there is very little reference to a practical television system, the wording of the claims is most important to the U.S. Patent Office. This decision was finally reversed when RCA took this case to a court of appeals, and Zworykin finally received his 1923 patent.

39. C.F. Jenkins, U.S. Pat. No. 1,683,137. Applied 2 June 1926; issued 4 Sept. 1928. Jenkins built this device, which appeared in May 1928. See Chapter 7, page 112.

40. *Bell Labs, 33089*, report from F. Gray, dated 21 June 1926.

41. "The Baird Televisor System," *The Electrician* **96** (25 June 1926): p. 672. See also H. de A. Donisthorpe, "With Description and Illustration of First Crude Results Secured by Means of the Baird Televisor," *Radio* **8** (Aug. 1926): pp. 9–10,

52; A. Dinsdale, "Television, An Accomplished Fact," *Radio News* **8** (Sept. 1926): pp. 206-207, 280-282; A. Dinsdale, "And Now We See by Radio!" *op. cit.* (n. 6.31), pp. 139-143; J.L. Baird, "Television," *op. cit.* (n. 6.31), pp. 730-739. There has been some controversy over this photograph. It has been claimed that it was faked or pieced together. However, after seeing later pictures taken from a moving disc, I have decided that this picture is genuine and shows what the Baird system was capable of transmitting at the time.

42. Archer, *Big Business and Radio., op. cit.*, pp. 250-276. See also Frank Waldrop and Joseph Borken, *Television: A Struggle for Power* (New York: Morrow, 1938), p. 177.

43. *Eng. Notes*, F. Gray, 16 July 1926.

44. *Eng. Notes*, F. Gray, 24 July 1926.

45. "Moving Images Sent by Wire or Wireless by Professor Belin before Paris Experts," *New York Times*, 29 July 1926, p. 1:4; P.C. [Pierre Chevallier?] "La télévision, par le procede Edouard Belin," *Le Génie Civil Revue Générale des Techniques* **89**, no. 25 (18 Dec. 1926): pp. 549-552; L. Fournier, "New Television Apparatus," *Radio News* **8** (Dec. 1926): pp. 626-627, 739; L. Lumière, *Comptes Rendus des Séances de l'Academie*, 28 Feb. 1927; Bernard Auffray, "Edouard Belin: Le père de lat télévision" (Paris: Les du Monde, 1981), pp. 98-102.

46. A. Dauvillier, "Sur le téléphote, appareil de télévision par tubes à vide; Resultats experimentaux preliminaires," *Comptes Rendus des Séances de l'Academie* **183** (2 Aug. 1926): pp. 352-354. Presented by L. de Broglie. Why electron beam acceleration after deflection didn't work for Dauvillier can only be guessed at. Just two years later Zworykin made this principle work, and it was the basis of his cathode ray tubes, for it allowed the electron beam to be deflected at low velocity and then accelerated for high brightness.

47. A. Dinsdale, "Television, An Accomplished Fact," *op. cit.* (n. 6.41), pp. 206-207, 280-282.

48. *Alexanderson/G.E. File*, letter from Alexanderson to Howland, dated 18 Sept. 1926.

49. A.A. Campbell Swinton, "Electric Television," *Nature* **118** (23 Oct. 1926): p. 590.

50. J.L. Baird, Br. Pat. No. 289,104. Applied 15 Oct. 1926; issued 16 Apr. 1928.

51. Hans Busch, "Calculation of the Path of an Electron Beam in an Axial Symmetrical Electromagnetic Field," *Annalen der Physik* **81** (1926): pp. 974-993. Presented 18 October 1926.

52. Ernst F.W. Alexanderson, U.S. Pat. No. 1,694,301. Applied 19 Oct. 1926; issued 4 Dec. 1928.

53. K. Takayanagi, "Research and Development of All Electronic Television System," publicity release, 1981, *Takayanagi File*, p. 6.

54. *Bell Labs, 33089*, letter from Gray to Ives, 10 Nov. 1926; *Bell Labs, 33089*, letter from Gray to Ives, 16 Nov. 1926; *Bell Labs, 33089*, letter from Ives to Arnold, 27 Nov. 1926.

55. Frederick W. Reynolds, U.S. Pat. No. 1,780,364. Applied 4 Dec. 1926; issued 4 Nov. 1930. A slightly different version, U.S. Pat. No. 2,055,593, was divided out of this and was issued on 29 Sept. 1936. This was the only electric camera patent to come from the Bell Labs for many years. It was not until 1929/1930 that Gray turned his attention to this subject. See Chapter 8, page 152.

56. J.L. Baird, "Television," *op. cit.*, p. 736; A. Dinsdale, "And Now, We See by Radio!" *op. cit.*, p. 141.

57. E.F.W. Alexanderson, "Radio Photography and Television," *General Electric Review* **30** (Feb. 1927): pp. 78-84; W. Kaempefert, "Science Now Promises

Us Radio Sight Across Seas," *New York Times*, 26 Dec. 1926, p. 8:4. *Alexanderson/G.E. File*, letter from Alexanderson to C.O. Howland, dated 24 Dec. 1926.
    58. Boris Rtcheoulouff, Br. Pat. No. 287,643. Applied 24 Dec. 1926; issued 16 May 1928. Boris Rtcheoulouff, Br. Pat. No. 288,680. Applied 4 Jan. 1927; issued 7 June 1928. See also U.S. Pat. No. 1,771,820. Applied 9 Mar. 1927; issued 29 July 1930.
    59. Philo T. Farnsworth. U.S. Pat. No. 1,773,980. Applied 7 Jan. 1927; issued 26 Aug. 1930. Divided on 7 Nov. 1927 to become U.S. Pat. No. 1,806,935; issued 26 May 1931. Most of the biographical background comes from George Everson, *The Story of Television, The Life of Philo T. Farnsworth* (New York: W.W. Norton, 1949).
    60. "Radio Movie in Home Forecast by Expert to Engineers Here," *New York Times*, 11 Jan. 1927, p. 1:1. See also "Moving Pictures by Wireless," *London Times*, 12 Jan. 1927, p. 12g.
    61. *Bell Labs, 33089*, memorandum from Ives, dated 17 Jan. 1927.
    62. J.L. Baird, U.S. Pat. No. 1,945,626. Conv. date 6 Jan. 1928 (applied 26 Jan. 1927); issued 6 Feb. 1934.
    63. Leon Thurm, U.S. Pat. No. 1,771,360. Conv. date 23 Jan. 1928 (applied 5 Feb. 1927); issued 22 July 1930.
    64. Etablissments Edouard Belin, Fr. Pat. No. 638,661. First addition no. 33,669, applied 4 Mar. 1927; issued 29 Nov. 1928. At the moment, I have not been able to find out who the actual inventor is. It is presumed to be either Fernand Holweck or, more likely, Pierre E.L. Chevallier, who was now working with Belin.
    65. L. Fournier, "Television by New French System," *Science and Invention* 14 (Mar. 1927): pp. 988, 1066.
    66. Hans Busch, "The Action of the Concentration Coil with the Braun Tube," *Archiv für Elektrotechnik* 18 (21 Sept. 1927): pp. 583-594. Presented March 1927.
    67. "Far Off Speakers Seen as Well as Heard Here in a Test of Television," *New York Times*, 8 Apr. 1927, p. 1:1. See also "Television: Its Development and Accomplishment" *Bell Lab Record* 4 (May 1927): pp. 297-325; A. Dinsdale, "Television Demonstration in America," *Wireless World* 21 (1 June 1927): pp. 680-686; H. Winfield Secor, "Television Perfected at Last," *Science and Invention* 15 (June 1927): pp. 108-109, 177; H. Winfield Secor, "Radio Vision Demonstrated in America," *Radio News* 8 (June 1927): pp. 1424-1426. For technical details see the following articles in *Bell System Technical Journal* 6 (Oct. 1927): Herbert E. Ives, "Television," pp. 551-559; F. Gray, J.W. Horton and R.C. Mathes, "The Production and Utilization of Television Signals," pp. 560-603; H.M. Stoller and E.R. Morton, "Synchronization of Television," pp. 604-615; D.K. Gannett and E.I. Green, "Wireless Transmission System for Television," pp. 616-632; Edward L. Nelson, "Radio Transmission System for Television," pp. 633-652.
    68. K. Takayanagi, "Experiments on Television," *Journal of the Institute of Electrical Engineers* (Japan), no. 482 (Sept. 1928): pp. 932-942. V.K. Zworykin, who was aware of the work being done on cathode ray receivers by the French, probably first knew of Takayanagi's work from this article.
    69. *Alexanderson/G.E. File*, letter from A.A. Campbell Swinton to Dr. Alexanderson, dated 20 April 1927.
    70. *Bell Labs, 33089*, memorandum from F. Gray, "Use of Cathode Ray Tube-Television Reception," dated 1 May 1927.
    71. Ray Kell, who had been working in the testing department at GE, had devised a means for maintaining synchronization of a picture by a hand control sometime in April 1927. He soon proved to be a valuable assistant to Dr. Alexanderson and was working on the television project full-time. See *Alexanderson/G.E. File*, 26 Apr. 1927, 11 May 1927, and 21 May 1927.

72. E. Taylor Jones, "Television," *Nature* **20** (18 June 1927): p. 896.

73. A. Dinsdale, "Television Sees in Darkness and Records its Impressions," *Radio News* **8** (June 1927): pp. 1422–1423, 1490–1492.

74. L. Fournier, "New European Television Scheme," *Science and Invention* **15** (July 1927): pp. 204–205. See also G. Valensi, "L'Etat actuel du problème de la télévision," *Annales des Postes Télégraphes et Téléphones* **6** (Nov. 1927): pp. 1047–1067.

75. "Television Developments of Edouard Belin," *Science and Invention* **15** (Sept. 1927): p. 410. See also "The New Belin Televisor," *Popular Radio* **12** (Nov. 1927): 347.

76. "Television at the British Association," *Wireless World* **21** (21 Sept. 1927), pp. .361–362. Baird's patent 288,882 described a form of spot-light scanning using infrared radiation. See J.L. Baird, Brit. Pat. No. 288,882. Applied 15 Oct. 1926 (divided out of 289,104) issued 16 April 1928. Dr. Ives applied for a patent involving flying-spot scanning with infrared rays in March 1927. See H.E. Ives, U.S. Pat. No. 2,082,339. Applied 2 Mar. 1927; issued 1 June 1937.

77. Much of this information comes from the notebooks of Philo T. Farnsworth, which were shown to me by Mrs. Farnsworth on 5 Nov. 1977. It is also confirmed in Everson's biography (see n. 6.59). The Farnsworth family is convinced that Philo built and operated the first camera tubes in the world. They have never accepted the fact that Zworykin did build and operate a tube earlier. (See pages 79–81.) Their doubt comes from the fact that the tube was never produced in any of the patent interferences. Only witnesses spoke of it and, as was pointed out, no one was quite sure when it was made, how it operated and with what success.

This created a problem for me until I discovered the Westinghouse Memo (see n. 6.16) dated 25 June 1926. It was actual evidence that tubes, both transmitting and receiving, had been built and operated. (I, of course, wish that it had gone into more detail.) In addition, there are many references to the existence of the tube by reliable witnesses, and this was never questioned. Finally, the tube still exists, so until there is concrete evidence to the contrary, I shall consider the case against Zworykin closed.

The fact is that Farnsworth had the only operating camera tubes in the world from September 1927 until July 1929, when Zworykin built his second tube. Dr. Zworykin's and Ogloblinsky's work on dissectors from 1930 till mid-1931 is recounted on pages 152, and 155–156. Further, it wasn't until late in 1931 that Zworykin built a storage tube that could work as well as the dissector. See Chapter 8, p. 173. Finally, Farnsworth never resorted to discs or drums and always used the cathode ray tube as a receiver. He was operating an all-electric system, i.e., electric camera tube, electric sweep generator, and magnetically focused cathode ray tube from July 1929 on, a feat of first rank. But his camera tube *was not* the first one to be built and operated.

78. Ralph V.L. Hartley and H.E. Ives, Br. Pat. No. 297,078. Conv. date 19 Mar. 1928 (applied 14 Sept. 1927); issued 19 June 1929.

79. Robert C. Mathes. U.S. Pat. No. 2,058,898. Applied 12 Nov. 1927; issued 27 Oct. 1936.

80. C. Francis Jenkins, "Radio Vision," *Proceedings of the Institute of Radio Engineers* **15** (Nov. 1927): pp. 958–964. Presented June 24, 1927.

81. August Karolus, U.S. Pat. No. 1,889,990. Conv. date 30 Nov. 1928 (applied 31 Dec. 1927); issued 6 Dec. 1932.

7. The Introduction of the Kinescope: 1928–1929

1. Alexandre Dauvillier, "La télévision électrique," *Revue Générale de L'Electricité* **23**: First Part (7 Jan. 1928): "Etude des divers procedes projetes ou realises," pp. 5–23. Second Part (14 Jan. 1928): "Téléphote et radiophote," pp. 61–73. Second Part (continued and finished, 21 Jan. 1928): "Téléphote et radiophote," pp. 117–128.

2. Philo T. Farnsworth, U.S. Pat. No. 1,970,036. Applied 9 Jan. 1928; issued 14 Aug. 1934.

3. "Radio Television To Home Receivers," *New York Times*, 14 Jan. 1928, p. 1:6; *Alexanderson/G.E. File*, memorandum from Alexanderson to Lunt, dated 28 Oct. 1927. It was indicated that the first test had been made to a "home receiver" located in Alexanderson's home on this date. He credited both Ray Kell and Paul Kober, who had operated the receiver.

4. P. Selenyi, "Use of Negative Charges of Kathode Rays as Means of Marking in the Kathode-Ray Oscillograph," *Zeitschrift für Physik* **47** (1928): pp. 895–897. Presented 20 Jan. 1928; P. Selenyi, "Electrical Charging of Glass by Kathode Rays and its Practical Application." *Zeitschrift für Technische Physik* **9** (1928): pp. 451–454. Presented 28 Sept. 1928. This article shows a high voltage anode which accelerated the beam while removing the positive ions. This was a positive step toward a bright television picture tube; P. Selenyi, U.S. Pat. No. 1,818,760. Conv. date 18 Jan. 1929 (1 Feb. 1928); issued 11 Aug. 1931. See also Br. Pat. No. 305,168. Conv. date 24 Jan. 1929 (1 Feb. 1928); issued 24 Oct. 1929.

5. "Device for Seeing by Radio Is Easily Attached to Sets," *New York Times*, 22 Jan. 1928, p. 14:1. This was reported by Capt. Hutchinson; "Persons in Britain Seen Here by Television As They Pose Before Baird's Electric 'Eye'," *New York Times*, 9 Feb. 1928, p. 1:3; A. Dinsdale, "Seeing Across the Atlantic Ocean," *Radio News* **9** (May 1928): pp. 1232–1233.

6. "Television Brings Fiancée's Living Image to Berengaria Radio Man 1000 Miles at Sea," *New York Times*, 8 Mar. 1928, p. 4:4. See also A. Dinsdale, "Seeing Across the Atlantic Ocean," *op. cit.*, p. 1233.

7. "Baird Puts Apparatus on Sale in London," *New York Times*, 21 Feb. 1928, p. 27:2; "TV Sets for Sale," *London Times*, 21 Feb. 1928, p. 13c; "A Television Challenge," *Electrician* **100** (23 Mar. 1928): p. 322; "Television Waves Pass Unnoticed," *New York Times*, 20 May 1928, sec. IX, p. 21:1; "England Goes in for Television," *Radio News* **9** (June 1928): pp. 1328, 1389; *Popular Wireless*, 10 Mar. 1928, p. 47; S.G. Sturmey, *The Economic Development of Radio* (London: Gerald Duckworth, 1958), pp. 192–193.

8. "New Device Shows Television Strides," *New York Times*, 26 Feb. 1928, p. 1:26; "New Devices in Television," *Bell Laboratory Record* **6** (May 1928): p. 215.

9. V.K. Zworykin, U.S. Pat. No. 1,837,746. Applied 3 Mar. 1928; issued 22 Dec. 1931. V. Zworykin and E.D. Wilson, "The Caesium-Magnesium Photocell," *Journal of the Optical Society of America* **19** (Aug. 1929): pp. 81–89. Presented July 24, 1929.

10. *Alexanderson/G.E. File*, memorandum from Alexanderson to Dunham, dated 17 Mar. 1928.

11. R.D. Kell, Br. Pat. No. 308,277. Conv. date 20 Mar. 1928 (20 Mar. 1929); issued 21 Nov. 1929.

12. *Zworykin File*.

13. P.T. Farnsworth, U.S. Pat. No. 1,986,330. Applied 17 Apr. 1928; issued 1 Jan. 1935. This immersing of a cathode ray tube in a magnetic field made possible the early low velocity tubes of the late 1930s built by RCA. This was another important first for Farnsworth.

14. P.T. Farnsworth, U.S. Pat. No. 1,844,949. Applied 25 Apr. 1928; issued 16 Feb. 1932. See Interference No. 73,103 (Iams vs. Ballard vs. Farnsworth), which Farnsworth won.

15. Ricardo Bruni, Br. Pat. No. 310,424. Conv. date 25 Apr. 1928 (applied 25 Apr. 1929); issued 3 Apr. 1930. Fr. Pat. No. 672,202. Conv. date 25 Apr. 1928 (applied 21 Mar. 1929); issued 24 Dec. 1929. R. Bruni, "System and Apparatus for Thermionic Television," *Revue de Télégraphie et TSF* 8 (Mar. 1930): pp. 218-225.

16. Arthur F. Van Dyck, "The Early Days of Television," *Radio Age* 15 (Apr. 1956): pp. 10-12. See also R.C. Bitting, Jr., "Creating an Industry," *Journal of the Society of Motion Picture and Television Engineers* 74 (Nov. 1965): pp. 1015-1023. *Alexanderson/G.E. File,* letters dated 9 May 1928.

17. "Broadcasts Pictures," *New York Times,* 6 May 1928, p. 3:2; "RadioMovies and Television for the Home," *Radio News* 10 (Aug. 1928): pp. 116-118, 173; "The Jenkins 'Radio-Movie' Reception Method," *Radio News* 10 (Nov. 1928): pp. 420, 492-493; C. Francis Jenkins, "The Drum Scanner in Radiomovies Receivers," *Proceedings of the Institute of Radio Engineers* 17 (Sept. 1929): pp. 1576-1583. The device used as a receiver was U.S. Pat. No. 1,683,137, filed 2 June 1926. It was issued 4 Sept. 1928.

18. K. Takayanagi, "Research and Development of All Electronic Television System," publicity release, 1981, *Takayanagi File,* pp. 7-8. See for instance, K. Takayanagi, "How to Make Television Equipment," *Radio of Japan,* Series 8 (January 1, 1929): p. 17.

19. G. Goebel, *op. cit.,* pp. 281-282. See also "50 Years of Fernseh 1929-1979," *Bosch Technische Berichte* 6 (25 May 1979): pp. 17-18.

20. *Bell Labs, 33089,* memorandum from Ives to H.D. Arnold, dated 11 May 1928. Also, memorandum from H.D. Arnold to E.E. Craft, dated 29 May 1928. This also mentioned that a 72-line apparatus was being built in the laboratory.

21. Ronald F. Tiltman, "Television in Natural Colors Demonstrated," *Radio News* 9 (Oct. 1928): pp. 320, 374. See also A. Dinsdale, *Television* (London: Television Press, 1928), pp. 161-162. But there is absolutely no notice of this "demonstration" in either the *New York Times,* the *London Times* or *Nature* for 1928. Three articles appeared in the English magazine *Television* after July claiming a daylight demonstration before the Bell Labs. This magazine was known to be the unofficial organ of the Baird Co. See J.R. Fleming, "Daylight Television — A Remarkable Advance," *Television* (London) 1 (July 1928): pp. 5-7; C. Tierney, "My Impression of Daylight and Colour Television," *Television* (London) 1 (Aug. 1928): pp. 7-8; A. Church, "Do We Encourage Genius?" *Television* (London) 1 (Aug. 1928): pp. 5-6, 26. It is understood that Baird's daylight demonstration was made possible by running the disc at about half-speed, i.e., about 5 frames/sec. This gave the photocells more output.

22. *Alexanderson/G.E. File,* letter from A.G. Davis to J.A. Cranston, dated 31 May 1928. The claim of a demonstration comes from Stephen F. Hofer, "Philo Farnsworth: The Quiet Contributor to Television," unpublished doctoral thesis, June 1977, Bowling Green University, p. 62. See also S. Hofer, "Philo Farnsworth: Television's Pioneer," *J. of Broad.* 23 (Spring 1979): pp. 153-165. Hofer quotes from "Philo T. Farnsworth, 'Daily Notes,'" San Francisco, 1928. I have not been able to get access to these notes as I would not agree with the Farnsworth family that Philo had priority over V.K. Zworykin. I told them that I must remain neutral and present the facts as I saw them. I did get a preliminary glance at the Farnsworth notebooks in Nov. 1977, but have not received any more information since that time. So all of my Farnsworth references must be secondary. Hofer was also determined to prove that Philo was "first," and all of his material is slanted in that direction. (Hofer's thesis is full of major errors and must be regarded with caution.)

23. A.A. Campbell Swinton, "Television by Cathode Rays," *Modern Wireless* 9 (June 1928): pp. 595-598; A.A. Campbell Swinton, "Television: Past and Future," *Discovery* 9 (Nov. 1928): pp. 337-339.

24. J.L. Baird, Br. Pat. No. 321,389. Applied for 5 June 1928; issued 5 Nov. 1929.

25. Lewis R. Koller, "The Photoelectric Cell — Radio's 'Eye'," *Radio News* 10 (Oct. 1928): pp. 305-307, 372-373. See also L.R. Koller, "The Photoelectric Cell," *General Electric Review* 31 (Sept. 1928): pp. 373-375; L.R. Koller, "Characteristics of Photo-Electric Cells," *Transactions of the Society of Motion Picture Engineers* 12 (1928): pp. 921-939.

26. Kolomon Tihany, Br. Pat. No. 313,456. Conv. date 11 June 1928, (applied 11 June 1929); voided and never issued. Fr. Pat. No. 676,546. Conv. date 11 June 1928 (filed 11 June 1929); issued 24 Feb. 1930. Br. Pat. No. 315,362. Conv. date 12 July 1928; voided and never issued. U.S. Pat. No. 2,158,259. Conv. date 11 June 1928 (applied 10 June 1929), divided 8 Mar. 1935; issued 16 May 1939. This information came from a personal interview in 1977 with Tihany's daughter (Katrina Glass), who lives in Los Angeles. She is convinced that her father "invented" the Iconoscope and that he has never gotten proper recognition for this. The fact is that RCA had to buy up his American patent as it did have certain claims that pertained to the operation and construction of a storage type tube that Zworykin built and operated. Again, I was faced with the fact that many inventors had the "ideas" that were so necessary to build a practical camera tube, but only one man, Zworykin, actually built and operated tubes of this type when almost all of the "experts" (see Schröter's remarks on pps. 187-188) claimed that such a tube could never work. Zworykin's faith in his ability to perfect an electric television system was his strength. With a superb technical staff he simply went ahead and made the system work.

27. "Television Method Shown in Chicago," *New York Times*, 13 June 1928, p. 32:2.

28. Coryton E.C. Roberts, Br. Pat. No. 318,331. Applied 22 June 1928; issued 5 Sept. 1929.

29. R.F. Tiltman, "Television in Natural Colors Demonstrated," *Radio News* 10 (Oct. 1928): pp. 320, 374.

30. "Television Shows Panoramic Scene Carried by Sunlight," *New York Times*, 13 July 1928, p. 4:1; "Progress of Television," *London Times*, 14 July 1928, p. 13b; "Radio 'Eye' Made Sensitive; Television Works Outdoors," *New York Times*, 22 July 1928, sec. VIII, p. 12:1; Frank Gray and Herbert E. Ives, "Optical Conditions for Direct Scanning in Television," *Journal of the Optical Society of America* 17 (Dec. 1928): pp. 428-434. Presented July 12, 1928.

31. C.F. Jenkins, U.S. Pat. No. 1,756,291. Applied 16 July 1928; issued 29 Apr. 1930.

32. *Alexanderson/G.E. File*, letter from Alexanderson to Dunham, dated 2 Aug. 1928.

33. "Radio Movies Demonstrated," *Science and Invention* 16 (Nov. 1928): pp. 622-623, 666; "Radio 'Movies' from KDKA," *Radio News* 10 (Nov. 1928): pp. 416-417.

34. There is a cathode ray tube on display at the Conservatoire Nationale des Arts et Métiers, Musée National des Techniques in Paris. It has a placard claiming that a tube "similar to the tube presented here" was used by Belin, Chevallier and Holweck in 1928 for reception of images. It is a demountable, two-piece glass tube that does have two anodes. It is obviously pumped and has only one set of deflection plates. The phosphor is almost gone, and there is no connection from the screen to the electron gun.

I visited the museum on 27 July 1984 in search of some documentation. I was shown a sheet of paper which stated only that the tube was received in 1966. Nothing as to who gave it or why. All my efforts to get any more information from the curator were in vain!

However, all my other evidence indicates that some kind of tube was in the Belin Laboratories in 1928 and that it certainly was shown to Dr. Zworykin. But the tube on display is not the one that is used in cathode ray television today. It remained for Dr. Zworykin to produce the first practical television tube in April 1929.

Strangely enough, I have never seen a French history of television that even mentions this tube or Chevallier. There is only an article by Marc Chauvierre entitled "Qui a invente la télévision?" in *La Liaison* (organ of old electronics) no. 127 & 128, p. 17 (date unknown but only goes up to 1939), furnished me by T. Bridgewater (the English television historian). This article does state that "the work of Holweck with the collaboration of M. Chevallier resulted in 1928 of a 36 line picture of remarkable quality."

35. The first mention of the work of George is R.H. George, "An Improved Form of Cathode Ray Oscillograph," *Physical Review* 31 (Feb. 1928): p. 303. However, this abstract gives very little information as to the tube's construction.

36. This information was given to me in an interview with Harley Iams on January 16, 1977. Harley Iams went to work at Westinghouse late in 1927 and was first assigned to Dr. Zworykin on his facsimile picture transmission project. He worked with Zworykin on the development of the Kinescope and the first all-electronic television receiver. He became ill late in 1929 and had to return to California. When he recovered, he went back to work for RCA Victor in Camden with Dr. Zworykin in April 1931. He was involved in the early development of the Iconoscope and was in charge of its production at Harrison, N.J. Later on, he collaborated with Dr. Albert Rose on the development of the RCA low velocity scanning tubes, which led to the Orthicon and the Image Orthicon. His information will be cited as the *Iams File*. See also Patent Interference #73,203 (Iams vs. Ballard vs. Farnsworth).

The addition of Gregory N. Ogloblinsky to Zworykin's staff in July 1929 was of the greatest consequence. Ogloblinsky (or "Oglo" as he was fondly called), was a trained physicist who was highly regarded by all who worked with him. There are even hints that he may have been responsible for most of the success of the Kinescope and future Iconoscope.

37. The story of the Dewar flask was described to me in a personal interview with Arthur Vance on December 22, 1976. Vance had gone to work for Westinghouse late in 1928 and was assigned to the Zworykin group in May 1929. He personally designed most of the deflection and high-voltage circuits for the first electronic receiver. He moved with Zworykin to RCA in April 1930 and worked with him on the early two-sided camera tubes. He participated in the development of the Iconoscope and worked with Zworykin and Hillier on the electron microscope in the early 1940s. His information will be cited as the *Vance File*.

38. Eugene Lyons, *David Sarnoff* (New York: Harper & Row, 1966), p. 209. This story had been repeated in dozens of sources. Lyons spoke of an "electric eye" as the device that was "operative." We know now that only a crude cathode ray viewing device was in existence. However, Sarnoff showed great courage in going ahead with a radical idea that was as yet nothing more than a laboratory experiment.

The source of all this seems to be *Television and David Sarnoff*, a history of the RCA television effort by its official historian, E.E. Bucher. It is to be found in the archives of the David Sarnoff Library in Princeton. Television is covered in

Part Twelve, "Black and White Television," Chapters 1–14. This history of television was occasionally found to be at variance with the stories that were described to me by the various pioneers who worked there, as well as the patent applications and newspaper stories. The Bucher work really was a romanticized version of television history. There was no way to check Bucher's sources as the private papers of Sarnoff were not available to me. Only his speeches are on file. (I did not go into other aspects of Bucher's history as I was concerned only with RCA's contribution to the history of television.) This source will be cited as *Bucher/RCA*.

39. Henroteau patent application of 29 May 1929. (See n. 7.76.) See U.S. Pat. Interference no. 69,135 (Henroteau vs. Zworykin vs. Farnsworth). Affidavit dated 21 Sept. 1936.

40. R.F. Tiltman, "How 'Stereoscopic' Television is Shown," *Radio News* **10** (Nov. 1928): pp. 418–419; "Stereoscopic Television," *Science and Invention* **16** (Nov. 1928): p. 621.

41. "Smith Rehearses for Camera Men," *New York Times*, 22 Aug. 1928, p. 3:4. Illustration shown in *New York Times*, 26 Aug. 1928, sec. V, p. 5:13. The remainder of this information comes from a personal interview with Ray D. Kell on 23 Mar. 1977. Kell went to work for GE in April 1927 and soon joined Dr. Alexanderson's television research team. It wasn't very long before Mr. Kell was leading the project. He joined the RCA research staff on television late in 1930. He participated in all phases of the development of the RCA television system. This source will be cited as the *Kell File*.

42. Devendra N. Sharma, Br. Pat. No. 320,993. Applied 24 Aug. 1928; issued 31 Oct. 1929.

43. *Bell Labs 33089*, letter from P.T. Farnsworth to Dr. E.B. Craft, dated 25 Jul 1928; letter from Mr. Fleager to E.B. Craft, dated 4 Sept. 1928.

44. "S.F. Man's Invention to Revolutionize Television," *San Francisco Chronicle*, 3 Sept. 1928, second front page; "New Television System," *New York Times*, 4 Sept. 1928, p. 20:1.

45. "Shown at Berlin Radio Exhibition," *New York Times*, 1 Sept. 1928, p. 6:8; Dr. A. Neuberger, "The Karolus System of Television," *Television* (London) **1** (Oct. 1928); pp. 35–37.

46. "Play Is Broadcast by Voice and Acting in Radio-Television," *New York Times*, 12 Sept. 1928, p. 1:3; R. Hertzberg, "Television Makes the Radio Drama Possible," *Radio News* **10**: pp. 524–527, 587–590; "Drama via Television," *Science and Invention* **16** (Dec. 1928): pp. 694, 762.

47. "Television Devices to Be Shown Here," *New York Times*, 6 Sept. 1928, p. 2:2; "Television Thrills Radio Crowd Show," *New York Times*, 21 Sept. 1928, p. 24:1; S. Mosely, "Television in 1930," *Television* **3** (Feb. 1931): pp. 479–480.

48. *Alexanderson/G.E. Files*, report of M.A. Trainer, dated 8 Oct. 1928.

49. Gillis Holst, DRP Pat. No. 535,208. Conv. date 4 Oct. 1928 (applied 24 Sept. 1929); issued 10 Oct. 1931. Br. Pat. No. 326,200, applied 5 Nov. 1928; issued 5 Mar. 1930.

50. "To Stop Television in Broadcast Band," *New York Times*, 23 Dec. 1928, p. 15:3.

51. J.L. Baird, Br. Pat. No. 324,049. Applied 10 Oct. 1928; issued 10 Jan. 1930.

52. George W. Walton, Br. Pat. No. 328,286. Applied 25 Oct. 1928; issued 25 Apr. 1930.

53. *Bell Labs, 33089*, letter from E.B. Craft to F.B. Jewett, dated 18 Sept. 1928; memorandum from F. Gray, dated 31 Oct. 1928; memorandum from H.D. Arnold to F.B. Jewett, dated 23 Nov. 1928.

54. P.T. Farnsworth, U.S. Pat. No. 2,037,711. Applied 26 Nov. 1928, renewed 21 Sept. 1931; issued 21 Apr. 1936.

55. J.H. Hammond, Jr., U.S. Pat. No. 1,867,542. Applied 6 Dec. 1928; issued 12 July 1932.

56. Max Knoll, Ludwig Schiff and Carl Stoerk, U.S. Pat. No. 2,036,532. Conv. date 12 Dec. 1928 (applied 18 Nov. 1929); issued 7 Apr. 1936.

57. *Alexanderson/G.E. File*, memorandum from R. Kell to J. Huff, dated 14 Dec. 1928.

58. Fritz Schröter, DRP Pat. No. 495,718. Applied 23 Dec. 1928; issued 10 Apr. 1930.

59. *Radio News* 11 (Jan. 1929): p. 637; "Disc-less Television," *Science and Invention* 16 (Jan. 1929): p. 840; "Invents New System Minus Disks," *Popular Science Monthly* 14 (Jan. 1929): p. 61; Patent Interference no. 73,203 (Iams vs. Ballard vs. Farnsworth), p. 9, testimony by Lubcke.

60. Lyons, *op. cit.*, pp. 145–147, 156. See also Archer, *Big Business and Radio, op. cit.*, pp. 339, 341.

61. *RCA Stockholders Annual Report—1929*.

62. Lyons, *op. cit.*, pp. 209.

63. V.K. Zworykin, U.S. Pat. Reissue No. 19,314. Original filed 26 Mar. 1929; reissue application 23 Dec. 1932; issued 11 Sept. 1934.

64. The first part of this material comes from a research memo 6-6705-1, dated 18 Jan. 1930, from V. Zworykin to Mr. W.A. Tolson of General Electric. This will be cited as *Westinghouse Research Memo 6-6705-1*. The remaining material was repeated in a Westinghouse Electric and Manufacturing Company Research Department report 6705-A, "Cathode Ray Television Receivers," by V. Zworykin. Closing report dated May 28, 1930. This will be cited as the *Westinghouse Report 6705-A*.

65. F. Gray and J.R. Hofele, U.S. Pat. No. 1,769,918. Applied 2 Feb. 1929; issued 8 July 1930. F. Gray and J.R. Hofele, U.S. Pat. No. 1,769,919. Applied 30 Apr. 1929; issued 8 July 1930.

66. "California Sees and Hears Griffith on Radio," *New York Times*, 4 Feb. 1929; p. 1:3.

67. *Bell Labs, 33089*, memo, "Recording Television Images on Movie Film at Television Speeds," from Frank Gray, dated 11 Feb. 1929.

68. Leon Nemirovsky, U.S. Pat. No. 1,941,618. Conv. date 11 Feb. 1929 (applied 7 Feb. 1930); issued 2 Jan. 1934.

69. Jean Thibaud, "Effet magnetique longitudinal sur les faisceaux d'électrons lents." *Journal de Physique* (Paris) 10, no. 4 (1929): pp. 161–176.

70. "Television Exhibition," *Electrician* 102 (15 Mar. 1929): p. 331. See also "The Television Society," *Television* (London) 2 (Apr. 1929): pp. 83–90.

71. "The Postmaster-General's Decision," *Television* (London) 2 (May 1929): p. 124. See also "Television—The Postmaster-General's Statement," *Wireless World* 24 (10 Apr. 1929): p. 380.

72. Sydney A. Moseley, "Writes from Berlin," *Television* (London) 2 (July 1929): pp. 244–246.

73. "Television Placed on Daily Schedule," *New York Times*, 22 Mar. 1929, p. 20:2; J. Weinberger, T.A. Smith, and G. Rodwin, "The Selection of Standards for Commercial Radio Television," *Proceedings of the Institute of Radio Engineers* 17 (Sept. 1929): pp. 1584–1594. On March 25, 1929, Goldsmith and Weinberger filed for a patent covering a television signal that combined sight, sound and the synchronizing signal within a 100 kc band. See A.N. Goldsmith and J. Weinberger, U.S. Pat. No. 1,770,205. Applied 25 Mar. 1929; issued 8 July 1930.

74. "Images Dance in Space, Heralding New Radio Era," *New York Times*, 14 Apr. 1929, sec. XI, p. 1:17; *Alexanderson File*, letter from J.G. Harbord to A.N. Goldsmith, dated 17 Apr. 1929.

75. R. Thun, Br. Pat. No. 355,319. Conv. date 18 May 1929 (applied 15 May 1930); issued 12 Aug. 1931.

76. J.W. Horton, Br. Pat. No. 353,471. Conv. date 25 May 1929 (applied 24 Apr. 1930); issued 24 July 1931.

77. Francis C.P. Henroteau, U.S. Pat. No. 1,903,112. Applied 29 May 1929; renewed 13 Aug. 1931; issued 28 Mar. 1933. F.C.P. Henroteau, U.S. Pat. No. 1,903,113. Applied 29 May 1929; divided on 8 Sept. 1930; issued 28 Mar. 1933. F.C.P. Henroteau, Br. Pat. No. 335,958. Applied 4 June 1929; issued 6 Oct. 1930. RCA later bought up the Henroteau patents.

78. "The Television Society," *op. cit.* (n. 7.70), pp. 355–356.

79. "Television in Color Shown First Time," *New York Times*, 28 June 1929, p. 25:1; H.E. Ives, "Television in Color," *Bell Laboratory Record* 7 (July 1929): pp. 439–444; H.E. Ives, "Television in Color," *Radio Engineering* 9 (Aug. 1929): pp. 34–36; H.E. Ives and A.L. Johnsrud, "Television in Colors by a Beam Scanning Method," *Journal of the Optical Society of America* 20 (Jan. 1930): pp. 11–22. Presented July 20, 1929; H.E. Ives, "Television in Color," *Science and Invention* 17 (Sept. 1929): pp. 400–401, 474.

80. "Large Television Images Broadcast by R.C.A." *Radio News* 10 (June 1929): pp. 1121; "Television Emerging from the Laboratory," *Radio News* 11 (July 1929): pp. 10–11.

81. Lyons, *op. cit.*, pp. 155–158.

82. T.A. Smith, Br. Pat. No. 349,773. Conv. date 27 June 1929 (applied 27 May 1930); issued 4 June 1931.

83. V.K. Zworykin, U.S. Pat. No. 2,361,255. Applied 5 July 1929, issued 24 Oct. 1944.

84. *Westinghouse Research Memo 6-6705-1, op. cit.* (n. 7.64).

85. T.A. Smith, Br. Pat. No. 356,880. Conv. date 19 July 1929 (applied 21 July 1930); issued 17 Sept. 1931.

86. *Westinghouse Report 6706-A*, "Cathode-Ray Television Transmitters," V.K. Zworykin, 28 May 1940; other information came from a letter to the author from W.D. Wright, dated 17 Nov. 1978. Wright worked with Zworykin on this first tube. It was confirmed in interviews by Arthur Vance and Harley Iams, who were with Zworykin at this time.

87. R.H. George, "A New Type of Hot Cathode Oscillograph," *Transactions of the American Institute of Electrical Engineers* 48 (July 1929): pp. 884–890; R.H. George, U.S. Pat. No. 2,086,546. Applied 14 Sept. 1929; issued 13 July 1937. (RCA took over processing of this patent on 7 Sept. 1934).

88. "Television at the Berlin Radio Exhibition," *Television* (London) 2 (Oct. 1929): pp. 379–383.

89. "Television Transmits British Talking Film," *New York Times*, 20 Aug. 1929, p. 5:2; "Talking Films by Television," *Television* (London) 2 (Sept. 1929): p. 353; "Voice and Image Go Together Over Wire," *New York Times*, 3 Sept. 1929, p. 29:8; "Baird's Newest Televisor," *Science and Invention* 17 (Dec. 1929): pp. 691, 732, 734.

90. "Television, First Experimental Broadcast," *London Times*, 1 Oct. 1929, p. 26a.

91. Pierre E.L. Chevallier, Fr. Pat. No. 699,478. Applied 25 Oct. 1929; issued 16 Feb. 1931; P.E.L. Chevallier, U.S. Pat. No. 2,021,252. Conv. date 25 Oct. 1929 (applied 20 Oct. 1930); issued 19 Nov. 1935; P.E.L. Chevallier, U.S. Pat. No. 2,021,253. Conv. date 25 Oct. 1929; divided on 25 Aug. 1932; issued 19 Nov. 1935; P.E.L. Chevallier, Br. Pat. No. 360,654. Applied 30 Oct. 1930; issued 12 Nov. 1931. A search of the Chevallier American Patent file showed that on June 16, 1931, Chevallier allowed an inspection of his file by RCA. On July 8, 1931, Grover of

RCA became his attorney. On July 29, 1931, the title of the patent was changed to "Kinescope." RCA then went to great lengths to prove that Chevallier was the first to use electrostatic focus. Obviously this was to protect RCA's interest in the vital picture tube that had been developed by Zworykin.

92. Manfred von Ardenne, "A Braun Tube for Direct Photographic Recording," *Experimental Wireless* 7 (Feb. 1930): pp. 66–70 (manuscript received in Oct. 1929); Hans von Hartel, "Eine neue Braun'sche Rohre," *Zeitschrift für Hochfrequenstechnik* 34 (Dec. 1929): pp. 227–228. This new tube was for sale for 200 marks; R.A. Watson Watt, *Applications of the Cathode Ray Oscillograph in Radio Research* (London: Her Majesty's Stationery Office, 1933/1943).

93. V.K. Zworykin, U.S. Pat. No. 2,109,245. Applied 16 Nov. 1929; issued 22 Feb. 1938. Westinghouse Electric & Manufacturing Company, Fr. Pat. No. 705,523. Conv. date 16 Nov. 1929 (applied 10 Nov. 1930); issued 9 June 1931. It has never been made clear as to why Westinghouse waited until November 1929 to file this application. Knowing that Zworykin arrived in the United States in September 1928 and allowing the usual 5–6 months to prepare a patent application, I have never understood why they couldn't have had this ready at least by March or April 1929. This would have given Zworykin an earlier filing date. It is possible that some kind of a deal had been worked out between Belin and Westinghouse, which could have fallen through. All pure conjecture. Certainly Chevallier's priority had been established: all that was needed was to produce a practical tube, and this of course is what Zworykin did. We shall never know for sure.

94. This probably comes from the *New York Times Index*, Oct.–Dec., 1929. On page 438 it states, "V. Zworykin demonstrates non–mechanical receiver, special cathode ray tube called 'kinescope.' N. 19, 32:3." Not only is this incorrect, but a search of the paper for Nov. 19, 1929, yields no information at all about the meeting or the so-called demonstration. (I have since found out that some items are carried in certain editions only and left out of later editions. This is possibly what happened in this case.) See "Institute Meeting," *Proceedings of the Institute of Radio Engineers* 18 (Jan. 1930): p. 4. "V. Zworykin presented a paper, 'Television with Cathode Ray Tube for Receiver.'" There was no mention of a demonstration. The meeting was held at the Sagamore Hotel in Rochester, New York. This paper was never printed in *Proceedings of the Institute of Radio Engineers*. It was printed in *Radio Engineering*. See V.K. Zworykin, "Television with Cathode-Ray Tube for Receiver," *Radio Engineering* 9 (Dec. 1929): pp. 38–41.

95. *Westinghouse Research Memo 6-6705-1, op. cit.*; "Television Film Goes on the Air," *New York Times*, 25 Aug. 1929, p. 15:7.

96. For instance, in reporting on the news of Dr. Zworykin's new receiver, see "The Cathode Ray Again," *Television* (London) 2 (Jan. 1930): p. 528. The comment was made in regard to this "utopian idea," that "we are not disposed to be prejudiced" and would "welcome any departure from existing practice."

H.E. Ives regarded Zworykin's television work as "chiefly talk" and "of very little promise." He concluded that its promise of a display of television to large audiences was "quite wild." This of course was the attitude of most of the television pioneers who had worked with cathode ray tubes and despaired of them ever becoming practical. See *Bell Labs, 33089*, memo from H.E. Ives to H.P. Charlesworth, dated 16 Dec. 1929.

97. W.J. Hitchcock, Br. Pat. No. 363,103. Applied 26 Nov. 1929; issued 17 Dec. 1931.

98. "Walker Televised at Demonstration," *N.Y. Times*, 21 Dec. 1929, p. 22:2.

99. Philo T. Farnsworth and Harry R. Lubcke, "Transmission of Television Images," *Radio* 11 (Dec. 1929): pp. 36, 85–86. K. Takayanagi had published pictures taken from his cathode ray tube in Sept. 1928 (see n. 6.68). But these came

from a mechanical "flying spot" scanner; Farnsworth's came from an electrical camera tube.

100. W.J. Baker, *A History of the Marconi Co.* (London: Methuen, 1970), p. 200.

101. His prime patent was R. Barthelemy, U.S. Pat. No. 2,023,505. Conv. date 27 Dec. 1928 (applied 20 Dec. 1929); issued 10 Dec. 1935.

8. Back to the Laboratory: 1930–1932

1. Lyons, *op. cit.*, p. 158.

2. Letter to the author from Albert F. Murray, dated June 14, 1978.

3. "Television Broadcast with Sound," *London Times*, 1 Apr. 1930, p. 28c; "Sight-Sound Program Broadcast in Britain," *New York Times*, 1 Apr. 1930, p. 17:3.

4. D.E. Replogle, "Where Television Is Today," *Radio News* 11 (Jan. 1930): pp. 629–631, 677; C.F. Jenkins, U.S. Pat. No. 1,844,508. Applied 14 Jan. 1930; issued 9 Feb. 1932. See also U.S. Pat. No. 1,984,682. Applied 1 Feb. 1930; issued 18 Dec. 1934.

5. *Alexanderson/G.E. File*, memorandum from Alexanderson to H.E. Dunham, dated 19 Feb. 1930; "Schenectady Flashes Picture to Australia: Gets It Back in One-Eighth of a Second," *New York Times*, 19 Feb. 1930, p. 1:6.

6. Obituary, "Mr. A.A. Campbell Swinton, F.R.S.," *Nature* 125 (8 Mar. 1930): pp. 356, 385.

7. P.T. Farnsworth, U.S. Pat. No. 1,969,399. Applied 3 Mar. 1930; issued 7 Aug. 1934.

8. Hans Hatzinger, Br. Pat. No. 358,411. Conv. date 25 Mar. 1930 (applied 16 Mar. 1931); issued 8 Oct. 1931.

9. "The Cathode-Ray Television Receiver," *Radio-Craft* 1 (Feb. 1930): pp. 384–385; V. Zworykin, "Television Through a Crystal Globe," *Radio News* 11 (Apr. 1930): pp. 905, 949; W.G.W. Mitchell, "The Cathode-Ray in Practical Television (Pt. 3)," *Television* (London) 2 (Feb. 1930): pp. 590–593; A. Neuberger, "Das 'Kineskop', ein neuer Fernseher," *Fernsehen* 4 (1930): pp. 175–179.

10. *Bell Labs, 33089*, memorandum from F. Gray, dated 26 Mar. 1930.

11. K. Takayanagi, Jap. Pat. No. 93,456. Applied 27 Dec. 1930; issued 4 Nov. 1931. See also Jap. Pat. No. 100,037. Applied 13 June 1932; issued 9 Mar. 1933.

12. U.S. Patent Interference No. 73,203 (H. Iams vs. R.C. Ballard vs. P.T. Farnsworth).

13. This material was obtained from a visit to the EMI Archives at Hayes, Middlesex, England, on September 18, 1978. I was the first television historian to see these records. This source will be cited as the *EMI File*.

14. Dietrich Prinz, U.S. Pat. No. 1,854,274. Conv. date 3 Apr. 1930, filed 4 Apr. 1931; issued 19 Apr. 1932.

15. "Second Annual Exhibition," *Proceedings of the Television Society* no. 15 (1930): pp. 12–14.

16. "'Visual' Conversations, Successful Demonstration in New York," *London Times*, 11 Apr. 1930, p. 13b; H.E. Ives, "Two-Way Television," *Bell Labs Record* 8 (May 1930): pp. 398–404.

17. Most of this material comes from Patent Interference No. 64,027, Zworykin vs. Farnsworth. It is repeated in Everson, *op. cit.*, see pp. 125–127.

18. *Alexanderson/G.E. File*, memorandum from Alexanderson to H.E. Dunham, Patent Dept., dated June 4, 1930. Alexanderson's attitude towards

cathode ray television was related to me in an interview with Mr. Ray Kell in 1977.

19. V.K. Zworykin, U.S. Pat. No. 2,246,283. Applied 1 May 1930; issued 17 June 1941. See also Fr. Pat. No. 715,912. Conv. date 1 May 1930 (filed 23 Apr. 1931); issued 11 Dec. 1931. Several new claims were made after November 23, 1938. This is the famous serial no. 448,834 (1930), which was part of many patent interferences (see pages 175–176). This patent was issued to Westinghouse for a "photoelectric mosaic." It took some 11 years to go through the Patent Office. For difficulties in building two-sided targets see V.K. Zworykin and G.A. Morton, *Television—The Electronics of Image Transmission* (New York: Wiley, 1940), p. 304.

20. *Iams File*, letter from Dr. Zworykin to Harley Iams, dated June 20, 1930. (Mr. Iams has given me several letters from Dr. Zworykin to him during this period.) This was also confirmed in my interviews with Arthur Vance and Les Flory. They were aware of Farnsworth's achievements and how useful his dissector was to their experiments at the time.

21. P.T. Farnsworth and Harry R. Lubcke, U.S. Pat. No. 2,059,219. Applied 5 May 1930; issued 3 Nov. 1936. P.T. Farnsworth, U.S. Pat. No. 2,246,625. Applied 5 May 1930; issued 24 June 1941. Harry Lubcke claimed that by 2 July 1929, all return scan lines had been eliminated. This is from Interference No. 73,203, p. 9. See also Interference No. 68,936 (Farnsworth vs. Vance), 10 July 1935. This was won by Farnsworth.

22. *Bell Labs, 33089*, memorandum for file, "Proposed Television Transmitters" (MM-10,020), Frank Gray, dated May 20, 1930. See Frank Gray's notebook for 29 Apr. 1929 for details of some ideas for camera tubes.

23. "Television on the Stage," *London Times*, 23 May 1930, p. 14b; "Television in the Theater," *Electronics* **1** (June 1930): pp. 112–113; "Television in the Theater," *Radio News* **12** (Aug. 1930): p. 100; Edgar H. Felix, "Television Advances from Peephole to Screen," *Radio News* **12** (Sept. 1930): pp. 228–230, 268–269. There have been several references to a large-screen demonstration that RCA was supposed to have given at the RKO 58th Street Theater on 16 Jan. 1930. Such references should be regarded with caution. There is no reference to this in either *Bucher/RCA* or *Alexanderson/G.E. File*. It of course would have taken priority away from General Electric. See Barton Kreuser, "Progress Report-Theater Television," *Journal of the Society of Motion Picture Engineers* **53** (Aug. 1949): pp. 128–136. Also in A.F. Van Dyck, "The Early Days of Television," *Radio Age* **15** (Apr. 1956): pp. 10–12.

24. "Trust Suit Filed on Radio Compacts," *New York Times*, 14 May 1930, p. 1:4; Lyons, *op. cit.*, p. 162–167; Archer, *Big Business and Radio, op. cit.*, pp. 349–351.

25. P.T. Farnsworth, U.S. Pat. No. 2,099,846. Applied 14 June 1930; issued 23 Nov. 1937.

26. P.T. Farnsworth, U.S. Pat. No. 2,085,742. Applied 14 June 1930; issued 6 July 1937.

27. *Bell Labs, 33089*, letter from Herbert Hoover, Jr., to Harry E. Young, Western Electric Co., dated 22 Sept. 1931. Also in Everson, *op. cit.*, pp. 120–121.

28. "40 Years Later," *Broadcast-Telecast* **70** (9 May 1966): p. 80.

29. *Bucher/RCA, op. cit.*, pp. 47–48.

30. "The First Play by Television," *London Times*, 15 July 1930, p. 12b; "Television Play Is Broadcast in Britain," *New York Times*, 15 July 1930; p. 1:2; Sydney A. Moseley and H.J. Barton Chapple, *Television, To-day and To-morrow* (London: Sir Issac Pitman, 1934), pp. 16–17, 154–158.

31. V.K. Zworykin, U.S. Pat. No. 2,157,048. Applied 17 July 1930 (renewed

30 Jan. 1937); issued 2 May 1939. Br. Pat. No. 369,832. Conv. date 17 July 1930 (applied 17 July 1931); issued 31 Mar. 1932. This appears to be the first Zworykin patent assigned to Marconi's Wireless Telegraph Co. According to Arthur Vance and Les Flory, several of these tubes were built and operated.
    32. Edwin H. Armstrong, U.S. Pat. No. 1,941,066. Applied 30 July 1930; issued 26 Dec. 1933. Also Pat. Nos. 1,941,067, 1,941,068, 1,941,069. See *Broadcasting* **18** (1 Apr. 1940): p. 19.
    33. Telehor Ak-Ges, Br. Pat. No. 364,003. Conv. date 5 Aug. 1930 (applied 21 Aug. 1930); issued 21 Dec. 1931.
    34. V.K. Zworykin, U.S. Pat. No. 2,025,143. Applied 15 Aug. 1930; issued 24 Dec. 1935. This receiving tube shows a bulb which became the shape of the not-yet-invented Zworykin single-sided camera tube.
    35. Alfred Gradenwitz, "Television in Germany Today," *Science and Invention* **3** (Jan. 1931): pp. 807, 857; "The German Radio Exhibition in Berlin," *Television* (London) **3** (Sept. 1930): p. 309; "The Exhibit of Fernseh A.G. as shown at the Berlin Radio Exhibition," *Television* (London) **3** (Oct. 1930): pp. 338–340.
    36. Alda V. Bedford, U.S. Pat. No. 1,849,818. Applied 19 Sept. 1930; issued 15 Mar. 1932. It was understood that these men requested to go to RCA, leaving Dr. Alexanderson with a very small staff. GE continued to work on Alexanderson's system for the next year or so. *Iams File*, letter from Zworykin to Iams, dated September 12, 1930.
    37. H.E. Ives, Br. Pat. No. 390,158. Conv. date 4 Oct. 1930 (applied 28 Sept. 1931); issued 28 Mar. 1933.
    38. H.E. Ives, "Television in Color from Motion Picture Film," *Journal of the Optical Society of America* **21** (Jan. 1931): pp. 2–7.
    39. George W. Walton, Br. Pat. No. 369,644. Applied 20 Oct. 1930; issued 21 Mar. 1932.
    40. E. Hudec, Br. Pat. No. 395,373. Conv. date 11 Nov. 1930 (applied 10 Nov. 1931); issued 10 July 1933.
    41. Philo T. Farnsworth, "An Electrical Scanning System for Television," *Radio Industries* **5** (Nov. 1930): pp. 386–389, 401–403. Also in *Radio-Craft* **2** (Dec. 1930): pp. 346–349. Farnsworth stated "50 kilocycles" in the original article. But he most often spoke of 15 kc for both picture and sound!
    42. L.R. Koller, "Photoelectric Emission from Thin Films of Caesium," *Physical Review* **36** (1 Dec. 1930): pp. 1639–1647. Received 22 Oct. 1930.
    43. See "A Radio Idea from the West," *New York Times*, 14 Dec. 1930, sec. X, p. 14:6. It was also reported by A. Dinsdale, "Television by Cathode Ray," *Wireless World* **28** (18 Mar. 1931): pp. 286–288, and in Everson, *op. cit.*, pp. 124–125. See also *Bell Labs, 33089*, in which H.E. Ives wrote a memorandum to O.M. Glunt, dated 19 Dec. 1930, stating that "if Mr. Farnsworth is doing what he says he is doing, we simply do not know how he does it." And, he continued, "the perplexing question with regard to Mr. Farnsworth's announcement is that we know him to be *an ingenious and sincere* experimenter." In spite of all of his accomplishments, this damage to his reputation was never quite rectified.
    44. P.T. Farnsworth, U.S. Pat. No. 2,026,379. Applied 4 Dec. 1930; issued 31 Dec. 1935.
    45. K. Takayanagi, Jap. Pat. No. 93,465. Applied 27 Dec. 1930; issued 4 Nov. 1931. He also applied for an electron-beam scanner. See Jap. Pat. 100,037. Applied 13 June 1932; issued 9 Mar. 1933.
    46. A. Konstantinov, Russ. Pat. No. 39,380. Applied 28 Dec. 1930; issued 30 Nov. 1934.
    47. *EMI File*.
    48. "Report Television Gains," *New York Times*, 7 Jan. 1931, p. 12:2; "A New

Television System," *Wireless World* **28** (14 Jan. 1931): pp. 38–39; W.G.W. Mitchell, "London Looks in at New Television Departure," *Science and Invention* **19** (May 1931): pp. 21, 78–79; C.O. Browne, "Multi-Channel Television," *Journal of the Institute of Electrical Engineers* (London) **70** (Mar. 1932): pp. 340–353.

49. H.E. Ives, "A Multi-Channel Television Apparatus," *Bell System Technical Journal* **10** (Jan. 1931): pp. 33–45.

50. "Schenectady-to-Leipzig Television a Success; Movie Also Made of Images Sent by Radio," *New York Times*, 18 Feb. 1931, p. 15:3. Two frames of the television film recording were shown in *New York Times*, 15 Feb. 1931, sec. VIII, p. 16:6.

51. *Bucher/RCA, op. cit.*, pp. 62–64; see *Broadcasting* (4 Dec. 1961) p. 5–33, for Engstrom. See also "Dr. E.W. Engstrom Elected President of RCA," *Broadcast News* **12** (Dec. 1961): pp. 4–5.

52. RCA patents: A.W. Vance, U.S. Pat. No. 2,137,039. Applied 17 June 1931; issued 15 Nov. 1938. W.A. Tolson, Br. Pat. No. 387,915. Conv. date 25 June 1931 (applied 27 June 1932); issued 16 Feb. 1933. V.K. Zworykin and J.C. Batchelor, U.S. Pat. No. 1,988,469. Applied 30 June 1931; issued 22 Jan. 1935. R.C. Ballard, U.S. Pat. No. 2,215,285. Applied 15 Aug. 1931; issued 17 Sept. 1940. R.D. Kell, Br. Pat. No. 407,409. Conv. date 30 Sept. 1931 (applied 22 Sept. 1932); issued 22 Mar. 1934.

53. C.J. Spencer visit to RCA. This is from the file of Patent Application No. 468,610, p. 3, dated 17 July 1931. Letter from Goldsborough to the Patent Office.

54. Horst Hewel, "Einzelheiten Amerikanischer Kathodenstrahl-Fernsehsysteme." *Fernsehen* **2** (Apr. 1931): pp. 123–128; A. Dinsdale, "Television by Cathode Ray," *op. cit.*, pp. 286–288; A. Dinsdale, "Television Takes the Next Step," *Science and Invention* **19** (May 1931): pp. 46–47, 72–73; W.G.W. Mitchell, "Developments in Television," *Journal of the Royal Society of the Arts* **79** (29 May 1931): pp. 616–642; "Visual Broadcasting Still an Experiment," *Radio News* **12** (Feb. 1931): p. 761; P.T. Farnsworth, "Scanning with an Electric Pencil," *Television News* **1** (Mar./Apr. 1931): pp. 48–51, 74; Arthur H. Halloran, "'Scanning' Without a Disc," *Radio News* **12** (May 1931): pp. 998–999, 1015.

55. M. von Ardenne, Br. Pat. No. 387,536. Conv. date 27 Mar. 1931 (applied 29 Mar. 1932); issued 9 Feb. 1933. M. von Ardenne, "Evolution of the Cathode-Ray Tube," *Wireless World* **66** (Jan. 1960): pp. 28–32.

56. Manfred von Ardenne, "New Television Transmitters and Receivers using Cathode Ray Tubes," *Fernsehen* **2** (Apr. 1931): pp. 65–80.

57. Manfred von Ardenne, interview with the author, Dresden, 3 Aug. 1984.

58. *EMI File*, Shareholder Report, dated 27 Nov. 1931; *1931 Stockholder Report*, Radio Corporation of America, 14 Mar. 1932, p. 4.

59. Letter to author from W.D. Wright, dated 18 Dec. 1978. See also C.O. Browne, "Technical Problems in Connection with Television," *Journal of the Institute of Electrical Engineers* (London) **69** (Oct. 1931): pp. 1232–1238.

60. "The Annual Exhibition," *Journal of the Television Society* **1** (1931/34): pp. 55–60; "Television Society Exhibition," *London Times*, 16 Apr. 1931, p. 12b.

61. Lee De Forest, U.S. Pat. No. 2,026,872. Applied 24 Apr. 1931; issued 7 Jan. 1936. Also U.S. Pat. No. 2,003,680. Applied 22 Sept. 1931; issued 4 June 1935. Lee De Forest, "Early Beginnings of Large Screen Television," *Journal of the Television Society* **4** (1944–1946): p. 147.

62. "Daylight Demonstration," *London Times*, 9 May 1931, p. 14g; "Broadcast Derby Stakes," *London Times*, 4 June 1931, p. 16b; H.J. Barton Chapple, "Televising a Horse Race," *Radio News* **13** (Mar. 1932): pp. 757, 812; "A Magic 'Gypsy' Caravan," *New York Times*, 13 Sept. 1931, sec. X, p. 14:1.

63. This information came from two important sources. In an interview with

the author on 2 Aug. 1981, Harley Iams confirmed that the first "direct vision" pictures came from a Wilson "Image Dissector" and not from an Iconoscope. It was also confirmed by Lesly Flory, who so kindly sent me the picture of an RCA "Image Dissector" camera on the roof at Camden. It is also discussed in the letter from Zworykin to Iams dated 20 June 1930, *Iams File* (see n. 8.20).

64. *Zworykin File.* Zworykin notebook. Entry dated June 12, 1931.

65. Harley Iams, interview with the author on 2 August 1981. Further details are from the Essig patent of 24 Feb. 1932 (see n. 8.106 and n. 8.107).

66. Everson, *op. cit.*, pp. 132–135. For details of the Sarnoff visit, see p. 199. More details were given in a two-part article by P. Schatzkin and B. Kiger, "Philo T. Farnsworth: Inventor of Electronic Television," *Television* 5 (1977): pp. 6–8. (Part 2, vol 5 [1977]: pp. 17–20.) Unfortunately, Schatzkin's enthusiasm for Farnsworth's cause taints all of his writings. He is reckless with his facts, and his shrill, abrasive attitude has done Farnsworth more harm than good. He will not accept the fact that Zworykin built and operated a camera tube before Farnsworth. In rejecting Zworykin's claim, Schatzkin has lost his credibility, and has thus diminished Farnsworth's credit for building and operating the first truly electronic television system, for which he is praised here. I hope that I have cleared up this point.

67. "Philadelphia to Look-In," *New York Times*, 20 Dec. 1931, sec. IX, p. 10:8.

68. Seimens-Schukerwerke Akt.-Ges., Br. Pat. No. 402,781. Conv. date 30 May 1931 (applied 30 May 1932); issued 30 Nov. 1933.

69. W.O. Osbon, "A New Cathode Ray Oscilloscope," *Electrical Journal* 28 (May 1931): p. 322–324; L. Sutherlin and A.J. Harcher, "Cathode-Ray Tubes," *Electrical Journal* 29 (Aug. 1932): pp. 388–389; "Cathode-Ray Oscillograph Tubes," *General Electric Review* 36 (Jan. 1933): p. 64. See also V.K. Zworykin, "Improvements in Cathode-Ray Tube Design," *Electronics* 3 (Nov. 1931): pp. 188–190.

70. G.B. Banks, Br. Pat. No. 380,109. Applied 2 June 1931; issued 2 Sept. 1932.

71. Philo T. Farnsworth, U.S. Pat. No. 2,051,372. Applied 14 July 1931; issued 18 Aug. 1936.

72. Philo T. Farnsworth, U.S. Pat. No. 2,140,284. Applied 14 July 1931; issued 13 Dec. 1938.

73. "Fifth Television Transmitter Planned for New York Area," *New York Times*, 19 Apr. 1931, sec. IX, p. 10:1; Samuel Kaufman, "Television Progress, New York Forges Ahead," *Radio News* 13 (Nov. 1931): pp. 375–376, 436.

74. "S.S. *Leviathan* Makes First Successful Demonstration of Shore-to-Ship Reception," *New York Times*, 24 July 1931, p. 20:4; Violet Hodgson, "Television Goes to Sea," *Radio News* 13 (Nov. 1931): pp. 386–387, 439–440.

75. Illustration of cathode ray television sender, *New York Times*, 16 Aug. 1931, sec. IX, p. 8:4; E.H. Traub, "Television at the 1931 Berlin Radio Exhibition," *Journal of the Television Society* 1 (1931/34): pp. 100–103; M. von Ardenne, "The Cathode Ray Tube Method of Television," *Journal of the Television Society* 1 (1931/34): pp. 71–74; Manfred von Ardenne, *Cathode-Ray Tubes* (London: Sir Isaac Pitman, 1939), pp. 482–484.

76. "Berlin Radio Show," *Wireless World* 29 (9 Sept. 1931): pp. 256–257; "Spiral Mirrors in New System Minimizing the Flickering of Images," *New York Times*, 13 Sept. 1931, sec. IX, p. 16:4; C. Kette, "Die Fernsehschau auf der Berliner Funkaus Stellung 1931," *Fernsehen* 2 (Oct. 1931): pp. 225–238.

77. "Cathode Ray Oscillograph," *Radio Engineering* 11 (Aug. 1931): p. 48.

78. R.H. George and H.J. Heim, U.S. Pat. No. 2,100,279. Applied 2 Sept. 1931; issued 23 Nov. 1937.

79. C.F. Harding, R.H. George, H.J. Heim, "The Purdue University Experimental Television System," *Purdue Engineering Bulletin*, Research Series no. 65, **23**, no. 2 (Mar. 1939): pp. 5–50.

80. M. Knoll and E. Ruska, "Beitrag zur geometrischen Elektronoptik," *Annalen der Physik* 12 (Feb. 1932): pp. 606–640, 641–661.

81. Frank Gray, Br. Pat. No. 406,672. Conv. date 16 Sept. 1931 (Applied 31 Aug. 1932); issued 28 Feb. 1934.

82. C.N. Katiev, Russ. Pat. No. 29,865. Applied 24 Sept. 1931; issued 30 Apr. 1933.

83. P. Shmakov, "Television in the U.S.S.R.," *Journal of the Television Society* 1 (1931/34): pp. 126–130. In October 1965, the Russians claimed that I. Belyansky and Boris Grabovsky actually demonstrated "the first cathode-ray television transmitter and receiver" on June 26, 1928. See *New York Times*, 25 Oct. 1965, p. 3:2. There is no mention of this world-shattering event in Rosing's 1930 survey of Russian television. (See n. 6.11.) In 1928, only Philo Farnsworth had a completely electrical television system operating.

84. "The Baird Television Arc," *Television* (London) 3 (Feb. 1931): p. 511; "New Modulated Arc," *London Times*, 25 Sept. 1931, p. 10a.

85. *EMI File*, p. 142. Capt. West's employment at EMI has been a secret until this time. It hasn't even been hinted at in any previous histories.

86. Jonathan Chambers, "Architects of Television — 1: The Story of Marconi," *International Television Technical Review* 3 (June 1962): pp. 310–317.

87. Manfred von Ardenne, Br. Pat. No. 397,688. Conv. date 6 Oct. 1931 (applied 5 Oct. 1932); issued 31 Aug. 1933. "Cathode Ray Television," *Journal of the Television Society* 1 (1931/34): pp. 69–70.

88. R.A. Watson Watt, *op. cit.*, p. 6.

89. Zworykin patent application, Serial No. 683,337, filed 29 Dec. 1923, p. 75 dated 8 Oct. 1931.

90. G.R.M. Garratt and A.H. Mumford, "The History of Television," *Proceedings of the Institute of Electrical Engineers* (London) 99 (1952): Pt. IIIA, p. 35; *Zworykin File*, Zworykin notebook. Entry dated 23 Oct. 1931; Harley Iams, interview with the author, 2 Aug. 1981.

91. V.K. Zworykin, U.S. Pat. No. 2,021,907. Applied 13 Nov. 1931; issued 26 Nov. 1935. See the original patent file for the claims given to Tihany. Tihany's patent became U.S. Pat. No. 2,158,259, originally filed 10 June 1929. There was the claim that the new single-sided target operated the same as the older two-sided target. This is not true; a two-sided target separates the primary beam from the photoelectric emission, so secondary electrons released from point of impact with the anode are separated from the electrons released from the photosensitive surface. The physical construction is different, with the two-sided target having more capacity. Finally, the single-sided target works on an unsaturated basis while a two-sided target works on a saturated basis.

92. The claim for Tihany having invented the Iconoscope was made by a Hungarian historian, Vajda Pal, in an article, "New Dates about Hungarian Pioneers of Telecommunication," *Technika-torteneti, Szemle*, published in VII/1973. He stated that "the iconoscope, the first image sensing tube making use of the charge storage principle was invented by Kolomon Tihany. On the other hand, we admit, that the realization of the Iconoscope in the RCA Laboratory is due to V.K. Zworykin..." This same claim was made by Katrina Glass (Tihany's daughter) in an interview in early 1977. This of course repeats the same statements made by F. Schroïer. See *Fernsehen* (Berlin: Julius Springer, 1937). (Reviewed by A. Murray, "Book Reviews," in *Proceedings of the Institute of Radio Engineers* 26 (Dec. 1938): p. 1565.

93. Interference No. 64,721.

94. Harley Iams, briefs on behalf of appellant, Vladimir K. Zworykin, paper no. 94, 11 Oct. 1934.

95. "Television Draws 1,700 to Theatre," *New York Times*, 23 Oct. 1931, p. 26:1; Robert Hertzberg, "Television Hits Broadway," *Radio News* 13 (Feb. 1932): pp. 654–655, 712–713.

96. "Baird Discusses His Magic," *New York Times*, 25 Oct. 1931, sec. IX, p. 10:1.

97. "Television in Japan," *Wireless World* 30 (11 May 1932): p. 491; "The Editor-to You," *Radio News* 13 (June 1932): p. 979. On 10 Nov. 1931, T. Nakajima and K. Takayanagi applied for a U.S. Pat. No. 1,933,219; issued 31 Oct. 1933. This was for an electronic scanning generator with return path blanking.

98. T. Thorne Baker, Br. Pat. No. 391,781. Applied 2 Nov. 1931; issued 2 May 1933.

99. G. Schubert, "Der Fernseh-Zwischenfilmsender der Fernseh-AKT-GES," *Fernsehen und Tonfilm* 3 (July 1932): pp. 129–143; Fernseh AKT. Ges., Br. Pat. No. 409,400. Conv. date 5 Nov. 1931 (applied 3 Nov. 1932); issued 5 May 1934.

100. Robert Harding, Jr., U.S. Pat. No. 2,112,527. Applied 7 Nov. 1931; issued 29 Mar. 1938.

101. Electric & Musical Industries, Br. Pat. No. 391,887. Applied 19 Nov. 1931; issued 11 May 1933.

102. This information comes from an unpublished article written by J.D. McGee entitled "The Early Development of the Television Camera." This will be henceforth cited as the *McGee File*.

103. Keith Geddes, "Broadcasting in Britain; 1922–1972," *A Science Museum Booklet* (London: Her Majesty's Stationery Office, 1972), p. 22–24.

104. Sydney Moseley, "This Month's Causerie," *Television* (London) 5 (Mar. 1932): pp. 3–4; G. Parr, "The Story of Baird and Television," *Discovery* 10 (Aug. 1952): pp. 1–3; Asa Briggs, *The Golden Age of Wireless, Vol. II*. (London: Oxford University Press, 1965), p. 558.

105. R.C. Ballard, U.S. Pat. No. 2,093,395. Applied 6 Jan. 1932; issued 14 Sept. 1937. See also Br. Pat. No. 394,597, issued 29 June 1933.

106. Sanford E. Essig, U.S. Pat. No. 2,065,570. Applied 24 Feb. 1932; issued 29 Dec. 1936. This patent was actually filed on 24 Dec. 1931 but was returned by the Patent Office for lack of a diagram. RCA asked for a date of 5 Jan. 1932 but was refused. See also Br. Pat. No. 407,521; issued 22 Mar. 1934.

107. Sanford E. Essig, U.S. Pat. No. 2,020,305. Applied 30 July 1932; issued 12 Nov. 1935. See also Br. Pat. No. 421,201; issued 17 Dec. 1934.

108. V.K. Zworykin and Gregory N. Ogloblinsky, U.S. Pat. No. 2,178,093. Applied 10 Mar. 1932; issued 31 Oct. 1939. Information from Patent Interferences Nos. 69,636 and 73,812.

109. From Patent Interference No. 64027.

110. "Test Television Progress," *New York Times*, 18 May 1932, p. 23:3; "Television Images Are Leaping From a Skyscraper Pinnacle," *New York Times*, 22 May 1932, sec. VIII, p. 10:1; "News from Abroad," *Television* (London) 5 (July 1932): p. 174. For details of the equipment used see E.W. Engstrom, "An Experimental Television System"; V.K. Zworykin, "Description of an Experimental Television System and Kinescope"; R.D. Kell, "Description of Experimental Transmitting Apparatus"; G.L. Beers, "Description of Experimental Television Receivers," all in *Proceedings of the Institute of Radio Engineers* 21 (Dec. 1933): pp. 1652–1706.

111. Harry Lubcke in an interview with Ed Reitan of ITT, 20 Nov. 1978.

112. Harry R. Lubcke, "Television Image Reception in an Airplane," *Proceedings of the Institute of Radio Engineers* 20 (Nov. 1932): pp. 1732–1740 (received 23 June 1932); Harry R. Lubcke, "Receiving Television in an Airplane," *Radio Engineering* 12 (Oct. 1932): pp. 12–13, 24.

113. "New Television System," *Wireless World* **30** (25 May 1932): p. 539.

114. G.F. Metcalf, "A New Cathode-Ray Oscillograph Tube," *Electronics* **4** (May 1932): pp. 158-159.

115. Allen B. Du Mont, "An Investigation of Various Electrode Structures of Cathode Ray Tubes Suitable for Television Reception," **20** (Dec. 1932): *Proceedings of the Institute of Radio Engineers* **20** (Dec. 1932); pp. 1863-1877. (Manuscript received 4 May 1932.)

116. "Derby Televised in London Cinema," *London Times*, 2 June 1932, p. 3c. Also Moseley and Barton Chapple, *op. cit.*, pp. 166-171.

117. K. Takayanagi, Jap. Pat. No. 100,037. Applied 13 June 1932; issued 9 Mar. 1933.

118. J.C. Wilson, Br. Pat. No. 404,281. Applied 7 Jul. 1932; issued 8 Jan. 1934.

119. Randall C. Ballard, U.S. Pat. No. 2,152,234. Applied 19 July 1932; issued 28 Mar. 1939. The Br. Pat. No. 420,391 was issued 30 Nov. 1934. The two prior interlace patents: (1) F. Schröter, DRP Pat. No. 574,085. Applied 27 Sept. 1930; issued 23 Mar. 1933. Schröter combined both interlace with long-persistence phosphors to minimize flicker. (2) M. von Ardenne, Br. Pat. No. 387,087. Applied 22 Dec. 1930, issued 21 Dec. 1931. This was simply a means for displacing the two sets of images.

120. W.D. Wright, "Picture Quality—The Continuing Challenge Towards Visual Perfection," *Journal of the Royal Television Society* **16** (Jan.-Feb. 1977): pp. 6-10.

121. Schubert, *op. cit.*, (n. 8.99), pp. 129-134; "New Film Devised to Aid Television," *New York Times*, 19 Aug. 1932, p. 20:8; A.T. Stoyanowsky, "A New Process of Television Out of Doors," *Journal of the Society of Motion Picture Engineers* **20** (Jan. 1933): pp. 437-443.

122. "Sound and Vision Broadcasting," *Radio Engineering* **12** (Oct. 1932): p. 22; Samuel Kaufman, "Television and Sound on One Wave!" *Radio News* **14** (Nov. 1932): pp. 270-271, 314-315.

123. V.K. Zworykin, U.S. Pat. No. 2,107,464. Applied 5 Aug. 1932; issued 8 Feb. 1938.

124. "News by Television, a New Marconi System," *Wireless World* **31** (5 Aug. 1932): p. 102.

125. Fritz Schröter, *Handbuch der Bildtelegraphie und des Fernsehens* (Berlin: Julius Springer, 1932), pp. 61-62.

126. William F. Tedham and Joseph D. McGee, Br. Pat. No. 406,353. Applied 25 Aug. 1932; issued 26 Feb. 1934. See also U.S. Pat. No. 2,077,442. Conv. date 9 Aug. 1933; issued 20 Apr. 1937.

127. *RCA Annual Stockholder Report, 1933; McGee File*, pp. 27-30.

128. *EMI File*. Also see "A.G.D. West," *Journal of the Society of Motion Picture Engineers* **53** (Nov. 1949): p. 604.

129. Letter dated 20 Sept. 1932, from Zworykin to Mitchell in *Journal of the Royal Television Society*, "50th Anniversary Issue" (Nov/Dec 1977): p. 93.

130. A. Dinsdale, "Television in America Today," *Journal of the Television Society* **1** (1931/1934): pp. 137-148.

131. W. Wenstrom, "The March of Television," *Radio News* **13** (Apr. 1932): pp. 852-853, 876-878.

132. C. Kette, "Die Fernsehschau auf der Berliner Funkaus Stellung 1931," *Fernsehen* **2** (Oct. 1931): pp. 225-238; E.H. Traub, "Television at the 1932 Berlin Radio Exhibition," *Journal of the Television Society* **1** (1931/34): pp. 155-166.

133. "Marconi Demonstration," *London Times*, 2 Sept. 1932, p. 10e; "Television Apparatus," *Electrician* **109** (9 Sept. 1932): pp. 311-312.

134. "The Marconi Co. and Television Research," *The Marconi Review*, no.

38 (Sept.–Oct. 1932): pp. 1–7; Baker, W.J., *op. cit.*, pp. 260–266.

135. *Bell Labs, 33089*, memorandum, dated 30 Sept. 1932.

136. M. Knoll and E. Ruska, "Electron Microscope," *Zeitschrift für Physik* **78** (4 Oct. 1932): pp. 5–6, 318–339.

137. W.D. Wright, Br. Pat. No. 399,654. Applied 12 Oct. 1932; issued 12 Oct. 1933. See also A.W. Vance, U.S. Pat. No. 2,006,063. Applied 15 Oct. 1932; issued 25 June 1935. A.V. Bedford, U.S. Pat. No. 2,004,099. Applied 15 Oct. 1932; issued 11 June 1935. R.W. Campbell, U.S. Pat. No. 1,995,376. Applied 29 Oct. 1932; issued 26 Mar. 1935.

138. Fernseh Akt.-Ges., Br. Pat. No. 428,227. Conv. date 15 Nov. 1932 (applied 9 Nov. 1933); issued 9 May 1935.

139. Briggs, *op. cit.*, pp. 569–571; *EMI File*, p. 165.

140. "Termination of Alleged Radio Combine Suit," *Radio Engineering* **12** (Dec. 1932): pp. 16–17.

141. F.J. Bingley, "A Half Century of Television Reception," *Proc. I.R.E.* **50** (May 1962): pp. 799–805. See also "Television as Good as Home Movies," *Radio News* **17** (Nov. 1936): p. 308; Everson, *op. cit.*, pp. 133–136.

9. The Iconoscope: 1933–1935

1. E.W. Engstrom, "An Experimental Television System, Part I — Introduction"; R.D. Kell, A.V. Bedford and M.A. Trainer, "Part II — The Transmitter"; R.S. Holmes, W.L. Carlson and W.A. Tolson, "Part III — The Receivers"; C.S. Young, "Part IV — The Radio Relay Link for Television Signals," all in *Proceedings of the Institute of Radio Engineers* **22** (Nov. 1934): pp. 1241–1294.

2. Gregory N. Ogloblinsky, U.S. Pat. No. 2,084,700. Applied 3 Jan. 1933; issued 22 June 1937. Ray D. Kell, Br. Pat. No. 431,207. Conv. date 3 Jan. 1933 (applied 3 Jan. 1934); issued 3 July 1935. Alda V. Bedford, U.S. Pat. No. 2,082,093. Applied 28 Jan. 1933; issued 1 June 1937. Richard L. Campbell, U.S. Pat. No. 2,092,975. Applied 28 Jan. 1933 (renewed 28 Jan. 1936); issued 14 Sept. 1937.

3. V.K. Zworykin, "On Electron Optics," *Journal of the Franklin Institute* **215** (May 1933): pp. 535–555.

4. "New 'Electrical Lens' an Aid to Television," *New York Times*, 5 Mar. 1933, sec. IX, p. 10:3.

5. O.E. Dunlap, Jr., "Faces That Lurk in Space," *New York Times*, 5 Mar. 1933, sec. IX, p. 10:1; Merle S. Cummings, "Television Advances," *Radio News* **15** (Oct. 1933): pp. 214–215, 245–247.

6. Harley A. Iams, U.S. Pat. No. 2,099,980. Applied 30 Mar. 1933; issued 23 Nov. 1937. Harley A. Iams, Br. Pat. No. 422,158. Conv. date 30 Mar. 1933 (applied 3 Apr. 1934); issued 7 Jan. 1935.

7. P.T. Farnsworth, U.S. Pat. No. 2,059,683. Applied 3 Apr. 1933; issued 3 Nov. 1936.

8. V.K. Zworykin, Br. Pat. No. 434,890. Conv. date 8 Apr. 1933 (applied 6 Apr. 1934); issued 11 Sept. 1935. See Patent Interferences Nos. 64,026 and 64,035, dated 19 May 1934.

9. Briggs, *op. cit.*, pp. 574–576. I visited the British Post Office Archives in Sept. 1979 to inspect their records of this era. To my chagrin, I found the files to be in great disorder. There were pages and sometimes whole sections missing, photographs and diagrams had disappeared, etc. As a result, I have had to depend on the findings of Briggs, who had access to these records before me.

10. "1933 Television Exhibition," *Journal of the Television Society* **1** (1931/34): pp. 209–216.

11. P.W. Willans, Br. Pat. No. 422,906. Applied 13 Apr. 1933; issued 14 Jan. 1935. J.D. McGee, Br. Pat. No. 419,452. Applied 5 May 1933; issued 5 Nov. 1934. (See also U.S. Pat. No. 2,100,259. Issued 23 Nov. 1937.) A.D. Blumlein, Br. Pat. No. 421,546. Applied 16 June 1933; issued 17 Dec. 1934. C.O. Browne, J. Hardwick and A.D. Blumlein, Br. Pat. No. 422,914. Applied 11 July 1933; issued 11 Jan. 1935.

12. Briggs, *op. cit.*, p. 576.

13. Albert F. Murray, interview with the author, 18 Apr. 1978. The information was also included in a letter to the author from Murray, dated June 14, 1978.

14. P.T. Farnsworth, U.S. Pat. No. 2,087,683. Applied 26 Apr. 1933; issued 20 July 1937. A Br. Pat. No. 489,199 was applied on 11 May 1937 and issued 21 July 1938.

15. Everson, *op. cit.*, pp. 135–136; Schatzkin and Kiger, *op. cit.*, p. 20.

16. R.K. Kilbon, "Pioneering in Electronics" (Princeton, N.J.: unpublished two-volume manuscript, Jan. 1960), Vol. I, p. 55. Kilbon claims that work on the relay was started in 1932 and went into test operation in 1933. For some rather vague reason, Kilbon's manuscript was not available to researchers for many years. I was finally able to secure permission to see it, and it turned out to be rather bland with no startling revelations. This information was also confirmed by Engstrom, *op. cit.*, pp. 1243–1245. However, the first publicity was "Television Sent 90 Miles in Test," *New York Times*, 30 May 1934, p. 15:6.

17. This was the original title as listed in "Institute News and Radio Notes," *Proceedings of the Institute of Radio Engineers* 21 (June 1933): p. 745. See also O.E. Dunlap, Jr., "Novel Radio Optic 'Sees'," *New York Times*, 25 June 1933, sec. IX, p. 7:1; W.L. Laurence, "Human-Like Eye Made by Engineers to Televise Images," *New York Times*, 27 June 1933, p. 1:1; O.E. Dunlap, Jr., "Outlook for Radio-Sight," *New York Times*, 2 July 1933, sec. IX, p. 6:1; V.K. Zworykin, "The Iconoscope—A Modern Version of the Electric Eye," *Broadcast News*, no. 8 (Aug. 1933): pp. 6–13; V.K. Zworykin, "The Iconoscope—A Modern Version of the Electric Eye," *Proceedings of the Institute of Radio Engineers* 22 (Jan. 1934): pp. 16–32 (paper received 14 June 1933); V.K. Zworykin, "Television with Cathode-Ray Tubes," *Journal of the Institute of Electrical Engineers* (London) 73 (Oct. 1933): pp. 437–451 (paper received 17 July 1933); V.K. Zworykin, "Système de télévision par tubes à rayons cathodiques." *L'Onde Electrique* 12 (Nov. 1933): pp. 501–539 (paper received 26 July 1933); V.K. Zworykin, "Fernsehen mit Kathodenstrahlrohren," *Hochfrequenztechnik und Elektroakustrik* 43 (Apr. 1934): pp. 109–121 (paper received 4 Sept. 1933); V.K. Zworykin, "Television," *Journal of the Franklin Institute* 217 (Jan. 1934): pp. 1–37 (paper presented 18 Oct. 1933).

18. Dr. Joseph McGee, who has always insisted that the work done at EMI was independent of Zworykin's research, admitted that the Zworykin paper was a momentous step forward. (See *McGee File*, p. 31.) This paper certainly started several laboratories into research into a storage-type camera tube. Thus it had the same effect as did Campbell Swinton's articles in *Wireless World* in April 1924. (See Chapter 5, pp. 67–68.)

19. *Bell Labs, 33089*, "Note on Zworykin's Iconoscope," dated 6 July 1933, by Frank Gray; memorandum to H.D. Arnold from O.E. Buckley and H.E. Ives, dated 6 July 1933.

20. *Bell Labs, 33089*, memorandum from H.E. Ives to O.E. Buckley, dated 20 July 1933; "Suggested Outline for Development Work on a Cathode-Ray Transmitter," by Frank Gray, dated 31 July 1933.

21. I have never been able to find an official date as to when Elmer Engstrom took over the RCA Television Project. But it seems to have occurred when the Empire State Building television project was temporarily shelved late in 1932.

22. *McGee File*, p. 33; J.D. McGee, "The Life and Work of Sir Isaac

Shoenberg, 1880-1963," *Journal of the Royal Television Society* **13** (May/June 1971): p. 210; *1934 RCA Stockholder Report* (it was reported that EMI "was engaged in the development of television transmitting and receiving apparatus"); A.D. Blumlein, "The Marconi-E.M.I. Television System, Part I. A: The Transmitted Wave-Form," *Proceedings of the Institute of Electrical Engineers (London)* **83** (Dec. 1938): pp. 758-766 (the 180-line standard was used until late 1934).

23. "'The Eye' Gains Prestige," *New York Times*, 16 July 1933, sec. IX, p. 7:5; Cummings, *op. cit.*, p. 215, 245-246.

24. W.S. Percival, C.O. Browne and E.C.L. White, Br. Pat. No. 425,220. Applied 8 Aug. 1933; issued 8 Mar. 1935. I have never been able to find out why EMI stopped having the patents issued in the EMI corporate name for those television patents applied for in Great Britain. They were still assigned to EMI in the United States.

25. "'Dumbest' $5000 Investment Brings Television," *San Francisco Chronicle*, 9 Aug. 1933; "Outdoor Test of Television Proves Merit," *San Francisco Chronicle*, 14 Sept. 1933; "Television Declared Ready to Broadcast Starting Sectionally, with Relays Later," *New York Times*, 11 Aug. 1933, p. 18:2.

26. J.C. Wilson, Br. Pat. No. 424,199. Applied 12 Aug. 1933; issued 12 Feb. 1935.

27. E.H. Traub, "Television at the 1933 Berlin Radio Exhibition," *Journal of the Television Society* **1** (1931/34): pp. 273-285; "Television in Germany; New Types of Transmitter and Receiver," *London Times*, 13 Oct. 1933, p. 12c.

28. L.H. Bedford and O.S. Puckle, Br. Pat. No. 427,625. Applied 4 Sept. 1933; issued 29 Apr. 1935.

29. "Development of Television; Proposed Experiments at Crystal Palace," *London Times*, 13 Sept. 1933, p. 5d; "Progress in Television," *London Times*, 14 Sept. 1933, p. 12a.

30. V.K. Zworykin, Br. Pat. No. 413,894. Applied 13 Sept. 1933; issued 26 July 1934.

31. Moseley and Barton Chapple, *op. cit.*, p. 24.

32. "High-Definition Television; B.B.C. Experiments," *London Times*, 13 Oct. 1933, p. 12c.

33. "Gain in Television Amazes Marconi," *New York Times*, 13 Oct. 1933, p. 25:5.

34. *Iams File.*

35. W.D. Wright, "Picture Quality — The Continuing Challenge Towards Visual Perfection," *op. cit.* (n. 8.120), p. 7.

36. Comp. pour la Fab. des Compteurs et Mat. d'Usines à Gas, Br. Pat. No. 431,827. Conv. dates 14, 17, 30, Nov. 1933; issued 16 July 1935.

37. *EMI File.*

38. W.F. Tedham, Br. Pat. No. 426,505. Applied 6 Dec. 1933; issued 4 Apr. 1935. Also U.S. Pat. No. 2,153,163. Issued 4 Apr. 1939. This patent was the subject of Patent Interference No. 77,619 with Iams of RCA. It was won by Tedham of EMI.

39. Telefunken Ges. für Drahtlose Telegraphie, Br. Pat. No. 431,904. Conv. date 12 Dec. 1933. Applied 12 Dec. 1934; issued 17 July 1935.

40. See n. 8.32. See also Lessing, *op. cit.*, p. 179. Also in Lyons, *op. cit.*, p. 251.

41. Comp. pour la Fab. des Compteurs et Mat. d'Usines à Gas, Br. Pat. No. 428,926; Conv. date 31 Jan. 1934 (applied 30 Jan. 1935); issued 21 May 1935.

42. Briggs, *op. cit.*, p. 579; *McGee File*, p. 35.

43. *EMI File; McGee File*, p. 35; Blumlein, *op. cit.*, pp. 448-449.

44. "Super-Microscope Uses Television to Open Vast Ranges for Science,"

New York Times, 25 Feb. 1934, p. 1:2. A picture and description of the device was shown in V.K. Zworykin and L.E. Flory, "Television in Medicine and Biology," *Electrical Engineer* 71 (Jan. 1952): p. 40–45.

45. L.H. Bedford and O.S. Puckle, "A Velocity Modulational Television System," *Journal of the Institute of Electrical Engineers* (London) 175 (July 1934): pp. 63–85.

46. Scophony and J.H. Jefree, Br. Pat. No. 439,236. Applied 3 Mar. 1934; issued 3 Dec. 1935.

47. This material was kindly furnished me by Solomon Sagall, the founder of Scophony, Ltd., on June 15, 1984. It is from a biography entitled *Scophony Limited*. This will be cited as the *Scophony File*.

48. Lessing, *op. cit.*, pp. 179–181.

49. Briggs, *op. cit.*, p. 577; "Meeting Addressed by Television," *London Times*, 21 Mar. 1934, p. 14e; "Television Demonstration to M.P.s," *London Times*, 29 Mar. 1934, p. 12c.

50. H.G. Lubszynski and S. Rodda, Br. Pat. No. 442,666. Applied 12 May 1934; issued 12 Feb. 1936. U.S. Pat. No. 2,244,466. Conv. date 4 May 1935; issued 3 June 1941.

51. Briggs, *op. cit.*, pp. 578–582.

52. "Marconi Co. in Merger to Promote Television," *New York Times*, 23 May 1934, p. 10:4.

53. Briggs, *op. cit.*, p. 578.

54. A.W. Vance and H. Branson, U.S. Pat. No. 2,147,760. Applied 24 May 1934; issued 21 Feb. 1939.

55. "Television Nears Technical Solution," *Electronics* 7 (June 1934): pp. 172–174.

56. *Selsdon Committee Report*.

57. *EMI File*.

58. *Bell Labs, 33089*, "Television Transmission System Using Cathode Ray Tubes," memorandum for file dated July 31, 1934, by John R. Hofele; Goebel, *op. cit.*, pp. 290–291; P. Shmakov, "The Development of Television in the U.S.S.R.," *Journal of the Television Society* 2 (1935/38): pp. 97–105. (Manuscript received 17 Jan. 1936.)

59. P. Mertz and F. Gray, "A Theory of Scanning and Its Relationship to the Characteristics of the Transmitted Signal in Telephotography and Television," *Bell System Technical Journal* 13 (July 1934): pp. 464–516.

60. Everson, *op. cit.*, p. 147. The agreement was made public in 1935. See "British Get Television," *New York Times*, 20 June 1935, p. 21:1; "Company Meeting, Baird Television Limited," *London Times*, 21 June 1935, p. 25a.

61. S. Sagall, "Television in 1934," *Television* (London) 7 (Jan. 1934): pp. 4–6; G.W. Walton, "The Stixograph and Scophony," *Television* (London) 7 (Mar. 1934): pp. 93–96, 134; "Scophony Projected Picture," *Television* (London) 7 (Aug. 1934): p. 332.

62. Alan D. Blumlein and James D. McGee, Br. Pat. No. 446,661. Applied 3 Aug. 1934; issued 4 May 1936. See also U.S. Pat. No. 2,182,578. Conv. date 2 Aug. 1935; issued 5 Dec. 1939.

63. "Tennis Stars Act in New Television," *New York Times*, 25 Aug. 1934, p. 14:4; Everson, *op. cit.*, pp. 142–145.

64. A.H. Brolly, "Television by Electronic Methods," *Institute of Electrical Engineers* 53 (Aug. 1934): pp. 1153–1160. (Submitted on April 24, 1934.)

65. E.H. Traub, "Television at the Berlin Radio Exhibition, 1934," *Journal of the Television Society* 2 (1931/34): pp. 341–351; E.H. Traub, "How Far Has Germany Progressed?" *Television* (London) 7 (Oct. 1934): pp. 453–456.

66. K. Takayanagi, "Recent Development of Television Technic in Europe and America," *Journal of the Institute of Electrical Engineers* (Japan) **55**, [no. 3] no. 560 (Mar. 1935): pp. 172–180.

67. L.H. Bedford and R.D. Kell, U.S. Pat. No. 2,108,097. Applied 31 Aug. 1934; issued 15 Feb. 1938.

68. E.C. Cork, M. Bowman Manifold and C.O. Browne, Br. Pat. No. 448,031. Applied 31 Aug. 1934; issued 2 June 1936; C.O. Browne, F. Blythen and A.D. Blumlein, Br. Pat. No. 449,242. Applied 18 Sept. 1934; issued 18 June 1936; J.D. McGee and L. Klatzow, Br. Pat. No. 447,819. Applied 20 Sept. 1934 (divided out of 446,664); issued 20 May 1936.

69. L.H. Bedford, U.S. Pat. No. 2,258,728. Applied 29 Sept. 1934; issued 14 Oct. 1941.

70. Patent Interference No. 74,655. It was decided in Bedford's favor on August 24, 1937. Thus the Image Iconoscope belonged to RCA and not to EMI!

71. L.H. Bedford, U.S. Pat. No. 2,166,712. Applied 26 Oct. 1934; issued 18 July 1939.

72. Philo T. Farnsworth, "Television by Electron Image Scanning," *Journal of the Franklin Institute* **218** (Oct. 1934): pp. 411–444. P.T. Farnsworth, U.S. Pat. No. 2,280,572. Applied 5 Nov. 1934: issued 21 Apr. 1942. See Patent Interference No. 76,571 (Farnsworth vs. Kell and Bedford), which was won by Farnsworth.

73. "Television: A Survey of Present-Day Systems," *Electronics* **7** (Oct. 1934): pp. 301–305.

74. "England on the Television Brink, Wonders Whether to Jump First," *New York Times*, 18 Nov. 1934, sec. IX, p. 13:1.

75. *Selsdon Committee Report*.

76. "The Television Committee in Germany," *Television* (London) **7** (Dec. 1934): p. 538.

77. *Selsdon Committee Report*; Everson, *op. cit.*, p. 146–148; T.H. Bridgewater, letter to author, dated 1 Apr. 1980. Bridgewater insists that the Farnsworth equipment was never demonstrated to the Selsdon Committee.

78. D.M. Johnstone, Br. Pat. No. 446,585. Applied 6 Nov. 1934; issued 4 May 1935. Goebels, *op. cit.*, p. 291.

79. C.O. Browne, J. Hardwick, F. Blythen, and E.L.C. White, Br. Pat. No. 450,675. Applied 19 Nov. 1934; issued 20 July 1936. W.D. Tedham, U.S. Pat. No. 2,153,163. Applied 23 Nov. 1934; issued 4 Apr. 1939.

80. "Film Records of Signals," *London Times*, 29 Nov. 1934, p. 19c.

81. Rolf Moller, U.S. Pat. No. 2,160,888. Conv. date 12 Dec. 1934 (applied 10 Dec. 1935); issued 6 June 1939.

82. W. Hickok, U.S. Pat. No. 2,047,369. Applied 21 Dec. 1934; issued 14 July 1936.

83. "The Television Committee's Report," *Television & Short-Wave World Supplement* **8** (Feb. 1935): pp. i to iv; "Text of British Television Report," *Electronics* **8** (Mar. 1935): pp. 76–77; "London Television Station," *London Times*, 7 June 1935, p. 13d; "The Advisory Committee Makes Its First Statement," *Television & Short-Wave World* **8** (July 1935): p. 393.

84. Moseley and Barton Chapple, *op. cit.*, p. 26; "A High-Definition Service Ready in London," *Television & Short-Wave World* **8** (Mar. 1935): pp. 117–121. The high hopes for success with the Farnsworth "Electron-Image Camera" by Baird Television Ltd. were reflected in two articles dealing with it. See J.C. Wilson, "The Electron-Image Camera," *Television & Short-Wave World* **8** (Apr. 1935): pp. 195–197; and "Producing Electron Images," *Television & Short-Wave World* **8** (Aug. 1935): pp. 467–470. A photograph of the Farnsworth film projector was shown in *Radio News* **17** (Sept. 1935): p. 139.

85. "A High-Definition Service Ready in London, *op. cit.*, p. 117, shows a photograph of the cathode-ray apparatus; "Television in the Cinema," *Television & Short-Wave World* 8 (Nov. 1935): pp. 647–648, 653. This was from a recent lecture by Capt. West, technical director of Baird Television, Ltd. In it, he promised that "good television pictures in one form or another will be shown in London cinemas before the end of the year."

86. H.G. Lubszynski and J.D. McGee, Br. Pat. No. 455,123. Applied 9 Feb. 1935 (divided out of 455,085); issued 9 Oct. 1936. H.G. Lubszynski and J.D. McGee, U.S. Pat. No. 2,150,980. Applied 17 Apr. 1936; issued 21 Mar. 1939.

87. A.D. Blumlein, Br. Pat. No. 458,585. Applied 20 Mar. 1935; issued 21 Dec. 1936; Leonard Klatzow, Br. Pat. No. 458,586. Applied 20 Mar. 1935; issued 21 Dec. 1936.

88. I. Kaar, "The Road Ahead in Television," *Journal of the Society of Motion Picture Engineers* 32 (Jan. 1939): p. 25.

89. *EMI File*, p. 310; J.D. McGee, "The Life and Work of Sir Isaac Shoenberg, 1880–1963," *Journal of the Television Society* 13 (May/June 1971): p. 213; Blumlein, *op. cit.*, p. 506; *EMI File*, p. 325; D. Birkenshaw, "Shoenberg: Faith in Electronic Television," *Journal of the Television Society* 18 (Sept./Oct. 1981): pp. 56–57.

90. "Berlin Television Begins," *London Times*, 23 Mar. 1935, p. 11d.

91. W.E. Schrage, "German Television," *Radio News* 17 (July 1935): pp. 9, 60; Review of M. von Ardenne, "Television Reception," Weidmannsche Bechhandlung, Berlin, 1935, in *Wireless Engineer* 12 (June 1935): p. 325; M. von Ardenne, "An Experimental Television Receiver Using a Cathode-Ray Tube," *Proceedings of the Institute of Radio Engineers* 23 (Mar. 1936): pp. 409–424 (paper received 30 Nov. 1934); H. Gibas, "Television in Germany," *Proceedings of the Institute of Radio Engineers* 24 (May 1936): pp. 741–750 (paper received 1 Nov. 1935).

92. "Alexandra Palace picked as British Television Site," *New York Times*, 4 Apr. 1935, p. 1:2; "London Television Station," *London Times*, 7 June 1935, p. 13c.

93. "High Definition Television Service in England," *Journal of the Television Society* 2 (1934/35): pp. 34–43; M. von Ardenne, "Interlacing and Definition," *Television & Short-Wave World* 8 (Dec. 1935): pp. 719, 721.

94. "The French 60-Line Transmissions," *Television & Short-Wave World* 8 (June 1935): p. 359; S. Kaufman, "Using Cathode Rays for High-Definition Television," *Radio News* 17 (Aug. 1935): pp. 76–77.

95. P. Hemardinquer, "Le progres de la radiovision en France et les systèmes cathodiques," *La Nature*, no. 2954 (1 June 1935): pp. 486–496; R. Barthelemy, "L'état actuel de la télévision," *L'Onde Electrique* 14 (June 1935): pp. 391–405; (July 1935): pp. 455–469; R. Barthelemy, "La télévision à l'exposition universelle de Bruxelles (1935)," *Revue Générale de l'Electricité* no. 38 (21 Sept. 1935): pp. 405–410.

96. "First Field Tests in Television, Costing $1,000,000, to Begin Here," *New York Times*, 8 May 1935, p. 1:2; "Television in U.S.A.," *London Times*, 9 May 1935, p. 18e; O.E. Dunlap, Jr., "Sky to Be the Laboratory," *New York Times*, 12 May 1935, sec. X, p. 11:1; "Television Progress in U.S.A., America to Follow Britain's Lead," *Television & Short-Wave World* 8 (Aug. 1935): pp. 436–439.

97. Gregory N. Ogloblinsky, U.S. Pat. No. 2,156,769. Applied 28 Feb. 1935; issued 2 May 1939. J.P. Smith, U.S. Pat. No. 2,132,655. Applied 28 Feb. 1935; issued 11 Oct. 1938. Ray D. Kell and Alda V. Bedford, U.S. Pat. No. 2,293,147. Applied 26 Mar. 1935; issued 18 Aug. 1942.

98. Lyons, *op. cit.*, p. 252; Lessing, *op. cit.*, p. 183.

99. V. Zeitline, A. Zeitline, and V. Kliatchko, Br. Pat. No. 478,121. Conv. date 9 May 1935 (divided out of Br. Pat. No. 476,865); issued 11 Jan. 1938. See also

Br. Pat. Nos. 478,641, 475,547, 477,326, and 478,499, all with the conv. date of 18 May 1935.

100. "Television from Wax Records: A Demonstration of 'Gramovision'," *London Times*, 16 May 1935, p. 9c. In June 1935 there was an account of a similar process by Major Radiovision Company of London. It was claimed that only still pictures had been recorded in order to get adequate definition. See "'Television' from Disc Records," *Television & Short-Wave World* 8 (June 1935): p. 308.

101. P.T. Farnsworth, U.S. Pat. No. 2,140,695. Applied 6 July 1935; issued 20 Dec. 1938. P.T. Farnsworth, U.S. Pat. No. 2,141,836. Applied 6 July 1935 (continued 7 Sept. 1937); issued 27 Dec. 1938. P.T. Farnsworth, U.S. Pat. No. 2,216,264. Applied 6 July 1935, issued 1 Oct. 1940.

102. *Bell Labs, 33089*. Memorandum entitled "Photo-conducting Television Transmitter," from Foster C. Nix, dated 6 Aug. 1935.

103. "Gain in Television is Demonstrated," *New York Times*, 31 July 1935, p. 15:4; "Television Transmitters Planned," *Electronics* 8 (Sept. 1935): pp. 294–295; S. Kaufman, "Demonstrates High-Definition Television," *Radio News* 17 (Nov. 1935): pp. 265, 308; "A Demonstration of the Farnsworth System," *Television & Short-Wave World* 8 (Nov. 1935): p. 628; S. Kaufman, "Farnsworth Television," *Radio News* 17 (Dec. 1935): pp. 330–331, 375.

104. E.H. Traub, "Television at the Berlin Radio Exhibition," *Journal of the Television Society* 2 (1935–1938), pp. 53–61; "Television Progress in Germany," *Television & Short-Wave World* 8 (Oct. 1935): pp. 564–567.

105. "The Wireless Exhibition and Television," *Television & Short-Wave World* 8 (June 1935): p. 330.

106. R.D. Washburne and W.E. Schrage, "World-Wide Television," *Radio-Craft* 7 (Aug. 1935): pp. 76–79, 80. The bulk of this information came from a book published in Japan in 1935. It was entitled *Transactions of the Television Engineers of Japan for 1935*. It was written in Japanese and was the most comprehensive report of the activities undertaken there. It was continued in 1936 by another report. These two volumes were kindly given to me by Harley Iams.

107. Fritz Schröter, U.S. Pat. No. 2,210,987. Conv. date 5 Aug. 1935 (applied 5 Aug. 1936); issued 13 Aug. 1940.

108. P.T. Farnsworth, U.S. Pat. No, 2,100,841. Applied 7 Sept. 1935; issued 30 Nov. 1937.

109. "B.B.C. Television Service," *London Times*, 22 Aug. 1935, p. 10c.

110. H. Miller, Br. Pat. No. 462,550. Applied 10 Sept. 1935; issued 10 Mar. 1937. H. Miller, Br. Pat. No. 463,297. Applied 24 Sept. 1935; issued 24 Mar. 1937. H. Miller, Br. Pat. No. 465,060. Applied 29 Oct. 1935, issued 29 Apr. 1937.

111. H.G. Lubszynski, Br. Pat. No. 464,919. Applied 24 Sept. 1935; issued 26 Apr. 1937.

112. "Sarnoff Off to Europe," *New York Times*, 27 July 1935, p. 16:5; "Sarnoff Denies Change in E.M.I. Set-Up," *Wall Street Journal*, 2 Oct. 1935, p. 84; *1936 RCA Stockholder Report*.

113. "Television Transmissions: Details of the Baird and Marconi-EMI Systems," *Wireless World* 37 (4 Oct. 1935): pp. 371–373; "High-Definition Television from the Alexandra Palace," *Television & Short-Wave World* 8 (Nov. 1935): pp. 631–634.

114. "Single-side band (transmission) was considered but no practical method was discovered." T.C. MacNamara and D.C. Birkenshaw, "The London Television Service," *Journal of the Institute of Electrical Engineers* (London) 83 (Dec. 1938): p. 759.

115. Briggs, *op. cit.*, p. 601.

116. "High Definition Television: Demonstration at Press Club Dinner," *London Times*, 9 Nov. 1935, p. 14e.

117. "Scannings and Reflections: At the Dominion Theatre," *Television & Short-Wave World* **8** (Dec. 1935): p. 707.

118. Eric L.C. White, Br. Pat. No. 471,731. Applied 4 Dec. 1935; issued 6 Sept. 1937.

119. P.T. Farnsworth, U.S. Pat. No. 2,153,918. Applied 31 Dec. 1935; issued 11 Apr. 1939.

10. The London Television Service: 1936–1939

1. H.G. Lubszynski, Br. pat. No. 468,965. Applied Jan. 15, 1936; issued 15 July 1937.

2. "The Telepantoscope, A New Cathode Ray Scanner," *Television & Short-Wave World* **7** (Jan. 1936): p. 14; "La télévision cathode," *La Nature* no. 2970 (1 Feb. 1936): pp. 105–113; "Television Progress in Italy," *Radio-Craft* **8** (Aug. 1936): p. 86; A. Castellani, "Telecameras Compared," *Television & Short-Wave World* **12** (Aug. 1939): pp. 470–472.

3. "Zworykin Shows New Electron Tube," *Radio-Craft* **7** (Jan. 1936): p. 391; "Dr. Zworykin on the Electron Multiplier," *Television & Short-Wave World* **7** (Mar. 1936): pp. 153–154, 191; "The Electron Image Tube," *Radio-Craft* **8** (Apr. 1936): pp. 594, 622; V.K. Zworykin, "'L'optique électronique' et ses applications," *L'Onde Electrique* **15** (May 1936): pp. 293–296; V.K. Zworykin, "Electron-Optical Systems and Their Applications," *Journal of the Institute of Electrical Engineers* (London) **79** (July 1936): pp. 1–10.

4. Briggs, *op. cit.*, pp. 595–596; D.C. Birkenshaw, "The Birth of Modern Television," *Journal of the Royal Television Society*, "50th Anniversary Issue," (Nov.–Dec. 1977): pp. 35–36.

5. "Baird Television Up-To-Date," *Television & Short-Wave World* **9** (Aug. 1936): pp. 436–439; "Technical Details of the Television Equipment Supplied by Baird Television Ltd. to the British Broadcasting Corporation at Alexandra Palace," *Journal of the Television Society* **2** (Jan. 1935/Dec. 1938): pp. 161–168; MacNamara and Birkenshaw, "The London Television Service," *op. cit.*, pp. 729–757.

6. "First Complete Details of the Marconi-E.M.I. Television System," *Television & Short-Wave World* **9** (Mar. 1936): pp. 132–136; "Marconi-E.M.I. Television," *Journal of the Television Society* **2** (Jan. 1935/Dec. 1938): pp. 75–77; "Marconi-E.M.I. Television Equipment at the Alexandra Palace," *Journal of the Television Society* **2** (Jan. 1935/Dec. 1938): pp. 169–176; "The London Television Station Alexandra Palace," *Journal of the Television Society* **2** (Jan. 1935/Dec. 1938): p. 156–160; MacNamara and Birkenshaw, *op. cit.*, pp. 742–745; Noel Ashbridge, "Television in Great Britain," *Proceedings of the Institute of Radio Engineers* **25** (June 1937): pp. 697–707.

7. J.L. Baird, Br. Pat. No. 473,323. Applied 9 Apr. 1936 (divided out of 473,303); issued 11 Oct. 1937.

8. See, for instance, V. Jones, Br. Pat. No. 473,028. Applied 8 Apr. 1936; issued 5 Oct. 1937. Also V. Jones, Br. Pat. No. 475,047. Applied 11 May 1936; issued 11 Nov. 1937. V.A. Jones, "The Baird Electron Camera," *Television & Short-Wave World* **9** (Sept. 1936): pp. 487–490; V.A. Jones, "The Baird Electron Multiplier," *Television & Short-Wave World* **9** (Oct. 1936): pp. 568, 605.

9. "Outdoor Scene Is Broadcast in Successful Television Test," *New York Times*, 25 Apr. 1936, p. 1:4; "Test of Television Started in Secret," *New York Times*, 29 June 1936, p. 17:3.

10. "Inauguration of Daily Television Broadcast Schedule," *Radio Engineering* 16 (June 1936): p. 24; Don Lee, "Television on the West Coast," *Radio-Craft* 8 (Aug. 1936): pp. 76, 110.

11. "Report of the RMA Television Committee," *Radio Engineering* 16 (July 1936): pp. 19–20; "Radio Progress During 1936," *Proceedings of the Institute of Radio Engineers* 25 (Feb. 1937): p. 203.

12. "Ring Fight Shown in Television Test," *New York Times*, 12 Aug. 1936, p. 21:8; "Philco Television," *Radio Engineering* 16 (Sept. 1936): pp. 9–10; A.F. Murray, "The New Philco System of Television," *Radio-Craft* 8 (Nov. 1936): pp. 270, 315.

13. "First Details of the Farnsworth Television Camera," *Television & Short-Wave World* 9 (July 1936): pp. 395–396; P.T. Farnsworth, "An Improved Television Camera," *Radio-Craft* 8 (Aug. 1936); pp. 92, 113; "Radio Progress During 1936," *op. cit.* (n. 10.11), pp. 205–206; "Television at Hand" (this is simply a photograph of a Farnsworth camera at work), *Electronics* 9 (Dec. 1936): p. 14.

14. L. Klatzow, Br. Pat. No. 480,946. Applied 25 June 1936; issued 25 Feb. 1938.

15. Dr. C.B. Joliffe. "Television," *RCA Institutes Technical Press*, **1936**, pp. 25–26. (From a speech delivered June 15, 1936.)

16. "Radio Receiver Off Tune Aids Clearer Television," *New York Times*, 29 Nov. 1936, sec. XII, p. 10:5; W.J. Poch and D.W. Epstein, "Partial Suppression of One Side Band in Television Reception," *Proceedings of the Institute of Radio Engineers* 25 (Jan. 1937): pp. 15–31.

17. "We See Scophony Television," *Television & Short-Wave World* 9 (July 1936): pp. 391–393. See also "Scophony Television," *Electronics* 9 (Mar. 1936): pp. 30–33; L.M. Myers, "The Scophony System," *Television & Short-Wave World* 9 (Apr. 1936): pp. 201–205; J.H. Jefree, "The Scophony Light Control," *Television & Short-Wave World* 9 (May 1936): pp. 260–264, 310; "Optical Methods of Television," *London Times*, 11 July 1936, p. 19c.

18. "Television of Olympic Games," *London Times*, 18 July 1936, p. 14a; "Television of the Games, Disappointing Results," *London Times*, 3 Aug. 1936, p. 12a; "Television Shows Relay," *New York Times*, 10 Aug. 1936, p. 12:6; "Fernsehen bei den Olympischen Spielen 1936," *Fernsehen und Tonfilm* 7 (Aug. 1936): pp. 57–59; W. Federmann, "Fernsehen wahrend der Olympischen Spielen," *Telefunken* 75 (1937): pp. 18–22; "La télévision aux jeux Olympiques et à l'exposition de T.S.F. de Berlin," *L'Onde Electrique* 15 (Nov. 1936): pp. 729–739.

19. "Television This Week," *London Times*, 24 Aug. 1936, p. 10e; "A Newcomer at Olympia," *London Times*, 26 Aug. 1936, p. 13c; "First Television Broadcast, Demonstration at Radio Show," *London Times*, 26 Aug. 1936, p. 12g; "The Wireless Exhibition, Television Exhibits Prominent," *London Times*, 26 Aug. 1936, p. 10b; "The Wireless Exhibition, Experiments in Television," *London Times*, 27 Aug. 1936, p. 10b; "London Views First Telecast," *New York Times*, 6 Sept. 1936, sec. IX, p. 10:6; "Images Over London," *New York Times*, 23 Aug. 1936, p. 10:7; "Television Programmes, Regular Service in October," *London Times*, 8 Sept. 1936, p. 10c.

20. E.H. Traub, "Television at the Berlin Radio Exhibition, 1936," *Journal of the Television Society* 2 (Jan. 1935/Dec. 1938): pp. 181–187; M.K. Taylor, "A Summary of Impressions of the Berlin Television Exhibition, 1936," *Journal of the Television Society* 2 (Jan. 1935/Dec. 1938): pp. 188–191.

21. "Japan Conducts Television Tests," *Radio-Craft* 8 (Aug. 1936): p. 70; "Research in Television Planned in Japan," *New York Times*, 25 Oct. 1936, sec. X, p. 10:4.

22. "B.B.C. and Television, Trial Programs for a Month," *London Times*, 15

Sept. 1936, p. 16e; "Broadcasting, Inauguration of Television," *London Times*, 2 Nov. 1936, p. 216; "Television in London, Opening of Regular Service," *London Times*, 3 Nov. 1936, p. 9a; "B.B.C. Television Programme," *London Times*, 3 Nov. 1936, p. 9c; Birkenshaw, *op. cit.*, pp. 35–36; L.M. Gander, "The First of Many," *Journal of the Royal Television Society*, "50th Anniversary Issue," (Nov./Dec. 1977): pp. 42–43. Information on the performance of the dissector came from T.H. Bridgewater in a letter to the author, dated 16 June 1984.

23. "Baird Laboratories Destroyed in Crystal Palace Fire," *Television & Short-Wave World* **10** (Jan. 1937): p. 14.

24. L.H. Bedford and K.J. Magnusson, U.S. Pat. No. 2,162,908. Applied 5 Nov. 1936; issued 20 June 1939.

25. "Television," J. Van Der Mark, *Philips Technical Review* **1**, no. 11 (Nov. 1936): pp. 321–325.

26. "New Television Screen," *London Times*, 7 Dec. 1936, p. 12c; "Baird Big-Screen Television," *Television & Short-Wave World* **10** (Jan. 1937): p. 26–28.

27. "London Television Service, E.M.I. Transmissions in Future," *London Times*, 5 Feb. 1937, p. 14c; "British Television Bars Baird System," *New York Times*, 5 Feb. 1937, p. 8:6; "Television, Single Standard Welcomed," *London Times*, 6 Feb. 1937, p. 10c; "Statement by Baird Company," *London Times*, 6 Feb. 1937, p. 10c; Noel Ashbridge, "The British Television Service," *Joint Engineering Conference*, **1937**.

28. "More Television Planned for Philadelphia Area," *New York Times*, 10 Jan. 1937, sec. X, p. 12:2; "Tests of Televisions 441 Line Images Begun," *New York Times*, 24 Jan. 1937, sec, X, p. 12:8; "Dionnes Seen on Tele-Screen," *New York Times*, 18 Apr. 1937, sec, XI, p. 12:3.

RCA claimed that they had converted from 343 to 441 lines in January 1937. But they also stated that it wasn't until June 1937 that the process was perfected. However, it was still double side-band transmission of 2.5 megacycles on each side of the carrier. See "'Empire State' Television shows Marked Advance," *Radio News* **18** (July 1937): pp. 7–8, 60; "Television Shows Big Gain in Clarity," *New York Times*, 12 Feb. 1937, p. 24:8; "441-Line Television," *Radio Engineering* **17** (Feb. 1937): p. 5; "Philco Shows 441-Line Television," *Electronics* **10** (Mar. 1937): p. 9.

29. Standard Television & Cables, Br. Pat. No. 498,721, Conv. date 31 Mar. 1937; issued 12 Jan. 1939.

30. "Farnsworth Television," *Radio News* **18** (May 1937): pp. 654–5, 679, 688.

31. "Moscow Television Center to Use American Devices," *New York Times*, 2 May 1937, sec, XI, p. 12:2.

32. "New Tele-Lens Aids Big Screen," *New York Times*, 9 May 1937, sec. XI, p. 12:7; "New Lens Projector Flashes Television on a Screen," *New York Times*, 16 May 1937, sec. X, p. 12:1; "The Projection Kinescope Makes Its Debut," *Radio-Craft* **9** (Aug. 1937): p. 83, 110; "Big-Screen Television Pictures," *Radio News* **19** (Sept. 1937): p. 143, 173; V.K. Zworykin and W.H. Painter, "Development of the Projection Kinescope," *Proceedings of the Institute of Radio Engineers* **25** (Aug. 1937): pp. 937–953; R.R. Law, "High Current Electron Gun for Projection Kinescopes," *Proceedings of the Institute of Radio Engineers* **25** (Aug. 1937): pp. 954–976.

33. V.K. Zworykin, G.A. Morton, and L.E. Flory, "Theory and Performance of the Iconoscope," *Proceedings of the Institute of Radio Engineers* **25** (Aug. 1937): pp. 1071–1092 (paper received 30 Apr. 1937).

34. "A Tele-Van for London," *New York Times* (17 Jan. 1937, sec. X, p. 10:7; "Television Will Be Used at Coronation Procession," *N.Y. Times*, 27 Feb. 1937, p. 7:3; "World Listens in on Crowning Today," *New York Times*, 12 May 1937, p.

17:4; "Seen 30 Miles From London," *New York Times*, 30 May 1937, sec. X, p. 10:3; *Wireless World* **40** (19 June 1937): p. 577.

35. "Television Exhibition, Science Museum, London, June–September 1937," *Journal of the Television Society* **2** (June 1937): pp. 265–273. All efforts to get information as to the "working Campbell Swinton camera" have been in vain. A letter to *Wireless World* received a negative reply. Even Drs. J. McGee and H. Miller of EMI have no knowledge of this exhibit.

36. H. Miller and J.W. Strange, "The Electrical Reproduction of Images by the Photoconductive Effect," *Journal of the Physical Society* **50** (2 May 1938): pp. 374–384 (paper received 10 Nov. 1937); M. Knoll and F. Schröter, "Translation of Electron Pictures and Drawings with Insulating and Semi-Conducting Layers," *Physikalische Zeitschrift* (Leipzig) **38** (1 May 1937): pp. 330–333; Harley Iams and Albert Rose, "Television Pickup Tubes with Cathode-Ray Beam Scanning," *Proceedings of the Institute of Radio Engineers* **25** (Aug. 1937): pp. 1048–1070.

37. "Tennis Games Telecast," *New York Times*, 14 July 1937, sec. X, p. 8:5; "Televising Wimbledon," *Journal of the Television Society* **2** (June 1937): pp. 278–279.

38. "Television Deal Signed," *New York Times*, 26 July 1937, p. 8:4; Everson, *op. cit.*, pp. 155–159.

39. Iams and Rose, *op. cit.*, pp. 1061–1066.

40. E.H. Traub, "Television at the Berlin Radio Exhibition, 1937," *Journal of the Television Society* **2** (Jan. 1935/Dec. 1938): pp. 289–296.

41. "Radio Show Features Television," *New York Times*, 5 Sept. 1937, sec. X, p. 10:8; "Radiolympia, 1937," *Journal of the Television Society* **2** (June 1937): pp. 280–284.

42. "Television in England Moves Forward—Sales of Video Sets Increase," *New York Times*, 8 Aug. 1937, sec. X, p. 10:5; M.P. Wilder, "Television in Europe," *Electronics* **10** (Sept. 1937): pp. 13–15; H.M. Lewis and A.V. Loughren, "Television in Great Britain," *Electronics* **10** (Oct. 1937): pp. 32–35, 60–62; A.B. DuMont, "Is Television in America Asleep?" *Radio-Craft* **9** (Nov. 1937): pp. 268, 306.

43. "Grand Central Is Site of Television Studio," *New York Times*, 22 Aug. 1937, sec. X, p. 10:6; "How Soon Television?" *Radio News* **19** (Dec. 1937): pp. 327–328, 361; "Reviewing the Video Art, 'CBS Prepares'," *Electronics* **11** (Jan. 1938): p. 10.

44. "New Camera Is Promised," *New York Times*, 5 Sept. 1937, p. 10:8.

45. "Super Emitron Camera," *Wireless World* **41** (18 Nov. 1937): pp. 497–498; "The Cenotaph Service," *London Times*, 11 Nov. 1937, p. 19d; "Cenotaph Ceremony," *London Times*, 12 Nov. 1937, p. 11d; "A New Emitron Camera," *Television & Short-Wave World* **11** (Jan. 1938): pp. 11–12; "The Latest Emitron Camera," *Television & Short-Wave World* **11** (July 1938): p. 397; J.D. McGee and H.G. Lubszynski, "E.M.I. Cathode-Ray Television Transmission Tubes," *Proceedings of the Institute of Electrical Engineers* (London) **84** (Apr. 1939): pp. 468–475 (presented 20 July 1938, revised Oct. 1938).

46. "Transmit Movies by Coaxial Cable," *New York Times*, 10 Nov. 1937, sec. XI, p. 6:3; "Electrified Movies," *New York Times*, 28 Nov. 1937, p. 12:1; "Bell Labs Test Coaxial Cable," *Electronics* **10** (Dec. 1937): pp. 18–19.

47. "RCA Describes Television System," *Electronics* **10** (Jan. 1937): pp. 8–11, 48; E.W. Engstrom, G.L. Beers and A.V. Bedford, "Applications of Motion-Picture Film to Television," *RCA Review* **4** (July 1939): pp. 48–61.

48. "Rochester, 1937: 'Resonant-Line' Television Modulation System Described by Parker," *Electronics* **10** (Dec. 1937): pp. 11–14.

49. "Television on a Large Screen," *London Times*, 10 Dec. 1937, p. 14c.

50. "Television on a Large Screen," *London Times*, 8 Dec. 1937, sec. X, p. 16f; "Movies Accept a Challenge," *New York Times*, 26 Dec. 1937, p. 12:3; "Scophony Demonstration on B.B.C. Television," *Television & Short-Wave World* 11 (Jan. 1938): pp. 23–25.

51. "Television Van Comes to Town," *New York Times*, 12 Dec. 1937, sec. XI, p. 14:1.

52. Allen Du Mont, U.S. Pat. No. 2,157,749. Applied 11 Jan. 1938; issued 9 May 1939.

53. Georges Valensi, Br. Pat. No. 524,443. Applied 17 Jan. 1938 (also 30 Apr. and 1 June 1938); issued 7 Aug. 1940.

54. "On a Storing Pickup Device with a Semi-Conducting Dialectric." *Zeitschrift für Technische Physik* 19 (Mar. 1938): pp. 63–73 (paper received 10 Jan. 1938).

55. G.V. Braude, Russ. Pat. No. 55,712. Applied 3 Feb. 1938; issued 30 Sept. 1939; "A New Type of the Mosaic for the Television Pick Up Tubes," *Journal of Physics* (U.S.S.R.), **1945**, pp. 348–350.

56. "First Colour Television," *London Times*, 5 Feb. 1938, p. 12f; "Color Is Transmitted in Television Program," *New York Times*, 5 Feb. 1938, p. 2:5; "Baird Colour Television," *Television & Short-Wave World* 11 (Mar. 1938): pp. 151–152.

57. "A. Du Mont Demonstrates New System," *New York Times*, 6 Feb. 1938, p. 7:5; "Lifting Radio's Blindfold," *New York Times*, 13 Feb. 1938, sec. X, p. 12:1; "Television Without Sync Signals," *Electronics* 11 (Mar. 1938): pp. 33–34, 68.

58. "Tests Projector to Televise Film," *New York Times*, 30 Mar. 1938, p. 18:1; H.S. Bamford, "A New Television Film Projector," *Electronics* 11 (July 1938): p. 25; "Latest Continuous-Film Television," *Radio-Craft* 10 (Aug. 1938): pp. 95–112; "Continuous Film Method," *Television & Short-Wave World* 11 (Aug. 1938): p. 452.

59. "High Definition," *Electronics* 11 (Apr. 1938): p. 32; "10×12 Foot, 441 Line Scan-Disc Television!" *Radio-Craft* 10 (Dec. 1938): p. 39.

60. Peter C. Goldmark, U.S. Pat. No. 2,287,033. Applied 28 May 1938; issued 23 June 1942.

61. "A New Farnsworth 'Pick-Up' Tube, Amplification Before Scanning," *Television & Short-Wave World* 11 (May 1938): p. 260; P.T. Farnsworth and B.C. Gardner, "Image Amplifier Pickup Tubes," paper presented at I.R.E. Rochester Fall Meeting, Rochester, N.Y., 14 Nov. 1938; "New Vacuum Tube Clears Television," *New York Times*, 15 Nov. 1938, p. 19:3; "Rochester 1938: Farnsworth's New Tube," *Electronics* 11 (Dec. 1938): pp. 8–9.

62. A.F. Murray, "RMA Completes Television Standards," *Electronics* 11 (July 1938): pp. 28–29, 55.

63. "Trooping the Colour," *London Times*, 19 July 1938, p. 14d; "The Baird Big-Screen Theatre Receiver," *Television & Short-Wave World* 11 (Aug. 1938): pp. 459–460; "The Radio Month in Review," Theatre Television, *Radio-Craft* 10 (Dec. 1938): p. 327.

64. "How the Derby Will Be Televised, Coming O.B.'s," *Television & Short-Wave World* 11 (May 1938): p. 291; "Television's Greatest Thrill," *Television & Short-Wave World* 11 (July 1938): p. 389.

65. "Wireless Exhibition at Olympia," *London Times*, 28 July 1938, p. 12d; "Cheaper Television," *London Times*, 6 Aug. 1938, p. 6g; "On the Television Front," *New York Times*, 7 Aug. 1938, sec. IX, p. 8:6; "British Try to Spur Television," *New York Times*, 21 Aug. 1938, sec. IX, p. 8:6; "Simplifying the Wireless Set," *London Times*, 24 Aug. 1938, p. 7a; "Television Demand at Olympia," *London Times*, 30 Aug. 1938, p. 7f; "Questions on Television," *New York Times*, 4 Sept. 1938, sec. X, p. 10:6.

66. H. Iams, G.A. Morton and V.K. Zworykin, "The Image Iconoscope," *Proceedings of the Institute of Radio Engineers* **27** (Sept. 1939): pp. 541–547. For the work of EMI on the Image Iconoscope, see also McGee and Lubszynski, *op. cit.*, pp. 468–482.

67. Harley Iams, U.S. Pat. No. 2,213,548. Applied 31 May 1938; issued 3 Sept. 1940. Albert Rose, U.S. Pat. No. 2,213,174. Applied 30 July 1938; issued 27 Aug. 1940.

68. Albert Rose and Harley Iams, "Television Pick-up Tubes Using Low-Velocity Electron Beam Scanning," *Proceedings of the Institute of Radio Engineers* **27** (Sept. 1939): pp. 547–555 (paper received 12 Sept. 1938).

69. Werner Flechsig, DRP Pat. No. 736,575. Applied 12 July 1938; issued 13 May 1943.

70. E.H. Traub, "English and Continental Television," *Journal of the Television Society* **11** (Jan. 1935/Dec. 1938): pp. 457–464; E.H. Traub, "Television at the Berlin Radio Exhibition, 1938," *Television & Short-Wave World* **11** (Sept. 1938): pp. 542–544; (Oct. 1938): Part II, pp. 606–607; "Flickerless Film-Television," *Radio-Craft* **10** (Jan. 1938): p. 395.

71. David W. Epstein, U.S. Pat. No. 2,251,786. Applied 30 Sept. 1938; issued 5 Aug. 1941.

72. "Enthusiastic Welcome for Mr. Chamberlain" (photograph), *London Times*, 1 Oct. 1938, p. 7e; "News by Television," *Television & Short-Wave World* **11** (Nov. 1938): p. 664; "Two Years of Television," *London Times*, 23 Dec. 1938, p. 11f; Gordon Ross, *Television Jubilee: The Story of 25 Years of BBC Television*, (London: W.H. Allen, 1961), photograph after p. 168 entitled "Peace in Our Time" shows the EMI Super-Emitron camera taking pictures of the event.

73. "Television Here and Abroad," *N.Y. Times*, 6 Nov. 1938, sec. IX, p. 10:5.

74. "Wins Basic Patent in Television Field," *New York Times*, 22 Dec. 1938, p. 38:6; "Notes on Television," *New York Times*, 25 Dec. 1938, sec. IX, p. 12:7; "Basic Television Patent Issued," *Broadcasting* **16** (1939): p. 71.

75. *Zworykin File.* This information comes from the original patent application no. 683,337 that Zworykin filed on 29 Dec. 1923. The file shows the progress of the patent through the U.S. Patent Office. It has all of the rejections, interferences, correspondence, etc., until the patent was finally granted on 10 Nov. 1938.

76. V.K. Zworykin, U.S. Pat. No. 2,280,877. Applied 26 Nov. 1938, issued 28 Apr. 1942.

77. V.K. Zworykin, U.S. Pat. No. 2,285,551. Applied 20 Dec. 1938; issued 9 June 1942.

78. Marconi's Wireless Telegraph Co., Br. Pat. No. 537,738. Conv. date 30 Dec. 1938 (1 Jan. 1940); issued 4 July 1941.

79. "Television Transmitters," *Electronics* **12** (Mar. 1939): pp. 26–29, 47.

80. "London Television Faces are Seen on Long Island in Freak Reception," *New York Times*, 5 Feb. 1939, sec. IX, p. 12:4; "London Faces Filmed Here," *New York Times*, 19 Feb. 1939, sec. IX, p. 12:3; "First Photographs of Transatlantic High-Definition Television," *Television & Short-Wave World* **12** (Apr. 1939): p. 224; "Telegossip, Transatlantic Results," *Television & Short-Wave World* **12** (Apr. 1939): p. 225.

81. "Television Images of Life-Size Shown," *New York Times*, 15 Feb. 1939, p. 14:4.

82. "Fight Telecast to Theatres," *New York Times*, 26 Feb. 1939, p. 10:6; "Television Here and Abroad," *New York Times*, 5 Mar. 1939. p. 10:8; "Notes on Television," *New York Times*, 12 Mar. 1939, sec. XI, p. 10:7; "Television Shows in Movies Planned," *New York Times*, 5 Apr. 1939, p. 27:6; "Gaumont-British

Plans Theatre Installation of Television in New York," *Broadcasting* **16** (15 Apr. 1939): p. 73.

83. "Notes on Television," *New York Times*, 12 Mar. 1939, sec. XI, p. 10:7; "The Race Televised," *London Times*, 25 May 1939, p. 10f; "Television Shows Derby to London," *New York Times*, 25 May 1939, p. 27:5; "Relay Television Service," *London Times*, 17 Apr. 1939, p. 17e; "Images Viewed on Big Screen," *New York Times*, 2 July 1939, sec. IX, p. 10:7; "The EMI Cinema Projector," *Television & Short-Wave World* **12** (July 1939): pp. 389–390.

84. "Portable Apparatus for Television Seen," *New York Times*, 8 Mar. 1939, p. 23:6; "Philco's Portable Video Transmitter Shown to Dealers at New York Session," *Broadcasting* **16** (15 Mar. 1939): p. 26.

85. "General Electric (U.S.A.) Television," *Television & Short-Wave World* **12** (Mar. 1939): p. 133.

86. "Television Receivers in Production," *Electronics* **12** (Mar. 1939): pp. 23–25, 78–81; "Plans Completed for RCA's Video Exhibition at Fair," *Broadcasting* **16** (1 Apr. 1939): pp. 31, 45; "Farnsworth Plans to Raise New Capital," *New York Times*, 10 Feb. 1939, p. 36:5.

87. "Dedication of RCA Seen on Television," *New York Times*, 21 Apr. 1939, p. 16:1; "New York Display Dedicated by RCA," *Broadcasting* **16** (1 May 1939): p. 21; "America Makes a Start," *Television & Short-Wave World* **12** (June 1939): p. 330; D.H. Castle, "A Television-Demonstration System for the New York World's Fair," *RCA Review* **4** (July 1939): pp. 6–13.

88. "Telecast of President to Start Regular Service," *New York Times*, 6 Apr. 1939, p. 22:3; "Telecasts," *New York Times*, 23 Apr. 1939, sec. X, p. 10:6; "Today's Eye-Opener," *New York Times*, 30 Apr. 1939, sec. XI, p. 12:1; "Ceremony Is Carried by Television as Industry Makes Its Formal Bow," *New York Times*, 1 May 1939, p. 8:3; "Television Motif Marks New York Fair," *Broadcasting* **16** (1 May 1939): pp. 20–21; "Act I Reviewed," *New York Times*, 7 May 1939, sec. X, p. 12:1.

89. O.E. Dunlap, "Watching a Battle," *New York Times*, 1 June 1939, sec. XI, p. 10:1; T.H. Hutchinson, "Programming the Television Mobile Unit," *RCA Review* **4** (Oct. 1939): pp. 154–161.

90. D.C. Espley and D.O. Walter, "Television Film Transmitters Using Apertured Discs," *Journal of the Institute of Electrical Engineers* (London) **88** (June 1941): pp. 145–169.

91. "Notes on Television," *New York Times*, 11 June 1939, sec. IX, p. 8:5; "New Faces and New Ways," *New York Times*, 23 July 1939, sec. IX, p. 10:5; "The Orthicon," *Electronics* **12** (July 1939): pp. 11–14, 58–59; Albert Rose and Harley Iams, "The Orthicon: A Television Pick-up Tube," *RCA Review* **4** (Oct. 1939): pp. 186–199.

92. "Television in Colour," *London Times*, 28 July 1939, p. 12e; "On the Television Front," *New York Times*, 13 Aug. 1939, sec. IX, p. 9:3; F.W. Marchant, "A New Baird Colour-Television System," *Television & Short-Wave World* **12** (Sept. 1939): pp. 541–542.

93. A.A. Gulliland, "Television in Germany 1939, by Our Berlin Correspondent," *Television & Short-Wave World* **12** (Sept. 1939): pp. 538–539.

94. See the following articles in *Journal of Applied Physics* **10** (July 1939): David Sarnoff, "Probable Influences of Television on Society," pp. 426–431; Knox McIlwain, "Survey of Television Pick-Up Devices," pp. 432–442; Pierre Mertz, "High Definition Television," pp. 443–446; Peter C. Goldmark, "Problems of Television Transmission," pp. 447–454; E.W. Engstrom, "Television Receiving and Reproducing Systems," pp. 455–464.

95. "Radio Exhibition: Opening To-day to Be Televised," *London Times*, 23 Aug. 1939, p. 8f; "Britain's World Lead in Television," *London Times*, 24 Aug.

1939, p. 8a; "New Industry Booms," *New York Times*, 19 Mar. 1939, sec. XI, p. 5:3; "Aspects of Television: Discussed at the Television Convention — Olympia 1939." *Electronics and Television & Short-Wave World* 12 (Oct. 1939): p. 588.

96. "Televiews of Pictures," *New York Times*, 17 Sept. 1939, sec. X, p. 8:8; "London 'Eyes' America," *New York Times*, 14 May 1939, sec. XI, p. 8:3.

97. "RCA-Farnsworth Pact," *Broadcasting* 17 (15 Oct. 1939): p. 75; Everson, *op. cit.*, pp. 242–247.

98. "Tele-Notes," *New York Times*, 18 June 1939, sec. IX, p. 8:7; "Don Lee Schedules," *Broadcasting* 17 (15 Nov. 1939): p. 86.

99. B. Robertson, "Reception of Television in Airplane over Capital Marks RCA Anniversary," *Broadcasting* 17 (1 Nov. 1939): p. 36.

100. "Television Notes: Farnsworth Exhibit," *Broadcasting* 17 (1 Nov. 1939): p. 65. A photograph of the Farnsworth television camera is shown.

101. Technische Hochshule of Zurich, Br. Pat. No. 543,485. Applied 8 Nov. 1939; issued 27 Feb. 1942.

102. "Limited Commercial Television May Be Recommended to FCC," *Broadcasting* 17 (1 Nov. 1939): p. 34; "Relax Video Rules, FCC Group Urges," *Broadcasting* 17 (15 Nov. 1939): pp. 17, 81; "Television Rules Given FCC Study," *Broadcasting* 17 (1 Dec. 1939): p. 25; "FCC Studies Commission Report," *New York Times*, 3 Dec. 1939, sec. IX, p. 16:7; "J.L. Fly, Outlook," *New York Times*, 10 Dec. 1939, sec. X, p. 12:7; "Hearing Ordered on Proposed New Television Rules," *Broadcasting* 17 (1 Jan. 1940): pp. 19, 58.

103. "The Diavisor: A New Type of Transmitting Tube," *Electronics and Television & Short-Wave World* 12 (Dec. 1939): pp. 686–689.

11. The First NTSC: 1940–1941

1. Photo (no caption) of Rose Bowl Parade telecast, *Broadcasting* 18 (1 Feb. 1940): p. 62.

2. Lessing, *op. cit.*, pp. 199–200; "Notes on Television," *New York Times*, 28 Jan. 1940, sec. IX, p. 10:4; "Future of Television in Lap of the FCC," *Broadcasting* 18 (1 Feb. 1940): pp. 24–27, 52; "FM Gets Its 'Day in Court'," *Electronics* 13 (Oct. 1940): pp. 14–16, 74–78.

3. "FCC Members Tour Television Stations," *New York Times*, 3 Feb. 1940, p. 8:3.

4. "See Television in Color," *New York Times*, 6 Feb. 1940, p. 18:5; "FCC Studies Television, Defers Action," *Broadcasting* 18 (15 Feb. 1940): p. 36; R.K. Kilbon, "Pioneering in Electronics," *op. cit.*, p. 221.

5. "Notes on Television," *New York Times*, 11 Feb. 1940, sec. IX, p. 10:5; "Faces in a Blizzard," *New York Times*, 18 Feb. 1940, sec. IX, p. 12:4.

6. "FCC Moves to Widen Use of Television," *New York Times*, 1 Mar. 1940, p. 13:1; "Hails Television Report," *New York Times*, 2 Mar. 1940, p. 25:7; "FCC Television Report to Release Ad Drive," *New York Times*, 3 Mar. 1940, p. 6:7; "Drive to Promote Video Set Sales Started by RCA," *Broadcasting* 18 (15 Mar. 1940): p. 86; "Lengthy Video Announcement Is Required at Station Breaks," *Broadcasting* 18 (15 Mar. 1940): pp. 37–68; "Text of New FCC Rules Governing Television," *Broadcasting* 18 (15 Mar. 1940): pp. 37–55; "FCC Reopens Television Hearings April 8," *Broadcasting* 18 (1 Apr. 1950): pp. 22–50; "Television Hearing Re-Opened," *Radio-Craft* 12 (June 1940): p. 714.

7. A.H. Rosenthal, "The Skiatron — A New Scophony Development Towards Large-Screen Television Projection," *Electronics and Television & Short-Wave World* 13 (Feb. 1940): pp. 522–555; (Mar. 1940): Part II, pp. 117–119; A.H. Rosenthal, "A System of Large-Screen Television Reception Based on Certain

Electron Phenomena in Crystals," *Proceedings of the Institute of Radio Engineers* **28** (May 1940): pp. 211–212.

8. "Photographing Television Programmes," *Electronics and Television & Short-Wave World* **13** (Mar. 1940): p. 124.

9. "Cathode-Ray View Finder for the Emitron," *Electronics and Television & Short-Wave World* **13** (Mar. 1940): p. 108.

10. V.K. Zworykin, *Engineering Notebook*, dated July 13, 1931. This was first described in an article by the author. See: Albert Abramson, "Pioneers of Television—Vladimir K. Zworykin," *Journal of the Society of Motion Picture and Television Engineers* **90** (July 1981), p. 586.

11. W.S. Brown, Br. Pat. No. 539,419. Applied 5 Feb. 1940; issued 10 Sept. 1941. W.S. Brown, Br. Pat. No. 541,860. Applied 5 Feb. 1940; issued 15 Dec. 1941. J.D. McGee and G.S.P. Freeman, Br. Pat. No. 542,488. Applied 2 May 1940; issued 12 Jan. 1942. J.D. McGee, H. Miller and G.S.P. Freeman, Br. Pat. No. 542,496. Applied 2 May 1940; issued 12 Jan. 1942. J.D. McGee, H. Miller and G.S.P. Freeman, Br. Pat. No. 542,497. Applied 2 May 1940; issued 12 Jan. 1942. J.D. McGee and H.G. Lubszynski, Br. Pat. No. 542,245. Applied 27 June 1940; issued 1 Jan. 1942.

12. "Recent Developments in Electron Engineering," Photo captioned, "B.T.H. Iconoscope Scanning Equipment in the Television Laboratory," *Electronics and Television & Short-Wave World* **13** (Apr. 1940): p. 157.

13. B. Robertson, "First Telecast from Plane Successful as RCA Demonstrates New Equipment," *Broadcasting* **18** (15 Mar. 1940): p. 24.

14. "FCC Stays Start in Television, Rebukes R.C.A. for Sales Drive," *New York Times*, 24 Mar. 1940, p. 1:6; "FCC Reopens Television Hearings April 8," *Broadcasting* **18** (1 Apr. 1940): pp. 22–50; "Freezing of Television Feared by FCC, Says Chairman Fly," *Broadcasting* **18** (1 Apr. 1940): p. 22.

15. S. Taishoff, "Flexible Television Is Urged by President," *Broadcasting* **18** (15 Apr. 1940): p. 18d; U.S. Senate, Committee on Interstate Commerce, *Development of Television*, Hearings Committee, 10 and 11 Apr. 1940 (Washington, D.C.: Gov. Printing Office, 1940), p. 38.

16. L.V. Gilpin, "Running Account of FCC Hearings on Television," *Broadcasting* **18** (15 Apr. 1940): pp. 74-A-D, 84–85; "Television Back on Experimental Shelf," *Broadcasting* **18** (1 June 1940): pp. 17, 88–89.

17. "Notes on Television," *New York Times*, 28 Apr. 1940, sec. IX, p. 10:7; "A New Tube Simplifies Television for Amateurs," *New York Times*, 9 June 1940, sec. IX, p. 8:4; "RCA Demonstrates Ham Video Tube," *Broadcasting* **18** (15 June 1940): p. 73; J.J. Lamb, "A New Iconoscope for Amateur Television Cameras," *QST* **24** (June 1940): pp. 13–14, 97–99; "An Experimental Miniature Iconoscope," *Electronics and Television & Short-Wave World* **13** (July 1940): pp. 292, 296.

18. "Projection 'Gun' Shoots Televiews: The Aim Is to Hit a Theatre Screen," *New York Times*, 12 May 1940, sec. IX, p. 10:5; "RCA Large-Screen Television with Clear Images Is Exhibited," *Broadcasting* **18** (15 May 1940): p. 32.

19. S. Taishoff and L.V. Gilpin, "Birth of Commercial FM This Year Seen," *Broadcasting* **18** (1 Apr. 1940): pp. 18–21, 80–83; "Summary of the Case for FM Broadcasting," *Broadcasting* **18** (1 May 1940): pp. 37, 70; "RCA Asks to Retain Present Television Bands," *Broadcasting* **18** (1 May 1940): pp. 37, 71; "Hints of Commercial Television Noted in FCC License Grants," *Broadcasting* **18** (1 July 1940): p. 28; L. Lessing, *op. cit.*, pp. 198–201; Lyons, *op. cit.*, pp. 257–258; "Dream Comes True," *Broadcasting* **18** (1 June 1940): p. 86.

20. "Coverage of GOP Convention to Include Television Pickups," *Broadcasting* **18** (15 June 1940): p. 22; O.B. Hanson, "RCA-NBC Television Presents a

Political Convention as First Long Distance Pick Up," *RCA Review* 5 (Jan. 1941): pp. 267–282.

21. "Television Audiences, Etc.," accompanied by a photo of a Philco television camera, *Broadcasting* 18 (1 July 1940): p. 16; S. Kaufman, "The Video Reporter," *Radio News* 24 (Sept. 1940): p. 29–58.

22. "FCC Pledges Help in Television Field," *New York Times*, 1 Aug. 1940, p. 23:5; "Ten Video Stations Granted by FCC as Interest Slackens," *Broadcasting* 18 (1 Aug. 1940): p. 101; "Standards Group Sets Course for Television Set-Up," *Broadcasting* 18 (15 Aug. 1940): p. 50; "New York Television Stations Adapting Plants to New Bands," *Broadcasting* 18 (1 Sept. 1940): p. 44; S. Kaufman, "The Video Reporter," *Radio News* 24 (Oct. 1940): p. 31; "News and Notes of the Advertising Field," *New York Times*, 14 Oct. 1940, p. 80:2; "Industry Accord Over Television Standards Seen," *Broadcasting* 18 (15 Oct. 1940): p. 102; "Video Standards Sought by Jan. 1," *Broadcasting* 18 (1 Nov. 1940): p. 80; "Video Panels to Report Their Progress Jan. 27," *Broadcasting* 18 (15 Nov. 1940): p. 76; D.G. Fink, *Television Standards and Practice* (New York and London: McGraw-Hill, 1943). This is the classic work on the organization, operation and results of the first NTSC committee. For the actual records see "Proceedings of the National Television Systems Committee," 27 Jan. 1941 (1940/1941, in four volumes).

23. "Television in Los Angeles," *New York Times*, 25 Aug. 1940, sec. IX, p. 10:4; see also *Broadcasting* 18 (1 Sept. 1940): p. 40.

24. "Color Television Success in Test," *New York Times*, 30 Aug. 1940, p. 21:3; "Color Television Achieves Realism," *New York Times*, 5 Sept. 1940, p. 18:6; "Painting Telepictures," *New York Times*, 8 Sept. 1940, sec. IX, p. 10:7; "New Color Television System Developed Secretly by CBS," *Broadcasting* 18 (1 Sept. 1940): p. 92; "Color Television by 1941 Is Forecast," *Broadcasting* 18 (15 Sept. 1940): pp. 38, 42; "Color Television Exhibited to FCC," *Broadcasting* 18 (1 Oct. 1940): p. 89; "Televiews on the Air," *New York Times* (13 Oct. 1940): p. 12:1.

25. "Color Television Demonstrated by CBS Engineers," *Electronics* 13 (Oct. 1940): pp. 32–34, 73–74; "Columbia Colour Television," *Electronics and Television & Short-Wave World* 13 (Nov. 1940): pp. 488–490.

26. P.C. Goldmark, U.S. Pat. No. 2,304,081. Applied 7 Sept. 1940; issued 8 Dec. 1942. P.C. Goldmark, U.S. Pat. No. 2,480,571. Applied 7 Sept. 1940; issued 30 Aug. 1949. P.C. Goldmark, Br. Pat. No. 647,714. Conv. date 7 Sept. 1940 (applied 11 Oct. 1946); issued 20 Dec. 1950. P.C. Goldmark, Br. Pat. No. 647,715. Conv. date 7 Sept. 1940 (applied 11 Oct. 1946); issued 20 Dec. 1950. "Goldmark Claims Pickups in Color," *Broadcasting* 18 (15 Nov. 1940); p. 87; "Rochester . . . 1940," *Electronics* 13 (Dec. 1940): pp. 25–27.

27. "Answer of CBS Denies Television Charge of Sarnoff," *Broadcasting* 18 (15 May 1940): p. 80; S. Kaufman, "The Video Reporter," *Radio News* 24 (July 1940): p. 29–43.

28. R.B. Janes, R.E. Johnson, and R.S. Moore, "Development and Performance of Television Camera Tubes," *RCA Review* 10 (June 1949): pp. 191–223.

29. A. Rose, Serial No. 357,543. Applied 20 Sept. 1940; no patent granted.

30. See A. Rose, U.S. Patent No. 2,506,741. Applied 20 Sept. 1940; applied 28 Nov. 1945; issued 8 May 1950. The May 10, 1940, date comes from this patent file. A. Rose, Br. Pat. No. 613,003. Conv. date 20 Sept. 1940 (applied 19 Sept. 1941); issued 22 Nov. 1948.

31. S. Kaufman, "The Video Reporter," *op. cit.* (n. 11.22); p. 58.

32. "Color Television Tested," *New York Times*, 22 Nov. 1940, p. 39:6; "Video Committee Busy in Experiments; GE Demonstrates Colored Television," *Broadcasting* 18 (1 Dec. 1940): p. 30.

33. E. Crosby, U.S. Pat. 2,296,908. Appl. 10 Dec. 1940; issued 29 Sept. 1942.

34. "Progress in Colour Television," *London Times*, 21 Dec. 1940, p. 7f.

35. "Industry Drafting Television Report," *Broadcasting* 19 (20 Jan. 1941): p. 54; "Television Progress Speeded Up," *New York Times*, 19 Jan. 1941, sec. IX, p. 10:8.

36. A.G. Jensen, "Film Scanner for Use in Television Transmission Tests," *Proceedings of the Institute of Radio Engineers* 29 (May 1941): pp. 243–249 (paper presented 11 Jan. 1941); "Television Process Speeded Up," *op. cit.* (n. 11.35); "Distance Record for Video Signals," *Broadcasting* 19 (20 Jan. 1941): p. 48.

37. "Baird High Definition Colour Television," *Journal of the Television Society* 3 (1939–1943): pp. 171–174 (included the colored picture from "Television in Colour," *Electronics and Television & Short-Wave World* 14 [Apr. 1941]: inset between pp. 152–153); "A Brief History of Colour Television," *Electronics and Television & Short-Wave World* 14 (May 1941): p. 228.

38. "Scophony Exhibits Video on Screen," *Broadcasting* 19 (20 Jan. 1941): p. 45; "Television Progress Speeded Up," *op. cit.*

39. "FCC Orders Hearing on Video Report," *Broadcasting* 19 (3 Feb. 1941); pp. 18, 36A; L.V. Gilpin, "FCC Paves Way to Commercial Television," *Broadcasting* 19 (3 Mar. 1941): pp. 14, 56; "NTSC Television Standards," *Communications* 21 (Feb. 1941): pp. 12–13; Fink, *Television Standards and Practice, op. cit.* (n. 11.22): pp. 18–24.

40. "Proposals to Change Television Standards," *New York Times*, 21 Mar. 1941, p. 22:3; L.V. Gilpin, "RCA Seeks Television Unity to Avoid More False Starts," *Broadcasting* 19 (24 Mar. 1941): pp. 16, 48–49; "Television Ready to Go, FCC Is Told," *New York Times*, 25 Mar. 1941, p. 25:2.

41. R.V. Jones, *The Wizard War* (New York: Coward, McCann & Geoghegan, 1978), pp. 174–178; A. Price, *Instruments of Darkness* (New York: Charles Scribner's Sons, 1979), pp. 47–51; B. Johnson, *The Secret War* (New York, Toronto, London, Sydney: Methuen, 1978), pp. 57–60.

42. "Color Television Given First Exhibition by NBC," *Broadcasting* 19 (5 May 1941): p. 41.

43. "Television Authorized by FCC on a Full Commercial Basis," *Broadcasting* 20 (5 May 1941): p. 12.

44. "Television Show Given in Theatre," *New York Times*, 10 May 1941, p. 17:6; "Latest Television Progress Is Shown During FCC Tour," *Broadcasting* 19 (27 Jan. 1941): pp. 47–49; "Some Recent Television Developments," *Communications* 21 (Feb. 1941): pp. 10–11, 23–25; "Engineers Send Theatre-Size Images," *New York Times*, 6 Apr. 1941, sec. IX, p. 12:1.

45. I.G. Maloff and W.A. Tolson, "A Resume of the Technical Aspects of the RCA Theatre-Television," *RCA Review* 6 (July 1941): pp. 5–11.

46. "Electronic Viewfinder for Television Camera," *Electronics* 14 (July 1941): pp. 58–59; "Electronic Viewfinder," *Review of Scientific Instruments* 12 (Sept. 1941): p. 451; R.L. Campbell, R.E. Kessler, R.E. Rutherford, and K.U. Landsberg, "Mobile Television Equipment," *Proceedings of the Institute of Radio Engineers* 30 (Jan. 1942): pp. 1–7 (paper presented 23 June 1941).

47. M.A. Trainer, "Orthicon Portable Television Equipment," *Proceedings of the Institute of Radio Engineers* 30 (Jan. 1942): pp. 15–19 (paper presented 25 June 1941).

48. A. Rose, "The Relative Sensitivities of Television Pickup Tubes, Photographic Film, and the Human Eye," *Proceedings of the Institute of Radio Engineers* 30 (June 1942): pp. 293–300 (paper presented 25 June 1941).

49. "Tests of Television Setups Are Made: Plans for July 1 Operations Uncertain," *Broadcasting* 19 (9 June 1941): p. 38; "Video Rate Card Prepared by NBC for July 1 Start," *Broadcasting* 19 (23 June 1941): p. 54; "Television Starts Today,"

New York Times, 1 July 1941, p. 15:4; "Regular Television On," *New York Times*, 2 July 1941, p. 17:8; "Imagery for Profit," *New York Times*, 6 July 1941, sec. IX, p. 10:7; "Novel Commercials in Video Debut," *Broadcasting* 19 (7 July 1941): p. 10.

50. J.L. Baird, Br. pat. No. 552,582. Applied 11 July 1941; issued 15 Apr. 1943; "New Progress in Television," *London Times*, 19 Dec. 1941, p. 2d; "Television in Colour and Stereoscopic Effect," *Journal of the Television Society* 3 (1939-1943): pp. 225-226; "Three dimensional color television" (abstract), *Electronics* 15 (May 1942): p. 76; "Colour and stereoscopic television," *Electrical Engineer* 15 (Aug. 1942): pp. 96-97; A.A. Gulliland, "John Logie Baird and Stereoscopic Television," *Radio News* 30 (Radionics Section) (July 1943): pp. 8-24.

51. P.C. Goldmark, J.N. Dryer, E.R. Piore, and J.M. Hollywood, "Color Television — Part I," *Proceedings of the Institute of Radio Engineers* 30 (Apr. 1942): pp. 162-182 (paper presented in part 3 Oct. 1940; manuscript received 2 Sept. 1941); P.C. Goldmark, E.R. Piore, J.M. Hollywood, T.H. Chambers, and J.J. Reeves, "Color Television — Part II," *Proceedings of the Institute of Radio Engineers* 30 (Sept. 1943): pp. 465-478; "CBS Field Tests for Color Video," *Broadcasting* 19 21 Apr. 1941: p. 49.

52. A.H. Rosenthal, "Storage in Television Reception," *Electronics* 14 (Oct. 1941): pp. 46-49, 115-116.

53. "RCA Sees Commercial Television Retarded by Defense Program," *New York Times*, 7 May 1941, p. 27:3; "RCA Studies Future of Video But Sees Rather Dim Future," *Broadcasting* 19 (12 May 1941): p. 92; Lyons, *op. cit.*, pp. 259-260, 1966.

Selected Bibliography

Abramson, A. *Electronic Motion Pictures*. Berkeley: University of California Press, 1955.
Aisberg, E., and R. Aschen. *Theorie et Pratique de la Télévision*. Paris: Chiron, 1932.
Archer, Gleason L. *History of Radio to 1926*. New York: American Historical, 1938.
_____. *Big Business and Radio*. New York: American Historical, 1939.
Ardenne, Manfred von. *Funk-Empfangs-Technik*. Berlin: Rothgiesser & Diesing AG, 1934.
_____. *Television Reception*. New York: D. Van Nostrand, Inc., 1936.
_____. *Cathode-Ray Tubes*. London: Sir Isaac Pitman & Sons, Ltd., 1939.
Baird, M. *Television Baird*. Cape Town: Haum, 1973.
Baker, T. Thorne. *Wireless Pictures and Television*. London: Constable, 1926.
Baker, W.J. *A History of the Marconi Co.* London: Methuen, 1970.
Barnouw, Eric. *A Tower in Babel*. New York: Oxford University Press, 1966.
_____. *The Golden Web*. New York: Oxford University Press, 1968.
Benson, Thomas W. *Fundamentals of Television*. New York: Mancall, 1930.
Blake, G.G. *History of Radio Telegraphy and Telephony*. London: Chapman and Hall, 1928.
Briggs, Asa. *The Golden Age of Wireless, Vol. II*. London: Oxford University Press, 1965.
Bruch, Walter. *Die Fernseh Story*. Stuttgart: Franckh'sche Verlagshandlung, 1969.
Burns, R.W. *British Television, the Formative Years*. United Kingdom: Peter Peregrinus Ltd., 1986.
Cameron, James R. *Radio and Television*. Woodmont: Cameron, 1933.
_____. *Television for Beginners*. Coral Gables, Fla.: Cameron, 1947.
Camm, F.J. *Newnes Television and Short-Wave Handbook*. London: Georges Newnes, 1934.
_____. *Newnes Television Manual*. London: Georges Newnes, 1942.
Ceram, C.W. *Archaeology of the Cinema*. New York: Harcourt, Brace & World, 1965.
Chapple, H.J. Barton. *Television for the Amateur Constructor*. London: Sir Isaac Pitman, 1933.
_____. *Popular Television*. London: Sir Isaac Pitman, 1935.
Cocking, W.T. *Television Receiving Equipment*. London: Iliffe, 1940.
Collins, A. Frederick. *Experimental Television*. Boston: Lothrop, Lee and Shepard, 1932.
Crawley, C. *From Telegraphy to Television*. London: Warne, 1931.

De Forest, Lee. *Television: Today and Tomorrow*. New York: The Dial Press, 1942.

Dinsdale, A. *Television*. London: Sir Isaac Pitman, 1926.

_____. *Television*. London: Television Press, 1928.

_____. *First Principles of Television*. London: Chapman and Hall, 1932.

Dunlap, Orrin E. *The Outlook for Television*. New York and London: Harper & Brothers, 1932.

_____. *Radio's 100 Men of Science*. New York and London: Harper & Brothers, 1944.

_____. *The Future of Television*. New York: Harper & Brothers, 1947.

_____. *Radio & Television Almanac*. New York: Harper & Brothers, 1951.

Dupuy, Judy, *Television Show Business*. Schenectady: General Electric, 1945.

Dowding, G.V. *Book of Practical Television*. London: Amalgamated, 1935.

Eckhardt, George H. *Electronic Television*. Chicago: Goodheart-Wilcox, 1936.

Eder, Josef M. *History of Photography*. Revised edition. New York: Dover, 1932.

Eddy, William C. *Television — The Eyes of Tomorrow*. New York: Prentice-Hall, 1945.

Eichhorn, Gustav. *Wetterfunk Bildfunk Television*. Leipzig: B.G. Teubner, 1926.

Everson, George. *The Story of Television, the Life of Philo T. Farnsworth*. New York: W.W. Norton, 1949.

Fahie, J.J. *A History of Wireless Telegraphy*. Edinburgh and London: Blackwood, 1901.

Felix, Edgar H. *Television, Its Methods and Uses*. New York: McGraw-Hill, 1931.

Fink, Donald G. *Principles of Television Engineering*. New York: McGraw-Hill, 1940.

_____. *Television Standards and Practice*. New York and London: McGraw Hill, 1943.

Friedel, W. *Elektrisches Fernsehen: Fernkinematographic und Bildfernubertragung*. Berlin: Herman Meusser, 1926.

Fuchs, Gerhard. *Die Bildtelegraphie*. Berlin: Georg Siemens, 1926.

Garratt, G.R.M., and G. Parr. "Television." *A Science Museum Booklet*. London: His Majesty's Stationery Office, 1937.

Geddes, Keith. "Broadcasting in Britain: 1922–1972." *A Science Museum Booklet*. London: Her Majesty's Stationery Office, 1972.

Gorokhov, P.K. *Boris L'vovich Rosing*. Moscow: Hayka, 1964.

Halloran, Arthur H. *Television with Cathode Rays*. San Francisco: Pacific Radio, 1936.

Hathaway, Kenneth. *Television: A Practical Treatise*. Chicago: American Technical Society, 1933.

Hatschek, Paul. *Electron-Optics*. Boston: American Photographic, 1944.

Hemardinquer, Pierre. *La Télévision et ses Progres*. Paris: Dunod, 1937.

_____. *Technique et Pratique de la Télévision*. Paris: Dunod, 1948.

Hendricks, Gordon. *The Edison Motion Picture Myth*. Berkeley and Los Angeles: University of California Press, 1961.

_____. *Eadweard Muybridge, the Father of the Motion Pictures*. New York: Grossman/Viking, 1975.

Hubbell, Richard W. *4000 Years of Television*. New York: G.P. Putnam's Sons, 1942.

Hutchinson, Robert W. *Easy Lessons in Television*. London: University Tutorial Press, 1930.

_____. *Television Up to Date*. London: University Tutorial Press, 1935.

_____. *Here Is Television: Your Window to the World*. New York: Hastings House, 1946.

Hylander, Clarence John, and Robert Harding, Jr. *An Introduction to Television.* New York: Macmillan, 1941.

Irwin, J.T. *Oscillographs.* London: Sir Isaac Pitman, 1925.

Jenkins, Charles Francis. *Animated Pictures.* Washington, D.C.: H.L.M. McQueen, 1898.

_____. *Vision by Radio, Radio Photographs, Radio Photograms.* Washington, D.C.: Jenkins Laboratories, 1925.

_____. *Radiomovies, Radiovision, Television.* Washington, D.C.: Jenkins Laboratories, 1929.

Jewkes, John, David Sawers, and Richard Stillerman. *The Sources of Invention.* London: Macmillan, 1958.

Johnson, B. *The Secret War.* New York, Toronto, London, Sydney: Methuen, 1978.

Jolly, W.P. *Marconi.* New York: Stein and Day, 1972.

Jones, C.R. *Facsimile.* New York: Murray Hill, 1949.

Jones, R.V. *The Wizard War.* New York: Coward, McCann & Geoghegan, 1978.

Kempner, Stanley. *Television Encyclopedia.* New York: Fairchild, 1948.

Korn, Arthur, and Bruno Glatzel. *Handbuch der Phototelegraphie und Telautographie.* Leipzig: Otto Nemnich, 1911.

_____, and E. Nesper. *Bildrundfunk.* 1930.

Kilbon, R.K. *Pioneering in Electronics.* 2 vols. Princeton, N.J.: unpublished manuscript, 1960.

Larner, E.T. *Practical Television.* New York: D. Van Nostrand, 1929.

Lee, Robert E. *Television: The Revolution.* New York: Essential, 1944.

Lessing, Lawrence. *Man of High Fidelity.* New York: Bantam, 1969.

Lieseqang, R. Ed., *Breitage zum Problem des Eletrischen Fernsehens.* Dusseldorf: R. Ed. Lieseqang, 1891.

Lohr, Lenox R. *Television Broadcasting.* New York: McGraw-Hill, 1940.

Lyons, Eugene. *David Sarnoff.* New York: Harper & Row, 1966.

McGowan, Kenneth. *Behind the Screen.* New York: Delacorte, 1965.

Mackenzie, Catherine. *Alexander Graham Bell, the Man Who Conquered Space.* Boston and New York: Houghton Mifflin, 1928.

MacLaurin, W.R. *Invention and Innovation in the Radio Industry.* New York: Macmillan, 1949.

Maloff, I.G., and D.W. Epstein. *Electron Optics in Television.* New York: McGraw-Hill, 1938.

Martin, Marcus J. *Wireless Transmission of Photographs.* London: Wireless, 1916.

_____. *The Electrical Transmission of Photographs.* London: Sir Isaac Pitman, 1921.

Mesney, Rene. *Télévision et Transmission des Images.* Paris: Librairie Armand Golin, 1933.

Mihály, Dionys von. *Das elektrische Fernsehen und das Telehor.* Berlin: M. Krayn, 1923.

Moseley, Sydney. *John Baird: The Romance and Tragedy of the Pioneer of Television.* Long Acre and London: Odhams, 1952.

_____, and H.J. Barton Chapple. *Television, To-day and To-morrow.* London: Sir Isaac Pitman, 1930.

_____, and Herbert McKay. *Television: A Guide for the Amateur.* London: Oxford University Press, 1936.

Moyer, J.A. *Practical Radio, Including Television.* New York: McGraw-Hill, 1931.

Myers, L.M. *Television Optics.* London: Sir Isaac Pitman, 1936.

Parr, G. *The Cathode Ray Tube and Its Applications*. London: Chapman & Hall, 1941.

Patterson, John C. *America's Greatest Inventors*. N.Y.: Thomas Y. Crowell, 1943.

Pfragner, Julius. *Eye of History*. Chicago, New York and San Francisco: 1964.

Pohl, Robert. *Die Elektrische Fernubertragung von Bildern*. Braunschweig: 1938.

Porterfield, John, and Kay Reynolds. *We Present Television*. New York: W.W. Norton, 1940.

Price, A. *Instruments of Darkness*. New York: Charles Scribner's Sons, 1979.

Proceedings of the National Television Systems Committee. 4 vols. 1940/1941.

Puckle, O.S. *Time Bases (Scanning Generators)*. New York: John Wiley, 1946.

Quigley, Martin, Jr. *Magic Shadows*. New York: Harcourt Brace & World, 1965.

Reyner, J.H. *Television: Theory and Practice*. London: Chapman and Hall, 1934; second edition, 1937.

_____. *Cathode Ray Oscillographs*. London: Sir Isaac Pitman, 1939.

Richards, Vyvyan. *From Crystal to Television*. London: A & C Black, 1928.

Rider, John F. *The Cathode-Ray Tube at Work*. New York: John F. Rider, 1935.

Robinson, David. *The History of World Cinema*. New York: Stein and Day, 1973.

Robinson, Ernest H. *Televiewing*. London: Selwyn & Blount, 1937.

Ross, Gordon. *Television Jubilee: The Story of 25 Years of BBC Television*. London: W.H. Allen, 1961.

Rowland, John. *The Television Man*. New York: Roy, 1966.

Secor, H. Winfield, and Joseph H. Kraus. *Television Including Experiments*. New York: 1927.

Sheldon, H. Horton, and Edgar Norman Grisewood. *Television: Present Methods of Picture Transmission*. New York: D. Van Nostrand, 1929.

Shiers, George, ed. *Technical Development of Television*. New York: Arno, 1977.

Sleeper, M.B. *The Television Handbook: Look and Listen*. New York: Norman W. Henley, 1939.

Sturmey, S.G. *The Economic Development of Radio*. London: Gerald Duckworth, 1958.

Schröter, Fritz. *Handbuch der Bildtelegraphie und des Fernsehens*. Berlin: Julius Springer, 1932.

_____. *Fernsehen*. Berlin: Julius Springer, 1937.

Television, Vol. I. New York: RCA Institutes Tech Press, 1936.

Television, Vol. II. New York: RCA Institutes Tech Press, 1937.

Television, Vol. III. Princeton: RCA Review, 1946.

Tiltman, Ronald F. *Television for the Home*. London: Hutchinson, 1927.

_____. *Baird of Television*. London: Seeley Service, 1933.

Trans. Television Engineers of Japan. 2 vols. 1935, 1936.

Tyne, Gerald F.J. *Saga of the Vacuum Tube*. Indianapolis: Howard W. Sams, 1977.

Waldrop, Frank, and Joseph Borken. *Television: A Struggle for Power*. New York: William Morrow, 1938.

Watson Watt, R.A. *Applications of the Cathode Ray Oscillograph in Radio Research*. London: Her Majesty's Stationery Office, 1933/1943.

West, A.G.D., et al. *Television Today: Practice and Principles Explained*. 2 vols. London: George Newnes, 1935.

Wilson, John C. *Television Engineering*. London: Sir Isaac Pitman, 1937.

Yates, Raymond F. *ABC of Television*. New York: Norman W. Henley, 1929.

Yearbook of the Television Scientific Society (Japan). 1934.

Zworykin, V.K., and E.D. Wilson. *Photocells and Their Application*. New York: John Wiley, 1930.

_____, and George A. Morton. *Television – the Electronics of Image Transmission*. New York: John Wiley, Inc. 1940.

Glossary of Terms

amplifier   An electrical device, usually consisting of an arrangement of thermionic tubes (or solid state devices), which increases the energy of a signal without altering its quality.

amplitude modulation   A process in which the amplitude of the carrier frequency is varied above and below its normal value in accordance to an input signal.

anode   The positive electrode in a thermionic tube (or solid state device) which attracts the majority of electrons emitted by the cathode.

aperture   The size of the scanning electron beam striking the target or mosaic of an electronic tube.

background level   *see*   **black level.**

bandwidth   The number of cycles per second between two specified limits. (Note: the measuring unit "cycles per second" is now called "Hertz.")

black level   Amplitude level in the video signal corresponding to the darkest part in the picture (*See also* **DC component**).

blacker than black level   The area below the video information where the synchronizing signals are placed.

black spot   *see*   **shading signals.**

blanking   The process of suppressing the return beam trace in a cathode ray tube by proper insertion of a special signal.

cathode   The negative electrode which emits an electron stream under certain conditions.

cathode ray tube   A vacuum tube utilizing a beam of electrons that can be guided toward a fluorescent screen, which glows when struck by the beam. The beam can be varied in position and intensity.

camera signal   The video output of an electronic camera.

camera tube   An electronic tube which converts the light and shade of a scene into electrical signals.

charge storage   The electrical energy stored in a capacitor, battery or held on an insulated plate.

cinematograph   The motion picture film camera or projector.

closed circuit   A television program not broadcast but confined to the studio. May be recorded for later use.

coaxial cable   A transmission line having at its center a wire supported by insulators capable of carrying high frequency wideband signals.

cold cathode tube   A vacuum tube in which electronic emission is caused by the attraction of electrons by electromagnetic or electrostatic forces.

color television   A television system that reproduces an image in its original colors.

composite picture signal   The complete television signal consisting of the video signal, blanking signal, and the horizontal and vertical synchronizing pulses.

contrast   The amplitude relationship between light and shade in a picture.

DC component   A fixed reference level in the video signal that represents the average illumination of the entire scene. (*See also* **black level**)

definition   The amount of detail in a picture. It depends on the number of picture elements and the contrast of the elements.

diode   An electric device (vacuum tube or solid state) having two electrodes, a cathode and an anode.

direct scanning   The form of scanning (either mechanical or electric) whereby the incident light from the scene goes directly to a transducer which converts the light into electrical impulses.

electromagnetic focusing   The focusing of an electron beam by means of an electromagnetic field.

electron beam   A concentrated stream of electrons focused into the shape of a beam by gas ionization or electrostatic or magnetic fields. Consists of negatively charged particles.

electron camera   The television camera in general. Originally was the brand name for any television camera that used the Image Dissector tube (*q.v.*).

electron gun   The structure of metallic cylinders in the neck of a cathode ray tube consisting of an electron-emitting cathode, and associated cathodes that concentrate, control and focus the stream of emitted electrons into a beam that produces a spot on a fluorescent screen.

electron multiplier A device for multiplying an electron emission by means of one or more bombardments of targets, each target releasing more secondary electrons than the primary ones hitting it.

electron optics The branch of electronics concerned with the behavior of an electron beam under the influence of electrostatic and electromagnetic forces.

electronic camera An electro-optical transducer which converts light waves from a scene into corresponding electrical signals.

electronic motion picture A moving picture in which the original photography is accomplished through the use of electronic cameras. The output of the camera may be stored by means of either photographic or magnetic recording.

electronic multiplication Electrical phenomenon which uses the principle of release of electrons from a surface when that surface is struck by other electrons.

electronic viewfinder The cathode ray monitor mounted on an electronic camera which shows the instantaneous output of that camera.

electrical wave forms The visual representation of certain electric signals with respect to time.

electrostatic focusing The focusing of an electron beam by means of an electrostatic field between two or more plates.

Emitron *see* **Iconoscope.**

explore To scan in some systematic manner.

facsimile The transmission of still photographs by means of wire or radio circuits. Also known as **phototelegraphy.**

Faraday effect The rotation of a beam of plane-polarized light through a transparent medium under the influence of a magnetic field.

field One set of scanning lines that makes up a television picture. In a 2-1 interlaced system, two fields make up one complete frame.

film camera A recording device for making a series of intermittent exposures on a strip of light sensitive film. (*See also* **cinematograph.**)

film scanning The process of converting motion picture film into corresponding electrical signals that can be transmitted by a television system. (*See also* **telecine.**)

fluorescence The physical property of certain substances giving off visible light different from their own during exposure to some form of excitation such as electrons, ultraviolet or X rays. Phosphorescence occurs when emission persists after excitation stops.

flying spot scanning A form of scanning (either mechanical or electrical) whereby light is directed through a scanning aperture to the subject from which it is reflected to a transducer. Also called **inverted scanning.**

frame   The total area occupied by the picture which is scanned while the picture signal is not being blanked.

frequency modulation   Modulation of a sine-wave carrier so that its instantaneous frequency differs from the carrier frequency by the amount proportionate to the instantaneous amplitude of the modulating wave.

galvanometer   An electrical device consisting of a mirror and coil suspended in a magnetic field. Variations in the magnetic field cause the mirror to move in such a manner as to cause light from the mirror to be reflected through a narrow slit.

gas focusing   A method of focusing the beam in a cathode ray tube by the action of a small amount of residual gas in the envelope, which on becoming ionized by collision forms a core of positive ions along the center of the beam and provides the necessary focusing field.

gramophone   The phonograph.

grid   A controlling electrode in a vacuum tube or solid state device.

Hallwachs effect   The ability of ultraviolet radiation to discharge a negatively charged body in a vacuum.

hard tube   Any electronic tube which has a high vacuum and no gas.

Iconoscope   A camera tube in which a high velocity electron beam scans a photoactive mosaic (or target) which has electrical storage capacity. Name developed by RCA. In England it was called the **Emitron.**

Image Dissector   A camera tube having a continuous photocathode on which is formed a photoelectric emission pattern whose electron image is scanned by moving the entire image past an aperture. Name developed by Philo Farnsworth.

Image Iconoscope   A camera tube in which the scene is projected onto a continuous photocathode. This emits electrons that are focused onto a secondary mosaic, which is then scanned by a high velocity electron beam. Name developed by EMI. In England it was called the **Super Emitron.**

intensity modulation   The method of modulating the electron beam by varying the intensity of the beam as it sweeps the fluorescent screen.

interlaced scanning   A form of television scanning in which every other horizontal line of the image is scanned during one downward movement of the scanning beam, with alternate lines scanned during the next downward movement.

intermediate film process   In the transmitting process, a scene is first filmed by an ordinary motion picture camera, quickly processed, and converted into a video signal by a film scanner. In the receiving process, the video signal is displayed on the face of a tube (or disc) which is photographed by a film camera. The film is quickly processed and then projected onto a screen by means of an ordinary film projector.

inverted scanning *see* **flying spot scanning.**

Kerr effect The rotation of a beam of plane-polarized light by means of an iron pole piece under a strong magnetic field.

Kinescope A television picture tube. Name developed by RCA.

lens disc A television scanning disc having a series of lenses in the apertures.

light chopper A device for interrupting a light beam.

light valve (modulator) A device which can control (vary) the amount of intensity of a light source corresponding to an input signal.

line A single horizontal scan across the picture containing highlights, halftones and shadow details.

lumen A unit of light energy. Four π lumens equals one candlepower.

lux A metric unit of illumination equal to the intensity produced by a standard candle on the surface of an object placed one meter from it and at right angles to the light radiation.

manometric device A device using gas (usually acetylene) in which the gas pressure is used to vary the intensity of the flame. (*See also* **speaking arc.**)

mechanical scanning Any process of dissecting an image done by means of mechanical parts, including discs, drums, belts, mirror screws, vibrating mirrors, and the like.

mirror drum A scanning device consisting of a series of mirrors fixed to its periphery. Each mirror is set at a slightly different angle from the one preceding it.

modulate To vary, as to vary the amplitude or frequency of an oscillation in some characteristic manner.

monitor screen The fluorescent face of a cathode ray tube.

monochrome Transmission of television signals in one color only. Consists of shades of gray and white.

mosaic The light-sensitive plate in an Iconoscope or Orthicon upon which the optical image is placed and then scanned by an electron beam. It consists of a multitude of individual elements. (*See also* **target.**)

Nicol prism A transparent form of calcium carbonate introduced from Iceland. It possesses the property of polarizing light rays passed through it.

Orthicon   A camera tube in which a low velocity electron beam perpendicularly scans a photoactive mosaic that has electric storage capability. (Short for **Orthiconoscope**, the name for the tube developed by RCA.)

pairing   Failure of lines to interlace, causing them to be superimposed or to overlap, leaving a dark line between successive pairs.

polarity   Referring to pictures, positive polarity has the correct tones, that is, black is black and so on; negative polarity has black tones being white and vice versa.

polarized light   Light that has been polarized by being passed through certain substances so that the transverse vibrations are in one plane instead of many.

photocathode   A cathode that emits electrons under the influence of radiant energy such as light.

photoconductive effect   The ability of a photocell to change its resistance under the influence of radiant energy.

photoelectric cell   Any cell whose electrical properties are affected by illumination; a device which converts variations in light into corresponding variations in voltage or current.

photoelectric effect   The emission of electrons from a body due to visible infrared, or ultraviolet radiant energy. The energy of a photon is absorbed for each electron emitted.

phototelegraphy   *see*   **facsimile.**

phototube   A vacuum tube in which the electric emission is produced directly by radiation falling on the cathode.

photovoltaic effect   The generation of a voltage as a result of exposure to radiant energy at the junction of two dissimilar metals.

picture elements   Name given to the minute areas in which a picture is to be dissected by any given means. All are of the same size but may differ in brightness. Also called **pixels.**

picture tube   The image-producing electronic tube in a television receiver. (*See also* **Kinescope.**)

pixels   *see*   **picture elements.**

pre-amplifier   An amplifier connected close to the source of a signal which amplifies it sufficiently for it to be transferred by cable to main amplifiers which may be some distance away.

pulse   A periodic or regular beat.

radio-relay   The transmission of television signals from point to point by means of ultra-high frequency waves.

regulator   Any device which maintains a desired quantity at a predetermined level or varies it according to a predetermined plan.

resolution   The sharpness or degree of reproduction of the detail in a scene after transmission through an electron, optical, or complete television system.

scanning   The process of analyzing successively, according to a predetermined method, the light values of picture elements constituting the total picture area.

scanning aperture   An opening in a scanning disc through which the scanning beam passes. In an electronic system, the size of the electron beam is determined by the electron gun.

scanning disc   A perforated disc usually having apertures spaced at equal angular intervals. Some discs have more than one row of holes, may be staggered, may be in a spiral, or may use lenses.

secondary emission   Liberation of electrons (**secondaries**) from an electrode when it is hit or bombarded by other electrons (**primaries**).

sequential scanning   A simple form of television scanning where the picture is scanned line by line only once during a complete frame cycle.

shading   The process of compensating for the spurious signals generated in a camera tube during the trace interval.

shading signals   Spurious signals from a camera tube caused by distribution of secondary electrons on the signal plate.

signal plate   A term applied to the plate of the Iconoscope tube on which is built a mosaic of minute light-sensitive cells on which the scene to be televised and converted into electrical signals is focused. (*See also* **target.**)

signal to noise ratio   The ratio of the intensity of wanted signals to the intensity of noise signals accompanying it.

solid state device   An active semiconductor device which may be used to control, amplify, or otherwise transform electrical signals.

speaking arc   A device that may use an electrical arc in a special circuit which when oscillating creates audible musical notes. A similar effect can be created by a device based on a gas flame which can be varied by means of gas pressure.

sweep   Motion of the electron beam across the face of a camera or picture tube.

switch   The instantaneous cut from one camera to another.

synchronizing generator   An electrical device that produces special pulses for keeping the electron beam at the receiver in step with the camera electron beam.

Super Emitron   *see*   **Image Iconoscope.**

target   The light-sensitive plate in a camera tube on which the picture is formed. It is usually traversed by an electron beam to retrieve the picture information. It may be either continuous or mosaic. It may also be single- or double-sided.

telecine   The term used for operations involving the sending of motion picture film in television.

television   The electrical transmission and reception of transient visual images. (The usual definition includes systematic scanning of the images, means for synchronization of camera and receiver and the use of the "persistence of vision" to recreate the picture.)

television camera   *see*   **electronic camera.**

thermionic tube   A vacuum tube in which electronic emission is produced by a heated cathode.

tilt and bend   *see*   **shading signals.**

triode   A vacuum tube (or solid state device) having three electrodes: a cathode, an anode and a control grid.

velocity modulation   The method of modulating the electron beam by varying the speed of the beam as it sweeps the screen. Slow speed will cause a bright screen and fast speed will cause a dim screen. Intensity of the beam is constant.

video disc   A phonographic disc on which video information may be preserved.

video recording   A process of preserving video information on a suitable medium, which can be either phonographic, photographic or magnetic.

white peak level   The maximum amplitude of the video signal in the white direction.

Index

339